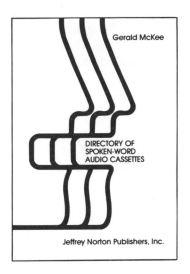

DIRECTORY OF
SPOKEN-WORD
AUDIO CASSETTES

Gerald McKee

Jeffrey Norton Publishers, Inc.
NEW YORK   GUILFORD, CT   LONDON

To the sisters —
Sharyn, Doris, and Gladys
— who aimed me through life.

DIRECTORY OF SPOKEN-WORD AUDIO CASSETTES

ISBN: 0-88432-118-5

Published by Jeffrey Norton Publishers, Inc.
On-The-Green, Guilford, Connecticut 06437 (203) 453-9794

New York Sales Office: 145 E. 49th St., New York, NY 10017 (212) 753-1783

London Sales Office: 31 Kensington Church St., London W8 4LL, U.K.

Contents

Introduction

Welcome to the 1983-84 edition of the Directory of Spoken-Word Audio Cassettes. Four years in preparation, this book lists the offerings of nearly 700 producers of spoken-voice audio-cassette programming in the educational, motivational, inspirational, and entertainment realms. All can be yours at minimum cost, and can provide hours of leisurely education or years of listening enjoyment.

Compared to past editions of the Directory, the descriptions are much more extensive, and the programs have been listed under topic headings, to permit 'browsing' among related programs. A comprehensive index permits easy access to any program topic.

In a sense, the world of spoken-word audio is almost infinite. Every radio and television station in the country —including those on college campuses and in local communities—make audio tapes of their broadcasts, copies of which frequently can be obtained merely for the asking. Every week, private and religious organizations record and distribute cassettes to specialized audiences. These too can get into the commercial mainstream or at least are available upon request. And this has been going on for decades. The annual output is vastly larger than that of printed books. Also, cassettes never really go "out of print"; they can continue to be made available even though the "demand" may be only a few copies a year.

All this makes it a practical impossibility to provide a complete "directory of spoken-word cassettes." The universe is just too vast. In general, therefore, cassettes listed are those from commercial organizations that *actively* promote and distribute spoken-word cassettes. Included also are materials offered by non-profit organizations and religious groups that regularly produce and distribute such programs.

With some more bountiful producers, the listings of their programs must be incomplete. If you seek more information, just write to the producers (a complete list of names and addresses appears at the end of the Directory). Almost all have brochures or catalogs (available without cost, unless otherwise indicated) that give complete descriptions of their programs.

All programs described in this Directory are aimed at the adult or college-level listener. Music cassettes have obviously been omitted, as have those 'instant cassettes' that are merely audio-transcripts of meetings.

Cassette programs that relate to slides or filmstrips are also excluded from the Directory, since our emphasis is on stand-alone audio-education programming that does not rely upon additional visuals. However, many of the listed cassette programs are accompanied by supplemental print materials.

The length of each cassette is given, whenever possible, either by the actual running time or by a 'C-00' designation. A 'C-60' cassette, for example, is 60 minutes long, consisting of two 30-minute sides.

With very few exceptions, all of the audio-cassette programs described in the Directory are available for purchase by mail order. A few are for rental only. All prices shown are prepaid and include postage and handling, unless otherwise stated. Appropriate state sales tax must be added when ordering from a source within your state.

Many professional education courses are income-tax deductible, if "an expense undertaken to maintain or improve professional skills" (see Treas. Reg. 1.162-5, and Coughlin vs. Commissioner, 203 F.2nd 307). Many of the professional courses are also acceptable for continuing education credit.

The Editors have tried to insure that all cassettes listed are currently available. We solicited and received review cassettes from most of the producers, and obtained other forms of confirmation from the remainder. A few companies responded neither to our formal requests or to our informal queries about information on their programs. Since they wouldn't respond to us, we felt they might not reply to our readers — and so their programs weren't included. Please let us know if any of the producers listed fail to respond to your requests for information, or to your orders.

We always welcome information about audio-cassette programs or producers that we have missed. Despite exploring every lead during the past four years, some sources have undoubtedly been overlooked. If you send us a valid new lead (one that hasn't been described in past issues of the Audio-Cassette Newsletter or in past editions of the Directory), we will send you a year's subscription to the Newsletter — with our compliments. See the last pages of this edition of the Directory for further details.

So here then is the 1983-84 Directory. Let us know how you like it, and especially how it could be made even more useful to you.

Jerry McKee

January, 1983

HOW TO USE THIS DIRECTORY

In organizing this Directory, every consideration has been given to helping the searcher to find the material that he or she is looking for among the rich varieties of spoken-word audio cassettes presented here. The organization and wording of the major headings and subheads have been carefully thought through to this end, but inevitably an existing program on a desired subject may be listed someplace other than the place where one is looking for it. This is because each item is listed only once, under only one heading, while the subject may well appear under other headings and subheadings as well.

After searching under the appropriate heading as listed in the Table of Contents, the best strategy may be summed up very briefly: USE THE INDEX. It is a subject or topic index, and every effort has been made to make it as inclusive and useful as possible.

You will, for example, find programs about "stress" (one of the all-pervasive and inescapable factors of life in our society today), in the sections titled BUSINESS, HEALTH SCIENCES, MANAGEMENT, and PERSONAL DEVELOPMENT. "Telephone techniques" may be found under major headings of BUSINESS, MANAGEMENT, and SALES. "Time management," "alcohol," "success," "sexuality," "motivation," and "communications" are only a few of the other myriad topics that may be found in several contexts as far as headings and subheadings are concerned. For instance, "Real Estate — Investment or Management" may be found under the heading of FINANCIAL MATTERS, while practically anything anyone might want to know about selling real estate comes under SALES.

Inevitably, there will be price changes, but those listed were as accurate as it was possible to make them up to press time for the book.

Probably no one library, however well stocked with spoken-word audio cassettes, will have all the titles in the Directory, nor even perhaps a majority of them, but the main purpose of a directory like this one is to let you know that a given taped program exists so that it may be requested. Many libraries of all types are eager to enlarge their collections of good audio tapes, so the individual seeker of a particular tape listed in this Directory will be doing the library being used a service by asking that programs be acquired permanently or borrowed on interlibrary loan.

Libraries of all types — public, school, college and special — should have this Directory on the reference shelves to serve as a finding tool.

One further word about the INDEX. It is a subject index, and does not list proper names either of the presenters or authorities of the tapes, nor of the well-known people many of them are about. If you are looking for material on Abraham Lincoln, it would most likely be found under HISTORY, or perhaps, LITERATURE. If you are looking for material by Dr. Norman Vincent Peale or Thomas Merton, you would know to search, and be fairly certain of finding their entries under RELIGION — probably under the subhead Sermons and Testimonies. If you want a presentation by a particular well known psychologist, however, be aware that it might be found under HEALTH SCIENCES, PERSONAL DEVELOPMENT, HUMAN RELATIONS AND COUNSELING, or even MANAGEMENT.

Finally, should you want to locate all the diverse kinds of programming available from a particular source — from Audio-Forum and Jeffrey Norton Publishers, Inc., for example — sources are listed with names, addresses and in many cases telephone numbers, with page citations of their offerings in the various categories.

Good hunting and good listening!

I.

Business

Accounting

NAA Self-Study Programs—Continuing education courses for CPAs and PAs that could benefit anyone making decisions that involve accounting and finance. There are three programs on *Management Accounting for Business Decisions*; the first (*A Contemporary Introduction*) includes management planning and control, reporting and budgeting, standard costs and responsibility accounting and costs $65 for a long cassette and workbook. The second program (*Cost Concepts and Cost Behavior Analysis*) covers different costs for different purposes, contribution analysis, and cost and price strategy, and it costs $65 for a 90-minute cassette and workbook. The final course (*Management Accounting in a Service Oriented Economy*) includes a series of case studies that focus on insurance, banking, office situations, price elasticity, and internal control. It is $90 for three 90-minute cassettes with workbook. Then, there are three self-study programs on budgeting: *Zero-Base Budgeting: What and How, Flexible Budgeting and Contribution Reporting*, and *Capital Budgeting: Concepts and Techniques*; these are, respectively, $65, $80, and $85 for a 60- to 90-minute cassette and workbook. Finally, *Auditable Internal Control Systems* (AUDICS) introduces audit concepts and objectives as they apply to the auditing of computer-based systems while still adhering to financial control requirements of the accounting profession, $395 for 10 cassettes, 400 pages of text materials, and an album. [Source: National Association of Accountants.]

Sobelsohn School CPA Examination Review Course—From the oldest and largest CPA training school in the nation comes a carefully programmed series designed for individual or small group study. It is presented in four parts: *Theory Review*, 11 cassettes, $155; *Business Law Review*, 12 cassettes, $155; *Accounting Practice* (*Problems*) *Reviews*, 17 cassettes, $235; and *Auditing Review*, 12 cassettes, $155. All cassettes are an hour long and all parts include a hefty manual (over 350 pages) and album. [Source: Protape, Inc.]

CPAudio Cassettes—A huge selection of cassette-workbook programs, from the American Institute of Certified Public Accountants, that cover all aspects of accounting and taxation. Most of the programs consist of one or two cassettes and comprehensive workbook for prices ranging from $35 to $80. Here we list just a few of the titles to show the diversity to professional topics offered: *Accounting and Reporting Systems for Banks, Tax Accrual Documentation, Accounting Changes, Accounting for Restaurant Operations, Audits of School Districts, LIFO Inventory Accounting, Introduction to Local Government Accounting* (six cassettes, $135), *Audit Diagnostic Review, Income Taxation of Estates and Trusts, Keogh and IRA Plans, Practical Approach to Preparing Form 1040, Advanced 1040 Problems, Subchapter C, Subchapter S, Federal Taxation of Partnerships*, and *Responsibilities in Tax Practice*. There are also a large series of programs to provide practical training for the new staff accountant or the newly promoted one, and for personal and professional management. [Source: AICPA]

National Book Company—*Accounting* (*Introductory*) is a completely individualized accounting course, equivalent to a one-year basic course. It comes in three major parts, an accounting cycle ($201.10 for 12 cassettes), special journals, adjusting, and closing ($248.15 for 15 cassettes), and special accounting procedures ($200.75 for 12 cassettes); all sets include student syllabus, tests, and teacher's aids. *Accounting* (*Advanced*) gives greater emphasis in the areas of receivables, payables, assets, payroll, partnership and corporate accounting, on 15 cassettes and printed materials for $255.10. Related programs cover *Business Law, Business Machines, Business Principles*, and *Data Processing*. [Source: National Book Company]

Tax-Saver Acounting System for Small Business—A simplified method to keep books on a business, on six cassettes. The first tapes guide the listener through the system, and the later tapes tell how to use the system to save taxes. Anyone who writes a check becomes the accountant and can instantly determine which items are tax-deductible and can easily handle disbursements, receipts, balancing, and closing. $129.95 for six cassettes in album-binder with enough forms for two years of complete record-keeping. [Source: Van Den Berg Publications]

Basic Accounting—A course specifically developed to supplement Accounting 101 courses at junior and community colleges by filling the void between classroom lecture and the exams. The emphasis is on 'the big picture' and not of the minutiae of specific examples, and is intended for slow learners, border-line students, and those who have missed classes. $98 for eight cassettes and study guides in album. *Managing Accounts Payable* and *Managing Accounts Receivable* ($12 each for a short cassette) can serve both to increase proficiency of beginning accountants and to offer step-saving shortcuts to more experienced personnel. [Source: Tutor/Tape]

CPA Review Course—A comprehensive course specifically designed for cassette education, with the aim of helping the candidate pass the CPA examination. Extensive workbook materials correlate with the cassette instruction. The program comes in four 12-cassette (except as noted) albums: *Business Law*, 14 hours, 600-page workbook, $110; *Auditing*, 13 hours, 450-page workbook, $110; *Accounting Theory*, 16 hours, 450-page workbook, $110; and *Accounting Practice* (24 cassettes), 22 hours, 1,025-page workbook, $170. The complete course of 64 cassettes and workbooks in five albums, $475. With the course comes a study guide, diagnostic and final exam practice, and free 'hotline' phone answering service. [Source: Totaltape, Inc.]

Contractor Information Services—Audio-cassette plus workbook courses, originally developed for Defense Contract Audit Agency (DCAA) auditors, and now used by accountants for government contractors to prevent and resolve accounting and audit problems. *Cost Accounting Standards* provides answers from both industry and DCAA viewpoints, covering all standards, rules, regulations and interpretations, updated yearly, on 12 cassettes and 600-page workbook in album, $350. *Contract Audit Orientation* explains and reviews contract auditing, government procurement procedures, and the role of the DCAA, updated semi-annually, on eight cassettes and 400-page workbook in album for $195. Toll-free 'hotline' telephone privilege comes with the purchase of either of these two programs. *DCAA Auditing Standards and Working Paper Procedures* gives an understanding of DCAA thinking and audit procedures by letting one adopt and review their procedures selectively in advance of the arrival of DCAA auditors, on six cassettes and 250-page workbook in album for $145. [Source: Totaltape, Inc.]

Administration

Washington Audio Journal—This twice-a-month audio-cassette service of the U.S. Chamber of Commerce provides early, inside information on the activities of congress, the administration, and the regulatory agencies, so that businessmen will know what is happening in Washington from a business point of view, and can apply these insights to their particular business needs. $150 a year (24 issues), $85 for six months (12 issues). [Source: Washington Audio Journal]

How To Start Your Own Business and Succeed—A program that answers such questions as what steps to take to launch a business, the personnel qualifications needed by the organizer, basics of market planning, and criteria for a sound business. Four cassettes, $109.95. [Source: Lansford Publishing Company]

Computer Cassettes—Home-study courses on operating personal, business, and industrial computers. There are four introductory short courses (two C-90 cassettes and workbook, for $29.95): *Introduction to Personal and Business Computing* ($24.95), *Introduction to Microprocessors, Designing a Microprocessor System*, and *Programming Microprocessors*. Then, there are two introductory comprehensive courses, each consisting of seven or eight C-90 cassettes and a 300-500 page workbook, for $99.95: *Microprocessors* and *Microprocess Programming*. Finally, four advanced courses on three or four C-90 cassettes with a 300-500 page workbook for $69.95: *Severe Environment/Military Microprocessor Systems, Microprocessor Interfacing, Bit Slice*, and *Industrial Microprocessor System*. [Source: Sybex Inc.]

Newstrack—A 'talking magazine' for business, with each twice-a-month, 90-minute issue containing narration of complete articles (occasionally excerpts) from The Wall Street Journal, U.S. News and World Report, Business Week, Forbes, Barron's, and other national and international business publications. Cost is $195 for one year (24 cassettes) plus four cassette profiles of vital business concerns throughout the year. [Source: Newstrack]

Control Your Business—Richard R. Gallagher D.B.A. defines control, explains the feedback loop concept, and applies control to finances, production, inventory, quality, and personnel. $15 for a 35-minute cassette. In *Business Management Tools*, he describes 20 tools to help businessmen evaluate their progress, including BE charts, budgets, normative values, quick ratios, PERT/CPM, 80-20 principle, and others. $15 for a 62-minute cassette. Other offerings by Dr. Gallagher include *Business Planning & Decision Making, Business Organization, Introduction to Business Law, Business Contract law*, and *Retail Store Location & Layout*, all one cassette each, $15 each. [Source: Tutor/Tape]

Small Business Planning Guide—In this start-up guide for getting into your own business, you'll hear advice from a lawyer, a banker, and an accountant, presenting practical information on how to organize your company. $29 for two cassettes, 114-page workbook, and action planner in album. [Source: Tutor/Tape]

Microcomputer Literacy Program—Before you buy, this kit offers solid advice on how much your business will actually benefit from having a desktop microcomputer, what a microcomputer will really do, how it does it, and what is necessary to make it work for your business or organization. It gives guidelines about buying peripherals, and pointers on the peril of buying equipment inadequate for future needs. Finally, brand name computers are evaluated objectively for their good and bad points. You get nine cassettes, 200-page text, programmed workbook, dictionary, comparison report, and computer simulator in two albums for $137.20. [Source: McGraw-Hill Continuing Education Center]

Business Opportunities—Single cassette talks on *Teenage Business Opportunities, How To Get Published, How To Supplement Your Income* (moonlighting), *Opportunities in Importing, Selling Toy and Game Ideas, Great Home Businesses*, and *How to Start a Home Business*—all $10.95 each. [Source: Jeffrey Norton Publishers, Inc.]

How To Start & Manage Your Own Business—Small-business consultants Arnold and Egon Van Den Berg offer a simple yet complete home-study course, taking up these subjects (each on one cassette): commitment, where to begin, starting vs. buying a business, finding and pricing a product, raising money, tax-saving angles, analyzing financial statements, and marketing strategies. All eight cassettes plus outlines, references, and workbook in album-binder for $129, individual cassettes with outline and references for $10 each. [Source: Van Den Berg Publishing]

Center for Entrepreneurial Management—High-quality programs for developers of new business and for their professional advisors, all given by Joseph R. Mancuso: *Five Greatest Marketing Blunders of the Century*, a fascinating and informative review of W. T. Grant and Corfam, among others (1½ hr); *Fun and Guts—Do You Have What It Takes To Be an Entrepreneur?*, common insights and goals of successful entrepreneurs (1 hr); *How To Raise Capital for a Growing Business*, either by debt (loans) or by equity (stock)(1½ hr); and *What Business Am I In?—Setting Meaningful Corporate Goals*, and if you are in the right business with meaningful goals, you'll succeed (1 hr). $11.95 each, or all four for $40. Also available are audio-cassette highlights of a three-day seminar on *Raising Capital*. The first day covers how to read and write a business plan, the second day is about sources of capital and making a deal, and the third day covers how to put the deal together. Each day covers over five hours of discussion. Any single day is $175, any two days $275, all three days $350, and any order includes the 450-page notebook. [Source: Center for Entrepreneurial Management, Inc.]

Starting Your Own Import/Export Business—A six-cassette course by Howard Goldsmith that gives such essentials as finding profitable products to import or export, buying them at a 'good' price, pricing goods for resale, establishing lines of credit, documentation, shipping restrictions, customs, and other 'inside' tricks of the trade. $95 including album and book. [Source: Professional Cassette Center]

Effective Dictation—A comprehensive, hands-on audio-cassette/workbook course in techniques of proper dictating, oriented primarily to the use of dictating equipment but with outlining and effective letter-writing segments helpful to all correspondence originators. The course, developed from Florence Rogers' successful workshops and seminars, is useful for anyone who generates paperwork, for executive trainees to corporate presidents, as well as doctors, lawyers, and other professionals. The time to complete the self-paced course is about five hours. $125 for three cassettes and 232-page workbook. [Source: BNA Communications Inc.]

Secretarial Skills

Speedwriting Shorthand—This is a shorthand system that uses the alphabet, rather than symbols. The basic *Speedwriting Theory Tapes* teach this system at the college level, with a text (*Principles of Speedwriting*) and 20 correlated tapes, each containing 30 minutes of dictation at speeds ranging from 60 wpm initially to 120 in the final lesson. $203.50 for the tapes, $10.95 for the text. *Speedbuilding Tapes* are 18 cassettes designed to enable students to take dictation at ever-increasing speed and accuracy, using any shorthand system; these are also $203.50, including a teacher's key. *Vocabulary Building Tapes* accomplish much the same thing on their 18 tapes, but the contents cover a much greater variety of subjects as the student progresses from 70 wpm to 140, $243 including a teacher's key. Finally, *Speedwriting Medical Dictation Tapes* gives special training in medical terms and other difficult words, on 13 cassettes for $175. [Source: Bobbs-Merrill Educational Publishing]

Transactional Analysis—TA authority Clay Hardesty discusses: *TA for Secretaries*, with examples in business situations; *The OK Secretary*, contrasting the qualities of winners and losers and of negative and positive scripts in the business world; and *What Games Do You Play?* that block communication and goal achievement. $47.50 for the three cassettes in album, or $17.50 each. [Source: Learning Consultants, Inc.]

Secretarial Seminar—Studio-recorded highlights of a popular seminar, stressing self-image, professional roles, and time management method. $69 for six 40-minute cassettes in album. Also available in the same format and price: *Advanced Secretarial Seminar*, emphasizing office effectiveness, new communication skills, and office automation; *Seminar for Executive Secretaries*, with counsel on managing your career, time management, problem solving, and management teamwork; and *Beyond the Typewriter*, with discussions of management styles, assertiveness skills, and management of stress. [Source: Professional Training Associates, Inc.]

Multimedia Individualized Instruction—Courses on a variety of secretarial and vocational subjects, usually accompanied by training booklet, tests, and other aids: *The Medical Secretary*, two cassettes, $40; *The Police Secretary*, five cassettes, $80; *The Technical Secretary*, four cassettes, $63; *The Education Secretary*, three cassettes, $50; *Useable English*, 15 cassettes, $15 each; *Business English Punctuation*, nine cassettes, $15 each; *Banking Skills*, five cassettes, $15 each; *Machine Transcription and Dictation*, eight cassettes, $105 for the set; *Accounting Skills*, 11 cassettes, $15 each; *Computing the Payroll* and *Writing the Payroll Check*, two cassettes, $35; *The Sales Slip*, one cassette $16; *Office Calculators*, five cassettes, $15 each. [Source: Cassettes Unlimited]

Seminar for Secretaries and Other Office Personnel—Recorded live in 1981, this edited album includes six 40-minutes cassettes and a workbook, and stresses strengthening self-confidence, improving human relations skills, and increasing personal effectiveness. $135. Also available in the same format and for the same price: *Seminar for Advanced and Executive Secretaries*, covering the professional relationship with executives, resolving common office problems, assessing career needs, and improving communications. [Source: Batten Institute]

Professional Secretary—A program aimed at giving the accomplished secretary, office manager, or administrative assistant additional versatility: organizational skills to get more done in less time; ways to work more effectively with people; and the ability to motivate self and others. $80 for eight cassettes and study guide in album, $20 for a one-hour cassette of highlights. [Source: Fred Pryor Resource Corporation]

Power Typing—A self-paced learning system designed to bring non-typists to a 40 wpm proficiency in 60 hours of audio-instruction, and to increase speed of intermediate typists to 60 wpm with minimal errors. This program is planned for in-house training, and can be monitored by any accomplished typist. $395 for 29 C-60 cassettes, plus $12.50 each for textbook and instructor's manual. A related program is *Power Stenography*—an individualized shorthand skill-building system that helps a company develop expert stenographers by upgrading the skills of intermediate stenographers, regardless of the shorthand method they use. Each student progresses at her or his own rate of speed; the program accommodates skill levels from 50 to 150 wpm. $295 for 10 cassettes (each increasing dictation speed by 10 wpm) and a pacer drill tape, plus $15 for student manual, $10 for instructor's manual. [Source: MIND]

Western Tapes—This source offers the business teacher a variety of multi-media instructional courses in the field of business and office education. Subject areas covered are word processing, shorthand, typing, general business and distributive education, and general office skills. One of the primary areas of emphasis at Western Tapes is instructional materials in word processing. Their offerings begin with fundamental programs which assume no more than the student's ability to type, and then proceed through the more complex area of medical and legal transcription as well as power typing. All of the attendant areas of word processing skills—grammar, punctuation, composition, and so forth—are also offered in cassette-plus-workbook format, suitable for either classroom or individual use at school or home. Most courses involve multiple cassettes; the cost is roughly $9.50 per cassette, usually including student workbook and leader's guide. [Source: Western Tape]

Stenographic Skill Dictation Test—Business letters of varying degrees of difficulty, dictated at 40 to 160 wpm, to aid in testing the shorthand skills of job applicants. With this set, anyone in the office can give the test and obtain accurate speed scores. $96 for five cassettes and printed texts in album, $24 for individual tapes. [Source: E. F. Wonderlic & Associates, Inc.]

Time Management for Secretaries—Planned to show the secretary how to save time both for herself and her boss, and at the same time make her job more interesting, rewarding, and productive. $350 for 9 cassettes and workbook in album [Source: AMR/ Advanced Management Reports, Inc.]

A Secretarial Career in the Medical Office—A complete training course for the medical secretary in machine transcription and dictation, as well as in medical office procedures, medical vocabulary, and general grammar. $99 for 12 cassettes, workbook, and forms in album. [Source: ESP, Inc.]

Office Education—A series of 26 cassettes ($150) that provides a condensed introduction to many different office-related fields, from surveying various office careers to improving correspondence and mathematical skills. [Source: ESP, Inc.]

Better-Faster Typing—Cassettes designed to help second-year typing students, with practical suggestions for improving typing speed and accuracy. $30 for five cassettes. Or, if the upgrading of a good typist is in order there's *Secretarial Training*, a course specifically designed to train the modern secretary in dictation, machine transcription, and word processing, as well as general office procedures, vocabulary, and grammar. The goal is to tranform a typist into a professional secretary. This course requires a cassette player with a foot control. $99 for twelve 60-minute cassettes and workbook in album. [Source: ESP, Inc.]

National Book Company—Many programs to help secretaries initiate or improve their stenographic skills. There are several sets of recordings designed to enhance dictation speed. One example is *Dictation & Transcription*, $93.55 for six cassettes with 90 letters and articles given at modest speeds (60-80 wpm) but increasingly challenging vocabulary. Then, they have a full selection of *Personal Shorthand* courses, an all-alphabetic shorthand system that uses conventional written letters. The basic course is $246.90 for 15 tapes, syllabus, tests, and teacher's manual; variant courses are available for the executive secretary and the journalist. Other secretarial skills programs cover filing, punctuation, spelling, and typewriting speed-building. [Source: National Book Company]

Steno Booster—Four cassettes of dictation—30 and 40 wpm, 50 and 60 wpm, 50 to 80 wpm, 90 to 130 wpm—provide practice with any type of shorthand to improve speed and accuracy. $7.98 each. [Source: Conversa-phone Institute, Inc.]

DDC Shorthand Dictation Cassettes—A collection of C-60 cassettes, each containing letters dictated at two different speeds—60/70 wpm, 70/80 wpm, 80/90 wpm, and so on up to 140 wpm. All are designed to force increased shorthand speed by frequent use of common business terms. $10 each, any two for $17.50, any three for $25. Another approach, the *Speed Development Programs*, consist of five cassettes (150 different letters) with speed ranges 90-110 wpm, 70-120 wpm, 80-130 wpm, and 90-140 wpm. These are $35 per set. Then there are some specialized items: *Legal Dictation Cassettes*, $25 for three tapes and transcript in album; *Medical Dictation Cassettes*, $17.50 for two tapes and transcript; *Spelling Conquered*, two cassettes for $15; *Punctuation Trainer*, one cassette in album, $10; and *Introduction to Machine Transcription*, $35 for three cassettes and booklet in album. [Source: Dictation Disc Company]

Typewriter Keyboard Response Program—This course uses positive repetitive learning reinforcement in successive series of controlled 'conditioning' sessions to train non-typists to subconsciously strike the proper key upon seeing the visual image. $89.50 for seven 40-minute cassettes (14 lessons) with student guide and instructor's manual in album. Having memorized the keyboard, *Typing Speed Development* guides the student toward higher speed plateaus and increasing finger dexterity, by means of tightly controlled pacing exercises. $73.50 for five cassettes with student and instructor's guides in album. *Production Typing* provides step-by-step instruction for the entry-level typist in realistic practice for on-the-job requirements, such as centering, tabulation, punctuation, numbers and symbols, business letters and forms, financial statements, and manuscripts. $128

for ten cassettes, student and instructor's manuals, and lesson projects in album. [Source: Reinforcement Learning, Inc.]

Reinforcement of Gregg Symbols & Theory—Not a shorthand course or dictation tapes, but a series of repetitive reinforcement sessions planned to provide instant, almost automatic response to every Gregg symbol, brief form, phrase, and word beginning and ending. $158 for 14 forty-minute cassettes and instructor's manual in album. *Reinforcement "500"* expands the conditioning program to encompass 500 of the words and phrases most frequently used in business correspondence, $128 for 10 cassettes and student guide in album, both for $245. Their program *Shorthand Speed Development* provides a rapid speed-building program that can be used with any shorthand system, with the objective of building speed from 40 to 135 wpm by means of varying speed sprints to increase memory/motor responses. $128 for ten cassettes and lesson plans in album. *Shorthand Speed Test Tapes* supply an additional source of practice dictation and speed development and/or appropriate test drills for evaluating student progress, in 5-word per minute increments from 45 wpm to 140 wpm. $128 for 10 cassettes in album, both programs for $218. [Source: Reinforcement Learning, Inc.]

Telephone Techniques for Secretaries and Receptionists—From a source that features distinguished trainers comes this program by Thom Norman on a two-cassette album for $30. [Source: Sales Communique Corporation]

Effective Telephone Techniques—Naomi Rhode and Thom Norman prepared this program especially to assist the dental or medical receptionist with the most important tool available to her, the telephone. $34.95 for three cassettes in album, telephone pickup microphone and mirror for practicing the techniques. [Source: Semantodontics, Inc.]

Audio Cassette Learning Programs—Top quality fairly priced seminars based on one-day programs presented nationwide by Applied Management Institute. Each program in comprised of six hour-long cassettes with seminar notes in album, for $75. *Time Management for Secretaries & Administrative Assistants*; also related is their *Seminar for Executive Secretaries, Senior Secretaries, Administrative Assistants & Office Managers*. [Source: Applied Management Institute, Inc.]

The Secretary as Manager—Just what it says...a program to train secretaries to keep on top of their jobs, rather than letting the jobs run them ragged, and their bosses crazy...all by setting priorities, avoiding conflicts, and scheduling tasks and activities. $125 for four audio-cassettes, seven trainee workbooks, and leader's guide. Related is *Time Management for Secretaries*, $75 for two cassettes and 10 workbooks. [Source: Management Resources]

Telephone Dynamics—A general telephone skills program, not tied to specialized applications, that can be completed by any employee in about 3½ hours without supervision. The skills covered include the best way to identify the caller, tactful screening, relaying information to others, and (when placing a call) getting through a screen, setting up appointments, and placing calls for a superior. $90 for two 60-minute cassettes plus a blank practice cassette, six 40-page workbooks, message pads, and supervisor's guide. [Source: Universal Training Systems Co.]

II.
Communication Skills

General

Improving Communication Skills—Supervisors and managers learn about overcoming the barriers to effective communication, the use of non-directive questioning techniques and active listening skills, generating descriptive feedback, and analyzing effective and ineffective self-expression. $150 for five cassettes (one a trainer's tape), seven trainee workbooks, and leader's guide. [Source: Management Resources]

Executive Writing, Speaking, and Listening Skills—A six-hour program that provides a unified approach to integrate an executive's understanding of the four parts of communication: speaking, writing, listening, and reading. $145 for six cassettes and workbook in album; two quizzes are included that can be returned for scoring and evaluation. [Source: American Management Association]

Psychology of Communication—In this two-cassette album, Dr. Richard P. Issel first gives some keys for using good and effective communication to revitalize and activate business function, and then discusses their practical applications with businessmen. $29.95 plus guide in album. [Source: Learning Consultants, Inc.]

Managing Change: A Blueprint for Productivity—A self-regulation course in cassette-workbook format, designed to initiate, involve others, and motivate others in the change process. The course teaches how to communicate change up, down, and across the organizational chart. $80 for four cassettes and workbook in album. [Source: Human Productivity Institute]

Learning Curve—One-hour mini-courses, each with a C-60 cassette, programmed exercises and tests: Creative Writing, College Preparatory Vocabulary, Public Speaking, and beginning, intermediate and advanced Speed Reading. Each one $9.98, any two for $15.98, any three for $22.98. [Source: Metacom, Inc.]

Powers of Persuasion—Jerry Richardson presents state-of-the-art communication techniques and strategies in a clear manner, showing how to take immediate control of any situation, establish trust and credibility and communicate clearly to others while avoiding being manipulated oneself. $74.95 for four cassettes and a workbook in album. [Source: Human Productivity Institute]

Listening

Listen Your Way to Success—The key leadership skill is active listening, says management consultant Dr. R. L. Montgomery. By the use of his program of 'fine-tuned listening skills' and his 'maxims for supercharged listening,' one should be able greatly to improve comprehension and retention. $85 for three cassettes, workbook, and test in album. [Source: Robert L. Montgomery & Associates, Inc.]

Systematic Listening—The ability to listen fully and retain what is heard is critical to the smooth operation of almost every business—yet most people retain less than 30% of what they hear. This course teaches the basic skills needed for good listening, by means of carefully sequenced practice skills to intensify response to auditory stimuli. $20 for an audiocassette with workbook. [Source: Systema Corporation]

Listening on the Job—A practical approach to a recurring problem in business and industry: oral communication and receiving information. Thomas E. Anastasi, Jr. and Sidney A. Dimond conduct this training package on how to listen effectively. $245 for three C-60 cassettes, leader's guide, and the workbook/reference books. [Source: Addison-Wesley Publishing Company]

Listen Up!—For $25, a package of two cassettes, reading materials, and checklists to provide a convenient reference and study tool to aid in improving listening skills. [Source: Cathcart, Alessandra & Associates, Inc.]

Art of Listening—Pointers on remembering and interpreting what you hear, how to eliminate the bias of emotions, and how to detect possible hidden meanings. Also how to determine how well you listen, and of course how to improve your listening ability. $27.50 for four cassettes. Related is *Memory*, a four-cassette course giving techniques for remembering different kinds of information, and so improving yourself socially and in business, $27.50. [Source: Associated Education Materials]

Reading

Speed Learning—Not just another course based on rapid eye movements, but a complete new concept, designed to develop improved thinking and learning skills, thereby increasing reading comprehension as well as speed. The concept was developed by Dr. Russell G. Stauffer, Director of the Reading Study Center at the University of Delaware. The cost is $99.95 for four cassettes in album plus three manuals and paperback books for practice. *Super Reading* is a less extensive adaption of the same course, with two cassettes and comprehensive instruction manual (280 pages) for $41.95. It also comes in a Junior Edition for children age 10-16. [Source: Learn Incorporated]

SRA Business Reading System—A speed reading course specifically applied to increasing business efficiency, by focusing on varying the rate with the material to be read; a technical rate for total comprehension of complex material; a general rate for extracting major ideas, points, and conclusions from reports; and a rapid rate for skimming 'required reading' and routine correspondence. $165 for three cassettes and workbooks in album. [Source: Science Research Associates, Inc.]

Power Reading—A simplified system, developed by the Kinder Institute, that can be used to improve both reading speed and comprehension. It is an eight-hour course (requiring about 10 minutes a day) on just two cassettes and workbook for $39.95. [Source: General Cassette Corporation]

Accelerated Reading Techniques—A compact self-instruction speed-reading course that can assist the average reader to double reading speed within 21 days. $12.60 for description of techniques on an audio-cassette, coordinated with worksheets that are included. [Source: Z Incorporated]

Rapid Reading and Comprehension Skills—A course that aims to help you read important business and professional correspondence and publications in half the time, with greater comprehension and retention. The program was developed in consultation with Dr. Alton L. Raygor, one of the nation's foremost reading experts. $81.95 for six cassettes in album, workbook, rate improvement charts, and two paperback novels. [Source: International Institute for Reading]

Reading: Sound and Sense—A two-part basic reading skills program for low-level readers, by Lloyd Besant, PhD. Part 1 (eight instructional cassettes plus blank practice cassette) teaches poor readers a decoding system and provides practice techniques to develop their skills. Part 2 (six instructional cassettes plus introductory tape) teaches the person who understands or remembers little of what is read some simple techniques of how to analyze and organize ideas for meaning. $76 for each part; both parts come with extensive booklets, workbook, user's guide, and other supplemental materials. [Source: Encyclopaedia Britannica Educational Corp.]

Speaking

Speech-Training Tapes—Twelve 30-minute talks aimed at improving self-expression skills. Topics covered include: the humorous speech, opening and closing with humor, overcoming stage fright, beginnings, audience involvement, building enthusiasm, persuasion, the how-to speech, proper delivery, the climax, visual aids, and speaking extemporaneously. $57 for 12 cassettes in album, or $9.95 each. [Source: Bureau of Business Practice]

Speaking Effectively—Experienced platform speaker and motivator Dave Yoho helps both beginners and professionals with tips on how to break the ice, get audience participation, get rid of stage fright, motivate the audience, and other speaking skills, on six cassettes in album for $69.75. [Source: Dave Yoho Associates]

Voice, Vocabulary and Delivery—A compact course on how to break bad speech habits, improve your voice, and select the words that best convey your meaning, on four cassettes for $27.50. [Source: Associated Educational Materials]

Effective Public Speaking—A nuts and bolts session with master platform speaker Zig Ziglar, on a single cassette for $9.95. Related is his cassette on *Using Voice Inflection Effectively*, also $9.95. [Source: Zig Ziglar Corporation]

Speak for Success—John T. Molly (author of *Dress for Success* and *Live for Success*) has prepared a comprehensive program to help average speakers communicate their ideas more effectively and confidently by learning good speaking habits, appropriate speech patterns, and other principles of successful communications. $95 for six cassettes, 100-page workbook, and album. [Source: Professional Cassette Center]

Effective Speaking for Managers—Master communicator Bob Montgomery shows how to learn the techniques that help one in conducting a meeting, discussion, or conference, making a presentation, giving a platform speech, and even (and perhaps, especially) when talking person-to-person. $85 for four cassettes and guide in album. [Source: Robert L. Montgomery & Associates]

Folkways—Tucked in among their ethnic music records, Folkways has some interesting spoken-word titles: *Mend Your Speech*, with Harry Fleetwood and Anne Burns; *American Pronunciation*, with Abe Lass, and *A Study in Regional Speech Patterns*, by Dr. James Golden. $9.98 each, with text. [Source: Folkways Records]

Speak Easy to One or One Thousand—Christopher J. Hegarty gives techniques that will improve effectiveness in all forms of public speaking and interviews, as well as in casual conversations, $55 for four cassettes in album. Also of interest in his single cassette, *Avoiding Calamities in Public Speaking*, for $10. [Source: Christopher J. Hegarty]

Does Anybody Listen, Does Anybody Care?—Do your words have the effect on people that you intend? Do your children tune you out? Does your spouse hear you? Do you often simply feel that you aren't getting your message across? Jacob Weisberg and Ginny Schecter-Weisberg explain the basic skills needed for effective communication on this 90-minute cassette, for $14.95. [Source: Creative Communications Associates]

No Fear Ta-Ta-Talking—The fear, anxiety, and the expectation of failure that is common to all people who stutter are actually defensive mechanisms designed to forestall what is perceived as impending failure, says psychologist Dr. Robert Rotella. He has produced an audio-cassette program that first introduces the six complementary goals to decrease blockage during speech, and then gives the listener a relaxation exercise to prepare for speaking. $9.95 with a booklet. [Source: Creative Media Group]

Earl Nightingale Toastmasters International Programs—In two 6-cassette albums, Earl Nightingale reveals little known secrets of effective communication. *Communicate What You Think* tells how to transmit your message without sacrificing intent or meaning, how to persuade others to agree with you, how to overcome the fear of facing an audience, and more. *The Compleat Speaker* draws upon both Earl Nightingale's vast experience and 50 years of Toastmasters' research to provide insights into every possible speaking assignment. $50 each album. [Source: Toastmasters International]

Stutter Therapy with the Double Tape Recorder Method—Developed over a ten-year study at Rutgers Medical School, this method has been shown to shorten the time required to correct stuttering by conventional means. The program contains 12 30-minute cassettes, each containing a lesson to be given by a speech therapist, physician, or psychologist. The stutterer receives the cassette for two weeks, and each day listens to it while recording his responses on another recorder. $150 for the 12 cassettes in album with transcripts and notes for the therapist. [Source: Bernard Lee]

Speech Power—Edited by Dr. Mario Pei, this self-administered program covers all the skills necessary for effective verbal communication—from good voice production and telephone speech to public speaking and profanity. There's even a section on the speech of love and a final one on when to stop talking. $90 for 11 hour-long cassettes (plus a blank one for practice), word lists and exercises, and album. [Source: Tape Productions, Inc.]

Speechmaker—Dr. George Fluharty, Director of Speech Communications at NYU, guides the user through this 10-cassette self-study program and toward developing into the kind of public speaker audiences enjoy. Each lesson has useful suggestions, demonstrations, and easy-to-follow speaking techniques, plus tips for success from well-known public speakers. $93.45 for 10 cassettes plus blank practice tape in album, with supplemental materials and exercises. [Source: Tape Productions, Inc.]

Improve Your English Pronunciation—Many adults learn correct English grammar and an extensive English vocabulary, but their pronunciation remains poor because they are applying to English the pronunciation rules of their native speech. In this innovative program, Jeffrey Bedell provides 42 listen-and-repeat lessons, each covering just one vowel or consonant sound of English, both isolated and in words and sentences. Each lesson has a corresponding lesson card, which recaps that lesson's sound and gives additional words using that sound. The album contains five instruction cassettes (4½ hours), another cassette with a personal welcome plus blank tape for practice, pictures showing exact position of teeth, tongue, and lips for more difficult sounds, and other printed materials to aid pronunciation and spelling. Total cost is $65. Mr. Bedell is a dynamic and forceful, yet friendly and personable instructor, and CIS recommends this album for those who feel their American English pronunciation is faulty. [Source: Bedell Speech Training International]

How To Speak Your Way To Success—Most successful people possess an ability to communicate orally that has carried them to the top. Nido Qubein gives pointers on how to speak effectively—be it to convey a point to a friend or to give a speech before a thousand people. $69.95 for six cassettes in album. [Source: Creative Services, Inc.]

Speaking Album—Four cassettes (in album) by a professional speaker for beginning stand-up speakers. His topics cover humorizing your talk, the anatomy of a speech, techniques for starting a speech, and planning an effective meeting. $49.50, including booklet and book. [Source: Art Fettig]

How To Enter the World of Paid Speaking—Dottie Walters tells you how to start, what to charge, and how to find paying customers, on four hour-long cassettes for $59. [Source: Royal Publishing]

Speech Impact—This course aims at improving speaking skills and confidence of executives, managers, and salespeople in large audience, small group, and one-on-one presentations. It focuses both on preparation (setting a results-oriented objective, planning the lead-in, emphasizing key points, and ending with impact) and delivery (improving articulation, using gestures, controlling pace). $39.95 for cassette, interactive workbook, and optional leader's guide in album-binder. [Source: Education Research]

'Mick' Delaney—In *Red Hot (But Clean) humor*, Mr. Delaney gives helpful hints on the use of jokes and one-liners to change pace, to salvage a failed joke, and to close the talk. *If You're Making A Speech . . . Start'Em Laughing* tells how to do just that. Both talks abound with anecdotes, of course. $15 for each 30-minute cassette, or both for $25. [Source: Clearing House for Speech Humor]

Facts for Stutterers: Finding a Clinician Who Can help—C. Woodruff Starkweather presents the indications for therapy, examines specific stuttering behavior of adults, evaluates the effectiveness and costs of treatment programs, and motivates the stutterer to work closely with the therapist, all on a 50-minute cassette for $13.95. [Source: Jeffrey Norton Publishers, Inc.]

Speech Improvement: Do It Yourself—A unique course designed to correct the major causes of unpleasantness in American speech: nasality, lack of resonance, faulty pronunciation of vowels and consonants, bad pitch, rasping and grating, excessive speed and improper volume. Like a private tutor, Phyllis Rooder Weiss gives firm but understanding guidance. $39.50 with booklet. [Source: Jeffrey Norton Publishers, Inc.]

Vocabulary Improvement

Vocab—The *Bergen Evans Vocabulary Program* presents 500 key words (such as anathema, coterie, eschew, hiatus, moot, risible) and more than 2,000 derivatives, not only to enlarge the recognition and comprehension vocabulary but also to expand spoken and written word choice. Five cassettes and manual for $39.95. The *Rapid Vocabulary Development Program* uses the same format of usage in context (with 256 key words such as cajole, ilk, cavort, trepidation), but aimed at the junior high school level and above, four cassettes and booklet for $35. The *Wordcraft* series present 700 new words for elementary students but can also be used remedially by older students and adults, for two cassettes $19.95, for three cassettes $29.95, all with manual. [Source: Vocab Inc.]

Vocabulary Program—ESP has vocabulary programs ranging from grade 7 through adult levels, and all present new words in isolation, in sentences, and in contextual exercises until each new word is mastered. The college prep set includes such words as abjure, paucity, culpable, limpid, and more. The college and adult course goes on to abrogate, encomium, propinquity, sapient, and 284 others. $80 per set of 12 cassettes in binder. [Source: ESP, Inc.]

Vocabulary Dynamics—"Words that forcefully communicate are the tools that build success," and this program will help add new and expressive words to your vocabulary—ubiquitous, dichotomy, ephemeral, invidious, and many more. $42.85 for three hour-long cassettes and manual in album. [Source: Kirkhon Publications, Inc.]

Writing

Business Communications—Business can be gained or lost by using, or failing to use, the most effective mode of communication. The key is often the proper choice of subjective vs. objective communications—and this program explains it all. $12.60 for cassette and worksheets. [Source: Z Incorporated.]

Effective Writing—This concise course, developed by Joel Bradke, covers when to use written vs. spoken communication, becoming clearer by being concise, and the value of using active verbs. $12.60 for cassette and worksheets. [Source: Z Incorporated.]

Action Writing—This cassette course aims at showing how to improve productivity by learning to write more clearly in half the time. Some of the topics covered are sizing up the audience, writing clear sentences, selling ideas to management, expressing complex ideas, and giving negative ideas a positive tone. $74.95 for four cassettes and workbook in album. [Source: Human Productivity Institute]

Writing Better Letters in Business—Intended for student use, these ten cassettes (18 to 24 minutes each) contain valuable pointers of use to anyone who writes business letters: how to handle the salutation (Ms? Dear?), use of active and conversational words, effective closings, how to say unpleasant things pleasantly, letter layout that invites reading, and much more. $113 for ten cassettes and study guide in album. [Source: Bergwall Productions]

Writing Album—Art Fettig based this six-hour course on the experience of years of trial and error, frustration and rejection. He helps budding writers avoid some of the anguish they face, by offering a 'positive living' approach to a successful writing career, together with an abundance of pointers, recommendations, leads, and advice. $49.50 for six cassettes in album. [Source: Art Fettig]

Writer's Voice—A collection of cassette programs that outline the "how-to" of all aspects of writing and selling manuscripts. Each selection gives professional, first-hand advice from experts like Arthur Hailey, James A. Michener, Art Buchwald, Gay Talese, Jesse Hill Ford (and many others), mostly through informal talks or interviews. Subjects include the basics of short story writing, novel writing, poetry, writing biography, science fiction writing. Most are about an hour long, cost $8.95, a few are shorter, for $7.95, some are longer, for $9.95 and $12.95. Fascinating stuff for any would-be writer. [Source: Learning Arts]

Write To Sell—Gordon Burgett tells how to do just that, on a four cassette-with-workbook program ($49.95) titled *How To Sell 75% of Your Freelance Writing*. Mr. Burgett has single cassettes on *How To*

Write Query Letters that Sell Articles and Books, Finding Ideas for Articles that Sell, and *Research: Finding Facts, Quotes, and Anecdotes for Articles that Sell,* all with printed summary for $9.95 each. *Ghostwriting: How To Define, Develop, and Market Your Skills for Profit* is Dr. C. E. Zoerner's collection of pointers for "the surest, quickest way for the freelancer to make money," three cassettes, $39.95. He also offers *Multiplying Your Writing Income by Increasing Your Productivity,* on one cassette for $9.95. [Source: Write To Sell]

Breaking That Writer's Block—How to overcome the hesitation that holds you back when it's time to write that special assignment, report, or article—and the deadline is approaching! $9.50 for one cassette. [Source: Mozelle Bigelow Kraus, Ed.D.]

Power Writing—A course designed by Robert Max to enhance writing skills of managers, professionals, and others whose careers demand clear and forceful writing skills. The course stresses the 'thinking processes' involved, by analyzing the object, subject, and purpose of written communications—letters, reports, proposals, etc. $99.95 for four cassettes, four study books, and three reference books. And for the correct way to put the thoughts into sentences, there is *Corporate Grammar,* in case you forgot the grammar you were taught in grade school, ignored it in high school, evaded it in college—but now find that errors in English usage, spelling, and punctuation on business correspondence are impeding your progress in the corporate world. This course uses a prescriptive/diagnostic approach to help rid you of the most common errors. $29.95. [Source: Learn Incorporated]

III.

Education

Adult and Continuing

How To Teach Grown-Ups—Help for the inexperienced instructor suddenly assigned to teach adults, giving crucial instruction on the differences in teaching adults (generally a self-learning process) vs. children (usually a teacher-led process). Important facets include the participative lecture, discussion methods, effective use of common instructional aids, lesson planning and developing objectives, experimental methods, one-on-one instruction, and testing. $250 for 12 cassettes in album, three sets of student interactive workbooks and binders, and an administrator's guide. [Source: Practical Management Associates, Inc.]

Complete Course in English Grammar—This eight-cassette course covers all areas and aspects of the language, suitable both for review and for those who need help at the senior high or college level. $245.95, including syllabus. [Source: Lansford Publishing Company.]

Math House Proficiency Review Tapes—An individual audio-tutorial program in basic mathematics that is thoroughly 'how to' and practical in its approach, with a minimum of reading required, yet mature enough in tone and content to appeal to adults. Unit A covers whole numbers and fractions, Unit B covers decimals and percents; $179.50 for each ten-cassette unit, both for $359. Unit C is devoted to measurements, Unit D to money math; again, $179.50 for each ten-cassette unit, both for $359—or the whole works for $665. Each unit also contains quizzes, workbook and instructor's guide in an album. [Source: Math House]

Automated Learning—College level courses (including cassette, text, and quiz) in: economics, biology I and II, world history I and II, vocabulary for literature, basic psychology, basic accounting, chemistry, plane geometry, American history I and II, college and intermediate algebra, business law I and II, business arithmetic, bookkeeping I and II, public speaking, American government, basic philosophy, basic sociology, English grammar and usage, and writing guide. They also offer short courses in Spanish I and II, French I and II, Hebrew, German, and Italian. [Source: Automated Learning, Inc.]

Pilots Audio Update—A monthly cassette designed to keep pilots informed and current on procedural changes, as well as giving practical information on flight safety, proficiency, and efficiency, $85 a year. Biennial flight reviews are available at $8.95 for General and $8.95 for Instrument, or both for $17.90. Icing tapes are also available in a series of three for $24.95, including binder. [Source: Educational Reviews, Inc.]

Physics—A new approach to physics, geared to the needs of a rapidly-changing world. It combines all the basic knowledge of conventional physics course objectives with many new ones, all in a way that makes the learning process easy. $295.95 for ten cassettes and a syllabus. [Source: Lansford Publishing Company]

Training Perspectives—Three top training specialists—Martin M. Broadwell, Ruth House, and Dugan Laird—combine talents to provide instruction and motivation for trainers through discussions, role-playing, and exercises. Six topics are covered, each on a 45-50 minute cassette: feedback in the learning process; determining training needs; evaluation of training efforts; principles and problems; supporting adult behavior change; and instructor training. $85 for six cassettes in album, or $14.95 per cassette. [Source: CBI Publishing Company, Inc.]

Lifelong Learning—Quality, advanced programming from the University of California Berkeley, mostly recorded conference proceedings, institutes, and workshops held at UCB. *Gifted Students: Teaching to Their Diversity* is captured on 19 cassettes for $138 in album, but individual lectures discussing aspects of the challenge are $10-$12 each. *Black English* is a complete course by Orlando L. Taylor, offering ways to improve the quality of education for black students whose nonstandard English is viewed as a disability that must be corrected, 13 hours, $110 with album. *Principles, Methods, and Materials of Adult Education* covers just that in 16½ hours of selected lectures, $125 in album. *How Tests Fail* provides what teachers, counselors, school psychologists, and administrators need to know about the limitations of standardized tests, 11 hours for $90, with album. [Source: University of California]

National Book Company—An extensive catalog of college-level courses (or advanced high school reviews) in many areas: algebra, basic calculus (covering both differential and integral), basic drafting, constructional geometry, statistics, and numerical trigonometry, among others in the mathematics category; biology, introductory chemistry, basic electronics, oceanography, physics, and weather analysis and maps in the science category. The language arts division covers English grammar, library orientation, punctuation, spelling, and vocabulary building, among others. Prices are modest for these complete courses; the physics course, for example, is $164.70 for 10 cassettes, syllabus, tests, and teacher's guide in album. [Source: National Book Company]

Educulture Audio-Tutorials—Mini-courses covering a spectrum of topics, with each course consisting of modules (each including two instructional cassettes and 12 student interactive response manuals) covering different or incremental aspects of the program's topic. The 'audio-tutorial' format is response-oriented to provide immediate feedback, perceptual involvement, and continuous evaluation. Subjects available include spelling, vocabulary development, speed reading, library skills, academic skills (reading), grammar, English, rhetoric and critical thinking, arithmetic, basic applied mathematics, business mathematics, think metric, pre-algebra, algebra, trigonometry, statistics and probability, inferential statistics, mathematics for allied health sciences, medical terminology, chemistry, psychology, insurance, and business reports. Costs range from $30 to $54 per module. [Source: Educulture Inc.]

College Preparation

Protape College Entrance Examination Review Course—More than seven hours of problems, principles, answers, and analyses, plus coordinated English and mathematics study manuals, to help prepare for and pass such examinations as PSAT, civil service, SAT, high school equivalency, ACT, scholarship, and LSAT. The emphasis is on sharpening powers of reasoning, and improving math and verbal skills, under simulated test conditions. $159 for six cassettes and two manuals with album. [Source: Protape, Inc.]

How To Take the SAT and PSAT Tests—A home tutorial study program that provides specific techniques for mastering both the verbal and the mathematical sections of the Scholastic Aptitude Tests, with advice on how to take the tests, how to recognize clues to answers, and how to develop a winning strategy. $23.95 for two 90-minute cassettes and 372-book [Source: Jeffrey Norton Publishers, Inc.]

Basic Skills—Two six-cassette study skills programs generally aimed toward helping college students raise achievement level while dealing with typical college assignments. The Level One course covers spelling, grammar and usage, diction and style, sentence structure, from paragraphs to term papers, and ways to use the program; the Level Two course has more emphasis on grammar and usage, how to write a critique, how to interpret prose and poetry-fiction, how to read a textbook, how to improve notetaking, and how to handle multiple research assignments. $98 for each course of six cassettes in album. Other single cassettes ($15 each) aimed at the college level listener: *How To Improve Your Listening*, *8 Steps to the Dean's List* and *Student's Survival Kit*. [Source: Tutor/Tape.]

How to Guarantee Success in College—Tips on choosing a college, financing an education, managing activities, planning schedules, getting the most from lectures, improving reading and listening comprehension, taking exams, and maintaining a winning attitude—all of which not only can help in college but also establish a lifetime of success behavior. $70 for six cassettes and guide in album. [Source: Nightingale-Conant Corporation]

Study Secrets: The Winning Edge for Students—Vernon Jacobs teaches students to "study smarter, not harder" on this recommended 40-minute cassette for $10.95. A related program is *How to Study*, a four-cassette (112 minute) course by Marianne L. McManus that requires active participation of the listener at each step toward the goal of developing effective study techniques. $39. [Source: Jeffrey Norton Publishers, Inc.]

How To Survive in College—Developed and tested at Purdue University, this program covers virtually every aspect of learning and success in college, from how to listen to a lecture to prepare for exams, aimed at the college-bound student with study problems. $99 for eight cassettes (five hours of lecture), workbooks and guide in album. [Source: Source: Educational Enrichment Materials]

Special Education

Specific Learning Disabilities—Designed for classroom teachers, school psychologists, speech and language therapists, and remedial learning specialists, this course helps to recognize the learning disabled child and to identify the best approach to remediation. $187 for ten cassettes and supplemental material. [Source: Paul S. Amidon & Associates]

Special Education Programs—*Innovations in Training Regular Classroom Teachers To Cope with the Handicapped* by Dr. Josephy Purdy, five cassettes with guide in album, $59; *Teaching Children with Learning Disabilities* by Dr. Stanley Krippner, six cassettes and guide in album, $69.95; *Career Education for the Mentally Retarded* by Dr. Sandra Boland, six cassettes and guide in album, $69.95; *Learning To Learn* (problems that interfere with effective learning) by Dr. Joseph Wepman, six cassettes in album, $68.45.

Some individual cassettes are offered, generally for $13.95: *Society's Responsibility for the Emotionally Disturbed*, *The Handicapped Are Here To Stay* ($15.95), *The Role of Psychology in Special Education*, *Learning Disabilities*, and *Hiring the Handicapped*. [Source: Instructional Dynamics, Inc.]

Special Education Series—Carefully planned cassette-plus-book courses for special education teachers, special school administrators, and others interested in mainstreaming handicapped children. The *Identfication and Evaluation Program* introduces theories and recent developments on assessing a variety of learning problems, $98 for three cassettes and four books. The *Emotional and Behavioral Program* shows how to help such students with their social, academic, and personal development, $96 for two cassettes and four books. *Gifted and Talented Education* and *Identification and Evaluation of Exceptional Children* are each $43.50 for two cassettes and a book. Finally, there are four overview programs, each consisting of a cassette and book, for $24.50: *Special Education*, *Learning Disabilities*, *Visually Handicapped Education*, and *Autism*. [Source: Special Education Corporation]

Skillstreaming the Adolescent—A skills training program for use with aggressive, withdrawn, immature, and developmentally lagging adolescents, led by Dr. Arnold P. Goldstein. It is planned to aid teachers or trainers in the use of the 'structured learning' approach, which consists of four facets—modeling, role playing, performance feedback, and transfer of training. $32.95 for three 60-minute cassettes in album. A related program is *Legal Challenges in Educating Handicapped Children*, recorded during an actual workshop on March 31, 1980, Reed Martin J.D. gives up-to-date information about current federal regulations and court decisions governing educational services to handicapped children. $59.95 for five 60-minute cassettes in album. [Source: Research Press]

Teacher Development

Staff Development—*Motivation in the Classroom* by Dr. Billy Sharp, six cassettes in album, $69.95; *Community Pressure Points in American Schools* by Dr. Luvern Cunningham, six cassettes in album, $68.45; *Education and Innovation* by Dr. Melvin P. Heller, five cassettes in album, $57.50; *Getting Back To Basics* by Dr. Willard J. Congreve, six cassettes in album with guide and manual, $79.45; *Choice and Change in Education* (a symposium of five outstanding educators), six cassettes in album, $68.45; *Administrative Patterns for Today's Education* (problems with 'building principals'), six cassettes in album, $68.45; *Advanced ESL Instruction* by J. William McVey, six cassettes in album with guide, $69.95; *Art for Today*, by Dr. Terence Tobin, six cassettes in album with guide and activity cards, $68.45; *Improv-*

ing Classroom Discipline by Dr. William J. Gnagey, six cassettes with guide in album, $69.95; *Nongradedness: How It Looks in the Real World* by Dr. Curtis Van Alfen, five cassettes in album, $57.50. And there are more. [Source: Instructional Dynamics]

Remedial Reading—An in-service program that gives concise coverage of the major topics involved in planning and implementing an effective remedial reading program. $167.45 for 15 cassettes, leader's manual, and participant handbook. A related program is *Teaching Reading in High School*, in which Dr. James Duggins raises questions fundamental to constructing reading curricula in the American secondary school—and then offers practical, down-to-earth suggestions for the teacher who isn't a reading expert. $40.15 for six cassettes, 25 teacher guides, and Dr. Duggin's text. [Source: Paul S. Amidon & Associates]

Basic Interaction Analysis Training Course—A course by Dr. Edmund J. Amidon for improving teacher effectiveness through Verbal Interaction Analysis. $206.50 for 17 cassettes, leader's guide and evaluation instruments. Also by Dr. Amidon is *Understanding Groups*. This authority on group dynamics outlines a systematic study of group structure, member roles, goals, norms, cohesiveness, and issues, to help meet the need for understanding the groups of which everyone is a part and with which teachers deal on a daily basis. $147.10 for 13 cassettes. Other programs available include: *Understanding and Improving School Faculty Meetings*, $8.75 for one cassette; *Counseling Interaction Profile Training Tape*, $9 for one cassette; and *Parliamentary Procedures*, $28.50 for five cassettes with content outlines and teacher notes. [Source: Paul S. Amidon & Associates]

How Teachers Control Behavior and Misbehavior in the Classroom—A six-cassette program that advocates a new technique of behavior modification in the classroom both for better discipline and greater motivation on the part of the students. The lectures cover also the scientific analysis of behavior, social reinforcement and the shaping and maintaining of behavior, superstitions, fears, and anxieties regarding behavior, and the relative value of choice, conflict, and control. $149 with teacher guide. [Source: Lansford Publishing Company]

American Montessori Society—Three albums presenting the best of three conferences featuring well-known educators, authors, and professionals. *Fantasy & Creativity in the Life of the Child* presents Bruno Bettelheim, John Blessington, Marilyn Ferguson, and 13 others. *Chance Favors the Prepared Mind* features Albert Reichert, Anne Sagendorph and 14 others. *Mind, Body, Movement: The Elements of Education* has George Leonard, Tim Seldin, and 14 others. $79 for each 16-cassette album, all three for $210. [Source: Professional Cassette Center]

Audio-Forum—Many topics dealing both with specific teaching goals and with education in general. Some examples: *Dealing with the Gifted Child* by Nathaniel Branden, *The Underachiever* with Rudolph Dreikurs, *Creative Ways of Teaching* with E. Paul Torrance, *The Deschooled Society* with Ivan Illich, and *The Effects of Federal Aid to Education* with Roger A. Freeman. These are all single hour-long cassettes for $10.95 to $11.95. Then, the Center for Constructive Alternatives (Hillsdale College) offers three symposia of talks by experts, generally of a conservative bent, on: *Education in America: Democratic Triumph or Egalitarian Disaster* (7½ hours, $44); *Decadence and Renewal in Higher Learning* (12 hours, $70); and *"Private vs. Public Education: Parental Control (1776) or Big Brother (1984)"* (8 hours, $51.50). [Source: Jeffrey Norton Publishers, Inc.]

How To Teach Eureka!—A highly acclaimed, carefully structured program to help teachers in grades 4-8 teach mathematic principles, by means of stories, games, and puzzles. Educator Louis S. Cohen recreates a classroom "chalktalk" with a discussion of techniques on Side 1, and on Side 2 of each cassette he is joined by a couple of classroom teachers playing devil's advocate about the procedures. $179.50 for 12 cassettes (each 24 to 48 minutes long) plus workbook in album. [Source: Math House]

Psychology of Learning—Psychologist Richard P. Issel discusses the factors that inhibit or enhance the learning process, and applies them both to school-based learning situations and to adult and life-long learning. $15.95 for a 50-minute cassette. [Source: Learning Consultants, Inc.]

Finding Career Alternatives for Teachers—Anne Miller adapted the material from her book and seminars to offer "everyting you need to know to help you find the most challenging and financially rewarding career for yourself in the least amount of time." The theme of this course is that teachers are skilled, intelligent, and talented individuals, who need only to learn how to identify, translate, and market their strengths into a new field. $48.95 for four cassettes plus workbook and additional printed material in album. [Source: Chiron Associates, Inc.]

Lifelong Learning—Advanced-level conference proceedings from the University of California Berkeley. *Advances in the Psychology of Thinking* is a collection of lectures on the cognitive processes, viewed from the perspectives of child study, linguistics, experimental psychology, neurology, education, and computer science, $97 for nine cassettes (10 hours) in album, $12 to $15 per cassette lecture. [Source: University of California]

Learning Theory and Personality—A series of cassettes that explores the input of Skinner, Thorndike, Guthrie, Pavlov, Tolman, Hull, Piaget, Freud, and Erikson into learning theory and personality, plus lectures on neurophysiology, implications of learning theory for education and for child-rearing, advice for parents, and more. $25.95 each. [Source: Lansford Publishing Company]

IV.
Financial Matters

Banking

Banking Series—Updates on the rapidly changing information about legislation, necessary for all those involved in providing bank services, in order to avoid serious penalties for non-compliance. Topics covered: bankruptcy law, consumer credit, regulations, consumer loans, pricing financial services, the professional teller, truth in lending. $45 to $130 for three to six cassettes, plus manual for $25 to $35. [Source: Professional Education Systems, Inc.]

RMA Cassettes—Live unedited recordings of Robert Morris Associates workshops for bankers, held around the country, on the general subject of the loan operations of a bank. Some specific titles: *Term Lending—Updated 1981* (three one-hour cassettes, $45); *Lending in Latin America* (four one-hour cassettes, $60); *Loan Quality Control* (three one-hour cassettes, $45); and *Foreign Credit Analysis* (two one-hour cassettes, $24). [Source: Robert Morris Associates]

Bank Marketing Association—Two programs for customer contact personnel. Those with limited banking experience would benefit from *Service Up to Par*, a basic program that teaches the PAR method of cross-selling: perceive, analyze, recommend, $200 for a cassette, leader's guide, and 10 student workbook. *The "Know" Program* is for employees with banking experience, teaching them the three selling steps: know your services, know your customers, know your selling situation. $225 for two lecture cassettes, one role-play cassette, 50 role-play cards, leader's guide, and five student workbooks. [Source: Bank Marketing Association]

Economics

Introduction To Free Market Economics—Sixteen lectures (each over an hour long), on basic free market economics, by Dr. Murray N. Rothbard, one of the foremost proponents of libertarian economics. $11.95 per lecture, all 16 in albums for $153. Also by Dr. Rothbard is *Cornell Lectures on Twentieth Century American Economic History*, a revisionist view of economic history that explains many of the economic problems being experienced today on ten cassettes (12 hours) for $85, and also available individually.

There is also the *Ludwig von Mises Lecture Series*, talks given by invited lecturers at the Center for Constructive Alternatives, Hillsdale College, all generally reflecting a conservative view of the national and world economy, $10.95 each, any ten titles for $85. [Source: Jeffrey Norton Publishers, Inc.]

Sound of the Economy—In this excellent monthly subscription service, top Citibank economists analyze the current forces—financial, political, technological—that are shaping the future of the economy. They give their interpretation of the latest shifts and trends in interest rates, government policy, the market, inflation, real growth, corporate profits, unemployment, inventories, and so forth. $124 for a year's subscription of twelve 40- to 50-minute cassettes, each with transcript. [Source: Citibank]

Audio-Forum—Single cassettes ($10.95 to $12.50 each) on various aspects of economics, but most propounding a conservative or libertarian viewpoint. There are two Nobel laureates represented: Milton Friedman on *The Role of Government in our Society* and *Long-Term Solutions to the Energy Crisis*, and Friedrich Hayek on *U.S. Policy Guarantees Inflation* and *The End of the U.S. Dollar Monopoly*. John Kenneth Galbraith offers his distinctly un-conservative views of *Economics and the Public Purpose*. Dr. Nathaniel Branden discusses *The Economics of a Free Society* and *Common Fallacies about Capitalism*, while Ludwig von Mises explains *Why Socialism Always Fails* and *The Spirit of the Australian School of Economics*. Dr. Murray Rothbard bluntly states *How Government Destroys Our Money*, George J. Viksnins gives *An Introduction to Economics*, and Dr. Charles Wolff describes *A Christian Approach to Business Economics*. And there are more listed in the free catalog. [Source: Jeffrey Norton Publishers, Inc.]

Bob Snyder Cassette Commentary—The controversial columnist and syndicated radio program producer gives his distinctly conservative, Christian viewpoints on money, finances, inflation, higher prices, government control, rationing, gun control, wage and price controls, gold and silver, and much more. Three of the monthly tapes for $25, six for $45, twelve (a year's subscription) for $82. Single tapes $10. [Source: Bob Snyder Enterprises]

Tutor/Tape—A series of talks that espouse the free enterprise, free market approach to economics, and a collection of short 'free-market essays' that promote the concept of the profit motive and private ownership as the foundation of free economics. $10 or $15 each cassette. [Source: Tutor/Tape]

How To Manage Your Money—A home budgeting system, written by Arnold Van Den Berg, on eight tapes, covering the psychology of money, personal budgeting, how to get out of debt, how to save money on insurance, how to buy a home, history of money and inflation, investment guidelines, and the best investment you can make. $95 for all cassettes plus budget book and album-binder, individual tapes $10. [Source: Van Den Berg Publishing]

Economics—A college-level course that gives a comprehensive overview of the subject, giving historical precedents, discussing the impact of technology, and covering some personal and consumer economics, 14 cassettes, syllabus, tests, and teacher's key in album, $222.45. Related are *Consumer Economics & Personal Finance*, 14 cassettes for $223.75, including syllabus and tests. [Source: National Book Company]

Investments

Commodities Trading Course—James H. Sibbet introduces his ten futures market predicting techniques that have proved to be highly effective for him. $75 for five tapes (8+ hours of material), and reference manual. Tips reflecting wide experience and success in another type of investment are to be found in *Real Estate Investment*, by James Nickerson, author of *How I Turned $1000 into Three Million in Real Estate . . . In My Spare Time*. This is a home-study for the beginning real estate investor, which tells Nickerson's secrets of financing, improving, operating, and selling for maximum profits. Six tapes plus a copy of the book for $75. [Source: Jeffrey Norton Publishers, Inc.]

What Every Woman Should Know About Investing, Estate Management and The Law—Five experts help women intelligently handle their financial affairs by acquainting them with estate planning, estate and gift taxes, life insurance, investment management, and sources of investment advice. Over nine hours of information on eight cassettes for $70. Two related programs, useful for men or women, are *How To Plan Your Retirement* and *Pitfalls and Benefits of Tax Shelters*. In the first you are shown how to figure your post-retirement assets, income and expenses, and the estate and income tax consequences of retirement are explained on two cassettes with booklet for $24.50; in the second, five accountants, lawyers and real estate specialists discuss the advantages of each type of shelter and its potential problems and how to avoid them. $50 for five tapes and a handbook in album. [Source: Jeffrey Norton Publishers, Inc.]

International Investments—*A Primer for Mideast Investments* gives five hours of advice on six cassettes ($10.95 each, the set for $55), with noted national and international financial and petrodollar experts. Then there's the *Bahamas 1979 Real Estate Seminar*, with everything you wanted to know about investing in Bahamas real estate—legal and tax advantages, how to buy in the volatile marketplace, and more on three cassettes for $65. Finally, there is the *1979 Swiss Money Seminar*, in which experts in economics, numismatics, real estate, gold and silver, and other fields talk about the virtues of living in Switzerland and transacting business there, on ten cassettes for $85. [Source: Jeffrey Norton Publishers, Inc.]

National Institute of Financial Planning—Mark O. Haroldsen has succeeded at the noble American goal of making a lot of money and paying very few taxes. He makes his money through real estate manipulations, as he modestly relates in *How To Make a Million Dollars* ($15.50 for one cassette) and expands in *Financial Genius* ($41 for six cassettes). Cassettes by other experts, all generally espousing real estate as the way to wealth, carry these titles: *Essentials in Property Management* ($31 for two tapes), *How To Borrow a Million Dollars* ($15.50), *Basic Law for Daily Living* and *Creative Real Estate Law*, (each $10.50), *Real Estate Money Machine* (two tapes, $31), *Develop Your Way to Success* (four tapes, $61), *Finance Your Way to Success* (eight tapes, $161), *Finding Super Deals*, *Trade Up Tax Free*, *Pay No Taxes Ever Again Legally*, *No Money Down Deals*, and *Buying Your First Investment Property* (all by Bill 'Tycoon' Greene, $14.50 each but please see caveat, p. 18), *Unlocking Your Real Estate Fortunes* (two tapes by David Cowan, $26), and more. [Source: National Institute of Financial Planning, Inc.]

Audio-Forum—A fascinating collection of individual tapes ($10.95 to $12.50 each) that covers the spectrum of investment opportunities. For example, Sigmund Rothschild discusses *Auction Buying Techniques*, *How To Buy Paintings*, and *Investing in Gems and Jewelry*. Vernon K. Jacobs offers *12 Unusual, Low-Risk Investment Ideas*, *How To Save 50% of your Lifetime Income*, and *An Easy System To Control Your Debts*. Alan Pope gets down to specifics with *How To Plan an Investment Program*, and Conrad Leslie gives *12 Laws for Successful Trading in Gold, Commodities and Stock*. Ira Cobleigh describes *Investment Opportunities in Uranium*, and Charles Stahl calls *Silver: The Super Investment of the Coming Decade*, while Michael West gives *An In-Depth Analysis of South African Gold Shares*. And there are many more; write for the free catalog. [Source: Jeffrey Norton Publishers, Inc.]

Winning Investment Strategies for Reaganomics—28 experts give their recommendations to help maximize profits on investments, avoid financial pitfalls, and capitalize on inflation. Speakers include Joseph E. Granville, Jack Anderson, Harry D. Schultz,

Robert M. Bleiberg, Martin Zweig, Joe Gandolfo, Donald H. Rowe, James McKeever, and Ralph Goldman. $70 for eight cassettes and study guide in album. [Source: Nightingale-Conant Corporation]

Investor's Hotline—Each monthly issue of this investment subscription service contains four interviews with leading sound money economists and monetary and financial experts—such as Harry Schultz, John Exter, Jerome Smith, James Dines, Henry Hazlitt, and E. C. Harwood, to name a few. They answer pointed questions on the stock market, inflation, gold and silver, commodities, bonds, art investments, taxation, and more—generally advocating a conservative, hard money approach. $140 a year for 12 monthly C-96 cassettes and printed summaries and charts. [Source: Audio Alert, Inc.]

Investment Economics—Eleven 90-minute tapes of talks by Richard R. Sylvester, J.D. Ph.D. and interviews with top-level experts on personal investment planning, including real property rental, estate taxes, tax-deferred exchanges, and technology changes. $219.45 for the set. [Source: Ph.D. Publishing Company]

Taxes

Tax Planning—Ten live recordings by Richard R. Sylvester J.D. Ph.D. that explain critical details of various tax minimization strategies in personal investment programs, all presented in a manner that can be understood and applied by all of us. $119.70 for ten 90-minute cassettes. Related is *Tax Strategy Under the New Tax Law*, with Richard R. Sylvester J.D. Ph.D. offering a detailed review of the major provisions of the Economic Recovery Tax Act of 1981, with suggestions for overall strategy, insights into the economic forecast, and highlights of basic decisions to be made. $20.95 for a 90-minute cassette. [Source: Ph.D. Publishing Company]

Keeping Current—In this subscription program, quarterly tapes provide a thorough analysis of the latest relevant IRS rulings, tax-related Federal Court decisions, and other Treasury promulgations. Each tape is accompanied by a comprehensive workbook supplementing the materials on tape. $100 a year (four cassettes). [Source: American Society of CLU]

CLU Cassette Library—Specially-recorded in-depth discussions providing insights into pertinent topics in the areas of estate planning, employee benefits, business and tax planning, and pensions, contributed by distinguished attorneys, CPAs, and CLUs. For example, Donald O. Jansen gives pointers on how to make the most of *The Economic Recovery Tax Act of 1981*, on one cassette and syllabus, $25. Four estate planning professionals give valuable and practical tips in *New Perspectives in Sophisticated Estate Tax Planning*, $100 for five cassettes plus workbook in

album. *Definitive Split Dollar* offers a comprehensive analysis of this subject, on a cassette with 100-page workbook for $25. In *Selective Compensation for the 1980's: Where We Are and Where We're Going*, four specialists provide an analysis of recent developments and imaginative application of new techniques in marketing employee benefit plans, $100 for five cassettes and 400-page workbook in album. Other single-cassette programs (except as noted): *The Technique of the Sales*, $7; *Use of Section 303 in Publicly-Held Corporations*, $12 with syllabus; *A Practical Approach to Estate Planning*, $7; *The Insured Stock Purchase Agreement*, $8; *Trusts To Receive Life Insurance Proceeds*, $8; *Employee Stock Ownership Trusts*, $12; *HR-10 Under ERISA*, $25; *Design Under ERISA*, $75 for three cassettes and workbook; *A New Look at Estate Planning for the Family-Owned Corporation*, $100 for five cassettes and workbook; and *Estate & Gift Tax Reform*, $25 with syllabus. [Source: American Society of CLU]

Estates, Gifts, Fiduciaries—Planning and Taxation—An excellent home study course on estate and gift taxation and how to minimize it. Just some of the topics covered are transfers, annuities, life insurance, powers of appointment, postmortem planning—everything to cover every situation. $195 for 20 half-hour lectures (10 cassettes) and manual in album. [Source: Protape, Inc.]

High Level Tax Knowledge Audiocassettes—Tax consultant Dr. Harold Wong shows how to prepare money-saving 1040 tax returns to help middle-income Americans minimize their tax burden, safely and legally. Going line by line through the 1040 forms of two typical families making $40,000 a year, he shows how one pays $8,495 in taxes, the other $891. You also hear how to deal with an audit, the advantages of itemization, the value of Schedule C, and the use of Form 2106, which the IRS doesn't supply because it saves you taxes. $140 for six cassettes (about three hours) and forms in album. [Source: Tax Perspectives]

Tycoon Tax Cassettes—Right up front, we rush to point out that these talks are produced by self-styled tycoon Bill Greene, who doesn't believe in paying federal income taxes, who likes to bait the IRS, and who unfortunately has been convicted of tax evasion. With that caveat, Mr. Greene offers these titles on cassette: *Buying Your First Investment*, *Think Like a Tycoon*, *Getting Organized as a Tycoon*, *No Money Down Deals*, *Pay No Taxes Ever Again, Legally!*, *Advanced Tax Avoidance*, *Trade Up Tax Free*, and *Finding Super Deals*. These are $11 each, or all eight in an album for $100. [Source: Bill Tycoon Greene]

Nuts & Bolts Tax Seminar—Four knowledgeable CPAs present a seminar to explain the latest changes in deductions, estate and gift tax provisions, Keogh plans, investment tax credits, and dozens of other tax law regulations (the course is updated yearly). $145 for eight 90-minute cassettes and interactive 200-page workbook in album. [Source: Professional Cassette Center]

Tax Shelter in Real Estate—A concise course on real estate shelters, covering all the rules with examples, showing how to compute the taxes, and giving explanations of alternative methods. Some topics covered include tax benefits of capital gains and losses, maximizing depreciation deductions, tax-free like-kind exchanges, deducting business uses, advantages of residence rentals and vacation houses, income averaging, and more. $49.95 for three cassettes and workbook in album. [Source: Totaltape, Inc.]

Complete Deferred Giving Tax Course—The tax law provides generous tax incentives for those who make deferred (life income) gifts to educational, hospital, religious, or charitable organizatons. This course describes the tax implications, advantages, and pitfalls of deferred gifts. $175 for five hour-long cassettes in album. Complementing this course is *Running a Deferred Giving Program Course*, which tells how to start, promote, and administer deferred giving programs. Also $175 for five C-60 cassettes in album. [Source: Taxwise Giving]

P-H Tax Professionals' Cassette—A monthly cassette service that brings new yet proved tax breaks to accountants and attorneys. The editors of Prentice-Hall use both top tax specialists and inside information gleaned from their network of contacts to show how to capitalize on the latest tax breakthroughs to increase after-tax earnings for the tax professional and his clients. The emphasis is on handling tax law changes, shortcuts in filing returns, tax incentives for executives, maximum deductions, and tax-free income. $198 for a year's subscription covering 12 hour-long programs, issued monthly. [Source: Prentice-Hall, Inc.]

Tax Highlights Quarterly—Comprehensive quarterly reviews of recent IRS rulings and regulations, court decisions, and legislation in the federal tax field prepared by three distinguished CPAs who point out the important news, analyze its practical effects, and point up potential problems and opportunities. $80 per year (four cassettes). [Source: AICPA]

Audilex—Specific, useful programs on taxation, accounting, auditing, and business law, of interest to accountants and tax lawyers and also to anyone else with an interest in these areas. The discussions are reasonably non-technical and are well-presented. Cassettes are generally one hour each, and all courses come in an album with supplemental materials. Titles include: *Individual Income Tax Refresher Course*, $70 for four cassettes and workbook; *Guide to Corporate Tax Planning*, $45 for two cassettes; *Estate Planning Course*, $70 for four cassettes, booklets, outline, and review quiz; *Preparers Liability*, $30 for one cassette and booklet; *Ins and Outs of IRS Practice and Procedure*, $50 for two cassettes and workbook; *Creating or Expanding an Estate Practice*, $40 for one cassette and quiz; *How To Turn Your Closely-Held Corporation into a Personal Tax Shelter*, $45 for two cassettes and booklet; *Pension and Profit-Sharing Course/IRA and H. R. 10 (Keogh) Plans*, $70 for four cassettes, booklets, workbook, and quiz; *Employee Benefits Under the 1981 Economic Recovery Act*, $30 for one cassette and booklet; *Tax Planning Opportunities for Businesses under ERTA*, $30 for one cassette, booklet, and resources; *The Tax Act of 1981*, $30 for two cassettes, outlines, and book; *Estate Planning Implications of the 1981 Tax Law*, $30 for one cassette, booklets, and book. Leaders on most Audilex courses are tax authorities Sidney Kess and George M. Schain. All courses published in 1982 or late 1981. [Source: Commerce Clearing House, Inc.]

Tax Views—A bimonthly subscription service, with Sidney Kess providing an analytic yet clear explanation of recent events in taxation. Each cassette comes with outline and bibliography. $85 a year for six cassettes (album sent with first cassette). In *Tax Shelters Quarterly*, a sophisticated quarterly service, Marvin Weinstein uses case studies and true-life examples to illustrate tax shelter planning techniques, including innovative and often-overlooked ideas to save valuable tax dollars. $70 a year for four cassettes with album. Finally there is *Estate Planning Quarterly*, a series of cassettes that meets the demand for concise, current information about estate planning, produced by Sidney Kess. $70 per year for four cassettes and album. An outline and bibliography accompanies each cassette sent at three-month intervals. [Source: Commerce Clearing House, Inc.]

V.

Health Sciences

Dentistry

Success In Dentistry—Leading dental clinicians in both the U.S. and Canada discuss their specialties in an informal, informative interview format. Speakers include Gen. S.N. Bhaskar, Dr. Wilmer B. Eames, Dr. Bernard Dolansky, Dr. George B. Robbins, Dr. Robert J. Samp, Dr. Sam Kucey, Dr. Harry Rosen, and Dr. Hugh Doherty. $12.50 for each conversation, mostly about an hour long, some shorter. [Source: Medifacts Ltd.]

Dentistry for Fun and Profit—Dr. Avrom King provides "the nitty gritty of whole person dentistry" on 10 cassettes in album for $136. Other programs of interest to the dentist are Dr. King's *A Survival Guide for Independent Dentists* (five cassettes in album for $144), *People Business in Dentistry* with Ken Olson PhD (six cassettes in album for $60), *Quality in Practice* with Dr. Bud Ham (11 cassettes in album for $125), and *Wet Fingered Advertising* by 'The Advertising Dentist' (six cassettes in album for $189). [Source: Semantodontics, Inc.]

Dentafacts—12 programs are issued each year in this subscription service. Each 60-minute program includes clinical presentations of various lengths (and occasional items on office or practice management) by prominent American and Canadian dental lecturers and teachers. $129 a year for Canadian, U.S., and overseas subscribers. [Source: Medifacts Ltd.]

ADA-Dentistry Update—In these specially recorded monthly programs, leading dental authorities join in panel discussions of pertinent clinical topics, to give listener-dentists the latest information regarding their practice. Each monthly program comes with complete transcript, quiz, and continuing education credits. $185 a year, $320 for two years. [Source: Medical Information Systems, Inc.]

Nutrition Counseling for Dental Caries Prevention and Control—An unrehearsed diet counseling session, with periodic explanations of the line of questioning the dentist is using. The program concludes with a brief follow-up interview with the patient. $26 for C-60 cassette with booklet. [Source: W. B. Saunders Company]

Holistic Health

Personal Enrichment Through Imagery—Arnold A. Lazarus, Ph.D. shows how a learned capacity to develop appropriate images can enhance general well-being as well as promote healing and coping responses. $35 for three cassettes and manual in album. [Source: BMA Audio Cassettes]

Awareness Through Movement—Audio-lessons by Ruthy Alon in the Feldenkrais method of overcoming poor posture and limited movement patterns to release greater ease and energy in their bodies and to relieve the pain and discomfort of misused joints and muscles. Separate cassettes ($9.50 each) cover breathing, the neck, eye training and proper sitting; and proper eating. Two-cassette programs ($18.20) are devoted to relieving lower back and neck compression and to helping the body re-align itself. A five-cassette *Primal Moving* package ($46) restores grace by re-experiencing the patterns of early infant movements. [Source: Creative Resources]

Comprehensive Weight Control Program—Drs. Albert R. and Marlene R. Marston offer a psychologically oriented approach to weight reduction, complementing calorie counting with principles learned from behavioral psychology. The result is a common sense approach to overeating and to the good-natured application of self-correcting techniques. Six hour-long cassettes with self-management and recordkeeping guides in album, $75. [Source: BMA Audio Cassettes]

ADA Audio Cassette Series—Subscribers receive ten new tapes each year covering administration, clinical nutrition, community nutrition, and education, given by outstanding authors in allied health fields, with the programs mailed as they are produced. $175 a year for the ten programs plus study guides and album. Individual programs are available for $18 each. The subscription plan is eligible for 20 ADA Continuing Education hours, and the individual cassettes each give two hours. All prices are less for ADA members. [Source: American Dietetic Association]

The High Fiber Diet—Dr. Robert A. Buyers discusses the possible role of fiber as a nutrient and its clinical applications in human disease. $9 for an hour-long cassette. [Source: Audio-Learning, Inc.]

Foods and Nutrition—College-level instruction on the basics of a well-balanced diet, the four food groups, nutrients in each food group and why they are important, and specific guidance for planning parties and dining out nutritiously. Three cassettes, syllabus, and tests in album for $58.10. Related is *Food Additives*, presenting an unbiased approach to the controversy of additions, explaining why they are used, safety and hazards, and how to read labels, all on two cassettes, syllabus, and tests in album for $39. [Source: National Book Company]

Audio-Forum—Down-to-earth topics covering health and the human body, each capsulized on a cassette for $10.95. Some of the titles: *The Wonderful Crisis of Middle Age, Growing Old with Grace, Self-examination and Understanding Breast Cancer, What You Should Know About Your Heart, Last Rights, How To Talk About Your Troubles, Lose Weight—and Enjoy It*, and *Having a Healthy Baby*. [Source: Jeffrey Norton Publishers, Inc.]

Managing Your Own Wellness Program—Barnet G. Meltzer M.D. gives 18 one-hour lectures explaining how all individuals hold the secret to their own health. There are eight lectures on improved nutrition (available for $55 with album), and other topics include physical fitness, lifestyles, personal relationships, and sexuality. The lectures are $7.95 each, any eight for $55, or all 18 with album for $120. [Source: Barnet G. Meltzer, M.D.]

Health World Cassettes—Hour-long cassettes that promote the laetrile and nutritional approaches to cancer. On one, the parents of Chad Green explain that nutritional therapy worked, since their son didn't die of leukemia. C. Edward Griffin discusses the science and politics of laetrile on three cassettes, Dr. Ernest T. Krebs, Jr. (the discoverer of laetrile) describes the origins of cancer and nature's treatment for it, and the late Adelle Davis tells how vitamin-rich diets prevent cancer. The last one is $7.60, the others are $8.45 each. [Source: Health World]

Health Care—A Way of Believing—A new view of holistic health and how we can help ourselves to better health, by orthopedic surgeon Robert L. Swearingen M.D., on this hour-long cassette, $8.95. [Source: Effective Learning Systems, Inc.]

Your Healing Power—Dr. Olga Worrall, a noted spiritual healer, offers a 90-minute self-look at our individual healing abilities and ability to consciously control healing energy. $7.95. Also available is a live healing workshop by Dr. Worrall, on three cassettes for $23.95—or all four tapes in an album for $28.95. [Source: Effective Learning Systems, Inc.]

New Dimension Tapes—Programs that offer internal solutions to the health of our society: David Commons on *Polarity Therapy*, Joseph Kamiya on *Biofeedback Basics*, Stanley Keleman on *Somatics/The Body and Beyond*, John Diamond on *Your Body Doesn't Lie*, Judith McKinnon on *Massage and Health*, Ruth Carter Stapleton on *The Nature of Inner Healing*, Irving Oyle on *Magical, Practical Medicine*, and more. $7.50 per cassette hour; most titles are 1-2 hours long. [Source: New Dimensions Tapes]

Facts of Life, Health, Happiness and Longevity—On four cassettes, Dr. Robert J. Samp of the University of Wisconsin Medical Center discusses disease prevention, well-being, and survival to a ripe old age. He first indicates the need for a life game plan with profiles of the long-lived, discusses the keys to longevity and survival strategies, analyzes the importance of stress in life, and then touches on important other aspects, including sex and nutrition. $38 for the set, including an album. [Source: Well-Being]

Cognetics Health Cassette Library—Talks by health experts on self-help health measures: *Acupuncture*; *The Bates Eye System* (of visual relaxation for improved vision); *Philosophy of Medicine for the Whole Man* (by Roy M. Menninger M.D.), *Holistic Healing*; *Role of the Mind in Cancer Therapy* (by O. Carl Simonton M.D.), *Mind as Healer, Mind as Slayer* (by Ken Pelletier M.D.); *Your Power to Heal* (by Olga Worrall Ph.D.), a host of specialized relaxation and mental imagery techniques for achieving specific goals, and a series of eight lectures by James Fadiman Ph.D. that offer help in restoring the balance between mind, body, and spirit. All cassettes $9 each, every sixth program free. [Source: Cognetics Inc.]

Spirit of Life—Self-help health programs, giving equal emphasis to the spiritual, mental, and physical nature of the person. *Nourishing the Life Force* (basic nutrition, including foods and supplements) and *Holistic Cleansing Program* (ridding the body of the toxic, negative conditions that impede the flow of healing) are 4½ hour programs on three cassettes for $15. One-hour holistic healing programs covering arthritis, weight loss, heart disorders, high blood pressure, and alcoholism are available for $5 each. Other one-hour programs cover healing, meditation, alignment training, stress and tension control, improved rest and sleep, also $5 each. [Source: Spirit of Life]

Taking Charge—Bevealy Nadller, author of the best-selling book by the same title, discusses in detail some of her basic tenets to help others enjoy 'total living.' Her emphasis on these four 50-minute cassettes is on nutrition stress, how the subconscious mind affects body and environment, and communication relationships and attitudes, all based on her 17 years of researching, correlating, and coordinating information on the 'whole' person. $52.45. [Source: Nadller Concepts]

Aletheia Foundation—Lectures by Jack Schwartz, a recognized authority of voluntary control of internal states, human energy systems (chakras), meditation, rebirthing, and other aspects of the holistic health movement. $7.50 to $15 per cassette, depending upon length. [Source: Aletheia Psycho-Physical Foundation]

Proseminar—Training and continuing education programs in human services and health care. Speakers and titles include: Gerald W. Piaget Ph.D., *Dealing with Difficult People, On the Job—In Daily Life*, four cassettes (one blank, for practice) and manual for $49.95; Janet W. Kizziar Ed.D. and Roger Moyer, *Burnout Prevention*, two cassettes, $23; Paul Lee Ph.D., *The Herb Renaissance*, one cassette, $11.50; Emmett E. Miller M.D., *Behavioral Change*, 13 cassettes, $11.95 each; William R. Miller Ph.D., *Alcoholism*, seven tapes, $69.50; C. Norman Shealy M.D. Ph.D., *Health Maintenance*, 10 cassettes, $9.95 each; O. Carl Simonton M.D. and Stephanie Matthews-Simonton, *Cancer Therapy*, four cassettes, $10 each; Robert L. Taylor M.D., *Organic vs. Psychological Diseases*, three cassettes, $11.50; Andrew Weil M.D., *Drugs & Higher States of Consciousness*, one cassette, $11.50; and Julian M. Whitaker M.D., *Prevention & Reversal of Heart Disease with Diet*, one cassette, $11.50. [Source: Proseminar]

Improve Your Eyesight Without Glasses—Some 80 years ago Dr. W. H. Bates developed some simple techniques for relaxing the ocular stress and strain that causes many vision problems. This program was created to guide the listener through the exercises at home. $15.95 for a cassette and six eyecharts. Related to the topic are *White Light Vision Improvement Cassette* with Martin Brofman offering gentle suggestion, affirmation, and visualization techniques to ease ocular stress and improve vision, $9.98. This tape was so successful that Mr. Brofman was asked to produce another, *Stay in the White Light and Dream Relaxation with Love*, on general relaxation, for $9.95 also. Finally, Pamela Whitney has her *Healing Tapes* (including one on healing your vision), each affirming the beauty and essence of one's true self, $10 each or all five cassettes for $39.95. [Source: Holistic Health Resources Center]

EWAHA Audio Cassettes—Lectures and panel discussions by noted experts in the field of holistic health, nurse-healers, Native American healing arts, and other cross-cultural approaches to health maintenance and disease treatment. In all, more than 125 topics are available, covering not only the specific techniques of various aspects of holistic medicine, but also insights into social, political, cultural, and ethical considerations. $10.50 each. [Source: East West Academy of Healing Arts]

Visionetics Tapes—Lisette Scholl presents her Visionetics program of vision improvement, based on the premise that common sight disorders (near-sightedness, far-sightedness, astigmatism) stem from

mental/muscular tension in the visual system. This causes both loss of proper coordination between the eyes and the brain and excess ocular stress so that the eyes are literally squeezed out of shape. Four programs are available in this area (mostly 60-minutes long) plus a 30-minute program on presbyopia for those who are growing older. These are $8.95 each, but should be used in conjunction with Ms. Scholl's book *Visionetics: The Holistic Way to Better Eyesight*, $4.95 plus $1 shipping and handling per order. Also available are a series of three *Yoga Etc. Tapes*, with stretching, limbering, and relaxing yoga postures supplemented with energizing Reichian exercises and stimulating massages, also $8.95 each. [Source: Clarity Tapes]

Wellness: Optimizing Health in Mind and Body—Experts examine the factors influencing wellness from the orientation of good health as well-being, rather than absence of disease: Benjamin Spock on children, Hans Selye on stress, Carl Simonton on cancer, Gerald Piaget on barriers, Roger Frager on exercise, Deane Shapiro on self-mastery, and Sue Rodwell Williams on nutrition. $73.50 for seven cassettes in album. [Source: BMA Audio Cassettes]

Mind as Healer, Mind as Slayer—Kenneth R. Pelletier, Elmer and Alyce Green, John E. Perry, and Carl and Stephanie Simonton all address the concept that individuals have certain psychological patterns that predispose them toward health and other patterns that predispose them toward disease, $58 for five cassettes (6¼ hours of material) in album. A related program from the same source is *Preventive Medicine and Health Maintenance: What Can You Do*—Six hours of insights into some ways to stay healthy, to reduce stress, and to alleviate the risks of arthritis, respiratory disease, cardiovascular ailments, and cancer, on six cassettes, $58. [Source: University of California]

UCSC Tapes—Recordings of live conferences at the University of California Santa Cruz, with most falling into the self-health category. Some conference titles are *Healing I* and *II, Birth and Rebirth, An Eastern View of Mental Health, From Stress to Success, 4th Annual Herb Symposium, Holistic Health and Children, The Human Dimension in Health Care, Intellect and Illness, Living the Rest of Your Life, New Ways of Being*, and *On the Nature of Reality*. $7.50 per lecture. [Source: University of California Extension]

Medical Adminstration

Management in the 80s—This live seminar is designed not only for hospital chief executive officers but also managers, department heads, and supervisors. Dr. Mark Silber stresses how to identify motivational problems and their cause, and how to return demotivated employees to productivity. $88.15 for six cassettes plus listener's guide and notebook in album. [Source: I P O Associates, Limited]

Audio Medical News—A twice-monthly socio-economic report on half-hour cassettes, covering professional liability, practice management, health legislation, medicolegal problems, cost containment, health insurance, money management, investment planning and more. The material comes from the news gathering services of the American Medical Association, plus wire services, journal articles, legislative analysts, and live interviews. $96 a year for 24 issues. [Source: Audio-Digest Foundation]

Medical Collection Study Course—A 'how to' cassette/workbook program designed to train medical assistants in the most effective methods of collecting overdue fees without offending patients. $33 for the set, $5 for additional workborks. [Source: American Medical Association]

Chief Executive Officer Tape Series—When chief executive officers of New Jersey's hospitals decided to do something about their own continuing education needs, they asked Dr. Mark Silber to speak to them on 'executive effectiveness.' The results are captured in this six-cassette album (three hours of material) by the noted authority in hospital management programs and consultation in the health care field. $78.35. [Source: I P O Associates Limited]

MGMA Audio Cassette Programs—Audio-cassettes relating to the administrative functions of managing a medical group practice are available from the Medical Group Management Association (MGMA). Some of the major subject areas covered are: financial management, general adminstration, communications, compensation and benefits, credit and collection, data processing, income distribution, and physician/manager relations. These tapes are taken from the proceedings of educational programs, section meetings, annual conferences, and interviews with group practice administrators. The tapes are lightly edited, vary in length from 30 to 60 minutes, and range in cost from $8 to $24. One recent program on cost containment is complete on four tapes with a booklet for $65. [Source: Medical Group Management Association]

ACHA Cassettes—The most helpful of the management seminars from the American College of Hospital Administrators' annual Congress of Administration are available on cassette for those wishing to improve their administrative skills and enhance their managerial competence. Typical subjects from this series, recorded over the past three years, include: competition, financial management, effecting change, marketing, quality assurance, employee relations, legislation, productivity, and mergers and acquisitions, to cite a few of the topics available. $12 each. [Source: American College of Hospital Administrators]

HFMA Audio-Cassette Programs—Sound practical advice from experts on important issues facing health care financial managers, all distilled from executive-level seminars sponsored by the Hospital Financial Management Association annual conferences. Some recent titles: *Cost Containment*, $48; *Introduction to Hospital Financial Management*, $48; *Annual Hospital Report*, $48; *Hill-Burton Regulations*, $24; *Financing and Accounting for P.A.M.s*, $48; *Accounts Receivable—Managing for Results*, $12; *Financial Ratio Analysis*, $12; *Improving Communications in Male-Female Management Relations*, $12; *Fund Management for New Construction*, $12; *Collections: Legal Aspects*, $24; *Management Accounting*, $48; *Managing the Financial Areas: Key Factors for Results*, $24; and *Planning, Managing, and Utilizing Computerized Systems*, $48. $12 for any individual cassette. All cassettes come in album. [Source: Hospital Financial Management Association]

Management Practice—A large collection of lectures and seminars aimed at the hospital administrator and financial officers. Just a few of the topics covered: malpractice, hospital cost containment, future of the small rural hospital, organizing for accountability, personnel cost savings, patient care audit, flexible budgeting, personnel administration and the law, ambulatory care. Cost is generally $10 per cassette. Of related interest to managers and administrators are the programs categorized as *Department Head Cassettes*, programs specifically intended to keep the chiefs of various hospital departments, and their co-workers, informed of new procedures, regulations, and techniques. A flock of titles are available, for $10 to $12 each, in these areas: purchasing and central supply, nursing supervision, food service management security, central service, medical records, operating room staff, respiratory therapy, IV therapy, and special care units. [Source: Teach'em, Inc.]

Tapes for Trustees—Cassette talks aimed to keep the hospital trustee informed of his duties and the duties of others. Among the topics covered: PSRO, how trustees can better serve their boards, role of trustee as an agent for change, quality assurance, federal planning laws, evaluation of trustee performance, fund raising, new accreditation developments, shared services, health care trends. There are generally $10 each; often several cassettes are combined in album with study guides. [Source: Teach'em Inc.]

Infection Control Cassettes—These cassettes offer both individual lectures covering individual aspects of infection control in hospital-based and outpatient practices ($10 each), a seven-cassette course ($65) especially prepared for the new infection control officer, and a five-cassette program ($100) providing a step-by-step report of new developments in control of hospital-associated infections. [Source: Teach'em, Inc.]

Medical Staff Consulting—Five contemporary cassette commentaries for hospital administrators and medical staff officers by Richard E. Thompson M.D., covering: quality assurance, working with physicians, who's in charge, medical staff privileges, and the competitive model. $65 for five cassettes in album, $15 per cassette. [Source: Teach'em, Inc.]

American Hospital Association—Many audio-cassette programs are available with topics covering all aspects of hospital management, and intended for administrators and supervisors at all levels. Many of the tapes are edited proceedings of conferences and symposia, some are specially recorded for the AHA. All cassettes are $12.50 per talk or title (discount to AHA members). A few of the offerings: proceedings from the *Third Annual AHA Trustee Forum* in 1980; *Spectrum on Aging*; *Effective Telephone Communications in Hospitals*, proceedings of a seminar of the *American Society for Hospital Personnel Adminstration*, a series of tapes on the role of the medical staff in controlling hospital costs, another series on nursing recruitment, several series on promoting community health and volunteer services, and a couple on disaster planning and emergency preparedness. The free catalog gives the entire spectrum of talks available. [Source: American Hospital Association]

Medicine

ACOG-Update—A monthly education subscription service, sponsored by the American College of Obstetrics and Gynecology with each 60-minute program featuring leading authorities in a panel discussion of a single clinical topic. Each program is eligible for three Category 1 AMA credit hours. Cost is $175 a year, $300 for two years, including an album. [Source: Medical Information Systems, Inc.]

ACOG Current Obstetrics—Highlights from post-graduate courses sponsored by The American College of Obstetrics and Gynecology, expertly condensed and skillfully edited onto six one-hour cassettes. The first volume features Jack A. Pritchard, M.D. on prenatal bleeding, Edward J. Quilligan M.D. on antepartum monitoring, Robert Resnick M.D. on primary and repeat Cesarean section, and F. Cary Cunningham M.D. on post-Cesarean infections, plus more on urinary infections in pregnancy, post-date pregnancy, hypertension, abnormal presentations. Other volumes are planned. Each volume gives 18 ACOG cognates and/or 18 AMA Category 1 credit hours. $59.95 for six cassettes, syllabus, and quiz in album. [Source: Audio-Digest Foundation]

The Electrocardiogram—In ten lectures, Dr. Emanual Stein covers all the important aspects: the normal EKG, right and left ventricular hypertrophy, repolarization (ST-T) abnormalities, myocardial infarction, ventricular conduction disturbances, arrhythmias, and digitalis. $85 for 10 cassettes (about 10 hours), plus $16.50 for 400-page manual. Of related interest from the same source is *Understanding Heart Sounds and Murmurs*, in which Ara G. Tilkian and Mary B. Conover explain it all, on one C-60 cassette with illustrated book for $19.95. [Source: W. B. Saunders Company]

Clinical Electrocardiography—A comprehensive multimedia learning program written by leading cardiologists and designed not only to upgrade skill at interpreting ECG tracings but also to provide pointers on correction of dysrhythmias and management of patients. $185 for 14 hour-long cassettes plus correlated text, transcript and quiz in album/binder. Acceptable for 14 CME Category 1 or AAFP prescribed hours. [Source: Post-Graduate Institute for Medicine]

ACS Clinitapes—Live unedited coverage of lectures, panels and post-graduate courses presented at recent clinical congresses and spring meetings of the American College of Surgeons. The topics cover the entire surgical subspecialty spectrum, with some two-hour panel discussions ($15), but mostly 4 to 12-hour post-graduate courses at about $7.50 an hour. An album is included if three or more cassettes are ordered. [Source: American College of Surgeons]

Dialogues in Dermatology—A monthly audio journal, produced by the American Academy of Dermatology, with each hour-long program containing the latest information on three to five timely topics—and then dermatologists expert on those topics are interviewed by other dermatologists for specifics of diagnosis and management. The aim is to keep the specialist current with all important issues and developments. $135 a year for 12 monthly cassettes, index, references and quiz, all in album. Each program is accredited for 2 hours of AMA Category 1 credit. [Source: American Academy of Dermatology]

Johns Hopkins Medical Grand Rounds—Each month the subscribing physician receives two C-60 cassettes containing four specially-recorded lectures on clinical topics originally presented at Johns Hopkins Medical Grand Rounds and Conjoint Clinics. Each monthly program is supplemented with a booklet containing illustrations, summaries, case histories, reading lists, and a self-grading quiz. A 10-month subscription (September-June) can earn the listener 40 hours of Category I AMA credit. $350. [Source: Johns Hopkins University]

Patient Care and Digestive Disease: An Update in Gastroenterology—11 lectures on four cassettes plus a printed booklet with illustrations, abstracts, reading lists, and a quiz. Subscribers returning the quiz can earn 10 Category I AMA credits. $75. [Source: Johns Hopkins University]

Echocardiography: Theory and Practice—10 lectures on eight cassettes plus a printed atlas of over 200 illustrations provide the listener with a good working knowledge of two-dimensional echocardiography. Subscribers returning the quiz can earn 24 Category I AMA credits. $150. [Source: Johns Hopkins University]

Current Views in Allergy and Immunology—Each month the subscriber to this series receives a 90-minute cassette, 10-20 35-mm slides with reproductions, outline and references, with a notebook provided yearly. Topics covered in the current volume include insect venom allergy, inhalation drugs for asthma, neonatal immunology, and complement disorders in man. A unique feature is that the last 30 minutes of each program is devoted to answers to listeners' questions on preceding programs. The course is approved for 30 AMA Category 1 credits. Cost is $285 a year before July 1, $325 after that date; those sharing another's education materials may enroll for $145. [Source: Medical College of Georgia]

Sportsmedicine Digest Audiotapes—60-90 minute tapes, recorded at various symposia and given by leading authorities. Topics covered: famous football injuries/three-sided knee instability; arthroscopic surgery/arthroscopy vs. arthrotomy for miniscus disease; synthetic knee ligaments; spinal cord injury from diving/distal tibial epiphyseal fractures; occult spinal dysraphism/EMG of posterior cruciate insufficiency; anterior-posterior instability in knee; laser research in orthopaedic surgery. $10 each. [Source: PM Incorporated]

Nutrition & the MD Audiotapes—Lectures by leading nutritionists on a wide range of nutrition topics: sugar and carbohydrate metabolism; dietary fiber; lipid research; micronutrients; food labeling; food safety; nutritional cultism; fasting; validity of vitamin therapy; fad diets and good nutrition; counseling the amateur athlete; nutrition advice for the professional athlete. $10 each. [Source: PM Incorporated]

Diastole, from Hospital Hill—Commentaries and philosophy by E. Grey Dimond M.D. on cardiology, the cardiologic literature, and world problems from a cardiologic standpoint—all aimed toward injecting some reason and common sense into the world of modern medicine. Accredited for 10 AMA Category 1 hours. $85 for 10 hour-long cassettes, sent monthly or so. [Source: Diastole-Hospital Hill]

Fluids, Electrolytes & Acid-Base Disorders—In this self-study course, eight hour-long cassettes of professional narration and another eight of clinical discussion and case studies give the listener a complete update on the diagnosis and treatment of patients with these conditions. Accredited for 16 AMA Category 1 or AAFP prescribed hours. $195 for 16 cassettes, correlated printed material, transcripts, and quiz in album/binder. [Source: Post-graduate Institute for Medicine]

ASA Audio Reviews in Anesthesiology—A monthly series of programs designed and developed by the American Society of Anesthesiologists. Each hour-long, professionally narrated program focuses on a single topic directly related to a specialized area in anesthesiology, and gives two hours of AMA Category 1 credit. $150 for 12 monthly cassettes plus study guide, quiz, and response sheet. Album/binder sent with first program. [Source: Audio Visual Medical Marketing, Inc.]

Dermatology—Direct Line—A news service that provides clinicians with their choice of lectures, discussions, and panels from virtually all of the dermatology meetings, postgraduate courses, and seminars held in this country. It works like this: the interested physician joins for $10, and gets his choice of a current recording in a 12-cassette album; and, he receives lists of all subsequent recordings as they occur. He can then order any of the presentations from any of these meetings for $10 for each cassette containing up to 60 minutes of lecture. Another free album comes with each 12th cassette order. Of related interest is *Dermatology*: *Front Row Center*—a monthly service that pinpoints all that is new in dermatology as reported at major medical meetings and seminars. $85 a year for ten cassettes. [Source: J. Schimmel Associates]

Orthopaedic Audio-Synopsis—Monthly hour-long teaching programs in the field of orthopaedic surgery, consisting of summaries of pertinent literature and excerpts from national and international orthopaedic meetings. Each tape eligible for one hour of AMA Category 1 credit. $85 a year ($42.50 for medical students, interns, and residents) for 12 programs, including album. Back issues $8 each. [Source: Orthopaedic Audio-Synopsis Foundation]

Intensive Review of Internal Medicine—54 professionally narrated lectures plus nine case studies, all correlated with an illustrated course book, and all organized largely by problems in diagnosis and treatment, rather than by disease entities. This course, prepared under the direction of Eugene Braunwald M.D., Stephen C. Schoenbaum M.D., and Peter F. Cohn, M.D., all of Harvard, is eligible for 45 hours of Category 1 AMA credit. $250 ($350 foreign) for 32 cassettes, course book, and quiz in box. [Source: Audio Visual Medical Marketing, Inc.]

Intensive Review of Cardiovascular Disease—31 leading physicians from Harvard Medical School provide information on the basics and on the latest developments in cardiovascular diseases—noninvasive and invasive methods of diagnosis, and mechanisms and management of dysrhythmias and other conduction disturbances, congestive failure, coronary and valvular heart disease, and hypertension. Meets the criteria for 40 hours of Category 1 AMA credit. $350. [Source: Audio Visual Medical Marketing, Inc.]

Holton Series of Self-Instructional Material in Physiology—Developed by the University of London Departments of Physiology, this excellent series of (mostly) one-hour courses is designed specifically for medical, dental, veterinary, and science as independent study material. The wide-ranging topics include indicator dilution, methods of contraception, glomerular filtration, the Fick principle, aqueous humour, enteropathic circulation of bile salts, concentration of urine, cardiac cycle, resting membrane potential, plasma proteins, intestinal absorption, cardiac output measurement, defenses of the lungs and airways, adrenal cortex, blood flow, thyroid, higher control of reflex activity, calcium metabolism, posterior pituitary, hormone action, sense of hearing, acid-base balance, skeletal muscle, arterial and venous systems, and autonomic nervous system. Most programs consist of a C-60 cassette, related workbook, transcript, and quiz, for about $13. A few courses—blood groups, cerebrospinal fluid, spinal reflexes, thermoregulation, fetal nutrition, and control of body fluid volume—consist of two cassettes and booklets for about $15. A course on physiology of exercise consists of four cassettes and booklets for about $21. [Source: BLAT Centre for Health and Medical Education]

Accel—A monthly service for cardiologists and cardiovascular surgeons, with relevant interviews, conference highlights, panel discussions, EKG interpretations, self-assessment quizzes, and highlights from the literature. $100 a year for 12 monthly hour-long programs, each with notebook. Also available are special supplement programs offering thorough discussions of specific topics—hyperlipoproteinemias, digitalis, congenital heart disease, heart sounds, drug interactions, hypertension, many more—for $8 to $30. [Source: American College of Cardiology]

ACS Conference Highlights—Each year the American Cancer Society sponsors (sometimes in conjunction with the National Cancer Institute) several conferences on some aspect of cancer. The recorded proceedings of these meetings are then skillfully edited and abridged onto two hour-long cassettes in an album, and are available on loan or for sale (usually at a modest fee) from most *local* units and divisions of the ACS. They are *not* available from their national office. [Source: American Cancer Society, Inc.]

Audiographic Series—Educational packages consisting of a cassette, illustrated workbook, self-evaulation quiz with answers, and bibliography. *Clinical Interpretation of Blood Gases*, including acid-base abnormalities and blood gas measurement and interpretation, is on a 60-minute cassette for $15. *Introduction to Breath Sounds* gives a concise presentation of normal and abnormal breath sounds, on a 23-minute cassette for $15. [Source: American College of Chest Physicians]

ACP Annual Session Tapes—Live unedited recordings of panel discussions and informal 'meet the professor' sessions from recent American College of Physicians' annual sessions, providing the internist's approach to the latest developments in the subspecialty fields—cardiology, gastroenterology, endocrinology, nephrology, pulmonary diseases, and others. $12 per 90-minute cassette; they give a free album if you order 12 tapes for $120. [Source: American College of Physicians]

Audio-Journal of Neuro-ophthalmology—In this monthly subscription service, the University of Miami's expressive Dr. J. Lawton Smith offers clinical discussions of materials helpful in office practice, interesting cases, overviews of interesting papers and interviews with other leading authorities on particularly timely topics. $175 for 12 issues a year plus album and summary and reference sheets, $90 to students and residents, $200 for hospitals and overseas. [Source: Neuro-ophthalmology Tapes]

Motor Speech Disorders—In this valuable guide to the differential diagnosis of motor speech disorders, ten separate neuro-anatomic types are demonstrated by voice recordings of mild to severe cases to show the spectrum of voice changes for all dysarthric types. $65 for three C-50 cassettes and supportive booklet. Also there is *Velopharyngeal Incompetence* in which Betty Jane McWilliams and Betty Jane Philips conduct an 'audio seminar in speech pathology' a difficult subject, on three hour-long cassettes and booklet for $125. From the same source is *Psychogenic Voice Disorders*—actual acoustic samples of major functional disorders of the voice, for use in learning or improving skill in recognizing and differentiating their acoustic properties. $75 for five C-60 cassettes and booklet. [Source: W. B. Saunders Company]

Medical Terminology—Five 12-cassette courses are available: *Anatomical Terminology* provides basic information, while *Cardiovascular, Respiratory, Orthopedic*, and *Gastroenterology Terminology* provide information about pertinent disorders, diagnostic procedures, and surgery for more advanced students. Each 10-hour course of cassettes, coordinated with illustrated study guides that interweave spelling, explanation, and pronunciation, has been designed for self- or group-instruction of students, technicians, and secretaries. $125 for each course. [Source: American Med. Tech.]

Practical Reviews—Monthly subscription services for physicians, providing reports from the current medical literature plus commentary. Separate services are available for anesthesiology, cancer, cardiology, emergency medicine, family practice, internal medicine, nuclear medicine, obstetrics/gynecology, pathology, pediatrics, psychiatry, radiology, and surgery. (The radiology series has two tapes and includes ultrasound.) Each monthly 60-90 minute cassette comes with index reference cards of pertinent points of the abstracts and references. $138 a year, except $175 for internal medicine (which has two cassettes each month). There are also three separate monthly C-60 programs available in radiologic technology, nuclear medicine technology, and ultrasound technology. $120 a year with study guide and quiz, or $150 a year for institutional use (with five study guides and quizzes supplied with each issue, plus an instructor's guide). [Source: Educational Reviews, Inc.]

Cardiac Auscultation Audio Tape Cassette Series—Auscultatory sounds of several common clinical disorders and conditions. The set includes six cassettes and booklet in album for $10. Each cassette contains 30 minutes of sounds and narration. [Source: Merck Sharp & Dohme]

AAOMS Audiovisual Programs—From the American Association of Oral and Maxillofacial Surgeons come a host of cassettes, generally covering the broad fields of medical management, anesthesia, trauma, professional issues, and practice management, $7 each. They also offer two special courses—*Drug Interactions in Oral and Maxillofacial Surgery* and *The Pharmacology of Intravenous Sedation*—each with two cassettes and a hefty workbook for $30. Finally, unedited cassettes of recent AAOMS annual meeting scientific programs are also available, again for $7 each. [Source: Allen Visual Systems, Inc.]

Heart Sounds with EKG Tracings.—Three cassettes full of heart sounds with descriptions of their significance, correlated with 134 tracings in booklet. $24 for the works, in an album. [Source: Career Aids]

Audio Education Service—Programs are issued up to 12 times a year, and each contains a 30-minute discussion of an important aspect of clinical medicine. Programs are sponsored by individual pharmaceutical companies and are provided to members of the American Osteopathic Association without charge. Programs are shipped individually or as a supplement to an issue of the *Journal of the American Osteopathic Association.* [Source: American College of Osteopathic Internists]

Spanish for the Health Professional—Basic health phrases needed by medical personnel to deal with Spanish-speaking patients, on four cassettes and illustrated text, for $99.95. [Source: Lansford Publishing Company]

Helping Cancer Patients Cope—Subtitled 'A Problem-Solving Intervention for Health Care Professionals,' this program by Harry J. Sobel Ph.D. and J. William Worden Ph.D. gives instructions in the use of powerful cognitive and behavioral techniques which have been proved effective in Harvard Medical School's Project Omega in assisting patients to deal with the stresses encountered in cancer. It both provides patients with useful self-help skills and gives practitioners a structured approach to treatment. $50 for four cassettes, manual, and problem-solving cards in album. [Source: BMA Audio Cassettes]

Basic Medical Terminology—Two cassettes that offer definitions, pronunciations, and review of over 350 commonly used nursing terms, useful for students, aides and office staff, as well as review for practicing nurses. $13.95. [Source: Career Aids]

Audio-Learning—*Orthopaedic Diagnosis and Treatment* is J. H. Cyriax's thorough discussion of the differentiation and therapy of the host of soft tissue lesions and musculo-skeletal disorders, on 12 cassettes with study guide for $155.50. *Clinical Advances in Pain Management* features presentations by experts representing the movement toward holistic pain managements, with insights and comments by co-editors John V. Basmajian M.D. and Wilbert E. Fordyce Ph.D., on 12 cassettes and album for $128.50. Marvin R. Goldfried Ph.D. takes up the *Behavioral Management of Anxiety and Self-Management of Anxiety* on two cassettes with instruction manual for $22.50. [Source: Audio-Learning, Inc.]

Basic Medical Terminology—An audio-course to give the beginning student in any allied health field a basic understanding of the language of medicine and medical science. The course is suitable for either independent or small-group study. The program consists of 60 lessons and 12 tests with a text ($13.50) and six one-hour cassettes in album ($105). [Source: Bobbs-Merrill Educational Publishing]

AAFP Home-Study Self-Assessment—A subscription continuing medical education course specifically designed for family physicians. Each monthly package includes a monograph, cassette, and testing materials, all pertaining to a single topic. Subjects include: growth and development, psychosomatic and behavioral disorders, drug actions and interactions, blood gases, geriatrics, ENT, CPR, arthritis, fluid and electrolyte balance, dermatology, contraception and abortion, coronary artery disease, and others. When completed as designed, the course earns 48 AAFP Prescribed Credit hours and 48 Category 1 AMA credit hours. Cost is $190 a year for AAFP members, $250 for non-members. [Source: American Academy of Family Physicians]

Audio Journal Review: Ophthalmology—A monthly C-60 cassette subscription service edited by Devron Char M.D. each containing abstracts of articles in the current ophtalmologic literature, sometimes focusing on a single topic, and featuring interviews by the authors about their papers and interpretations by experts of the implications of recent findings to everyday clinical practice. $85 for 12 monthly tapes. [Source: Grune & Stratton, Inc.]

Graves Medical Audiovisual Library—Over 100 lectures, talks, interviews, and demonstrations, covering all medical specialties, plus some titles for nurses, other paramedical workers, and patients. The emphasis is on practical, down-to-earth presentations.

These cassettes are available for rent in Great Britain, but only for sale overseas; write for the complete list of titles and prices. [Source: Grave Medical Audiovisual Library]

MediSom—Live proceedings of Brazilian medical meetings, recorded in Portuguese, with pharmaceutical messages interspersed on each hour-long tape. Twelve separate editions by specialty, each issued every other month, for $50 a year. QBD also produces management training albums, including Peter Drucker on management and John Humble on management by objectives, mostly in Portuguese and some Spanish. Finally, QBD also produces evangelical material for several churches, yoga programs, and courses for the study of English and Arabic. [Source: Grupo Editorial QBD, Ltda.]

Audio-Digest—Separate, twice-a-month subscription services for *Anesthesiology, Family Practice* (also available monthly), *Internal Medicine, Obstetrics-Gynecology, Ophthalmology, Otolaryngology-Head and Neck Surgery, Pediatrics, Psychiatry, Surgery*, and monthly services of *Orthopaedics* and *Urology*. Each hour-long program consists of live recordings from major medical conventions or courses, usually giving a thorough discussion of a single important aspect of practice in the specialty, carefully edited to remove irrelevant material, extraneous noises, and undue pauses. $119 a year for 24 C-60 programs ($238 for the weekly *Family Practice* service, 48 issues, and $59.50 for the monthly *Orthopaedics* and *Urology* services, 12 issues). Back issues for $7.20 each. [Source: Audio-Digest Foundation]

Medical-Dental Terminology—Neither a list of medical words and phrases nor a medical transcription course, this program gives background information into the formation of medical terms and concepts, which are then expanded to cover the necessary terminology. Ultimately, terms relating to the physiology and diseases of the entire body are covered, on 11 cassettes, with syllabus, tests, and teacher's guide album, $177.70. [Source: National Book Company]

Audiotape Teaching Aids—The University of Pittsburgh School of Medicine tape-records all of their continuing education courses in medicine and related topics and makes them available to physicians, hospitals, and medical libraries. The recordings are lightly edited and cost $6 per cassette, regardless of length—60, 90, or 120 minutes. There are over 75 conference titles listed in their current catalog, available for $2. Recent titles cover family practice, orthotics for children, hormone receptor research, otolaryngology, respiratory failure, head and neck oncology, chronic pain, evaluation of the vestibular system, infectious diseases, high-frequency ventilation, rehabilitation of brain-injured children, and contemporary problems in surgery. [Source: University of Pittsburgh]

Innovations in Athletic Conditioning and Sports Medicine—The training and assessment of athletes (adolescents to professionals) are discussed by experts in exercise physiology and sports medicine, and intended for medical and physical education specialists, coaches, trainers, and sports enthusiasts. 14 cassettes with 13½ hours of material in album for $165, $13-$15 each. [Source: University of California]

Ethical Issues in Biomedical Science and Health Care—Highlights of a 1975 symposium at the University of California Berkeley, covering experimentation on the unborn, prenatal diagnosis and therapy, artificial organs, informed consent, lifestyles, aging, and a national health policy. Note the date. $12-$16 per cassette, $120 for all 14 cassettes (15 hours) in album. [Source: University of California]

Neurosurgery Review and **Neurology Review**—Two separate subscription services that bring to the practicing neurosurgeon and neurologist the latest developments in their fields, featuring both established authorities and rising newcomers in lectures, panel discussions, 'how-I-do-it' sessions, and interviews. $105 a year for 12 one-hour programs sent monthly, both services for $190 a year. Past issues are available for $12.75 per tape. [Source: Professional Information Library]

Heart Sounds and Murmurs—An audiovisual presentation of five 10-minute cassettes (each demonstrating six heart sounds and murmurs), a special stethoscope that connects directly to a tape player, and a booklet that explains the diagnostic significance of each sound—all prepared by Indiana University's Dr. Morton E. Tavel. $185 for the set in an album. [Source: Year Book Medical Publishers]

Audio Veterinary Medicine—Continuing education subscription services for veterinarians, with each hour-long program containing two to three lectures by prominent veterinary authorities to provide current clinical information. The tapes are carefully edited to remove extraneous noises—a sign of quality. Monthly services are available for small animal practice ($90 a year) and equine medicine ($96 a year). Bi-monthly services ($54 a year, for six issues) cover dairy medicine, beef medicine, and swine medicine. Specialty courses are available in small animal nutrition, anesthesia, behavior (each $44.95 for six cassettes in album), small animal heartworm disease, small animal endocrinology, and bovine immunology (each $24.95 for three cassettes in album), and good business management for veterinarians ($31.95 for four cassettes in album). A host of back issues and other special programs are available; write for their 10th anniversary catalog. [Source: Audio Veterinary Medicine]

Football Injuries—Based on the edited proceedings of workshops sponsored by *The Physician and Sportsmedicine* and intended for doctors serving as team physicians or caring for individual athletes, but much is suitable for coaches and trainers. The 12 tapes cover a spectrum of topics, from conditioning, equipment, and legal aspects to the prevention, examination, treatment, and rehabilitation of injuries in all areas of the body. $15 each, all 12 cassettes in album for $175. Also, *Baseball Injuries*—edited workshop proceedings, with advice from team physicians, sports medicine specialists, and other kindred experts. The topics cover: equipment and conditioning; lower back, groin, hip, and thigh injuries; knee, leg, ankle, and foot injuries; head, neck, forearm, wrist, and hand injuries; and shoulder and elbow injuries. $15 each, all five cassettes in album for $70. [Source: Teach'em, Inc.]

Tennis Medicine—Two-cassette programs ($30 each) on: objectives as a sport, biomechanics, and tennis elbow; use of physical therapy, exercise, and surgery for tennis elbow; problems of the competitive player; and lower extremity problems. $115 for all eight cassettes in album. [Source: Teach'em, Inc.]

Medical Aspects of Strength Conditioning—A complete learning program, with noted experts examining strength training for specific sports, equipment strength testing, and many other important aspects. Specific program topics: physiology of strength, strength testing for sports (each two cassettes, $30 each), methods measurement, and problems in strength training (each three cassettes, $45 each). All ten cassettes in album for $140. [Source: Teach'em, Inc.]

Running, Jogging, and the Marathon—Programs for physicians, coaches, and trainers who need to keep current in these sports, each prepared by a leading authority in sports medicine. Cassette programs cover: caring for the otherwise healthy runner, biomechanics of running, pathomechanics of running injuries, aerobic exercise and its effect, cardiovascular adaptation to aerobic exercise, jogging and running shoes, flexibility exercises and the use of orthotics, pharmacologic and nutritional aspects (all $15 each), and recognition and management of basic 'over-use syndromes' (two cassettes, $30). All ten programs in album for $140. [Source: Teach'em, Inc.]

Medifacts—Produced in association with the College of Family Physicians of Canada, each 60-minute cassette (published every two weeks) contains one indepth discussion plus a number of short talks on the etiology, diagnosis, and treatment of various medical conditions by leading Canadian and other authorities. Each tape contains pharmaceutical advertising (maximum of nine one-minute ads per cassette). Distributed in Canada on a controlled circulation basis; for physicians outside Canada, the yearly subscription rate is $65. *Clinimed* is a French-language sister program of Medifacts. Each hour-long cassette contains one thorough discussion of a medical topic, plus shorter presentations on the etiology, diagnosis, and treatment of important medical conditions, all by major Canadian and French

physicians. Each tape contains pharmaceutical advertising (no more nine one-minute ads per program). Distributed on a controlled circulation basis in Canada, available to physicians outside Canada for $65 per year. [Source: Medifacts Ltd.]

Specialist Program Series—This innovative new division of Medifacts produces hour-long programs for specialists in dermatology, obstetrics-gynecology, internal medicine, cardiology, gastroenterology, general surgery, psychiatry, endocrinology, and ophthalmology. Each program, produced at irregular intervals depending on availability of speakers, includes both specially recorded materials and live recordings of symposia. Cost per program is $2.50 each. [Source: Medifacts Ltd.]

ACP-Psychiatric Update—This subscription service, prepared monthly by the American College of Psychiatrists, brings the listeners "structured yet unrehearsed" panel discussions of single important topics in psychiatric practice. Each program eligible for three Category 1 AMA Credits. Cost is $125 a year, $200 for two years, for one tape a month, plus a 12-cassette album. [Source: Medical Information Systems, Inc.]

AAP-Pediatric Update—A "clinical continuum in pediatrics," each monthly program in this subscription service features a panel discussion of noted pediatricians giving views on an important pediatric topic. Each program is eligible for three Category 1 AMA credits and 36 elective PREP credits. The cost is $110 a year, two years for $250. [Source: Medical Information Systems, Inc.]

The Language of Medicine—Eight 60-minute cassettes (about eight hours) of pronunciations and brief definitions of more than 1770 key medical terms, intended to accompany Davi-Ellen Chabner book by the same title, but can be used with other medical terminology texts. $69. There is also *Medical Transcribing*, three hour-long cassettes to be used in conjunction with the book of the same title by Marcy Otis Diehl and Marilyn T. Fordney. $98.50 for the cassettes and instructor's guide, $19.95 for the book. [Source: W. B. Saunders Company]

Internal Medicine: Board Review/Recent Advances—This thorough review, consisting of live lectures by Emory University internists, is geared to successful completion of the Board examination in internal medicine, and emphasizes both basic material and recent advances most likely to appear on the examination. The course consists of 40 cassettes (46 hours of material), a book containing summaries of each lectures, graphs and illustrations, and self-assessment quiz, all on a box. The program meets the criteria for 50 Category 1 AMA credit hours. Cost is $295, or $345 in Canada and Mexico. [Source: Science-Thru-Media, Inc.]

Radiation Accident Preparedness—Developed by four experts in the field of radiation accident management, this course provides the key elements needed by physicians, nurses, health physicists, nuclear plant managers, and all others involved in the care of individuals exposed to radiation. Topics include administrative aspects, acute radiation syndrome and local irradiation injuries, decontamination, federal regulations and requirements, and public relations aspects. $205 ($300 in Canada and Mexico) for ten lectures on four audio-cassettes, plus detailed manual (can serve as a quick reference during emergencies), and quiz in box. Eligible for 18 Category 1 AMA credit hours. [Source: Science-Thru-Media, Inc.]

Heart Sounds: What They Teach Us—Dr. Antonio C. de Leon, Jr., of Georgetown University, leads a 7-½ hour course on cardiac anatomy and physiology, basic heart sounds, systolic and diastolic sounds and murmurs, specific cardiac abnormalities, and bedside diagnostic techniques, all with special emphasis on the shading and grading of murmurs. $275 for 12 cassettes in album with 100-page illustrated text. Of related interest is *The Chest: Its Signs and Sounds*—Dr. George Druger leads this study course on the examination and interpretation of the physical signs of the chest, plus hearing the actual pulmonary sounds—breath, voice, percussion, and adventitious—and the auscultatory findings in pneumonia, bronchiectasis, asthma, pleural effusion and most other thoracic and pulmonary diseases. Designed for medical students, nurses, physical and inhalation therapists, paramedics. $275 for 12 cassettes (about 4-½) plus 112-page text and album. [Source: Humetrics Corporation]

Nursing

Nursing and the Law—In this era of more acute attention to patients' rights and huge liability settlements, higher salaries and lower budgets, greater demands and few resources, all nurses must be up to date on the legal aspects of their work. And that's what Willian A. Regan J.D. provides complete in *Psychiatric Nursing and the Law*, two volumes for helping nurses with psychiatric responsibilities to apply the information on a day-to-day basis. Price is $78.35 (or $83.15 if billed) for either volume (each containing about four hours on six cassettes) in an album, or both albums for $141. There is another program from the same source which deals with another area of practice in which nurses must know what they are doing to avoid liability: *Operating Room Nursing and the Law*, in which Mr. Regan tells nurses what they have to know about the legal aspects of working in the OR, by means of informative talks interspersed with case presentations and on-the-spot questions and answers in an edited version of a live presentation. Five hours of material on six cassettes in album for $78.35. [Source: I P O Associates Limited]

Nursing Resources—Programs recorded at conferences sponsored by the *Journal of Nursing Administration* and *Nurse Educator*, and covering nursing education, administration, and practice. Some of the single cassette titles ($10 each) include: *Coaching, Counseling and Interviewing; Building Skills in Disciplining and Grievance Handling; How to Communicate with Physicians and Surgeons; Cost Containment in the Nursing Department; Maximizing Your Personnel Performance; Personnel Administration and the Law; How to Use Rewards to Motivate Employees* ($12); and more. Some two-cassette programs ($20 each): *Managing Your Time; How To Meet the Challenge of the Union Organizer; Budgeting and Productivity Improvement; Comparative Cost of Team Nursing vs. Primary Nursing; How To Organize Orientation and Skills Training Programs; Staff Burnout*; and more. Then there are some multi-cassette programs: *How To Communicate Effectively*, four cassettes and printed materials in album, $75; *The Sociology of Hospital Care* (part I, four cassettes, $85; part II, two cassettes, $40, both with study materials and album); *Nursing vs. Medicine: Avoiding Legal Collisions*, four cassettes, $45; *What Nurses Should Know About Oncology Nursing*, five cassettes and study guide, $55; *Complete Course in Infectious Disease* (how to combat and control hospital-associated infections), five cassettes and much supplemental material in album, $100; *What Nurses Should Know About Adverse Drug Reactions and Interactions*, two cassettes and print materials, $22; and many more. [Source: Teach'em Inc.]

r.n. tapes—Programs designed, written, and narrated by nurses, to provide a review for new RN state board examinations. *State Board Review Tapes: Nursing Process* gives about 25 hours review on health care during: childhood and adolescent years, young adult and reproductive years, and behavioral and emotional problems through the life cycle (five cassettes and workbook, $70 each) and acute and chronic problems in the adult years (six cassettes and workbooks, $115), all 21 cassettes for $300. *State Board Review Tapes: Nursing Content* offers 28 hours of review in five clinical areas—medicine (eight cassettes), pediatrics (six cassettes), surgery (six cassettes), maternity (seven cassettes), and psychiatry (four cassettes)—for $65 each, or the entire set for $300. *Review of Pharmacology* emphasizes nursing process on two C-60 cassettes and booklet in album for $30. *Review of Diets* also uses the nursing focus on a single cassette and booklet in album for $15. *Relaxation Approaches for Nurses* offers four exercises by Dr. George Fuller on one cassette for $10. *Strategies for Success on Nursing School Exams* gives hints on taking multiple-choice exams, on cassette with booklet and album for $15. Finally, there's *Effective Test-Taking Techniques for State Boards*, a single tape for $10. [Source: r.n. tapes, inc.]

Nursing Care: A Problem Solving Approach—Both a creative refresher in current nursing principles and practice and an aid in reviewing for RN licensure examinations, all research, developed, and reviewed by professional nurse educators. $69.95 for 10 cassettes and manual. This source also features several other single cassettes and albums in the nursing field: *Legal Liabilities on RN's in the OR*, two cassettes, $30, and *What Nurses Should Know About Their Legal Rights and Liabilities*, five cassettes, in album, $55, among others. [Source: Career Aids]

Audio Anthology—Under this collective heading Trainex has several offerings. First are two volumes of Nursing Audio Journal. Volume 1 has 4 lectures: *Psychopathology of Anxiety*; *Death and Dying* (with Dr. Kubler-Ross); *Management of the Depressed Patient*, and *Management of Schizophrenia*, each with program guide, for $9.95 each, or all 4 in album for $39.80. Volume 2 has these lectures: *National Perspectives and Legal Aspects of Rape*, *Nursing and Medical Management of Rape Victims*, *Psychological Crisis of Rape*, and *Crisis Intervention with a Rape Victim*, each with program guide, $14.95 each or $59.80 in album. Finally, they have some individual programs: *More Alike than Different*, a candid discussion of puberty in mentally retarded children, $9.95; *Baby Cries*, with Dr. Murray Feingold demonstrating how infant vocalizations can be used to diagnose congenital abnormalities, $9.95; and *Process Recording Guide*, a training course for evaluating nurse-patient interactions, $44.45 with cassette, instructor's guide, and student workbooks. [Source: Trainex Corporation]

Nursing Audio Tape Programs—Short (14 to 42 minute) cassette programs, sometimes with a handout or pamphlet, on various aspects of general nursing, acute care nursing, patient care, and care of the aged patient. The price per cassette varies from $14 to $24.45. They also offer longer programs on pharmacology, which run a bit longer, some cost a bit more. [Source: Communications in Learning, Inc.]

Holistic Assertion—In these programs aimed at women, especially nurses, Dr. Sonya J. Herman RN offers holistic communication skills to help integrate mind, body, and spirit. Easy, relaxed breathing is emphasized to promote awareness of one's conscious and subconscious thoughts, thereby developing a positive inner environment. Besides two programs on assertion, she offers several tapes on relaxation, one on images of holistic health, and one titled *As a Woman Thinketh*. $7.50 each. [Source: Assertive Training Institute]

Fundamentals of Nursing Law in the 80's—Legal authority William A. Regan J.D. updates legal aspects of nursing practice, applicable for nurses working in hospitals, nursing homes, HMOs, or other facilities or agencies. In essence, he clarifies and reassures nurses about both their rights and their responsibilities in a way that makes sense to practicing professional nurses. He offers many practical methods of handling difficult situations in a professional manner. $93.15 for six cassettes (5½ hours) in album. [Source: I P O Associates Limited]

Making Nursing Stress Work For You—A nurse, a health educator, and a stress management psychologist combine talents in this three-cassette course on coping with nursing stress and avoiding nurse burnout. The course covers how to handle feelings of guilt and anxiety stemming from daily decisions, how to relieve personal stress, how to help patients deal with their own stresses, and how to incorporate stress management into nursing training programs. $25.95. [Source: Creative Media Group]

Patient Education

How To Live Longer and Love It—Kenneth Cooper M.D. (author of Aerobics) gives pointers on how to stay healthy, on a single cassette for $9.95. [Source: Zig Ziglar Corporation]

Orthopedics for the Layman—Orthopedic specialists discuss the present and future of the wide array of illnesses and injuries that involve bones, joints, tendons, and their related structures. The target audience are those who suffer from such illnesses, those who need to know more about these diseases, and those who must deal with rehabilitation of orthopedic disorders. Topics cover disc problems and laminectomies, sports medicine, new joints, fractures and dislocations, control of pain, rehabilitation, and medico-legal considerations. $116 for nine cassettes in album (13 hours), $13-$15 per cassette. [Source: University of California]

Patient Education Cassettes—Individual cassettes to help patients learn more about their illness. Topics include emphysema, diabetes, benign prostrate hypertrophy, peptic ulcer, hypertension, angina, myocardial infarction, gout, osteoarthritis, anorexia nervosa, depression, gallbladder disease, hyperthyroidism, hypothyroidism, multiple sclerosis, retinal detachment, rheumatoid arthritis, and diverticulitis. Also available is a two-cassette album with study guide ($40) on how alcoholic patients can help themselves, and a four-cassette package to amuse young hospitalized patients, $45. [Source: Teach'em Inc.]

ACOG Patient Information Library—Two libraries (one in obstetrics, one in gynecology, each comprising 10 cassettes with accompanying booklets) that help explain various medical conditions to patients. Each cassette consists of a 10-12 minute dramatizatin of a woman and her doctor discussing one subject. Topics in the gynecology library cover various types of contraception, infertility, hysterectomy, abnormal pap smear or uterine bleeding, and menopause. Topics in the obstetrics library include the three trimesters of pregnancy, childbirth, abortion, anesthesia, and breastfeeding. $100 for each library. There's also a single tape on abortion, $10. [Source: Medical Information Systems, Inc.]

Patient Education Tapes—Six tapes provide basic information about health and illness to patients. *Growing Up* (adolescence, 46 min); *Birth Control* (41 min); and *Teenage Drinking and Drugs* (37 min)—all $6.95 each. Longer programs include: *Your Heart and Heart Attacks* (68 min); *Your Blood Pressure* (66 min)—both 8.95 each—and finally, *Talking About Sex* (89 min), $9.95. All tapes include a glossary of medical terms and, when needed, diagrams of relevant anatomy.   [Source: Medifacts Ltd.]

Preparing for Easier Childbirth—To help with the LaMaze experience, Elisabeth Bing speaks directly to expectant mothers and their partners, teaching them to limber and strengthen the body, relax more effectively, and breathe properly in the three stages of labor. $9.95 for one cassette with illustrated practice guide.   [Source: BMA Audio Cassettes]

Health Insights Cassette Library—Audio-consultations with leading medical experts give fresh, entertaining, stimulating insights into various medical problems. $13.75 for each 25-30 minute cassette. Topics include: alcohol abuse (medical consequences, teenage alcoholism, women alcoholics, sex and booze, fetal alcohol syndrome, social drinking); consumer health (prescription drugs, over-the-counter drugs, keeping good health), dental health (cavities, gum diseases); drug abuse (marijuana, tranquilizers, sleeping pills, street drugs); eye injuries, hearing loss; family problems (domination, discipline, divorce, senior citizens, child abuse); heart care (diet, exercise, Type A behavior), nutrition and diet (weight control, vegetarianism, balanced diets, vitamins, organic food); physical fitness (sports, aerobics, jogging, heatstroke, injuries, stress); psychology (suicide, identity crises, many more); sex (unmarried pregnancy, sex and children and teens, rape, gay world, abortion and contraception); smoking, feminine hygiene, inherited diseases, headache, epilepsy, strokes, acne—and nearly 50 more.   [Source: Spenco Medical Corporation]

Soundwords—An excellent source of health information and patient education programs, each prepared and given by a knowledgeable doctor to communicate factual advice about a disease or disorder in an easy-to-understand manner. Patients uninterested, unmotivated, or educationally unequipped to read and understand patient education literature can gain much from these cassettes. Over 110 separate 40-50 minute programs are available (generally $10.95 each). Some of the areas included: healthy and diseased skin, various venereal diseases, various sexual disorders, diabetes (diet, juvenile diabetes, complications), pulmonary problems (cancer, asthma, emphysema and bronchitis, hay fever, pneumonia, flu, and TB), digestive disorders, kidney diseases, prostate disease, many programs on drug abuse, breast cancer, mental disorders (psychotherapy, phobias, psychosomatic disorders, schizophrenia, depression, suicide, grief, death and dying), hearing

problems, alcoholism, various types of cancer, autism, dyslexia, hyperactivity, anorexia nervosa, Tourette's syndrome, Hodgkin's disease, leukemia, multiple sclerosis, menstruation and menopause—and many, many more.   [Source: Soundwords, Inc.]

Medical Digest—Practical information regarding various functions of the human body, categorized into heart, lungs, children, women, arthritis, venereal disease, birth control, pregnancy, drugs, and miscellaneous. $6 each (two topics), or all 30 cassettes for $180. Of related interest is the group of programs on *Diseases*, graphic explanations of numerous human diseases: detection, symptoms, incubation, communicability, and prevention. Two 15-minute descriptions of two diseases on each cassette—from allergy/asthma and bubonic plague/cholera to frostbite/gangrene and mumps/poliomyelitis. $6 each, all 78 diseases on 39 cassettes for $230.   [Source: ESP, Inc.]

Herpies—The New VD Around Town—Written by an obstetrician, this presentation features a dialogue between a health educator and a character named 'Herpie,' the virus responsible for genital herpes. By means of frank conversations, audience questions, and humorous asides, the listener learns the facts about this newest and perhaps most widespread of all sexually-transmitted diseases. $7.70 for the cassette with written script and study guide.   [Source: Creative Media Group]

Creative Learning Center—Consumer-oriented talks on drug abuse, VD in general, VD for the young, VD for parents, tuberculosis, youth and alcohol, birth control methods, how to avoid surgery (the famous 'Shopper's Guide to Surgery' prepared by Herbert S. Danenberg, Pennsylvania Insurance Commissioner), growing old, menstruation, and menopause. These are $9 each. *Game Without Winners* is a four-cassette series on drug abuse, $9 for each cassette. *Alcoholism—the Disease* is a six-cassette series that explains the disease and offers an enlightened approach to it, $59.95.   [Source: Creative Learning Center]

Personal Health Education Cassettes—Individualized self-instructional programs for patient teaching. Topics include basic human sexuality, the pill, prenatal care, lower back pain, stomach distress, diabetes, and hypertension. $14.95 for each cassette with illustrated flip-chart book.   [Source: Career Aids]

Informed Homebirth Cassette Tape Course—Rahima Baldwin gives a 12-lesson course that provides pregnant couples with the medical data and the support they need to have a safe and successful delivery of their child at home. Topics include the advantages and risks, finding a birth attendant, normal labor and delivery, relaxation, breathing and pushing techniques, complications and emergencies, the homebirth team, psychologic aspects, and the newborn and postpartum periods. $49.75 for six cassettes in album, plus the book *Special Delivery*, a year's membership in Informed Homebirth, and information on how to form a study group using the tape course. [Source: Informed Homebirth]

Promoting Long-Term Health Behaviors—Eight experts offer new methods for dealing with an old problem: patient non-compliance with therapeutic recommendations prescribed to overcome medical and psychological illnesses. The speakers cover how to gain greater patient cooperation, ways to enhance effectiveness of practice, and methods to identify causes of poor compliance. $85 for eight cassettes and study guide in album. Lectures available individually for $10.50 each. [Source: BMA Audio Cassettes]

Informed Consent Cassettes—Brief descriptions of a number of procedures—lararoscopy, hysterectomy, early or saline abortion, vasectomy, use of the IUD or the pill—with a questionnaire (extra) to be completed by the patient after hearing the talk. $24.95 each, any six in album for $129.50. [Source: Pfarrago Information Systems]

Post-Coronary Patient Education—A program designed for use in the hospital, that provide the post-coronary patient with basic information about a heart attack, its causes and contributing factors, subsequent care and exercise, going home, and return to normal activities, including sexual activity. $129 for six cassettes in album, individual cassettes $24.95. [Source: Pfarrago Information Systems]

OB/GYN and Family Planning and **Human Sexuality Patient Teaching Audio Cassettes**—Short, to the point messages for patients, in the hospital or in the office. Topics include various aspects of contraception, sterilization, the pelvic examination, venereal disease, breast feeding, sexual response, masturbation, and sex after a heart attack. $24.95 each, any six in album for $129.50. [Source: Pfarrago Information Systems]

Post-Partum Patient Teaching Audio-Cassettes—Various aspects of post-partum care—handling the baby, breast feeding, contraception, sexual response, going home—on 12 short cassettes (90 minutes of information) for $195, or $250 with 100 copies of a coordinated, illustrated booklet ($1 each). These are intended for in-hospital use. [Source: Pfarrago Information Systems]

Pharmacology

Voices—A monthly cassette subscription service for pharmacists, produced for (with editorial content controlled by) the American Society of Hospital Pharmacists, providing up-to-the minute reports on important developments in pharmacy. $96 a year for 12 cassettes. Also available under the ASHP banner

are these six-cassette courses for $70 (except as indicated): *Financial Management, Geriatric Pharmacy Practice, Intravenous Therapeutics and Admixture Services, Hospital Pharmacy Practice, Laws, Standards, and Regulations* ($80), *Acute Poisoning and Overdose, Hospital Pharmacy Design* ($80), *Pharmacist Burnout* ($24 for two cassettes) and *Unrecognized Salicylate Intoxication* ($24 for two cassettes). [Source: Teach'em Inc.]

AMA Complete Drug Compendium—Highlights of an American Medical Association theme meeting on Current Drug Therapy, available by drug or indication categories: *Anticonvulsants* (1 hour, $10); *Psychotropic Drugs, Headache and Analgesic Drugs, Drugs in the Elderly, Drug Interactions, Hypolipidemic Drugs, Endocrine Drugs, Drug Overdose and Accidental Poisoning, Antirheumatic Drugs* (all 2 hours, $19); *Antimicrobial Drugs* (3 hours, $28); and *Cardiovascular Drugs/Diuretic-Antihypertensive Drugs* (4 hours, $37). All programs qualify for hour-for-hour AMA Category 1 credit. Price includes album and syllabus. [Source: Audio-Digest Foundation]

Extension Services in Pharmacy—Courses designed to meet the personal and educational needs of pharmacists and related health professionals, with ACPE/CME credit given in many states. All are 16-hour courses (except as noted), and some might be a bit dated, so the year of publication is given. Topics: cardiovascular diseases and their management (1979); the health professional's role in diabetes mellitus (1975); fluids and electrolytes (1976); geriatric considerations of drug therapy (1976); human lungs in health and disease (14 hours) (1978); introductory aspects of clinical pharmacy (1974); mental health and disease (1979); neurologic disorders and their treatment (1980); pediatric considerations of drug therapy (1977); pharmacology of over-the-counter preparations (1978); a rational approach to drug selection (14 hours) (1975); recent developments in chemotherapeutics (1978); renal and urinary tract diseases (1981); and obstetrics and gynecology (1981). Each course is $50. [Source: University of Wisconsin-Extension]

Psychology and Psychotherapy

Le Grand Day—*Jungian Hypnotherapy*, intended for professionals but interesting to the laity, describes the synthesis of Jung's personality theory with Erickson's hypnosis technique. For professionals only is *Special Meditation for Psychotherapists*. $10 each. [Source: Le Grand E. Day]

Dave Elman Course in Medical and Clinical Hypnosis Here are 27 hours of medical hypnosis training, five hours of hypnoanalysis, and four special purpose studies of weight control, medical relaxation, techniques for children, and childbirth training—36 cassettes, two workbook/manuals in albums for $195. [Source: Gil Boyne]

The Professional Hypnosis Course—A workshop designed for doctors, dentists, lawyers, ministers, police personnel and counselors, providing step-by-step, word-for-word hypnotic techniques and advice on their use in professional contexts. Program contains 12 sessions on six cassettes in album for $69.95. [Source: Human Development Training Programs]

ASCH Tape Cassettes—Complete lectures, dialogues, and panel discussions from the Society's annual workshops and scientific meetings with special emphasis on the clinical use of hypnotherapy in medicine, dentistry, psychology, and pediatrics, plus specific applications in surgery, obesity, smoking, and sexual problems. $11 per cassette. [Source: American Society of Clinical Hypnosis]

Audio Colloquies—Leading behavioral and social scientists discuss their research, their findings, and their opinions in developmental psychology, experimental and physiological psychology, parapsychology, social psychology, therapy and personality, and cognition, perception, and language. Some of the speakers include B.F. Skinner, Jerome Kagan, Stanley Milgram, Philip Zimbardo, Margaret Mead, Judith Bardwick, Ashley Montagu, William Glasser, Albert Bandura, Michael Gazzaniga, Noam Chomsky, J. B. Rhine, and many more. Also available are some of the psychology/anthropology programs produced by MCI: *Why People Hate: The Origins of Discrimination*, on six cassettes; *Ashley Montagu Speaks . . .* on four cassettes; *Women Today: Options, Obstacles, Opportunities*, on six cassettes; and *Myths to Live By*, on eight cassettes. All cassettes are about 45 minutes long, cost $12.95 each. [Source: Harper & Row Media]

Agoraphobia: Multiform Behavioral Treatment—A program for both therapist (giving guidelines for modifying the behavioral, cognitive, and affective components of the fear of open spaces) and client, (with guides to understanding agoraphobia, sensory awareness to overcome negative preoccupations, and home exercise instructions). $42 for four cassettes and client manual in album. [Source: BMA Audio Cassettes]

Assertiveness—How To Fight Fair: Understanding Aggression—Dr. George R. Bach (co-author of *Intimate Enemy*) shows how to deal creatively when confronted with human anger and violence, especially related to those you love. In *Therapeutic Aggression—Another View of Assertiveness*, Dr. Bach shows professionals how to use hostility as a therapeutic measure. Both programs on ten C-30 cassettes in albums for $84.50. [Source: Instructional Dynamics, Inc.]

Laymen Level Interventions—A program of therapeutic timesavers, intended to provide a means of explaining complex psychological dynamics to cli-

ents in therapy and counseling, in terms that laymen will understand and thus will facilitate communication in the counseling process. $69.95 for six cassettes. [Source: Instructional Dynamics, Inc.]

The Search for Meaning—Five albums by psychotherapist Dr. Sheldon Kopp. The titles (and subtitles) are: *Myself and Others* (a tough and tender dialog) and *The Search for Happiness* (what kind of help helps!), each $39.95 for five C-30 cassettes in album; and *Nothing to Hide* (become who we are), *Companions and Helpers Along the Way* (metaphors from a psychotherapist), and *Therapists Are People Too* (fragments from the notebooks of a psychotherapist), each $47.95 for six C-30 cassettes in album. Of related interest is the program on *The Real Self*, a three-part program, by Dr. Sterling G. Ellsworth, that guides both the individual and the professional toward identifying the real self, explaining styles of substitute self, and helping the real self emergence. $89.50 for 12 cassettes, with album. [Source: Instructional Dynamics, Inc.]

Counseling and Psychotherapy with Adolescents—Unique insights and techniques of a therapist—Joy Johnson—who has spent a professional lifetime helping adolescents and training those who counsel teenagers. Her topics: the nature of the beast, do's and don'ts, engaging the adolescent, adolescent smokescreening, resistance, and differential treatment methods. $69.95 for six cassettes in album. [Source: Instructional Dynamics, Inc.]

Psychology of Romantic Love—Dr. Nathaniel Branden deals with one of the most crucially important aspects of human life, integrating the theoretical and practical aspects of romantic love into an understanding and appreciation of its meaning and value and of the conditions necessary for its growth. 19 hours of material on 16 cassettes for $144 in albums, or $11.95 each. Dr. Branden also has *Discussions of Man-Woman Relationships* (four hour-long cassettes for $50), *Self-Esteem and Personal Evolution* (20 tapes, 26 hours, $188.95), and many others. [Source: Jeffrey Norton Publishers, Inc.]

Audio-Forum—Many single cassette titles covering issues in psychology and psychiatry, often of a controversial nature. For example, Dr. Peter Breggin talks about *The Politics of Psychosurgery* and *Psychiatry and the Free Market*. Charlotte Buhler describes her *Humanistic Psychology* and Drs. Miriam and Otto Ehrenberg discuss *The Ins and Outs of Therapy: A Consumer's Guide*. Karl Hess evaluates *The Psychology of the Ruling Class*, and Gardner Murphy gives an *Introduction to Parapsychology*. These and many more are available for $10.95 to $13.95 each. [Source: Jeffrey Norton Publishers, Inc.]

Outcome of Psychotherapy: Benefit, Harm or No Change—Lectures on this highly-charged and controversial topic, by Thomas Szasz, Allen E. Bergin,

Hans H. Strupp, Jerome D. Frank, Sol L. Garfield, Lester Luborsky, and Hans J. Eysenck, eight cassettes in album, $84. Cassettes also available individually. [Source: BMA Audio Cassettes]

Androgynous Perspectives on Psychotherapy—Alexandra G. Kaplan Ph.D. shows how the combined presence of socially valued masculine and feminine characteristics can influence therapy, on one cassette for $10.50. Related single cassette titles (also $10.50) include: *Issues in Applied Ego Psychology*: *Diagnostic and Treatment Implications, Psychotherapy with Women*: *Contemporary Approaches, Diagnostic Interview Techniques for Short-Term Psychotherapy, Paradoxes of Freedom* (Rollo May Ph.D.), *Time-Limited Psychotherapy*, and many more. [Source: BMA Audio Cassettes]

Rational Emotive Therapy—Albert Ellis Ph.D. offers: *Rational Emotive Therapy in the Treatment of Severe Mental Disorders* on six cassettes in album for $63; *Rational Emotive Therapy*: *Clinician's Guide, Dealing with Sexuality and Intimacy*, and *Discomfort Anxiety* (all single cassettes for $10.50), and *Rational Emotive Workshop* (two cassettes, $21). [Source: BMA Audio Cassettes]

Dream Series—An overview tape covers the historical significance of dreams as depicted in the Old Testament and in ancient records, and then discussions of the dream theories of Freud, Jung, and Perls, described in terms of their interrelationship and significant differences. Four cassettes, $25.95 each. [Source: Lansford Publishing Company]

Psychological Control of Pain—Dr. Ronald Melzack, developer of the 'gate control' theory of pain, reviews the theoretical and practical aspects of this concept, and then Dr. Campbell Perry shows how hypnosis and biofeedback can be used to augment it. $21 for two cassettes. A program of related interest is *Cognitive Therapy for Pain*, featuring Dr. Dennis Turk who believes that patients can be guided to use available psychological resources to combat the debilitating effects of chronic pain, and shows how therapists can accomplish that goal on these two cassettes for $21. [Source: BMA Audio Cassettes]

Behavioral Assessment: A Clinical Approach—An overview cassette defines the innovative approach, a second cassette gives a guiding framework with a five-stage heuristic model, and then there are separate tapes on adult and on child assessment, with pointers on use of questionnaires, multiple data sources, and sharing conferences. Four cassettes in album, $42. [Source: BMA Audio Cassettes]

Seminar in Gestalt Therapy—Eric Marcus M.D. leads mental health professionals and paraprofessionals through a challenging seminar designed to show how gestalt techniques apply to very human situations in counseling and therapy. $59.50 for six cassettes (four hours) in album. [Source: Instructional Dynamics, Inc.]

Differential Diagnosis of Anxiety—Discussions of how anxiety affects various organ systems of the body—genitourinary, respiratory, cardiovascular, gastrointestinal, endocrine, and central nervous systems, as well as skin and eye—in health and disease, all prepared to enable clinicians to better recognize, intervene, and treat anxiety appropriately in various clinical settings. Eligible for 20 hours of Category 1 AMA credit. $50 for 16 cassettes, syllabus, and quiz in album. [Source: Audio Visual Medical Marketing, Inc.]

Survey of Psychiatry—Lectures presented at the 1979 APA meeting provide an overview of neuropsychiatry, psychopathology, psychopharmacology, major treatment approaches, forensic psychiatry, and psychologic testing, all planned to reinforce previous learning and to update knowledge of current concepts in psychiatry. Eligible for 24 Category 1 AMA credit hours. $50 for 14 cassettes, illustrated syllabus, and quiz in album. Also there is *The New Psychiatry*, an album of 22 lectures that integrate new biological, diagnostic, neurophysiological, genetic, and pharmacologic research with traditional psychosocial approaches to mental and psychiatric disorders. Prepared under the direction of Harvard's Shervert H. Frazier M.D. and eligible for 22 Category 1 AMA credit hours. $250 for 22 cassettes, illustrated syllabus, and quiz, in album. [Source: Audio Visual Medical Marketing, Inc.]

Psychiatry Home Study Courses—12 selected courses from the 1980 and 1981 annual meetings of the American Psychiatric Association, carefully edited to delete extraneous material and slide references. There is one 6-hour course, *Child and Adolescent Psychiatry* for $59.95, and one 5-hour course, *Neurology for Psychiatrists*, at $49.95. Among the 3-hour courses for $29.95: *New Treatments for Phobic Patients, Psychiatric Syndromes Induced by Medications, Treating the Child or Adolescent with Minimal Brain Dysfunction, Depression in Medical Patients, Emergency Psychiatry* and *Right to Refuse Treatment*. Finally, some 2-hour courses for $19.95: *The Adult Life Cycle, Chronic Pain Therapy, Legal Regulation of Psychiatric Practice*, and *Family Therapy*: *Theory and Technique*. All prices slightly higher in Canada. Price includes album and syllabus. [Source: Audio-Digest Foundation]

How To Practice Bio Scream Psychotherapy—For psychotherapists and students, a complete course containing theory and detailed description of a supportive, direct, responsible way to help patients feel safe with their deepest feelings. The two cassettes include illustrative excerpts recorded in actual psychotherapy sessions. $20, with booklet. [Source: Nolan Saltzman, Ph.D.]

DSM-III for Clinicians—Six hours of lectures from the 1980 APA meeting offer a 'how-to' guide for the new DSM-III, the most important revision of psychiatric nomenclature in the past decade. Eligible for 10 hours of Category 1 AMA credit. $75 for six cassettes, syllabus, case studies, and quiz. [Source: Audio Visual Medical Marketing, Inc.]

Training in Psychosomatic Illness—R. Alec Ramsay M.D. developed this program to give health professionals an insight into the dimensions and complications of psychosomatic illness. He covers the meaning of 'psychosomatic,' the doctor-patient relationship, psychosomatic aspects of pain, and the role of the family and of stress in psychosomatic illness. $59.50 for six 30-minute cassettes in album. [Source: Instructional Dynamics, Inc.]

UCLA Extension—*Stations of the Mind* is Dr. William Glasser's explanation of how the functioning of the brain affects the way people think, act, and feel, on six cassettes for $51. The *Psychology of the Self* is a series of analytically-oriented presentations in areas of topics for mental health practitioners, with individual cassettes $6.95 to $12.95 each. Other multi-cassette programs cover *Borderline Conditions—Diagnosis and Treatment* and *Images, Myths and Fairy Tales*, both $10.95 to $12.95 per cassette. [Source: UCLA Extension]

Lifelong Learning—Katharine Whiteside Taylor and Crittenden E. Brookes discuss *Relationships and the Growth of Love*, especially from the Jungian point of view, $140 for 13 cassettes (14 hours) in album. *Escaping the Therapeutic Sanctuary: Psychodrama versus Gestalt* is debated by Richard Korn and George Lane, on a single two-hour cassette for $20. [Source: University of California]

Psychology Today Cassettes—Provocative interviews with foremost social scientists, offering insights into issues that concern us all in our daily lives. Among a few of the titles: *Constructive Anger*, by George Bach; *21 Ways to Stop Worrying*, by Albert Ellis; *Client-Centered Therapy*, by Carl Rogers; *Reality Therapy*, by William Glasser; *Rational-Emotive Therapy*, by Albert Ellis; *Gestalt Therapy*, by Robert W. Resnick; and *Behavior Therapy*, by Joseph Wolpe. There are a lot more, all for $10.95 each, with a 15% discount when 4 or more are ordered. A few cassettes are specially discounted to $3.98, and some albums are offered at great savings. [Source: Psychology Today Cassettes]

AAP Tape Library—Recordings of actual psychotherapy sessions, conference and workshop demonstrations, and discussions of psychotherapeutic techniques, theories, and experiences, for use in teaching, continuing education, and research. The more than 105 titles represent an important archive of contemporary psychotherapy, including talks by such experts as Carl Rogers, Albert Ellis, Fritz Perls, Carl Whitaker, Joseph Wolpe, Erika Fromm, Hans Strupp, Virginia Satir, Harold Greenwald, and many others. The presentations range from 20 minutes to nearly six hours in length, with prices ranging from $11 to $44 per title. Most programs are accompanied by a verbatim transcript. These are for sale only to professionals and to qualified institutions. [Source: AAP Tape Library]

Cognitive Behavior Therapy: Applications and Issues—Single cassettes (10.50 each) giving an overview, use in phobic and obsessive-compulsive disorders, obesity, addictions, sexual problems, depression, anxiety and impulse disorders. The whole works on eight cassettes with study guide in album for $84. *Cognitive Treatment of Depression: Live Demonstration of Interview Procedures* is another offering, on a single cassette for $10.50; *Controlling Depression Through Cognitive Therapy* consists of one tape for the therapist and two tapes for direct client use, with workbooks for $35. There's also *Behavior Therapy*, a group of single cassette programs covering the behavioral management of anxiety, insomnia, depression, weight control, phobias in women (all $10.50 each), and chronic alcoholism, which is on two cassettes for $21. [Source: BMA Audio Cassettes]

BMA Audio Cassettes—Many tapes for therapists, by one of the leaders in the field: *Selecting Patients for Biofeedback Therapy* by Kenneth R. Gaarder M.D., *Biofeedback Procedures* by Charles F. Stroebel MD, *Systems Approach to Biofeedback Training* by Thomas H. Budzynski Ph.D., and *Introducing Patients to Biofeedback Assisted Relaxation* by Mark S. Schwartz Ph.D. (all $10.50 for one cassette). Other cassettes ($11.50 each) cover other applications and the technology of biofeedback. [Source: BMA Audio Cassettes]

Clinical Biofeedback-Review Course—An overview of the evolving status of clinical biofeedback as a therapeutic modality, with nationally recognized authorities discussing basic theoretical issues, instrumentation considerations, and current clinical applications. This course has been planned for physicians, psychologists, physical therapists, nurses, and other allied health professionals who wish to understand more about clinical biofeedback as either primary or adjunctive therapy. $270 for 10 one-hour cassettes, course syllabus, and pre- and post-study tests in album, $25 more if continuing education credit is sought. [Source: UCLA Extension]

Thought Technology—Biofeedback programs by some of the leaders in the field: George D. Fuller Ph.D. on developing a biofeedback clinic; Thomas H. Budzynski Ph.D. on the systems approach to biofeedback training; Barbara B. Brown on stress and biofeedback; Hans Selye M.D. on the functional concept of stress; Seymour Diamond M.D. on biofeedback and headache; Ronald Melzach Ph.D. on the psychological control of pain; and others. Any six cassettes in album for $63, any eight in album for $84. [Source: Thought Technology Ltd.]

Biofeedback Patient Training Programs—Patient education tapes by Theodore Bradley M.D. that generally consist of an explanation about biofeedback and the psychophysiology of the patient's specific problem, and then of encouragement to respond while using biofeedback monitors (GSR, EMG, thermal training). This not only gives the patients uniform professional guidance, but also saves the therapist the need for repeated explanations. There are specific tapes for: alcoholism, asthma, arthritis, bruxism (teeth grinding), cardiac arrhythmia, childbirth, cancer, hypertension, headache, impotence, insomnia, narcotic addiction, obesity, peptic ulcers, smoking, menstrual cramps, Raynaud's disease, regional ileitis, ulcerative colitis, vaginitis, and stress. Cost is $9.95 for each C-90 cassette, generally available only to physicians, psychologists, and therapists. [Source: Biofeedback Recordings Inc.]

Psychofeedback—Deep in the brain is a structure called the reticular activating system that some believe underlies a person's awareness of the world and the ability to think, learn, and act. 'Psychofeedback' is a method of controlling this system by inserting into it the results of past and present experience, and thereby initiating purposeful behavior toward specific goals—a form of practical psychocybernetics. All this is explained on four cassettes and a book in an album for $59.95. [Source: Psychofeedback Institute]

Substance Abuse

The Drug Decision—A six-cassette commentary by psychiatrist Daniel Freedman MD, aimed at counselors, teachers, and parents, covering facts and myths about the use of drugs, categories of drugs, historical contexts, and patterns and motives for drug use. He covers not only hard drugs but also marijuana, alcohol, and nicotine. $84.50 for six cassettes in album, plus a copy of the book *Narcotic Plants*. [Source: Instructional Dynamics, Inc.]

The Drug Problem—A program planned to give students a thorough understanding of drugs and the drug problems by means of interviews with government officials, businessmen, law enforcement officers, doctors, clergymen—and drug users themselves. $112.25 for 10 cassettes, $13.95 per single cassette. [Source: Instructional Dynamics, Inc.]

Industrial Program for Alcoholism—Mr. Don Lew presents a step-by-step plan for identifying and combating some of the difficulties encountered in industrial and institutional settings. $39.95 for five cassettes in album. [Source: Instructional Dynamics, Inc.]

Comprehensive Smoking Cessation Program—The first tape in this series is for therapists, with specific pointers for improving motivation, selecting the best approach, and maintaining gains. The remaining four tapes are directed to the smoker and cover preparing to quit, quitting, and maintaining freedom from smoking; the patient approach is both relaxation and aversion. $52.50 with instruction guide. [Source: BMA Audio Cassettes]

Hazelden Cassettes—An outstanding collection of low-key talks for alcoholics, their family and friends, reflecting the Alcoholics Anonymous point of view. Except as noted, all albums contain six cassettes for $34.95; all individual cassettes (including those in most albums) are $5.95. There are three albums of talks on: culture, personality, and physiology; recovery; and the concepts of AA. One album features various speakers giving explanations and interpretations of the Twelve Steps of AA, others have talks by Phil Hansen (eight cassettes, $39.95) and by Joe Klass (four cassettes, $24.95) on the Twelve Steps. Another album features the Steps for Al-Anon, another has talks on other topics for Al-Anon. The *Golden Tapes* are a collection of 30 talks by Father Ralph Pfau, founder of the National Clergy Conference on Alcoholism, $5.95 each or all 30 for $159.95. Yet other cassettes take up other aspects of AA, alcoholism, and other forms of chemical dependency. [Source: Hazelden Educational Services]

New Directions–Alcoholism—23 lectures (many recorded live, with provocative questions-and-answers) that provide the latest insights into diagnosis and treatment of alcoholism, for program administrators, alcoholism workers, trainers, even students. Subjects covered include: the alcoholic script, drinking practices and problems, diagnosis and referral, differential selection and treatment, alternatives to abstinence, the doctor's role, acupuncture, agapé therapy, detoxification, ethics and politics, many more. Cassettes average 45 minutes each. $9.95 each, any eight for $68 with album, all 23 for $200 with three albums. Of related interest is *The Father Joseph C. Martin Tape Cassette Series*. With insight, humor, and a down-to-earth style, Fr. Martin outlines and discusses the guidelines for working with alcoholics. Recorded live. $36.50 for four cassettes in album. [Source: Faces West Productions]

Drug Abuse—A comprehensive drug-study program that takes an objective look at such drugs as alcohol, marijuana, LSD, and narcotics—their uses, effects, and hazards. The series is designed to inform youths about drugs so that they are able to make intelligent and reasonable decisions regarding their personal involvement with drugs. $6 for each cassette, $90 for all 15 cassettes in the series. [Source: ESP, Inc.]

Understanding Alcoholism and Problem Drinking—Authoritative information on the nature of alcoholism and problem drinking, alcohol and the body, the causes of alcoholism, approaches to abstinence, and self-control training for moderate drinking. $95.95 for five cassettes. [Source: Lansford Publishing Company]

Compulsive Habit Disorders—To Mehl McDowell MD, smoking, alcohol abuse, and compulsive over-eating are addictions with critical physical roots; the psychological components are carried by the bio-chemical forces of the addictive process. Dr. McDowell treats these three habits by helping the individual create two new permanent specific atti-tudes: (1) a positive self-image as a liberated, fit, ex-addict, and (2) an aversion to the particular sub-stance by converting the craving for it into a hate. Much of the body-mind training on the tapes is experienced while the subject is in a relaxed, hypnot-ic-like state of mind. The *Stop Smoking* album contains three cassettes, instructions, and visual aids for $67. The *Stop Alcohol Abuse* album contains four cassettes plus instructions and visual aids for $82. Finally, the *Appetite Control* album contains four cassettes, instructions, and a 'thin eating style' cook-book, all for $87. [Source: Westerly Institute]

A Smoking Clinic on Tape—This program promises to teach the smoker how to eliminate completely the craving for cigarettes, and thereby how to quit smoking without becoming tense and irritable and without gaining weight. There are pointers on over-coming withdrawal symptoms, on easing 'smoker's tension,' and the danger points leading to backslid-ing—all in a step-by-step approach for $21.15. Simi-lar is *A Weight Clinic on Tape*, showing how to lose weight easily, safely—and permanently, by overcom-ing faulty eating habits and alleviating the situations that often lead to over-eating. $21.15. [Source: Au-dio Health Services]

Father Joseph C. Martin—Talks on various aspects of alcoholism by Fr. Martin, for $9.50 each: *Alcohol-ism in Industry, Family, Counseling, Chalk Talk on Alcohol* (also in Spanish), *Prevention, Symptoms of Sobriety, The Twelve Steps of AA, Spirituality and Religion, Feelings, Spiritual Aspects, Parenthood, Values, Caring, Live and Let Live, One Day at a Time, Gratitude,* and *Alcoholism Among the Elderly.* Album included with orders of four or more cassettes. [Source: Kelly Productions, Inc.]

Training

Emergency Care Cassettes—These programs are in-tended for emergency room personnel who must cope with the spectrum of ER presentations: ear ailments, dental emergencies, burns, alcoholism, bleeding, penetrating chest trauma, blunt abdominal trauma, the battered child. There are several pro-grams on staffing the ER. Most are $9 for each 30-60 minute lecture. [Source: Teach'em Inc.]

Emergency Care Cassettes—A four-cassette program for paramedics on emergency room procedures and personnel with specifics relating to particular kinds of emergencies. It's $31 for the set. [Source: Teach'em Inc.]

Death and Dying Services in the Acute Care Hospital—Current concepts, new knowledge, and refined skills for all practitioners in acute care hospitals, particularly the personnel in the hospice program. Except for an introductory program (two cassettes, $20), the cost is $10 for each of 15 cassettes covering various aspects of this timely subject. [Source: Teach'em Inc.]

The Geriatric Aide—An instruction course for aides, orderlies, and other health service assistants crucial to a satisfactory geriatric care program, designed to develop communication skills and professional atti-tudes, compassion and concern. The use of "situa-tion-example" vignettes provides the motivation and knowledge critical to an aide's success. $285 for 27 C-30 cassettes (54 lessons) with instructor's guide-book. [Source: W. B. Saunders Company]

Patient Care—As an aid to in- or pre-service training of all health care workers, 19 patients describe the problems that arose during their illnesses and their reactions to doctors, nurses, hospitals, nursing homes, and medication. $125 for 12 cassettes with teaching guide in album. [Source: American Med. Tech.]

Learning To Speak Again After a Stroke—A series of six audio-cassettes, an introductory cassette, visual aids, and instructional booklet—all designed and prepared by two senior qualified speech therapists to show voluntary helpers, relatives, and friends the best way to help stroke patients suffering from speech and language difficulties. This program should be used under the guidance of a speech therapist. $65. [Source: Chest, Heart and Stroke Association]

Audio-Learning—Continuing education programs intended especially for physical and occupational therapists: *New Methods in Physical Rehabilitation* explores the use of biofeedback in improving the function of neurological patients with voluntary movement disorders, on seven cassettes in album for $74.50; *Human Physiology* is a review of body func-tions relevant to paramedical professionals, on two 12-cassette albums with workbooks, $110.75 each. *Human Anatomy and Bio-Mechanics* has been pre-pared by Eleanor J. Carlin Sc.D. specifically for physical and occupational therapists, 12 cassettes in album for $110.75. *Recovery of Function Following Injury to the Nervous System* is planned to cover material pertaining to the recovery of function fol-lowing lesions in the peripheral, autonomic, and central nervous systems, on 10 cassettes in album for $95. [Source: Audio-Learning, Inc.]

Communications in Learning—Five separate catalogs of audio-tape programs are available, running from as short as 11 minutes for $16.15 to 60 minutes for $14. You figure it out. The main headings are dietetics & nutrition (covering patient care, diet therapy, and managing the dietary department), occupational therapy (subdivided into patient care, professional issues, communication in institutional life, and management aids), respiratory therapy (covering RT practitioners, ventilator procedures and techniques, oxygen therapy, anesthesia, patient care, interactions with patients, death and dying), medical technology (with programs on hematology, blood banking, instrumentation, special chemistry, and microbiology), medical records (covering the basics, management aids, and social issues). [Source: Communications in Learning, Inc.]

VI.

History

Revolutions—Eugene Kamenka, Professor of the History of Ideas at Australian National University, Canberra, first discusses the theoretical basis of any revolution, and then on successive cassettes takes up the French, Russian, and Chinese revolutions. A$37 for four C-90 cassettes, A$32 if payment accompanies order. [Source: Rigby Publishers]

Sourcetapes—A fascinating collection of eyewitness accounts, radio reports, and oral history interviews clustered into groupings that reveal dimensions of a human experience that cannot be captured by the printed page. All sets include an album and most a listener's guide; the $39 ones contain three cassettes, the $76 ones six cassettes. *The Decades Series* covers the 1930s, 1940s, 1950s, and 1960s, $39 each. *Black Diamonds* is an oral history of Negro baseball, $39; *Project Blue Book* contains eyewitness accounts of UFOs, $39; *Eyewitness* is a potpourri of human experiences, from the San Francisco Earthquake and Custer's last stand to the Iwo Jima Landing and the Hungarian Uprising, two albums, $76 each. *Grass Roots* and *They Choose America* (two albums) contain over 200 vivid first-person accounts of ethnic heritage and folk tradition, $76 each. Still other titles: *Peace for Our Time: The Causes of World War II*, $76; *Atomic War/Atomic Peace: Life in the Nuclear Age*, $76; *Voices of World War II*, 12 cassettes, $119; *Print Journalism*, $76; *Broadcast Journalism*, $76; and *China*, $76. The *American Economy Series* has two parts: *1929-1945, From Breadline to Frontline* and *1945-1959, From Frontline to Picketline*, $76 each. *Speaking for America* are *Six Presidents* (Hoover through Johnson), *12 Activists* (Bond, Coffin, DeCrow, Nader, Wilkins, and others), and *12 National Leaders* (Gardner, King, Lippman, McGovern, Meany, Moynihan, Stevenson, and others), $76 each. [Source: Visual Education Corporation]

"...our Lives, our Fortunes and our sacred Honor"—The lives of the 56 signers of the Declaration of Independence—not only John Hancock and Thomas Jefferson, but also Thomas Nelson and Lewis Morris and *all* the others—on eight cassettes (over seven hours of narration by Bob Lockwood). $98.50 in album with hardbound textbook in newspaper format. [Source: Harrison Tyner International, Inc.]

Ivan Berg Cassettes—Dramatized biographies of history makers such as Napoleon, Lenin, Luther, Drake, Mao and others from various periods and countries. There's a series of scientists (Einstein, Darwin, Edison, Fleming, and others), famous women (Elizabeth the First, Florence Nightingale, Emma Hamilton, Mary Baker Eddy and others), and a series of U.S. founding fathers and patriots (Henry, Franklin, Jefferson, Paine, Hamilton, Hancock, Madison and others), and Civil War heroes (from both sides) including Lincoln, Davis, Grant, Lee and Jackson. Another group of cassettes from this noted English producer covers dramatized recreations of great disasters of history (sinking of the Lusitania and the burning of the Hindenburg) as well a famous battles such as Gettysburg, Waterloo, Midway, and the Spanish Armada's attack on England, and others. Each program on a single cassette for $8.95. [Source: Spears Communications International, Inc.]

Excursions in American History—Historian Kenneth Bruce makes history come alive in his series of six-cassette albums ($68.45 each): *The Beginnings of Our Nation*; *The Westward Movement*; *The War Between Brothers*; *An Economic Giant: Growth and Problems* (from the industrial beginnings to the great depression), *Challenges, Crisis, and Calamities* (generally, from 1868 to 1912); *Conquering Space and Time: Development in Transportation and Communication*; *The Great War: Prelude, Conflict, and Aftermath*; and *Our Nation in the Pacific and the Kennedy Era* (two separate segments). Mr. Bruce also has a ten-cassette series on *Some Critical Periods in World History*, bring to life such events and eras as the fall of Constantinople, Louis XIV, Rousseau and the Enlightenment, the French revolution, Napoleon, the Russian revolution, and the rise of fascism. $112.25 for ten cassettes in album. [Source: Instructional Dynamics, Inc.]

American History and Heritage—Audio-Forum's vast collection of single cassettes and series covers the whole spectrum of America's past. Write for their catalog for we can list here only a few of the titles ($10.95 per cassette): *Looking Back at Hiroshima* by Jacob Beser; *America, An Outside View* with Alastair Cooke; *The True Story of Pearl Harbor*, with Percy L. Greaves; *The Assassination of Robert F. Kennedy*; and *The American Revolution as Seen by a*

British Historian with Edmund Wright. *Voices of the Old West* contains memories of frontier life by a rancher, housewife, prospector and others who lived in the period, and its $59 for five cassettes and a discussion guide. [Source: Audio-Forum/Jeffrey Norton Publishers, Inc.]

History Makers—Capsule biographies of noted leaders of history which give not only what they did but also how and why they did it. A few of the individuals covered are Einstein, Washington, the Wright Brothers, Thomas A. Edison, Charles Darwin, Mary Baker Eddy, Martin Luther and Mao Tse-Tung. $10.95 for each 60+-minute cassette. [Source: Jeffrey Norton Publishers, Inc.]

America in the 1920's—Discussions of American life from the end of World War I to the Great Depression, with analysis of the Harding, Coolidge, and Hoover administrations, and of such heroes and anti-heroes as Lindbergh, Capone, Bryan and Darrow, Dempsey, Tilden, and Babe Ruth, and such authors as Lewis, Fitzgerald, and Hemingway. $135.95 for eight cassettes. [Source: Lansford Publishing Company]

Dramatized American Heritage—Great moments in American history dramatized, featuring Columbus, Powhatan, Roger Williams, Lord Baltimore, William Penn, Benjamin Franklin, Daniel Boone, Lafayette, Justice Marshall, Noah Webster, Robert E. Lee, William Sherman, Susan B. Anthony, George Washington Carver and George Washington himself, the Wrights, Samuel Gompers, and Lindbergh, to name just a few of the stars in this series of 36 one-hour programs. The Revolutionary War, the making of the Constitution, the coming of the railways and telegraphy, the Civil War are just a few of the events covered. $239.20 for the set with three albums, or $18 for two tapes sent monthly. [Source: Living Scriptures Inc.]

History—Three two-cassette packages by Professor Al Stokes, for $29 each. Series I covers America before the Revolution, Series II surveys America from the Revolution to Jefferson, 1775-1783, and Series III covers the Federalist period, 1788-1800. All three series in album for $79. [Source: Tutor/Tape]

Simplified Texts—An eclectic collection of programs, generally 30 minutes long, $10 each. The *Holocaust* series has studies of the rise of Hitler, the Third Reich and the master race, the Warsaw ghetto, Hermann Goering, Nazi aims and methods, the underground, the death camps, and more. The series on *Europe* has profiles on Bismarck, the Dreyfus Case, Czarist Russia, the Russian Revolution, the Weimar Republic, Mussolini, the outbreak of WWII, Karl Marx, Leopold and the Congo, and more. Series on *American Presidents* and the *Presidency* covers everything from Washington, Jefferson, Jackson, and Polk to the Harding scandals, Teddy Roosevelt, Wilson, FDR, Truman, Eisenhower, and a lot on JFK. [Source: Simplified Texts]

Vital History Cassettes—An audio history of our times, as the spoken words of the world's leaders and would-be leaders are heard in speeches, press conferences, briefings and interviews, selected to achieve proper balance between current relevance and historical significance. $281 a year for three C-60 cassettes a month (36 a year), plus study guides, index and binder. Individual cassettes $12 each. Grolier has also released three other collections: *American Crisis* (the last days of the Nixon presidency), three C-60 cassettes and supplements, $29.50; *The Cold War*, eight C-60 cassettes plus extensive supplemental material, $92.50; *World War II*, nine C-60 cassettes plus supplements and book, $123. [Source: Grolier Educational Corporation]

Kaleidoscope—Based on his Peabody Award-winning radio programs on WJR, Mike Whorf presents over 1,000 informative 'visual sounds' narratives and documentaries. Topics in the six categories of subjects range from biographies of famous men in the *History and Heritage* group to the life and times of poets, authors, and painters in the *Arts and Letters* category. The *Social* category deals with the lives of Americans from all walks of life, including a 34-part series on the American Revolution. There is a collection of narratives on the lives of great spiritual leaders of our time under the *Religious* grouping and under the *Science* heading, stories of medical researchers, developers, and physicians. Each cassette runs about 40 minutes, costs $8.95. [Source: Mike Whorf Inc.]

United States History: An Audio Chronology—A comprehensive presentation of important milestones in the growth of America, with narration, music and special effects. A few topics included in the 60 programs of the series are: Christopher Columbus, the Coming of the Pilgrims, Paul Revere, The Winter at Valley Forge, the Lewis and Clark Expedition, the War of 1812, Florida and the Seminoles, the Alamo and San Jacinto, the Pony Express, Custer, several programs on the Civil War, the Alaska Gold Rush, the Gay 90s, Henry Ford, World War I, the Great Depression, FDR, two programs on WW II, the Atomic Age, the Korean Conflict, Vietnam, and the Space Age. $12.95 each. [Source: Educational Record Sales]

The Decades—Interviews, speeches, and eyewitness reports bring to life important events from: The 1930s, The 1940s, The 1950s, and The 1960s. Each decade of excepts consists of three cassettes with guide in an album for $39. [Source: Educational Record Sales.]

Our Fifty States—50 cassettes (one on each state in the Union) that describe the past heritage, present status, and future characteristics and growth of the individual state. $6 for each 30-minute cassette, all 50 for $300. Related are *Our Constitution* and *Our*

Flag (each with two 30-minute cassettes, $12), and *Our Electoral College* ($6 for one cassette). [Source: ESP, Inc.]

The American West: The Frontier Era—12 lectures by leading authorities in the field of western American history, dealing with the important issues (exploration, mountain men, Mormons, mining, Indian affairs, farmers and cattlemen, populism, women, violence) of the trans-Mississippi West of the 19th century. $12 each, $120 for complete set of 12 titles. Also as a follow up, there's *The New Frontier: The 20th Century West*, with major social and political events of this century, as they affected the American West: reform politics to the depression, WWI, New Deal, Japanese Americans, Indians, Chicanos, conservation, urbanism, the literary West. $12 each. [Source: Everett/Edwards, Inc.]

VII.
How To Do It

Bark Alarm—For those interested in foiling intruders there is an endless-loop six-minute cassette offered by two different sources for this purpose. Both are filled with ferocious growls and snarls, barks and ominous pauses. One is $15.95. [Source: Professional Cassette Center] The other is $15.98. [Source: Metacom, Inc.]

We've Got Your Number—Gives a choice of five telephone answering tapes with impersonated celebrity voices giving zany and funny (and in one case serious and dignified) responses to put on your telephone answering machine. They're $8.98 each, any three for $19.98. [Source: Metacom, Inc.]

How to Meet Intelligent and Beautiful Women—Eric Weber gives a 90-minute seminar that offers hope for sagging social lives. $12.95. [Source: Professional Cassette Center]

How to Select and Install the Right Computer System for Home or Business—Designed for persons with no technical background in computers, this course gives the necessary information to make the proper selection of a mini-computer for home or office needs. It's $19.95 for two cassettes in an album. [Source: Professional Cassette Center]

ESP—A major producer of cassette education packages intended for use in schools, ESP produces some programs clearly of adult interest. They have these mini-courses on a single cassette with workbook, for $8 each: *Beginning Public Speaking, Corrective Practices in Speech Therapy, Basic Facts of Astrology, Business Mathematics, Algebra, Geometry, The Metric System, Sex in Marriage, Basic Practices in Weight Control, Starting and Managing a Business, Getting and Keeping a Job, Developing Your Personality, How To Study, Secrets of Beauty and Charm, The Successful Secretary, Drug Abuse, Understanding Politics, How To Write, Planning a Will*, and more. *The Baby Sitter* offers practical help for this poorly trained group, four C-30 cassettes for $24. *Skillful Business Management* is complete on 20 cassettes, $120, while *Success in Life Insurance* is on six cassettes, $40. And you could do worse than get their general self-improvement course, *Successful Living*, 24 cassettes for $140. The *World of Astrology* is on six cassettes, $36, as is *The World Religions*. And there are more; write for their catalog. [Source: ESP, Inc.]

Michigan Media—This source has a vast library of entertainment and education program, and although much of it is aimed toward primary and secondary education, there are many titles of college and adult-level interest (and all titles are coded as to educational level). They also have available audio-cassettes to accompany foreign language textbooks developed at the University of Michigan, including Arabic and Hebrew. Write for their free 'Audio Tape Recordings' catalog. Costs are exceptionally low, and customers can also supply their own high quality cassettes, if desired. [Source: University of Michigan]

Learning Curve—Henny Youngman tells you *How to be a Comedian* in a one-hour mini-course consisting of a C-60 cassette, programmed exercises and tests. $9.98. [Source: Metacom, Inc.]

Basic Guide to Better Photography—On four cassettes, the course leads you through an illustrated study guide, all in laymen's language, that enables one to begin taking better pictures with a 35mm single lens reflex camera. Intended for the amateur, hobbyist, or occasional picture taker, it covers camera control, focusing, shutter speeds, aperture, depth of field, meters, flash, film, lenses, filters, and more. $49.95 for four cassettes and study guide in binder. [Source: American Institute of Photography]

Montaigne Ltd.—An eclectic collection of one-hour cassettes ($10.95 each) on diverse topics: *How To Start and Operate a New Photography Business* (two cassettes) by a successful commercial photographer; *How To Make Money With Your Camera*, and pay for film and new equipment in your spare time; *Photographing Weddings* inside and outside of the church; *How To Sell Real Estate*, by one of Canada's top real estate brokers; *How To Make Love*, with 'Lynda' describing what pleases a woman in lovemaking; *Flower Arranging*, original yet practical ideas by a professional florist; *How To Ski*, by Canada's chief ski instructor, Real Charette; *Yoga*, in four 15-minute sessions, covering exercises, breathing, and relaxation; the *5BX plan*, with progressively more difficult 10-minute exercises; and the only English language *Mass by Pope John Paul II*, recorded live in Washington, DC. [Source: Montaigne Ltd.]

Sounds of Shortwave—Here is a 60-minute cassette that will be intriguing to any shortwave enthusiast: examples of the strange sounds and signals heard throughout the shortwave spectrum, with a clear explanation of what each sound represents. There's also an authoritative discussion of receivers, antennas, accessories, and other help for the shortwave neophyte. $6.45. [Source: Grove Enterprises, Inc.]

Morse Code Practice Tapes—30 minutes of 5 wpm and another 30 at 7.5 wpm on one cassette, and another of 30 minutes of 10 wpm and 30 minutes of 13 wpm—$5 each, both with booklet ('ARRL Code Kit') for $8. There is another tape of 30 minutes of 15 wpm and 30 minutes of 20 wpm for those really adept, also $5. Finally, *Hola CQ* is a cassette with 16-page booklet to help communicate with Spanish-speaking radio amateurs, $7. [Source: American Radio Relay League]

Radio Code by the Word Method—This course of instruction for Morse code is unique in that it begins at a moderate rate of transmission speed (13 wpm) using simple material. It continues at this same speed through the course, because instead of increasing the transmitting rate, the complexity of the material is increased. $10.95 for volume one (ER 1004) on a C-90 and C-60 cassette. Volume two (ER 1005) consists of a life sketch of Nikola Tesla in Morse code, on a C-60 cassette at 20 wpm, for $4.98. [Source: Epsilon Records]

Whirlpool Technician Training Materials—Programs intended for whirlpool appliance repairmen, but anyone with a mechanical bent should be able to follow the cassette instructions ($6.95 per topic), and those in doubt can order the correlated filmstrip ($6.95) and booklet ($1.95). Some of the topics covered: compact laundry appliances, service procedures for mechanical systems in dryers, diagnosing the wash, understanding laundry electrical controls and components, understanding and servicing solid-state electronic controlled washers (and also, dryers), refrigeration electrical controls, fundamentals and diagnosis—refrigeration, room air conditioner fundamentals (and another on 'diagnosis'), trouble-shooting trash compactors, servicing the SHU9900 dishwasher, and microwave oven problem diagnosis and repair. [Source: Whirlpool Corporation]

Chek-Chart Automotive Mechanics Refresher Course—A programmed audio-text refresher course for auto mechanics, designed not only to keep them up-to-date on the latest service and repair procedures for most U.S. cars, but also to prepare for the pass NIASE certification examinations. There are five cassette-plus-text segments, covering: ignition and fuel injection; engine, lubrication, and cooling systems; electrical systems plus heating and air conditioning; transmission and drive train; and brakes, steering, suspension, wheels, and tires. The complete course of six cassettes (including introductory cassette) and books in album is $79.95; individual cassette-with-book sets are $21.70. [Source: Gousha/Chek-Chart]

How to Operate the Apple II Plus—Three hour-long lessons guide the listener through the essentials of computer operation: how to run programs, enter

data, save files, make back-up copies, modify programs, and much more. The audio format lets the listener run the computer and watch the screen while listening to the instructions. These programs are in the FlipTrack format, giving optional instruction in color video, second disk drives, and printers—all without interrupting training for those desiring only basic information. $49.95 for three cassettes and operator's guide in binder (requires an Apple II Plus computer with the System Master 3.3 diskette). [Source: Math House]

How to Do—Have you ever wondered how to plan a party, choose a sorority, make a decision, select a physician, care for children, buy insurance, enjoy a concert, care for your car, or refinish furniture? These 30-minute cassettes (each with two 15-minute instructions) are given in simple, easy-to-understand terms. $6 each, the complete set of 48 cassettes for $280. ESP also offers *very* basic courses in carpentry, plumbing, heating/air-conditioning, electricity, electronics, auto mechanics, drafting/blueprint reading, and home economics. 12 cassettes in an album for $80. [Source: ESP, Inc.]

Sabine Voice Strengthening Technique—In the first part of this one-hour program, voice coach Elizabeth Sabine explains that we have lost our ability to 'roar' from the chest, and instead we 'whisper' from the throat. In the second part, she provides exercises to drive the origins of the voice back into the chest, keeping stomach muscles tense and making speaking resonant and effortless. $15. [Source: Elizabeth Sabine]

Cassette Tapes for the Interior Designer—Four discussions written and narrated by A. Allen Dizik, F.A.S.I.D.: *Furniture Arrangements*, an analysis of physical and psychological considerations in space planning and interior environments; *Color/Color Psychology*, exploring and identifying the principles of color technology and psychology; *Window Treatments and Textiles*, the design of window treatments using fabric, shades, blinds, and shutters, with some practical solutions for problem windows; and a guide, *Furniture Styles and Periods*. $11 for each tape. [Source: Stratford Publishing Company]

Instant Learning Courses—A good collection of fundamental "how-to-do-it" courses, all with a C-60 cassette and instruction booklet, for $14.95 each. Some of the titles: *Instant Memory Power, Listening and Concentration, Instant Math, Double Your Reading Speed in One Week, Skyrocking Your Child's Grades in School, Instant Shorthand, Successful Secretarial Course, Writing Articles that Sell, Double Your Power to Learn, Instant Piano* and *Instant Guitar, Instant Yoga, Instant Meditation, Relax Your Way to Success, Eat Your Way Out of Fatigue, Shed Pound After Pound, How to Avoid Lawyers, Astrological Horoscopes, Witchcraft Powers, Instant Word Power, Self-Hypnotism* and *Good Health and Vigor After 50*. [Source: Automated Learning, Inc.]

VIII.
Human Relations and Counseling

Questions and Answers on Aging and Retirement—Psychologist Harold Geist, Ph.D. presents current information and help in retirement planning, especially for executives and other hard-driving individuals. $25.95 for a single cassette. [Source: Lansford Publishing Company]

Stigma—A group of severely physically disabled people talk openly about their self-image, dependency, sexuality, social interactions, mobility, and survival skills—to provide insight for both counselors and disheartened disabled patients. $11.50 for a single cassette. [Source: Faces West Productions]

Transactional Analysis in Social and Communications Training (TASC)—A kit consisting of a cassette, manual, games book, and other materials, intended to give a group of up to 15 participants insights into why they are the way they are and why others react to them in the way they do. *Advanced TASC— Higher Levels in Transactional Analysis* is a kit intended for those who have gone through TASC or another introductory course in TA, using the same format. $49.50 for either kit. Of related interest is *TA in the Key of C* in which Dr. Warren Welsh uses carefully selected remarkably pertinent lyrics of certain popular and folk songs to communicate the ideas of TA in a way that is as effective as it is surprising; with it one can often reach groups otherwise resistant to transactional analysis. Six cassettes and support materials in album for $54.50. [Source: Instructional Dynamics, Inc.]

TA for Creative Living—The important ideas of transactional analysis in simple language on 60-minute cassettes, prepared by senior members of the International Transactional Analysis Association. The programs are designed for professionals, para-professionals, and interested lay persons, all with the intent to transmit knowledge of TA and its application to learning as well as to problem situations. 19 tapes are offered in five categories: basic TA; self-improvement; TA and daily problems; special uses of TA; and new concepts. $9.95 for each C-60 cassette. [Source: American Life Foundation]

Toward Emotional Health—Bonaro W. Overstreet Ph.D. shares her insight and experience in helping students, teachers, counselors, and parents to work together to achieve emotional health in relation to the world around them. $54.50 for six half-hour cassettes and leaders guide. [Source: Instructional Dynamics, Inc.]

APGA Cassette Tapes—A cassette library of distinguished speakers offering original thoughts on guidance and counseling, suitable for classrooms, workshops, seminars, preservice and inservice training, and as the basis of community-oriented programs. Twenty-five titles are available, under the headings of careers, minorities, drugs, women, counseling, testing, program planning, sexism and sexuality. Recorded at past annual meetings of the guidance counselors professional association, some of these are not too current. $8 each, any three for $23. [Source: American Personnel and Guidance Association]

Insight Cassettes—Intended to help students and teachers learn from the life experience of others, these 50 cassettes feature real people talking about their life-wrenching experiences: the convict, the abused child, the young diabetic, the widower-suicide, the father of a Down's syndrome child, the rape victim, the unwed mother, the welfare mother, the ex-Moonie, the homosexual, the divorced father. One message per cassette (each plays about 15-20 minutes, repeated on second side.) Price is $6.98 per cassette, free album with an order of ten cassettes for $69.80. [Source: Greenhaven Press]

The LEAR Approach To Working With Irate People—After analyzing the techniques used by those successful in handling conflict situations, Ted Dreier has developed this approach for dealing with irate persons: customers, employees, and even family members. One cassette is devoted to each of the four components of the LEAR approach: *L*istening, developing *E*mpathy, *A*sking questions, and then *R*esponding. When correlated with workbook exercises, the course provides new insights into improving employee communications and building customer relations. $129.95 for four cassettes (1-¾ hours) and workbook in album. [Source: C.D.S., Inc.]

Teens to the Top—Mark Rhode and Lisa Nock offer pointers to teenagers to help them improve their self-image by eliminating negative attitudes, handling peer pressure, communicating more effectively with parents, and identifying hidden qualities. $49.95 for four cassettes and action guide in album. [Source: Semantodontics, Inc.]

Effective Personality Interactions—Especially intended for dental and medical office staffs, this course by Naomi Rhode and Don Thoren supplies strategies for improving interpersonal relationships and for enabling one to identify and deal successfully with the different social styles of both patients and other staff members. $69.95 for eight cassettes and study guides in album. On *Say 'Yes' to Living*, Ms. Rhode gives an inspirational message on value clarification as a tool in personal growth. $12.95 for two cassettes in album. [Source: Semantodontics, Inc.]

Family Meeting—A series of five cassettes ($36.25) covering parent-teen communications, providing 'talk starts' to help bridge the communications gap. *The Cheaper Life* is a six-cassette 'postgraduate course,' that takes a look at the kind of people we create and become when we accept the lonely, defensive life we live when we are afraid of loving and being loved right in our own homes. $43.50. [Source: Family Enrichment Bureau]

Crisis Intervention—David R. Burke Ph.D. explores the problems faced by paraprofessional or volunteer helpers at hospitals, clinics, or crisis centers. He covers: creative listening, dealing with depression, the suicidal caller, and dealing with dangerous patients. $19.50 for two cassettes in album. [Source: Instructional Dynamics, Inc.]

Self-Control Systems—In *Understanding Relationships: How To Relate to People*, Dr. James W. Jolliff shares his insights into practical, everyday communication practices. In *Using Effective Management Techniques: Ways To Have a Smooth Running Organization*, Dr. Merritt F. Felmly shows how to put 'human relations' into an organization. In *Effective Communication Between Parents and Teenagers*, Dr. C. Eugene Walker gives pointers on how to bridge the sometimes insurmountable gaps between adolescents and their parents. In *Creative Parenting: Helping Children Learn To Be Happy Adults*, Dr. Walker discusses the principles of childbearing and how to cope with typical childhood problems. These are all $23.95 for two cassettes and manual in album. Dr. Jolliff's program (in the same format) titled *Too Much of a Good Thing* is subtitled 'It's no picnic living with a nitpicker, much less being one,' provides a satirical attack on self-defeating attitudes, and costs $25.95. [Source: Self Control Systems, Inc.]

Understanding and Predicting Human Behavior—Insights into understanding and predicting the behavior of those people with whom we live and work are revealed in this course of eight cassettes and study guide album for $80. Topics covered include

recognizing the motivation for the action of others, reversing one's own negative feelings, dealing with aggression, and when and how to give recognition and gain control in a relationship. [Source: Fred Pryor Resources Corporation]

Elisabeth Kubler-Ross—Dr. Ross, renown author and authority on death and dying, offers three hour-long presentations: *Life, Death and Life after Death*, the basic teaching tape; *Elisabeth Kubler-Ross Talks to High School Students* about the quality of life, how to live more fully, and with fewer anxieties about life and death; and *The Santa Barbara Lecture*, on the importance of unconditional love, with practical examples for the enhancement of life (fidelity is not the best). All $8.95 each. [Source: Shanti Nilaya]

Coping With Death and Dying—Dr. Elisabeth Kubler-Ross, the renown author of *On Death and Dying*, relates on the first three cassettes the 'three languages' used by dying patients to communicate their knowledge of impending death, with special reference to symbolic verbal and non-verbal language. She also covers the five states—denial, anger, bargaining, depression, acceptance—through which terminally ill patients and their families pass. On the fourth cassette she takes up the special problem of children who are facing death and who convey in their own way their concept and understanding of their status. The final cassette deals with sudden, unexpected death for which neither patient nor family is usually prepared. $40 for five 30-minute cassettes in album in the U.S., $43 in Canada. [Source: Ross Medical Associates]

The American Family: Current Perspectives—11 leaders in the field of family relations discuss changing patterns and developments in this all-important social group. The series includes: Urie Bronfenbrenner on the ecology of the family; Robert Coles on a social and racial perspective; George W. Goethals on the family life cycle; Robert S. Weiss on the single-parent family; Beatrice B. Whiting on various methods of child-rearing; Barrie S. Greiff on the high-pressure executive family; Mary Jo Bane on marriage and divorce rates; T. Berry Brazelton on the bonds between mother and infant; John Demos on past and present images of the family; Patricia K. Light on the dual-career family; and Douglas H. Powell on strengthening relationships among family members. $49.50 for six cassettes and pamphlet. [Source: Harvard University Press]

Handling People for Fun and Profit (Theirs and Yours)—In four hours of live recording, Roy Hatten describes the characteristics of people who are skilled in dealing with people, for $35 in album. Other albums of live performances by Mr. Hatten: *The Magic of Communications*, the important, overlapping roles of communications in management, three hours, $25; *People, Pins, Pumps, & Balloons*, two hours of lively discussion and specifics on working with people in a harmonious way, $20; two hours of *The Humor of Roy Hatten*, $20; and *The Magic of Believing* in yourself and in others, one hour, $10. [Source: Roy Hatten Enterprises]

Child Abuse: Causes and Prevention—A comprehensive set of lectures that cover the history of child abuse, the underlying causes of the maltreatment of children, what is being done by professionals and concerned lay people to prevent child abuse, and what still needs to be done. $99.95 for four cassettes, book, and resources. [Source: Lansford Publishing Company]

Interpersonal Communications—Lectures that examine the factors influencing our contacts with others, the nature of nonverbal communications, the psychological dispositions of people involved in a communication process, and ways to deepen and enrich interpersonal contact. $149.95 for six cassettes and printed materials. A related program is *Communications Lectures* (covering the communication process, persuasion and attitude change, human listening, and audience analysis), $99.95 for four cassettes, outline, and text. Also relevant is *Oral Communication Skills* (speech making, voice improvement, reading aloud, parliamentary procedure, group discussion, debate), $25.95 for each cassette. Finally, there's *Improving Your Helping and Communication Skills with Mental Practice*, providing experiential situations to practice communication or counseling skills on their own, on three cassettes and guide for $88.95. [Source: Lansford Publishing Company]

Thanks for Listening—Dr. Ralph G. Nichols offers three 50-minute talks on aspects of communicating: *He Who Has Ears*, covering the ten factors that separate good and poor listeners; *Barriers of Communication*, including the 'Good News Syndrome' and three others; and *Psychology of Persuasion*, based on the five steps Marc Antony used to gain willing cooperation of the Romans through persuasion. $12.95 each, all three for $35. [Source: Telstar]

Creative Learning Center—A potpourri of programs dealing with human interactions, covering sex in the classroom, the divorce experience, non-traditional marriages, death of a small town, the identity search of Terry Braun, the forces that shaped Hemingway's life and work, and the many faces of love (with Eli Wallach and Anne Jackson). All $9 each. [Source: Creative Learning Center]

Foundation of Praise—Talks by Merlin R. Carothers on the blessings and the benefits of praise, both praise given and praise received. $3.95 donation for each talk, $12.95 for an album of three cassettes of talks on a specific theme, and $23.95 for six-cassette album on *Prison to Praise* or *Power in Praise*. [Source: Foundation of Praise]

The Way of a Transsexual—Programs produced by Confide—Personal Counseling Services on counseling of men and women with gender identity problems, for physicians and therapists, and for the transsexual and his or her family. Four titles are available: *Joanne's Story*, the serious, yet often funny, and always optimistic first-person report of a man named George who became a woman named Joanne, 50 minutes, $12; *The Hardest Decisions*, an interview with the Rev. Canon Clinton R. Jones, a distinguished Episcopal counselor-priest who relates his experiences in helping troubled transsexuals, 35 minutes, $8.95; *How the Doctor Can Help*, with Dr. Leo Wollman describing his criteria, his modes of treatment, his results and his philosophy in helping more than 1,600 transsexuals. 41 minutes, $10.45; and *Avoiding the Legal Pitfalls*, with attorney Richard D. Levidow offering practical solutions to the legal pitfalls facing sex changers, 42 minutes, $10.45. Of related interest is a program on *The Male Transvestite*, a 54-minute program in which Dr. Garrett Oppenheim and Fae Robin of Confide give clear, simple answers to the questions most often asked by transvestites and those close to them: What is transvestitism and what are its causes? Does cross-dressing really provide satisfaction? What about heterosexual relations? What will estrogens do? How do you get rid of facial hair? What if arrested or taken to a hospital? and many others. $12. [Source: Confide]

Death, Grief and Bereavement—Lecture, interview, dialogues and panel discussions on death-related matters by knowledgeable speakers: Dr. Elisabeth Kubler-Ross on *Stages of Dying*; Dr. Jeannette Folta on *Social Reconstruction after Death*; Dr. Robert Fulton on *Terminal Care and Anticipatory Grief*; Dr. Helena Lopata on *The Widow in America*; Dr. George G. Williams on *Talking to Children about Death*; and 19 others. Lengths range from 21 to 59 minutes. The series has been prepared by the Center for Death Education and Research of the University of Minnesota. Cost is $15 each; an album is included with orders of six or more. [Source: Charles Press Publishers]

Achieving Counseling and Personal Understanding—A series of eight cassettes, by Charles A. Curran, Professor of Psychology at Loyola University of Chicago, that focuses on ways and skills of bringing about genuine understanding and open communication among persons. With guest authorities, he considers recent research into the self, the place, the importance of values, and the value of such operational aids as behavior modification. In a second series, *Group and Individual Skills in Understanding Communication*, Dr. Curran offers advanced presentations to further develop some of the concepts of the first series. Included are more subtle considerations of social and group situations, learning conflicts and anxieties, and personal difficulties. $48 for each set of eight cassettes, or $7 per cassette. [Source: Counseling-Learning Institutes]

Affective House—Six-hour programs prepared and narrated by counseling professionals who provide useful commentary and examine the problems under discussion in a positive way, then giving helpful information and suggestions for resolving them. All programs are in albums, and cost $72.50 except as indicated. Course titles and instructors include: *How To Use TA Concepts*, by Ronald H. T. Owston; *Realities of the Physically Handicapped*, by Helen Jones and Dick Farr; *Interpersonal Communication Skills and Crisis Intervention Training*, by Mike Lillibridge and Gary Klukken; *Stress Reduction: Personal Energy Management* ($82.50), by James Greenstone and Sharon Leviton; *Value Clarification*, by Dale Hill; *Counseling Inventory Resource Kit* and *How to Separate Successfully*, by Ronald Y. T. Owston and David S. Abbey; *Human Relations Workshops*, by Terry Seamons with David Seamons; *Self Concept Dynamics and Interpersonal Processes* ($82.50), by Don E. Hamachek; *Middle Years: Career Options and Educational Opportunities*, by Alan Entine; *How to Use Biofeedback Training*, by Steven L. Fahrion; *Lessons for Living: Psychology of Self-Interest* ($82.50), *Overcoming Emotional Problems with Rational Emotive Therapy*, and *Short-Term Therapy with RET*, by Paul A. Hauck; *Crisis Management and Intervenor Survival*, by James Greenstone and Sharon Leviton; *Social Effectiveness Training* ($82.50), by Dale Hicks and Mike Lillibridge; *Women and Work*, by Dennis Nord and Doris Weigel; *Building the Guidance Community, Realities of Classroom Management, How To Build Modules and Learning Packets*, and *Educational Administration: A Drive-Time Review of the Principal's Job*, by Ward Weldon; *Behavioral Cybernetics*, by Paul Jones; *Discussions with Parents of Exceptional Children*, by Norman E. Bissell; and *Transactional Analysis for Counselors and Teachers*, by Terry Seamons. [Source: Affective House]

Family Living Series—Two albums prepared by Dr. Gerald R. Patterson and Marion S. Forgatch to show the applications of behavior management in family life. Part 1 covers positive reinforcement, pinpointing and tracking, time out, negotiation, and contracting—five 30-minute cassettes in album for $44.95. Part 2 takes up counting and record-keeping, advanced contracting, and dealing with noncompliance—three 30-minute cassettes in album for $26.95. [Source: Research Press]

Helping Couples Change—The first two cassettes in this program are designed for counselors and cover social learning strategies for marital therapy with a clinical demonstration of a first interview; the second two cassettes are for client use, informing couples of common marital problems, preparing them for short-term therapy, and instructing them on maintaining gains made during therapy. $46 for four cassettes and manual in album. [Source: Research Press]

The New Look Toward Marriage—A three-cassette program ($27.50) of value not only to prepare engaged couples for the realities of married life, but also useful in marriage counseling and training of counselors for family life programs. [Source: Family Enrichment Bureau]

Counseling for Personal Mastery—In eight one-hour sessions, two accomplished counseling practitioners and educators—Dr. John Vriend of Wayne State and Dr. Wayne W. Dyer of St. John's—provide a no-excuse therapy for living now and the specific procedures for accomplishing that goal. Titles of the sequenced, integrated programs are: *The Counselor*; *A Person in Charge of Self*; *Goals for the Counselor and Client*; *Counseling: What It Is and Why It Works*; *Learning to Diagnose Thinking and Behavior*; *Being a Non-Evasive Counselor*; *The First Counseling Session*; *Continuing the Counseling*; *Goal Achievement*; and *Avoiding Common Counseling Pitfalls*. $50 to APGA members, $60 to nonmembers, $1.50 for a preview tape. [Source: American Personnel and Guidance Association]

Creative Widowhood Adjustment—Eight 20-minute messages (an introduction and then messages for each day of the week), designed to help widowed people understand and move through the normal grieving process through relaxation and healing images, so that the recently-widowed can emerge from the crisis with new confidence and strength to assume their responsibilities. The authors are Dr. Helen Antoniak, Director of the Widowed to Widowed Program, Inc. and Dr. Ann Sturgis, Director of the Stress Management Training Institute. $50 for the set. Another program is *Creative Divorce Adjustment*. Dr. Helen Antoniak and Dr. Ann Sturgis believe that divorce and separation bring grief and challenges not unlike widowhood, so offer these eight 20-minute cassette messages to help those people experiencing this life crisis, also for $50. They also offer, for $5 each, *Widowhood Adjustment* and *Divorce Adjustment* (each in versions for professionals and for clients) that give an explanation of the development, purpose, and use of the Creative Adjustment cassettes on one side, and a complete 'introduction to relaxation' on the other side. [Source: Helen Antoniak]

La Familia Sana—Originally produced for radio, these Spanish-language cassettes each contain ten 5-minute discussions of healthy family relationships. They are best suited as discussion starters in counseling sessions on marriage problems, child development or abuse, youth work, drug abuse programs, home visiting, and basic education for low-income mothers. The programs have an easy-to-listen-to format; the message is direct and simple, but not condescending. [Source: Paulist Communications]

Illness: A Spiritual Crisis—Chaplain Curtis Holland designed this program by pastoral care professionals to train laymen for hospital visitation, and covers courtesies to be considered, basic ministerial essentials, and emotional and spiritual needs created by illness. $23.95 for two cassettes and manual in album. [Source: Self Control Systems, Inc.]

How To Get Your Children to Do What You Want Them to Do—A program by Dr. Paul Wood that offers effective techniques to help parents who are "tired of threatening, punishing, bribing and endlessly reasoning with your kids." Application of the principles presented can result in important behavioral changes on the part of both parents and children. $16.95 for two cassettes in album. [Source: Professional Cassette Center]

Coupling Skills: A Cognitive Behavioral Systems Approach—Specific guidelines by Dr. Robert L. Weiss for identifying and managing deficits in intimate relationships. Dr. Weiss emphasizes four core skills: objectively labeling behavior and its controlling stimuli; developing support/understanding; problem-solving; and behavior change. $21 for two cassettes and manual. [Source: BMA Audio Cassettes]

How Others See You And What To Do About It—On four cassettes and aided by worksheets and a Behavior Style Profile, Jim Cathcart and Dr. Tony Alessandra and others show how you come across, and then demonstrate what can be done about what's not good about it. $80. [Source: Cathcart, Alessandra & Associates, Inc.]

Single Again—Six tapes that deal with questions important to adults who are widowed, divorced, or separated and who are living single after their marriage experience. These questions include dating as an adult, sex, preparation for remarriage, religion, children in the one-parent home, and the need for a generic term for the once-again-single status. $10.95 each, all six tapes for $55. [Source: Jeffrey Norton Publishers, Inc.]

Word—Resources for counselors and for couples and individuals in need of counsel, from one of the most prestigious sources of Bible-based guidance. *Enriching Your Marriage* features respected marriage expert Dr. David Mace talking about communication, conflict, anger, and intimacy, on 12 cassettes with transcripts in album, $89.95. James C. Dobson MD offers several albums: *Straight Talk to Men . . . and Their Wives*, the meaning of Christian manhood, three cassettes, $39.95; *Preparing for Adolescence*, an analysis of the problems parents and pre-teens face, eight cassettes, $59.95; *Focus on the Family*, with information to enable all family members confront the problems that face them, 12 cassettes, $79.95; *Questions Parents Ask About Rearing Children*, four cassettes, $24.95; *30 Critical Problems Facing Today's Family*, 12 cassettes, $89.95; all these sets include album and discussion materials. Keith Miller and Andrea Wells Miller honestly and squarely face *Faith, Intimacy, and Risk in the Single Life*, $89.95 for 12 cassettes and guides in album. Then there's

Charlie Shedd, lecturer, counselor, and minister: *Straight Talk on Love, Sex and Marriage* for high school and college audiences, four cassettes in album, $24.95; *Good Times with the Bible*, 12 unique Bible studies which help resolve some of the most pressing issues facing families today, 12 cassettes in album, $69.95; and *Fun Family Forum*, six down-to-earth tapes dealing with parent/child relationships, and six more covering husband/wife relationships, $69.95 including album. [Source: Word, Inc.]

Results with People—On eight cassettes with a workbook, Keith DeGreen has recorded an interesting, results-producing program on dealing with people. He covers breaking through the mediocrity barrier, reverse performance appraisal, monitoring personal and professional effectiveness, and how to effectively present yourself and your ideas. $95 including album. [Source: DeGreen Corporation]

Encouragement Cassettes—Dr. Lewis E. Losoncy is the country's foremost advocate of 'encouragement counseling,' which he defines as an optimistic and practical approach to developing responsible, confident, and courageous people. He offers three hour-long programs to help counselors assist the client's willingness and determination to change: *You Can Do It* (achieving personal goals through self-encouragement), *On Becoming an Encouraging Person* (helping others develop self-confidence through encouragement), and *Encouraging Yourself by Using the Powers of Prophetic Psychology* (to make self-realized predictions). $9 each. [Source: Encouragement Associates]

Modern Cassette Library—Inspirational talks and discussions primarily (but not exclusively) of Roman Catholic interest, covering marriage, family enrichment, prayer and confession, penance, and many other topics. Some are planned for the ministry, to provide help with counseling and liturgical preparation; others are aimed at parishioners, and provide meditation themes and other self-enrichment materials. $5.95 per cassette (each generally about an hour long). [Source: Ave Maria Press]

University Associates—Tape programs planned to increase awareness of human interactions in business. In *Communicating Empathy*, John Milnes and Harvey Bertcher show that accurate empathic understanding is a key interpersonal skill associated with perception, communication, and sensitivity to the feelings of others, $44.95 for two cassettes, booklet, and response forms in album. In *Appraising Performance*, Norman R. F. Maier describes the very specific yet subtle skills and methods needed for effectively communicating appraisal of a person's work performance, on two cassettes and guide for $44.95. Lawrence N. Solomon and Betty Berzon focus on basic interpersonal skills required in the work environment in *Employee and Team Development* and Ms. Berzon and Jerome Reisel's *Effective Interpersonal*

Relationships provide an educational experience in personal growth; each course is on four cassettes with facilitator's guide in album for $54.95. [Source: University Associates]

UCLA Extension—Tape series for self-development and personal relationships. In *Good Relationships . . . and the Other Kind*, Harriet Braiker Ph.D. describes the qualities of good, close interpersonal relationships, with particular emphasis on heterosexual coupling, $51 for six cassettes. In *The Vulnerable American Male*, Albert E. Ross probes the tendency of men to deny their inner feelings, and thus hinder their ability to develop gratifying and meaningful relationships, seven cassettes, $70. In *Finishing our Parents' Business*, Dr. Ross gives pointers on how to overcome our parents' role in molding our adult lives, on six cassettes, $51. *Making Marriage Work* is Walter E. Brackelmanns' program for those who have, have had, or wish to have a stable marital relationship, on eight cassettes for $67.25. [Source: UCLA Extension]

SASHAtapes—SASHA (Self Automated Series on Helping Alternatives) has been developed by Gerald Goodman Ph.D. of UCLA as a method of developing interpersonal communication skills among para-professional counselors, mental health practitioners, hot-line workers, community mental health counselors, families, couples, and volunteers in the human services. Each session focuses on some single aspect of communications, using structured exercises, lectures, demonstrations, and outside practices; the tapes work best when studied with a group or at least one other person. $66 for three C-90 cassettes and ten participant manuals in album. [Source: UCLA Extension]

Helping Couples Change—On two cassettes, Dr. Richard B. Stuart demonstrates the core elements of this approach to short-term marital therapy with both live examples and lucid explanations. Then there are two more cassettes designed for direct client use with models to maximize couples' collaboration and exercises for home assignment. Four cassettes and practitioner manual in album, $42. If these don't work then there's *Separation, Divorce, and Beyond: Challenges for Today's Therapist*—presentations by James Framo, Richard A. Gardner, Emily Visher, John Visher, Jean Goldsmith, Judith Wallerstein, and Robert S. Weiss, on six cassettes with study guide in album for $70. [Source: BMA Audio Cassettes]

Helping Families Change—Family therapy through the life cycle, with sage advice from Murray Bowen, Carl Whitaker, Alan Gurman, James Framo, Peggy Papp, and Donald Bloch, on six cassettes with study guide in album for $63. Related is *Therapeutic Paradox: "Restraint From Change" Techniques in Family Therapy* in which Lynn Hoffman shows how to use 'paradoxical' techniques in family therapy (by which

the therapist 'prescribes' the symptom) as an effective tool for counteracting resistance within the therapeutic process. $11.50 for one cassette. [Source: BMA Audio Cassettes]

Cassette Communications—This producer, no longer in business, published some valuable single cassette titles: *Fathering* (the importance of the father's role in the emotional development of his children), *Children of Divorce* (the psychological effects and how to avoid them), and *Teaching Children About Sex*, with sex educator Dr. Sol Gordon giving the what, when, and how. All $10.95 each. [Source: Jeffrey Norton Publishers, Inc.]

Making Marriage Work—Dr. Carl Whitaker, nationally prominent husband-wife counselor, explains what married (and unmarried) couples can do to ensure a lasting physical and emotional bond, $78.95 for ten cassettes in album. *Husband-Wife Counseling* is a course by Dr. Whitaker for marriage counselors and psychologists, on three albums of ten 30-minute cassettes for $78.95 each, or the whole works for $214.95. In *Negotiating a Divorce* he talks with a lawyer about the legal aspects, $47.95 for six C-30 cassettes in album. [Source: Instructional Dynamics, Inc.]

Dimensions of Divorce—David Burke Ph.D. puts the problem in perspective by reviewing and anticipating divorce-related problems: considering it, counseling, finding the balance, the divorce experience, and the children. $27.95 for three cassettes in album. Of related interest is *Life After Divorce*—Clinical psychologist Dr. John Otterbacher discusses life after divorce, stages of divorce recovery, divorce and children, and building a new life. $56 for four cassettes ($14 each). [Source: Instructional Dynamics, Inc.]

Marriage Enrichment Program—An aid to therapists, clergymen, and counselors in cutting down on the amount of time spent in getting constructive processes started; the program is designed to get significant data to the surface and to start the couple working through it. $89.50 for five cassettes and supplemental materials. [Source: Instructional Dynamics, Inc.]

Loving Relationships—Subtitled 'Bonding Experiences for Gay Men and Lesbian Women,' this course is planned to help homosexual couples gain awareness and confidence in their intimacy concepts and love relationships. $54.30 for four cassettes and workbooks for two couples. [Source: Instructional Dynamics, Inc.]

Provocative Therapy—Frank Farrelly, the originator of this startling technique, shows how a combination of empathy, humor, banter, and role modeling goads patients into expressing and the acting on feelings and insights to grow emotionally. 12 C-60 cassettes and guide in album for $95.50. A three-cassette mini-version is also available for $27.95. [Source: Instructional Dynamics, Inc.]

IX.
Language Instruction

Alpha Recorded Tape—A series of eight C-48 cassettes (two each in Vietnamese, TaGaLog, Mandarin, and Cantonese) intended to help the new, non-English-speaking student (and his teacher) in making the transition from his native language to English. Each two-cassette program covers a welcome to the U.S., welcome to school, recreational activities, and useful words—with pauses on the tape to permit the student to repeat the new English words and phrases. $56.50 for the complete set. [Source: Alpha Recorded Tape, Inc.]

Assimil Cassettes—Instruction in the continental manner: you think in the language and 'assimilate' it naturally by listening to lively everyday conversations while following along in an illustrated 400-500 page book. The cassettes are entirely in the language being studied, the texts are in the learner's native language. English text courses are available in German, Spanish, Greek, Italian, Portuguese, Latin, Arabic, French, Corsican, and Breton (three cassettes, $110), and in Dutch, Russian, Serbo-Croatian, and Esperanto (four cassettes, $125). There are courses with texts in other languages (generally $110 for three cassettes plus the workbook): Dutch for German speakers; Russian for Spanish speakers; English or German for French speakers; and Arabic for Dutch speakers, for example. Advanced courses are also available in German, Spanish, and Dutch. [Source: French & Spanish Book Corporation.]

Berlitz Comprehensive Cassette Course—50 teaching sequences that involve the student in culture and conversation while gradually increasing speaking facility and vocabulary. Available in French, German, Italian, Spanish. $125 for six cassettes (one C-90, five C-60) with manuals, rotary verb finder, and album. [Source: Berlitz Publications]

Berlitz Basic Cassette Course—Learn to speak French, German, Italian, or Spanish by speaking—not by reading, writing, or translating. $49.95 for three cassettes (one C-90, two C-60) with lesson book, rotary verb finder, dictionary, and album. [Source: Berlitz Publications]

Berlitz for Travelers—300 basic phrases, recorded by native speakers, for pre-trip preparation or for use while there. Available on C-50 cassette in Arabic, Danish, Dutch, Finnish, French, German, Greek, Hebrew, Italian, Japanese, Norwegian, Portuguese, Russian, Serbo-Croatian, Spanish (both Castilian and Latin American), and Swedish. Also available in this format is English for Foreign Visitors: Danish, Dutch, Finnish, French, German, Italian, Japanese, Norwegian, Spanish, and Swedish. $7.95 with phrase book. [Source: Berlitz Publications]

Biblical Hebrew and New Testament Greek—These curricula-on-cassette programs move from an introduction to the basics of language study to a working knowledge of these significant languages. Designed for pre-seminary or seminary students, practicing clergy for a brush-up, or laymen interested in original-language Biblical studies. Each set $40 for three cassettes and workbook. [Source: Thesis]

Blasad Gaidhlig—Literally 'a taste of Gaelic,' this cassette offers instruction in Gaelic for beginners, with 250 simple phrases spoken in Gaelic and then in English, with translations in an accompanying booklet. $12. [Source: Gordon Wright]

Cassette Language Courses—Five-cassette structured courses (with each cassette more advanced than the previous one) covering conversation, vocabulary, grammar, and sentence structure, while an accompanying booklet gives the complete text of each lesson. Languages covered are Spanish, French, German, Italian, and English for Spanish-speaking people. $49.95 for each course; individual cassettes (each with booklet) are $9.95 each. [Source: Institute for Language Study]

Conversa-phone Modern Method Language Courses—100 lessons on two cassettes for the traveler, student, or businessperson who wants a basic language knowledge. Available for Spanish, French, German, Italian, Russian, Swedish, Portuguese, Modern Greek, and English for Spanish-speaking persons. $16.98 each with instruction manual and quiz booklet. [Source: Conversa-phone Institute, Inc.]

'Round the World' Language Courses—One-cassette 'see-hear' programs (for travel or brush-up) that helps you speak a new language in minutes. Available for Spanish, French, German, Italian, Russian, Swedish, Portuguese, Arabic, Modern Greek, Japanese, and English for Spanish, French, or German speaking persons. $7.98 each with instruction manual. [Source: Conversa-phone Institute, Inc.]

Exotic Languages on Cassette—Conversa-phone has now made language courses in some of the less familiar languages: Mandarin Chinese, Cantonese Chinese, Danish, Hungarian, Norwegian, Hebrew, Dutch, Polish, and Finnish. $11.98 for two cassettes and instruction book. Also available for the same price are two-cassette programs for children in Spanish, French, German, and Italian. [Source: Conversa-phone Institute, Inc.]

Conversa-phone Three Cassette Courses—*Intermediate English for Spanish-speaking Persons*, with two manuals; *Advanced English for Spanish-speaking Persons*, with manual; *Basic English for Portuguese-speaking Persons*, with manual and dictionary; and *Mandarin Chinese*, with two manuals. All courses $18.98 each. [Source: Conversa-phone Institute, Inc.]

Conversational Arabic—Specifically designed to meet the needs of businessmen, contractors, engineers, journalists, and anyone who must master basic Arabic quickly and be able to use the common words and phrases encountered in daily situations. The complete course consists of three C-60 cassettes giving correct pronunciation of all words and phrases with 43 matched topic cards, plus reference cards giving sample dialogues and a text including trade and customs information—all for $59. [Source: Inter Amar Specialties]

Conversational Spanish—A two-part program leading the student through a series of sequentially arranged exercises that results in rapid acquisition of basic Spanish speaking and reading skills, using conventional techniques and a slower-paced Americanized pronunciation approach. Each part (Spanish I and II) consists of 24 lessons on 12 cassettes in album for $80. Also available for $8 each are some one-cassette-with workbook courses covering *Beginning* and *Intermediate Conversational Spanish*, and *Tourist Conversational Spanish* and *French*. [Source: ESP, Inc.]

Cortina Master Linguist Courses—A comprehensive approach to foreign language instruction. The heart of the course is eight audio-cassette recordings of native instructors in everyday conversations—no memorizing of lists of words or rules of grammar. Supplementing these are a text, exercise book, study guide, supplemental conversation book, and dictionary in album. The $149.50 price also includes two test recordings (you send your answers to Cortina for scoring and evaluation), and a year's personal guidance and consultation service from Cortina. Languages available include Spanish, French, German, Italian, Modern Greek, American English, and French and English for Spanish-speaking people. [Source: Cortina Institute of Languages]

Cortina Home Study Courses—Cassettes, textbook, supplementary practice book, bilingual dictionary, and a guide to language study in an album. The six-cassette Brazilian Portuguese course is $99.50, the eight-cassette Japanese course is $129.50. [Source: Cortina Institute of Languages]

English for Special Purposes—These programs, derived from the BBC's popular English by Radio Programmes, use dialogue and dramatizations of practical situations to apply English learned as a foreign language to specific situations: Scientifically Speaking, 6 cassettes, $79.50; Export English, 3 cassettes, $49.50; English for International Cooperation, on 3 cassettes, $49.50; Wavelength: English for Marine Navigation, 3 cassettes, $49.50; English for the Oil Industry, 3 cassettes, $49.50; Aviation English, 3 cassettes, $49.50; Language of Business, 4 cassettes, $59.50; Take a Break: The English You Need for Travel, 3 cassettes, $49.50; Seafaring in English, 2 cassettes, $35.50. All sets come with one or two comprehensive texts. [Source: Jeffrey Norton Publishers, Inc.]

Foreign Service Institute Language Courses—Prepared by the Foreign Service Institute of the Department of State, courses of varying length are available in many languages: Amharic, Arabic, Baluchi, Bulgarian, Cambodian, Cantonese, Chinyanja, Finnish, French, Fula, German, Hausa, Hebrew, Hungarian, Igbo, Italian, Japanese, Kirundi, Kituba, Korean, Lao, Lingala, Luganda, Mandarin (Standard Chinese), Moré, Portuguese, Serbo-Croatian, Shona, Sinhalese, Spanish, Swahili, Swedish, Thai, Turkish, Twi, Urdu, Vietnamese, and Yoruba. The number of cassettes vary for each course, and the prices are generally quite low: $50.25 for nine cassettes and text offering a basic course in Twi (in case you're off to Ghana), up to $256 for 50 cassettes with texts for the complete course in basic Hungarian. The first cassette and text of any course are available for $7.50, to provide a perspective of the complete course. Some languages are organized into modules that focus on particular situations or language topics. [Source: National AudioVisual Center]

Fünf Aktuelle Deutsche Gespräche—Live interviews with interesting German-speaking persons, recorded on location and covering Germany's division, Berlin's Wall, Switzerland's banking, and Hitler's native Austria. The responses provide an enriching change of pace for students of the German language, as well as insights into the variations of 'Hochdeutch'. Four cassettes and a guide in box for $36. [Source: Encore Visual Education, Inc.]

Getting Along in English—Mario and Mrs. Pei have four separate on-cassette-with-text courses for French, Spanish, Italian and German-speaking people, at $9.98 each. [Source: Folkways]

Hear America Speak!—English as a second language is never mastered until the idioms are mastered. Here are two volumes (each with two cassettes and text, for $52.75) that provide a guided topical approach to 600 essential idioms as they are used naturally in everyday American English. [Source: Science Research Associates, Inc.]

JAL Jet Age Language Courses—Japan Air Lines designed these courses in Japanese or Chinese especially to provide the beginner with a working knowledge of essential conversational elements most likely to be of use to the person traveling to Japan or China on business or pleasure. Obviously, these courses don't go into complicated grammar, but rather stress the pronunciation and meaning of a few well-chosen phrases. $10 each for an hour-plus cassette plus cue-cards. [Source: Japan Air Lines]

Language/30—Ninety minutes of instruction in the foreign words and phrases that business and other travelers need to communicate in foreign lands. The courses cover greetings, introductions, asking questions, and making requests at hotels, restaurants, banks. Available in 22 languages: Arabic, Chinese, Danish, Dutch, French, German, Greek, Hebrew, Indonesian, Italian, Japanese, Korean, Norwegian, Persian, Portuguese, Russian, Serbo-Croatian, Spanish, Swahili, Turkish, and Vietnamese ($14.95 each) and *El Ingles Practico* (English for Spanish-speaking people, $16.95) for two cassettes and phrase book/dictionary in pocket-size album. [Source: Educational Services]

The Learning Curve—60-minute mini-courses including cassette, programmed exercises, and tests, covering beginning, intermediate, and tourist conversational Spanish, French, and German. $9.98 each, any two for $15.98, any three for $22.98. This source also has the Pimsleur courses created for the U.S. State Department program for foreign service officers: Latin American or Iberian Spanish, $220; French, $220; German, $125; and Modern Greek, $200. [Source: Metacom, Inc.]

Living Language Courses—The world's best-known 'listen and repeat' language instruction courses, available for French, Spanish, German, Italian, Russian, Japanese, and Hebrew, each with two cassettes, 40-lesson conversation manual, and common usage dictionary for $15.95. Also available in the same format and cost is instruction in English for French, Spanish, German, Italian, and Chinese speaking people. Finally, 20-lesson advanced French and advanced Spanish courses are available for $11.95 each. Extra manuals or dictionaries are $3. [Source: Crown Publishers, Inc.]

Longman English Language Teaching—For those to whom English is a foreign language, Longman offers structured courses to benefit students at any level of comprehension, from elementary to polishing idioms in American English. The cassettes run from $9 to $20 each, depending on how much visual material accompanies them. [Source: Longman Inc.]

Medical Spanish: A Conversational Approach—A course developed for health professionals who must deal with Hispanic patients but who understand little or no Spanish. Use of this 12-cassette plus 256-page text/workbook kit develops conversational skills as one learns both grammar and medical/technical terminology. Dialectal variations in Cuban, Mexican, and Puerto Rican Spanish are also covered. $145. [Source: Jeffrey Norton Publishers, Inc.]

Modern Spoken Italian—A comprehensive course by Elaine Vertucci Baran, using faculty from different parts of Italy. Periodic tests provide immediate feedback, and 'culture capsules' throughout the course give insights into language usage and social customs. In two parts: each part $125 for eight hour-long cassettes and text. [Source: Jeffrey Norton Publishers, Inc.]

Foreign Service Institute (FSI) Language Courses—Created by the State Department for use by diplomatic personnel who must learn a foreign language both quickly and thoroughly. Each FSI course includes an album of 8 to 20 tapes, text, and sometimes an instructor's manual, and are intended for intensified study. They are available in Saudi Arabic, French, German, Greek, Spanish, or Mandarin ($125), Hebrew ($195), Portuguese ($149), Russian ($195), and Swedish ($245). [Source: Jeffrey Norton Publishers, Inc.]

Beginning Japanese—A comprehensive course in two parts developed by Eleanor Harz Jorden of Cornell University. It is concerned only with the spoken language and teaches the "standard" dialect of educated inhabitants of Tokyo. Part I: 8 cassettes and 409-p. text, $125; Part II: 16 cassettes and 512-p. text, $175. [Source: Jeffrey Norton Publishers, Inc.]

NCAT Languages—With 16,000 separate titles under their roof, the National Center for Audio Tapes can easily claim to be the largest repository of audio-cassette programming in the country. Alas, budget cuts limit their activity only to their language programs. And rather than instructional courses, most of their programs are readings and recitations, often without written translation, and are intended to improve comprehension and pronunciation. This is especially true of their Chinese, French, German, Italian, Latin, Continental and Brazilian Portuguese, and Spanish. The large collection of Japanese tapes are intended for use in conjunction with a University of Hawaii text. Beginning instructional courses are available in German, Russian, Spanish, and the Pacific languages (Chamorro, Hawaiian, Marshallese, Palauan, Ponapean, Trukese, Yapese). Finally, they have an excellent collection of programs on general semantics. Write for their free language catalog ... for you can't beat their price: $3.50 for any cassette up to 30 minutes long, $4.50 for any cassette from 31 to 60 minutes. [Source: National Center for Audio Tapes]

No-Time Method of Speaking Many Languages—These language instruction courses are unique: no reading, no writing—just listening repetitively to cassettes of the foreign language being learned (with minimal on-tape instruction in English). Each language course consists of three two-hour tapes, one each emphasizing conversation, vocabulary, and speaking. The publishers claim that listening to the cassettes each day for 45 minutes (preferably while jogging, commuting, or performing some routine boring task) will master the language in two months. Courses are available for High German, French, Spanish, Italian, Brazilian Portuguese, Russian, Hebrew, and Tagalog. Modified courses (with more on-tape explanations) are available for Czech, Bulgarian, Modern Persian, Modern Greek, Turkish, Hungarian, Japanese, and Chinese. Cost per course (three tapes, six hours of listening) is $48, single tapes $16.95. For $148 you can order any 10 cassettes. [Source: 200-Language Club]

No-Time Language Method—No texts, just tapes of conversations and translations to be played over and over until the vocabulary, structure, and grammar are absorbed and comprehended. Six-hour courses are available in German and Japanese for $72 each, as well as eight-hour courses in French and Spanish for $96 each. [Source: Jeffrey Norton Publishers.]

Pimsleur Language Programs—These foreign language instruction courses have been designed to avoid mindless repetition of words and phrases. They use 'graduated interval recall' to create a mental set that allows the student to recall words and phrases when needed and to combine them creatively, through a variety of cues. Moreover, all the teaching on these courses is on the tapes, so that you learn the foreign language as you learned English—with your ears, not your eyes. The Spanish and French courses are $230, the German one is $135, and the Modern Greek course is $195. [Source: American Management Associations]

Russian Pronunciation—Five tapes and a manual provide a brief but thorough coverage of the sounds of Russian, all presented in contrast with their nearest English equivalents. The approach is semi-programmed and doesn't require the presence of a teacher. $49 for five C-32 cassettes and a manual. [Source: Encore Visual Education, Inc.]

Speak and Read Essential Series—In these courses, developed by Dr. Paul Pimsleur, the student converses with native speakers with step-by-step guidance in English by an expert American teacher.

Emphasis is on high-utility vocabulary, fluency, and word recombinations, in the language of everyday 'survival' situations—asking directions, ordering food, securing lodging, making purchases, and asking and giving personal information. Five languages are now available, all on C-60 cassettes and including a reading booklet: French, Spanish, and Hebrew, $220 for 15 cassettes; Modern Greek, $200 for ten cassettes; German, $125 for five cassettes. A testing program (manual and two cassettes) is available with the French and Spanish courses, $30.92. [Source: Heinle & Heinle Publishers, Inc.]

Speak & Read French—Armand and Louise Begue cover basic and intermediate French on three cassettes with text for $29.94, and take up conversational French and French literature each on two cassettes with text for $19.96. [Source: Folkways]

Spoken Language Series—A large series of self-teaching courses for beginners, each with a text and six cassettes having four hours of instruction for $65 (except as noted), prepared under the aegis of the Linguistic Society of America and the American Council of Learned Societies. Languages include: Albanian, Amharic ($135 for 26 cassettes), Amoy Hokkien ($110 for eight cassettes), Arabic (Iraqi or Saudi), Armenian, Bulgarian ($110 for 19 cassettes), Burmese, Cambodian ($100 for 19 cassettes), Cantonese ($80 for 15 cassettes), Chinese, Danish, Dutch ($55 for five cassettes), Finnish ($45 for three cassettes), French, German, Greek, Hausa, Hebrew ($170 for 31 cassettes), Hindustani, Hungarian, Indonesian, Italian, Japanese, Kashmiri, Korean, Lao, Malay, Norwegian, Persian ($90 for five cassettes), Polish ($95 for 19 cassettes), Portuguese, Romanian, Russian, Serbo-Croatian, Sinhalese ($105 for 21 cassettes), Spanish, Swahili, Swedish ($145 for 24 cassettes), Tagalog, Taiwanese (nine cassettes), Tegulu, Thai, Turkish, Urdu ($95), Vietnamese, Yoruba ($165 for 34 cassettes). Advanced courses and reading practices are available in some languages. [Source: Spoken Language Services, Inc.]

Spoken English as a Foreign Language—Courses in English grammar, vocabulary, and construction, with instructions written in the language of the learner. Courses are available for those whose native language is Burmese, Mandarin Chinese, Greek, Indonesian, Iranian, Serbo-Croatian, Korean, Spanish, Thai, Turk, and Vietnamese. Each course consists of nine cassettes and a text for $90 (the Spanish course has six cassettes and text, costs $65). [Source: Spoken Language Services, Inc.]

Think Language—Ninety-minute cassette plus illustrated 'concept cards' provide a handy kit for learning spoken languages. The method bypasses rote study, instead getting the student to think in the language, associating what is heard with readily understandable situations. Available for German,

French, and Spanish, and in two different levels—Level I for beginners, Level II for students with one year of high school study or one semester of college experience. Cost is $11.95 per set. [Source: Visual Education Association]

Tutor Tape—An extensive collection of British-produced courses, mostly planned to teach English as a second language. The courses begin at the very elementary level, and progress to programs designed to familiarize adult students of English with the terminology of various professions: statistics, banking, economics, and so on. There are also quite a few short stories and abridged novels on cassette, planned to aid in listening comprehension but enjoyable in their own right. Finally, this source also produces a large collection of German language courses, and several series of language instruction in Italian, Russian, French, Spanish, and even Portuguese, Modern Greek, Arabic, Hebrew, and Chinese. All cassettes are 60-minutes long, cost about $8. A book accompanies most courses, and it is extra. [Source: Tutor Tape Company Ltd.]

X.
Law

Law Enforcement

Police Officer Stress—Dr. Robert Flint, a consultant for psychological evaluation for national law enforcement agencies, deals with the symptoms, causes, and methods of coping with the day-to-day stress in the police officer's work and family situations, and adds a cassette of relaxation exercises especially designed for police officers. $19.95 for three cassettes. [Source: Greatapes]

Child Abuse and Neglect for Police Officers—Dr. Robert ten Bensel developed and gives this training course, covering five aspects of child abuse and neglect: history and background; intra-family violence, effect of media; terminology; and dynamics and outcomes. $12 each, $65 with training manual, $49.95 without manual. A related series covering other family and emergency matters, the *Crisis Intervention Series* is an instructional package designed for independent self-study by law enforcement officers, mental health para-professionals, nurses, and others who can benefit from learning experience geared to professional problems. Topics of the 14 tapes in the series include introductions to mental health, schizophrenia, suicide, depression, personality disorders, alcoholism, disaster intervention, and family disturbances. $8.95 each, all 14 with study guide for $99.95. [Source: Greatapes]

Personnel Planning, Selection and Development—Everett M. Christensen developed this course for those involved in hiring police personnel. Topics of the six cassettes include: effective use of an application form; effective interviewing techniques; developing personal relations through communication; time planning, developing productive behavior; and counseling and performance evaluation. $8.95 each, all for $38.50. [Source: Greatapes]

Practical Conversational Spanish for Policemen and Firemen—Covering practical and basic Spanish expressions on five cassettes and illustrated text keyed to the tapes. $129.95. [Source: Lansford Publishing Company]

Investigative Procedure and the Intelligence Function—The specialized investigative procedures and the evidence needed to secure convictions in crimes both against persons and property and against persons involved in vice activities, on four cassettes for $99.95. [Source: Lansford Publishing Company]

Legal Education

CEB Audio Cassette Programs—Each program focuses on a single legal topic and provides a thorough discussion of important new decisions and statutes in California law that affect that subject. The service is primarily aimed at California attorneys. These are generally $15 per hour programs, $30 per 2-hour programs, and $60 per 4-hour programs, all with accompanying written materials. Another series, *Developmental Cassettes*, provides an annual 60-minute update in: business law, commercial law, civil procedure, criminal law, family law, probate and estate planning, real property law, tax procedure, torts, and workers' compensation. $15 for each cassette and syllabus. [Source: Continuing Education of the Bar]

Sum & Substance—Analytical summaries by some of the nation's most outstanding legal authorities designed to aid law students: *Antitrust Law*, Phillip Areeda, four cassettes, $36.95; *Commercial Paper*, Douglas Whaley, three cassettes, $29.95; *Criminal Law*, Michael Josephson, four cassettes, $36.95; *Professional Responsibility*, Donald Burris, four cassettes, $36.95; *Secured Transactions*, Douglas Boshkoff, two cassettes, $18.95, and many more, including *Getting Into and Surviving Law School*, John Dobbyn, one cassette, $9.95. All cassettes are 90 minutes long. [Source: Josephson Center]

How To Take Legal Exams—In *How To Take Essay Exams*, Michael Josephson focuses on general study and writing techniques discussed in the context of first-year law courses, three hours on two cassettes, $18.95. In *How To Take Objective Exams*, Professor Josephson discusses the problems of analyzing objective law school exam questions, how to recognize the 'best' answer, and how to guess intelligently. $9.95 for one 90-minute cassette. Also in the all important area of exams and how to pass them is the *Multistate Professional Responsibility Course*, by Donald Burris, intended for use as a preparation for the Multistate Professional Responsibility Exam, on four cassettes (six hours of material), written summary, and self-testing materials, for $44.98. [Source: Josephson Center]

Understanding Our Courts—Three actual trials are re-enacted—a grand jury hearing, a sex discrimination trial, and a murder trial—and the listener is asked to be the jury, debate the testimony, and reach a verdict. The actual verdicts are provided. $29.95 for three cassettes. *Understanding Your Constitutional Rights* has dramatizations of some recent Supreme Court decisions, all following the case in chronologic order: the issue, the arguments, and the Court's majority and dissenting opinions. Some of the ten issues covered: The George Carlin 'Filthy Words' case, the public school Bible reading case, the Amish compulsory education case, the reverse discrimination case, and the parental consent for abortion case. $7.95 for each cassette, all ten for $49.95. And yet another series designed to educate the layman in legal matters is *Public Education Cassettes*, a variety of single-cassette programs ($8 to $10 each) that explain the realities of the criminal justice system. There's an eyewitness account of an execution in a gas chamber, racism in prisons, an interview with Sirhan Sirhan and another with a psychopathic criminal, and conversations with convicted shoplifters, streetwalkers, arsonists, embezzlers, and rapists. An interesting two-cassette program ($20) covers the law of implied and expressed warranties. [Source: Greatapes]

Audio Research in the Law—A self-teaching series that provides the tools for legal research by giving the researcher a solid background and understanding for finding the law. Series I: *Basic American Law* guides the listener through a legal problem, describing the way solutions are sought, on five cassettes and 360 pp. printed text for $150. Another Series I program, *How To Use Government Documents in Legal Research*, is on a single cassette with printed material for $30. Other Series I programs on Canadian and English law are planned. Series II programs cover international law, and one program—*International Trade, Business and Investment: The Sources of Public and Private International Law*—is available on seven cassettes and 200 pp. of material for $175. [Source: Condyne/The Oceana Group]

Condyne Law Tapes—Condyne offers tapes in all areas of trial practice, and are especially good in commercial and business corporation law, tax practice, estate planning, and negligence. Their concept is simple: take the very latest in law, use the best legal minds available, and produce cassettes that are easy to listen to and are packed with facts. The Condyne offerings fall under nine major headings: real estate, estate planning, corporate, banking & business law, tax law, criminal law and urban problems, personal injury law and litigation, trial practice, constitutional law, and multinational/international law. The cassettes cost approximately $20 each, usually with a syllabus. Some recent offerings: *Brief Writing and Oral Argument*, by Judge Edward D. Re, $35 for cassette and 400 pp. book; *Psychology of a Trial*, by Jacob D. Fuchsberg, $40 for two cassettes; *Hospital Liability* by Neil Galatz, $20; *Estate Freezing*, by Frank S. Berall, $40 for two cassettes and syllabi; *Law and the Television of the 80's*, six programs, $20 each. [Source: Condyne/The Oceana Group]

Counseling Cassettes—Currently available are volumes 8B and 9B, dealing with contemporary criminal defense techniques, $20 for 8B, $10 for 9B, each consisting of three cassettes (six talks) in album. Other titles and price include: *Product Liability Litigation* ($35), *Persuasion in Advocacy I* ($20) and *II* ($35), *Tom on Torts* ($60), *Professional Liability-Medical Negligence* ($15), *Psychology of Trial* ($85), *Philo on Tort Liability* ($105), and *Proof of Damages* ($55). [Source: Association of Trial Lawyers of America]

ATLA Cassettes of the Month—Ten programs to provide the trial lawyer with in-depth examinations of current issues in jurisprudence. The topics cover jury selection, qualifying the expert witness, sports injuries, dynamic persuasion through analogy, handling damages in the opening statement, class actions in tort litigations, employment discrimination litigation, recognition of a plaintiff's antitrust suit, psychology in the courtroom, and family law. $20 for each cassette with supplemental printed materials. [Source: Association of Trial Lawyers of America]

Sabo Law Series—Law lectures, covering agency and partnership, civil procedure, conflicts, constitutional law, contracts, conveyances, corporations, criminal law, evidence, real property, and torts. Each topic is on three to eight cassettes, and costs $16.95 to $29.95. Some topics come with law study cards, at $6.50 each. [Source: Law Distributors]

Creative Educational Service—In-depth lecture presentations, designed to aid the hard-pressed law student gain a meaningful level of comprehension of the law. 22 topics are available, including: bankruptcy, by Boshkoff, 4½ hours, $32.95; criminal law, by Josephson, 6 hours, $32.95; equitable remedies, by A. Miller, 4½ hours, $27.50; and secured transactions, by Hawkland, 3 hours, $14.95. Also available are a 3-hour tape on writing essay exams ($17.50) and a 1½-hour tape on writing objective exams ($12.50). Finally, Donald Burris offers a multistate professional responsibility course (book, tapes, and testing) for $39.95. [Source: Law Distributors]

Legal Tapes—Tape-recordings made at various seminars of trial lawyer associations throughout the state of California, available for $6.50 each. Subject matter includes criminal law, domestic relations, workers' compensation, personal injury, business litigation, plus other topics. Free catalog available. [Source: Infonetics Corporation]

Construction Law Series—Detailed discussions of construction contracts, mechanics lien law, and other topics important to building contractors and their attorneys. Titles specific to state law are available for over 30 states. $45 to $95 for three to six cassettes, plus manual for $20-$30. Also there is the *Collection Law Series*, thorough discussions of state collection laws (30 states are individually covered), collection procedures, and bankruptcy—all from the creditors' point of view, all planned to aid credit or collecting managers in maintaining current accounts receivable and in collecting delinquent accounts. $50-$55 for three cassettes plus $25-$30 for manual. [Source: Professional Education Systems, Inc.]

ALI-ABA Audio Cassettes—A large selection of continuing legal education programs recorded at ALI-ABA Courses of Study, ABA Section of Taxation mini-programs, and Association of the Bar of the City of New York lectures. Over 350 titles are available, with topics related to estate, environmental law, law management, international practice, estate planning and pensions, Uniform Commercial Code, government regulation, trial and appellate practice, taxation, and business law. Program sets consist of one to 20 90-minute cassettes, many packaged in albums and accompanied by written study materials. All programs can be purchased, at prices ranging from $10.44 to $250; some are available for rental. [Source: American Law Institute-American Bar Association]

NPI Cassette Lecture Series—Leading attorneys lecture on major topics in their fields, almost all with correlated manual, outline, and supplementary text material. A few of the 30 courses available: Irving Younger, *Credibility and Cross Examination*, six hours, $90; Gerald Williams, *Effective Negotiation and Settlement*, eight hours, $95; Arthur Miller, *Judicial Control of Litigation*, two hours, $30; F. Lee Bailey, *Opening & Closing Statements in a Criminal Trial*, three hours, $45; Louis Loss, *Securities Regulations: Current Developments*, 10 hours, $75; Robert Levey, *Uniform Child Custody Jurisdiction Act*, one hour, $10; and Harry Rein, *Weight of Medical Evidence*, 12 hours, $95. [Source: National Practice Institute]

University of Bridgeport—Unedited audio-cassettes of recent UB seminars: *Medical Malpractice* (standards of care, informed consent, assessment of pain and suffering, defense), six tapes, $75; *Zoning* (exclusionary zoning, appeals, recent decisions), three tapes, $60; *Legal Ethics* (confidentiality, conflict of interest, tactics, advertising, fees), four tapes, $49; and *Law for the Artist* (gallery agreements, copyright, estate, recent developments), three tapes, $10. [Source: University of Bridgeport Law Center]

National Institute for Trial Advocacy—They have produced 18 series (comprising over 80 individual audio-cassettes), all reflecting the expertise of some of the country's foremost lawyers, judges, and law teachers. There are from three to 15 tapes in each series; the tapes are $15 each, sometimes less when the larger collections are purchased as a complete series. All come with outlines. Topics of the series are: evidence (mostly with Irving Younger), evidence

update (with Faust Rossi), negotiations, depositions, appellate arguments, advocacy, criminal trial advocacy, James Jeans trial advocacy, demonstrations, jury selection, opening statements, direct and cross examination, exhibits, expert witnesses, closing arguments, master advocate's series, teacher training series, and public education series. [Source: National Institute for Trial Advocacy.]

ATS-CLE Audiocassettes—These are recordings of the (mostly) one-day programs on current legal topics sponsored recently by the State Bar of Wisconsin's Advanced Training Seminars-Continuing Legal Education. All feature prominent Wisconsin attorneys, all consist of three or four cassettes and cost $25 for the set (except as noted). The topics cover: accounting for lawyers, discovery, torts update, probate law, proof of damages, estate planning, negotiating and preparing marital and non-marital agreements, bankruptcy update, basic corporate practice, health issues, securities law, annual tax school (December, 1981) (seven cassettes, $50), handling administrative law cases, real estate transactions, psychology and the law (two cassettes, $12.50 each for criminal law, civil law, and family law, or the complete set for $37.50), retirement benefits in divorce (two cassettes, $12.50), life insurance in estate & business planning, and evidence (general provisions, hearsay). Printed materials required for each seminar are sold separately, for $7 to $17 each ($40 for basic corporate practice). [Source: ATS-CLE Audiocassettes]

MCLE-NELI Audiotapes—A bountiful number of self-study audio-cassette programs, produced by the Massachusetts Continuing Legal Education-New England Law Institute and dealing with specific aspects of Massachusetts law, but with much material applicable to all states. All speakers are practicing attorneys or judges specializing in the area of law about which they speak. They have 90 titles available, running anywhere from one to 15 hours (tapes are priced at $7 per hour of instruction). Just a few of the topics offered, and the price: banking law: regulation of traditional activity, $21; basic bankruptcy, $7; franchising and licensing, $21; secured transactions, $28; immigration law, $42; condominium conversions, $21; fundamental real estate transactions, $80; personal income taxation, $7; advocacy in an eminent domain case, $42; structured settlements, $21; medicine and the law, $21; and arbitration law, $42. Books are available separately to accompany each course. [Source: MCLE-NELI Publications]

ICLE Educational Seminars—Audio-cassettes of seminars sponsored by Michigan's Institute of Continuing Legal Education. Some topics are of interest only to Michigan lawyers, but others are of universal interest: how to introduce evidence in court, divorce trial techniques, occupational cancer, suing the government, no-fault auto accident update, wrongful death, economic recovery tax act of 1981, and more. These are generally $45 for three cassettes. [Source: ICLE]

Plain Talk From The Bench—A subscription series (eight tapes a year for $154.50) featuring pointed, probing interviews with leading state Supreme Court judges, giving practical suggestions on various aspects of the trial and pre-trial processes. [Source: Condyne/The Oceana Group]

Lawyer's Management Principles—Not for the attorney but for his/her assistant, this course gives very basic details about the role of a legal assistant or other paralegal careers, $86.90 for five tapes and syllabus. The *Legal Secretarial* course covers both background information and extensive typing practice in general legal vocabulary, corporate vocabu-

lary, wills and probate, taxes, and litigation, $102.55 for six cassettes, syllabus, and teacher's guides. [Source: National Book Company]

LSAT Review Course—An authoritative program, designed to improve the student's performance on the Law School Admission Test (LSAT) administered by ETS. The emphasis is on the basic skills, definitions, methods, and short-cuts that are absolutely necessary for LSAT success. Practice exams to simulate the actual LSAT cover: logical reasoning, practical judgment, quantitative comparison, data interpretation, cases and principles, error recognition, sentence correction, and experimental . . . in all, 1448 questions with 1193 detailed explanations. $99.95 for 10 hours of cassette, 400-page workbook, diagnostic and final exams in album. Free introductory cassette and 24-hour question answering service. [Source: Totaltape, Inc.]

XI.
Literature

Cassette Book Library—Distinguished actors (Marvin Miller, Lew Ayres, Ronald Colman, Thomas Mitchell, among others) narrate such literary classics as: *Walden, Immortal Speeches of Abraham Lincoln, Heart of Darkness, Meditations of Marcus Aurelius, Tales of Edgar Allan Poe, The Red Badge of Courage, The Time Machine, Alice in Wonderland, Treasure Island, Pinocchio, Leaves of Grass*, and many others. Also available are current literary selections: *The World According to Garp, Wifey, The Thornbirds, A Stillness at Appomattox, Stained Glass, Condominium, The Coup*, and others. These are $5.95 per cassette (and most titles involve multiple cassettes). [Source: Audio Book Company]

Audio-Visual Productions—An excellent selection of prose and poetry from the Middle and Elizabethan Ages, the 17th and 18th Century, the Romantic and Victorian Ages, and the 20th Century. They have eight cassettes, each of a contemporary poet—John Betjeman, Robert Graves, Lawrence Durrell, and five others—reading their own poetry, and they have on cassette the Jupiter Anthology of Twentieth Century Poetry. Prices are about $9 to $12 per cassette. [Source: Audio-Visual Productions]

Poets' Audio Center—As a service to the literary community, this source seeks, finds, and distributes poetry cassettes by little known and well known poets, such as Matthyas Jenny ('a German Bukowski'), the Owen Sound poetry ensemble from Canada, James Baldwin, Robert Penn Warren, and Alfred Lord Tennyson reading from 'Maud.' They also have the seven-volume *Treasury of American Jewish Poets* and serve as distributors for the *Audio Arts* tape magazine from England and *Mag Magazin* from Vienna. All tapes run between $8 and $10 each, generally. [Source: Poets' Audio Center]

Women's Audio Exchange—Cassettes of plays, poetry, story readings, and letters, selected for their content, quality of performance, and because they are for, by, and about women. Among the plays are: *I'm Getting My Act Together and Taking It on the Road*, by Gretchen Cryer; *Hedda Gabler*, with Joan Plowright and others; and *A Raisin in the Sun*, by Lorraine Hansberry. Prose includes readings of *Jane Eyre* with Claire Bloom, *Wuthering Heights* with Dame Judith Anderson, *Diary of Anne Frank* with Julie Harris, and *The Lottery*, read by Shirley Jackson. Maya Angelou, Erica Jong, Marianne Moore,

and Dorothy Parker (and many others) all read their own poetry. Most of these selections are produced by others, but two are exclusives: Viveca Lindfors in her one-woman show *I Am a Woman*, and Lyn Lifshin's poetry, *Offered by Owner*. Generally $10 per cassette. [Source: Natalie Slohm Associates Inc.]

Lifelong Learning—*A Mouth that Speaks* is a collection of poets reading their own works: Alta, Susan Griffin, Roberto Vargas, David Henderson, Jessica Hagedorn and Ntozake Shange, Adrienne Rich, Lynn Sukenick, Nanos Valaoritis, and Stephen Vincent; $10 per cassette, $75 for all nine in album. Other single cassettes ($10) feature John Laurie, Vernon Watkins, Gary Snyder/Nanao Sakaki, and Allen Ginsberg/Michael McClure, Uri Alter/Chana Bloch, and Joel Rosenberg/Marlene Tait. Some other titles: *Trends in Arabic Poetry, Afro-American Children's Literature*, and *Truth and Poetry in the Works of Thomas Mann*. [Source: University of California]

Toward the Future—From 1909 to the 1930s, the Italian Futurists created abstract and obtuse theatrical works, often compressing their plays into compact 'sintesi' (syntheses) and using sounds to go beyond the meaning and connotations of the written word—although one sometimes wonders what one has heard. 12 of these highly compressed dramas are captured on this 36-minute tape. *Soundings* is a 31-minute cassette program of contemporary sound poetry that is both amusing and alarming—and certainly not Longfellow, nor even e. e. cummings. $10 for either program. [Source: Audio Players]

The Poet's Voice—13 of the most important American poets read selections from their own poetry, offering not only the incontestable authority that comes from a poet reading his own work, but also with comments and witty asides: T. S. Eliot, Auden, Wallace Stevens, Theodore Roethke, Robinson Jeffers, Marianne Moore, Sylvia Plath, Frost, Lowell, Randall Jarrell, John Berryman, Ezra Pound and William Carlos Williams, each reading for about 30 minutes. $60 for six C-60 cassettes in album. [Source: Harvard University Press]

Folkways—*Directing a Play*, a lecture by Tyrone Guthrie; *Early English Ballads*, read by Kathleen Danson; *Understanding and Appreciation of the Essay*, and *Understanding and Appreciation of the Short*

Story, both by Dr. Morris Schreiber; and *Great Short Stories of the World*, also by Dr. Schreiber. $9.98 each, with text. [Source: Folkways Records]

Hear-A-Book—Abridgments or excerpts from public domain books (*Around the World in 80 Days*, *The Scarlet Letter*, *Robinson Crusoe*, *Red Badge of Courage*, *Treasure Island*, *War of the Worlds*, *Captains Courageous*, *Tom Sawyer*, *Two Years Before the Mast*, *Ben Hur*) and complete short stories (*Pit and the Pendulum*, *Island of Dr. Moreau*, *Picture of Dorian Gray*). They also have many of the Sherlock Holmes stories of Arthur Conan Doyle. A generous collection of children's stories are also available. Most programs run 60 to 90 minutes on a single cassette, for $7.95 each; a few longer ones are on two cassettes, for $9.95. [Source: Hear-A-Book, Inc.]

Recorded Books—Full-length books narrated by professional actors on multiple C-90 cassettes, available for 30-day rental, shipped in a pre-stamped carton for easy return. A few of the titles now available (with number of cassettes and rental fee): *The Sea Wolf* (seven, $8.95); *Guadalcanal Diary* (two, $4.50); *1066: The Year of the Conquest* (five, $7.25); *Desperation Valley* and *The Hardy Breed* (westerns, each four cassettes, $4.95 each); *North Star* (seven, $9.50); *Diary of a Young Girl* (six, $8.50); *Looking for Mr. Goodbar* (X-rated, seven cassettes, $8.75); *Pride and Prejudice* (eight, $9.75); *The Zimmerman Telegram* (five, $7.75); *An Ambassador's Wife in Iran* (five, $7.50). All books are also available for purchase. They also have some abridged books and excerpts on two cassettes for sale at $13.95. [Source: Recorded Books]

Caedmon Cassettes—No mere description here would do justice to the over 1000 spoken-word cassettes available from this pioneer producer of spoken-voice recordings in literature and history; you have to get their inch-thick free catalog. It lists these headings under the adult section: American, English, and world literature (*The Gold Bug*, *Green Mansions*, and *Anna Karenina*), short stories (from *The Scarlet Letter* to *The Lottery*), Old English and Middle English literature (*Beowulf* and Chaucer), American poetry (from Longfellow and Vachel Lindsay to Ezra Pound and e. e. cummings), English poetry (from William Blake to Noel Coward), world poetry, drama (practically all of Shakespeare and everyone else), biography, American and English history (such as great speeches), black and women's studies, philosophy and religion, and foreign language literature (Isaac Bashevis Singer reading his stories in Yiddish, Collette reading Collette in French). All cassettes $8.98. *Caedmon Soundbooks*— Four-cassette collections in box for $29.95: *Dylan Thomas Soundbook*, some of his best poetry and prose, including *A Child's Christmas in Wales* and *Fern Hill*, read by the author; *Beatrix Potter Soundbook*, stories of that 75-year-old bunny, Peter Rabbit and his friends, read by Claire Bloom; *Science Fiction Soundbook*, with the best of Bradbury, Asimov, and Heinlein; *Sherlock Holmes Soundbook*, with Basil Rathbone reading three of the greatest stories, including *Silver Blaze*; *Ogden Nash Soundbook*, with the author reading his immortal Portrait of the *Artist as a Prematurely Old Man*, and others; and the *J. R. R. Tolkien Soundbook*, with the author reading highlights from his Middle Earth trilogy and his son reading excerpts from *The Silmarillion*. Finally from this outstanding source are the *Spoken-Word Classics*, which make listening become an active art. This new series has over 300 titles from Caedmon. The diversity runs from the very American letters of Abigail Adams to the romantic Spanish of Don Juan; from the exuberance of Homer to the acerbic satire of Heller, plus observations from Disraeli, Mencken, and Thoreau, praise from nature poets like Wordsworth and Hopkins, comments from Agee and Joyce. To show the quality of the Caedmon recordings, Sir John Gielgud's *Ages of Man* won the 1980 Grammy Award, and Pat Carroll's *Gertrude Stein, Gertrude Stein, Gertrude Stein* won it in 1981. All Spoken-Word Classic cassettes come in an album, cost $12.95. [Source: Caedmon]

CMS Cassettes—Primarily a spoken-word record producer, CMS offers many of its programs on cassette as well. Titles range from Jack London's *To Build a Fire* to *James Baldwin Reads James Baldwin*, from *A Treasury of the Greek Myths* to a three-cassette edition of *Alice in Wonderland*, from *Norse Folk and Fairy Tales* to *The Monkey's Paw*, from *Peter Rabbit and his Friends* to *The Mouse That Roared*. $8.98 per cassette. [Source: CMS Records, Inc.]

Communications Institute Cassettes—Dramatized biographies of great artists (Shakespeare, Dickens, Verdi, Mozart, Tchaikovsky, Haydn, and others), crime and mystery dramas (all true, solved and unsolved), dramatic abridgments of Shakespeare plays (*Macbeth*, *Romeo & Juliet*, *Julius Caesar*, *Henry V*, *Twelfth Night*, *Othello*, *Midsummer Night's Dream*, *Merchant of Venice*), and some hours of dramatic readings, with Damon Runyon, Edgar Allan Poe, O. Henry, and Dr. Faustus, among others. All programs complete on one cassette, for $8.95 each. [Source: Spears Communications International, Inc.]

Spoken Arts Cassettes—An excellent selection of literature programs for adults, including classic literature from the Greek myths, British Middle Ages, 17th and 18th century British and American literature, American poets and short story writers, the Romantic and Victorian Ages, modern English poetry, and English and American Drama. Many of the modern works are read and discussed by the authors, the remainder are read by prominent actors and professional narrators. There is also a selection of favorites from the international literature, some presented in their native tongues. All cassettes are $9.95 each. [Source: Spoken Arts]

America Audio Prose Library—Contemporary American prose authors read from their own works (on one cassette) and then (on a second cassette) discuss their lives, works, careers, work habits, and other matters of interest to serious readers, writers, and students of contemporary prose. The 17 writers now available include Jack Conroy, Stanley Elkin, James B. Hall, Norman Mailer, Speer Morgan, Tillie Olsen, David Wagoner, and Alice Walker. $8 for each 45- to 90-minute cassette, all 17 cassettes of readings for $119, $238 for complete series of readings and interviews. [Source: American Audio Prose Library]

Remarks on the Novel—The only known recording of John O'Hara's voice, recorded at his 1956 lecture at the Library of Congress. $10. [Source: Bruccoli-Clark Publishers]

Audio Arts—Quarterly audio-journals devoted to the creative arts, and comprising an eclectic collection of interviews, readings, talks, and performances in the creative arts. The topics cover art, architecture, poetry, avant garde music, drama; the discussants range from Marcel Duchamp and Buckminster Fuller to contemporary artists such as Ian Breakwell, Conrad Atkinson, and Mario Merz. Each program is at least an hour long, and a volume of four programs costs about $42 (in the U.S. and Canada) including postage. Supplements are also available, each usually devoted to a single work by a contemporary artist, poet, or playwright, published at irregular intervals, about $10 each including postage. [Source: Audio Arts]

Listening Library—A good selection of prose, short stories and novels, plus anthologies and critiques from various literary periods. There are also good sections on essays, discussions and philosophy and on English language skills (grammar, speech, vocabulary, debate). The extensive poetry section ranges from Chaucer to Dylan Thomas, and the drama section includes an extensive list of both complete and abridged performances, and criticisms. They also offer a variety of foreign language literature selections. And finally there are cassette programs available on history, government and social studies, and secretarial skills. Most cassettes are $8.95 each. [Source: Listening Library, Inc.]

Books on Tape—Books recorded in their entirety by professional readers and actors on multiple cassettes, then rented for a month at modest prices, ranging from $6.50 to $16.50, depending on the number of cassettes. Some of their most popular recent recordings have been *The Winds of War* and *War and Remembrance*, by Herman Wouk, *The African Queen* by C. S. Forester, *The Second World War* by Winston Churchill, *The Effective Executive* by Peter F. Drucker, and *The Origin* by Irving Stone. The scope of the books recorded range from classics like *Barry Lyndon* and *Kidnapped*, biographies like *Edgar*

Cayce: *The Sleeping Prophet* and *My Life and Hard Times* by James Thurber, to such current best sellers as *Bech*: *A Book*, *Rabbit Redux*, and *The Honourable Schoolboy*, plus mysteries by John D. MacDonald, Adam Hall, Kingsley Amis, and William F. Buckley Jr. All of these are superbly narrated. In addition, B-O-T also sells selected taped programs of Auto Tape Tours, American Management Associations, Caedmon, Listen for Pleasure, BMA, SMI, and New Dimensions. [Source: Books on Tape]

My Ship, My Navy, and Me—In what is probably the first 'book' published initially in the audio-cassette medium, Navy flyer Edward L. White tells of his World War II adventures aboard the U.S.S. Enterprise, with eyewitness accounts of Guadalcanal, Midway, and the Marshall Islands campaigns, in a salty narrative, full of personal reminiscences peppered at times with the healthy vulgarity of Navy men. $19.95 for two cassettes in album. [Source: Jeffrey Norton Publishers, Inc.]

Literature and Great Writers—Gilbert Highet provides masterful, and exciting, introductions to the great works of literature, with two 15-minute talks on a cassette for $10.95. A few of the many paired topics available: Wordsworth and Macaulay, Dickens and Tolkien, Dylan Thomas and Orwell, Dante and Don Quixote, sonnets and haiku, proverbs and slang, and first words and final words of a book. [Source: Jeffrey Norton Publishers, Inc.]

Exeter Tapes—Talks by British scholars who share with the listener their expertise in British literature, arts, politics, and language. Some representative topics: social structure, English law, buildings, music, films, 16th and 17th century poetry and prose, painting, sculpture. Also available are some French-language talks on French politics, Moliere, Camus, and Barthes. $9 each. [Source: Teach'em Inc.]

Sherlock Holmes—Excellent dramatizations of four novels—*Hound of the Baskervilles*, *Sign of the Four*, *Study in Scarlet*, and *Valley of Fear*—each on a C-90 cassette, $7.95 each or all four boxed for $25. Dramatized versions of most other Holmes short stories are also available, two on a C-60 cassette for $6.95. [Source: Lava Mt]

H. P. Lovecraft—Four cassettes of dramatic interpretations of the horror fantasies of the master of the genre: *The Rats in the Walls/The Outsider*, *The Music of Erich Zann*, *The Picture in the House*, and *The Haunter in the Dark*, $7.75 each. *Dreams in the Witch House* is a three-hour reading of the classic Lovecraft horror tale, $21. [Source: Lava Mt]

The Hobbit—A four-hour dramatization of J. R. R. Tolkien's classic tale of Middle Earth, by the Marleybone Players of London, on four C-60 cassettes, for $25. [Source: Lava Mt]

The Foundation Trilogy—Isaac Asimov's renowned tale of power politics in the world of the future, in an 8-hour dramatization, $35. [Source: Lava Mt]

Contemporary Drama Service—An interesting collection of dramatized "interviews" with noted literary and historical personalities: Sophocles, Shakespeare, O'Neill and Keats, Wordsworth, Byron, each $17.50 for three cassettes and study guide in album: Ibsen, Checkhov, Shaw, Maugham, and Thoreau, Poe, Lewis, Steinbeck, each $17.50 for four cassettes with study guide in album. [Source: Contemporary Drama Service]

British and American Poetry—The important poems of the British Romantics and the major American poets of the 19th century, with oral interpretations and also brief introductions that fit each poem into the poet's total body of work and alert the listener to the poem's special features and meanings. *The Romantic Period in British Poetry, Part I* covers Burns, Gray, Blake, Wordsworth, and Coleridge; *Part II* includes works by Byron, Shelley, and Keats. *The 19th Century Revolution in American Poetry* deals with Emerson, Whitman, and Dickinson. $63.25 for each program of six cassettes in album. [Source: Educulture Inc.]

Cassette Library of Shakespeare Plays—22 of the Bard's great plays. *Antony and Cleopatra, As You Like It, Julius Caesar, Macbeth, The Merchant of Venice, Midsummer Night's Dream, Othello, Romeo and Juliet, Taming of the Shrew, Tempest,* and *King Henry IV—Part I* are each on three cassettes, each $26.98. *Hamlet, King Lear, King Richard III,* and *King Henry IV—Part 2* are each on four cassettes, $35.98. [Source: Educational Record Sales]

Prose Cassette Library—Each six-cassette program contain some complete works and other highlights of: Poe, Charles Dickens, O. Henry, Faulkner, Sherlock Holmes, Ray Bradbury, Isaac Asimov, Jack London, Nathaniel Hawthorne, Joseph Conrad, Stephen Crane, Hemingway, Mark Twain, Fitzgerald, and H. G. Wells, plus the complete *Martian Chronicles* and *Lord of the Flies,* and anthologies of *American Humorists, Great Novels, American Short Stories, Great Poetry,* and even *The Presidents Speak.* $49.95 each. [Source: Educational Record Sales]

Listen for Pleasure Talking Books—Favorite works of fiction and nonfiction, classic tales, and plays, skillfully abridged to 2-2½ hours and narrated by expert readers (such as Sir John Mills, Edward Fox, and Leo McKern). Some of the titles in the fiction category: *Upstairs Downstairs, Guns of Navarone, The Odessa File, Shane, Doctor Zhivago, Day of the Jackal, African Queen,* and *Tinker, Tailor, Soldier, Spy.* Nonfiction titles include *The Moon's A Balloon* (read by author David Niven), *Running Free* (read by runner Sebastian Coe), *An Actor in His Time* (read by Sir John Gielgud), and *Let Sleeping Vets Lie* (read

by author James Herriot). Among the classic tales: *Great Expectations, Tale of Two Cities, Lady Chatterley's Lover, Jane Eyre, Call of the Wild,* and *Pride and Prejudice.* Finally, they have three plays: *Hamlet* (with Gielgud and the Old Vic), *Romeo and Juliet* (with Claire Bloom), and *The Importance of Being Earnest* (with Dame Edith Evans). $14.95 for each album of two cassettes. [Source: Listen for Pleasure]

The Cassette Library—Skillful readings of great short stories (Guy de Maupassant, Bret Harte, and Burnham Carter, each $6.50 for one cassette); famous books; *The Alice Books* by Lewis Carroll, four cassettes, $15; *A Christmas Carol* by Charles Dickens, two cassettes, $9; *Delta of Venus, Erotica,* by Anais Nin, six cassettes, $24; *The Maltese Falcon,* four cassettes, $16; *Persuasion,* by Jane Austen, six cassettes, $16; *Murder Games* by Lionel Davidson, six cassettes, $18; a selection of Sherlock Holmes stories, ($6.50 for each cassette), poetry (*Psalms and Sonnets from the Portuguese,* each $6.50 for one cassette), classic horror stories by Edgar Allan Poe ($6.50 for each cassette) and Henry James (*The Turn of the Screw,* four cassettes, $15), and some nonfiction (*How To Be Your Own Best Friend* and *How To Take Charge of Your Life,* by Mildred Newman and Dr. Bernard Berkowitz, each on a cassette for $7.50; *The Peter Prescription,* four cassettes, $16; and Ralph Waldo Emerson's *Self-Reliance,* $6.50 for one cassette). [Source: SBI Publishers in Sound]

Simplified Texts—A varied collection of dramatized short stories (*The Monkey's Paw, Niemoller and the Nazis, Jacob and the Indians, Some Time with Thurber*) and narrated essays (*Utopianism and History, Carnegie,* Adlai Stevenson on *Democracy,* Mark Twain on *Antisemitism,* and others), for $10 each. Another collection of short stories is narrated, and includes Rip Van Winkle, many of Poe's famous stories, some of Hawthorne's little known ones, *Alibi Ike* by Ring Lardner, *The Most Dangerous Game, The Lady or the Tiger,* and many others, also for $10 each. [Source: Simplified Texts]

Classic Books—Each two-cassette album gives over two hours of listening pleasure. Titles include: *Walden, Favorite Stories, American Masterpieces, Tales of Horror and Suspense, The Best of Mark Twain, American Humorists, Alice in Wonderland, Benjamin Franklin,* three *Adventures of Sherlock Holmes, Storytime Favorites, Gulliver's Travels, Tom Sawyer, Pinocchio, Wizard of Oz,* and *Black Beauty.* $9.98 per album, any two for $15.98, any three for $22.98. [Source: Metacom, Inc.]

Cassette Curriculum—A remarkable collection of provocative commentary and criticism on a large number of literary works, with each 30-50 minute cassette generally covering one writer or literary work. The cost is $12 per cassette, except as noted. Series include: American Literature, 300 titles; Early

American Literature, 35 titles; Western American Literature, 29 titles; British Literature, 175 titles, including much Shakespeare; World Literature, 139 titles; Science Fiction, 6 titles; Classic Films, 7 titles; Women in Literature, 60 titles; the Humanities, 25 titles; and American Folklore, 47 titles. Also available are these sets: *The Meaning and Methods of Poetry*, Lawrence Perrine, six cassettes, $12 each; *Western Civilization: Origins and Directions*, Harold Schultz, five cassettes, $50; *Reading Imaginative Literature*, $100 for ten tapes and a workbook; *Metaphor and Meaning*, Weller E. Embler, 12 tapes, $120; and *Heritage of American Ideas*, John Hague, seven cassettes, $70. Finally, their library on semantics and linguistics: *Principles of General Semantics*, S. I. Hayakawa, five cassettes, $45; *General Semantics*, Joseph A. DeVito, $100 for nine cassettes; and *Linguistics*, Robert E. Callary, nine cassettes, $95. [Source: Everett/Edwards, Inc.]

The Mind's Eye—Dramatized radio programs that include famous stories, novels, and adventures from the world's best literature: *The Hobbit* on six cassettes for $19.95; *Lord of the Rings* on 12 cassettes for $39.95; *Time Machine, Jekyll & Hyde,* and *Hound of the Baskervilles*, each one cassette, $3.98; *Great Expectations*, three cassettes, $9.95; *Oliver Twist*, two cassettes, $7.95; *Christmas Carol*, one cassette, $3.98; *Connecticut Yankee in King Arthur's Court* and *Adventures of Huckleberry Finn*, each on three cassettes, $9.95 for the set; *Scarlet Letter* and *Red Badge of Courage*, two cassettes each, $7.95 each title; *Turn of the Screw*, Ambrose Bierce short stories, Poe tales, one cassette each, $3.98 each; Greek classics, four cassettes of the *Odyssey* ($12.95) and two each of *Agamemnon, Oedipus the King, Antigone,* and *Execution of Socrates* ($7.95 each); and finally, one-hour adaptations of great movies, novels, plays, and short stories, featuring Hollywood and Broadway stars, for $4.75 each. All cassettes are an hour long. [Source: Mind's Eye]

Recordings in World Literature—Over 100 classic novels, histories, biographies, essays, and poems are offered in this series, mostly narrated by Robert L. Halvorson. All tapes are 90 minutes long. A sample of selections: *Essays* of Francis Bacon, four cassettes, $16.95; *Alice in Wonderland*, by Lewis Carroll, two cassettes, $8.95; *Critique of Pure Reason* by Immanuel Kant, four cassettes, $16.95; Charles Dickens' *A Tale of Two Cities*, ten cassettes, $40.95; Hippocrates' *Medical Works*, six cassettes, $24.95; Nietzsche's *Genealogy of Morals*, four cassettes, $16.95; Plato's *Protagoras*, two cassettes, $8.95; *Travels of Marco Polo*, eight cassettes, $32.95; *Wealth of Nations* by Adam Smith, ten cassettes, $40.95; and Mark Twain's *The Prince and the Pauper*, four cassettes, $16.95. [Source: Halvorson Associates]

XII.
Management

Professional Development

The Right Place at the Right Time—The 'good luck' of many top professionals is actually the result of their consciously or unconsciously practicing success skills. Adele Scheele Ph.D. shows how folk wisdom can be translated into skills and strategies that are crucial to having successful careers. $32.50 for three cassettes in album. [Source: UCLA Extension]

Turning Point Programs—*Generating People Power*, with Dr. Ron Brown showing how to close the communications gap between you, your employees, and the public; *New Dimensions in Business and Life*, with Christopher J. Hegarty covering a host of management problems: poor communications, lack of leadership, apathy, boredom, and unproductive stress; *Getting More Productivity and Profit From Your People*, with Jim Hooker pointing out that understanding human behavior is the key to achieving corporate goals; *Matching and Meshing of Personal and Company Goals*, with Mike McCaffrey showing how to achieve personal goals by working in tandem with organizational goals and plans; *New Dynamics of Achievement: Releasing Human Potential*, with James W. Newman describing how to release creative energies, how to make pressure a turn-on, and how to use empathy to build understanding; *Adventures in Creative Thinking* and *Adventures in Creative Leadership*, with Mike Vance giving tips on motivation, creativity, communications, personal growth, leadership, and selling. All these are $69.95 each for six cassettes in album. [Source: Turning Point Programs]

How To Become a More Effective Supervisor—A four-hour course designed to develop motivational skills, strengthen leadership qualities, and promote team effectiveness. Two similar offerings are *Getting Organized* (managing time, improving personal productivity, controlling interruptions, increasing efficiency) and *Improving Your Communication Effectiveness* (working with the office team, increasing self-confidence, resolving conflicts and building working relationships). $135 each for six cassettes and workbook in album. [Source: Batten Institute]

Burnout—All the materials for a one-day workshop on burnout, although it can be used individually. The prime causes are generally felt to be constant stress coupled with a lack of independence, but Dr.

Richard P. Issel shows that it is diagnosable, treatable, and preventable. $115 for four cassettes (100 minutes of material), participants manual (more available, 10 for $50), and leader's guide in album. [Source: Learning Consultants, Inc.]

Women in Management—Clay Hardesty covers three aspects: *The Woman as Effective Executive*, describing the qualities of leadership and how to attain them; *Interpersonal Communications*, the simple yet difficult tasks of talking and listening to those around you; and *Practical Decision Making*, giving principles of determining when, how, and where to make decisions. $47.50 for the three cassettes in album, or $17.50 each. [Source: Learning Consultants, Inc.]

Everyday Creativity—12 steps to innovative thinking to give a fresh outlook on business problems and sometimes the competitive edge, provided by Dr. Ernest Dichter, $115 for seven C-30 cassettes, text, and workbook in album. [Source: American Management Associations]

Women as Leaders—A comprehensive analysis of the problems confronting the high-achieving woman manager: staff development, delegation, conflicts with coordinates, and balancing personal and professional lives. $24.95 for cassette, transcript, workbook in album. [Source: Performance Group Incorporated]

Management Performance Improvement System—Pointers on becoming a high-performance manager, by mastering time, working with people, making decisions, solving problems, and delegating authority, $24.95 for cassette, transcript, and workbook in album. [Source: Performance Group Incorporated]

Management by Objectives and Results—George L. Morrisey gives the principles and techniques of the MOR concepts that he developed, on six cassettes with workbook in album for $80. In *Introduction to Management by Objectives and Results*, he offers a one-cassette overview of its key issues, for $10. Two other programs by Mr. Morrisey focus on determining, setting, and achieving goals: *Women and MORe—Winning Techniques for Goal Setting*, with Dru Scott, dealing with the special psychological factors women face in contributing to results using the MOR approach, and *Practical Self Management*, with Fred Clark, emphasizing how individual managers and specialists can apply the three essential steps in the MOR process to their jobs and their personal lives; these are each $35 for two cassettes and workbook in album. Finally, George Morrisey and Karen Wilson provide the principles, techniques, and the motivation to achieve whatever is important to you in your personal and business life, in *Getting Your Act Together: Goal Setting for Fun, Health and Profit*, on eight cassettes in album plus text for $75. [Source: MOR Associates]

Development Publications—Self-administered learning programs for management training covering the consulting process, role-playing methods, and life goals: *The Consulting Process in Action Skill-Development Kit* thoroughly covers the skills needed in both working with and becoming a consultant, on six cassettes and exercises in binder for $155; *Reality Practice: Theory and Skills of Role Playing Methods* shows how to set up and lead role-playing activities in all kinds of training programs, on six cassettes for $70; and *The Life/Work Goals Exploration Workbook Kit* shows an individual how to collect information about self, to develop realistic goals that best satisfy self-values, needs and wants, and then formulate action plans to achieve these goals, all on six cassettes and workbook in binder. Cost $155. [Source: Development Publications]

Managing Time—Longer hours is not the way to get work done. Rather—as this course shows—it is development of individual time-management techniques: improving effective work time, banishing 'time wasters,' improving planning and decision-making skills, scheduling according to body metabolism, and others. $80 for eight cassettes and study guide in album. [Source: Fred Pryor Resources Corporation]

Professional Development/Interpersonal Communications—A six-cassette program developed (and given) by Jim Cathcart and Dr. Tony Alessandra. Titles are: *Who is Responsible (For your Career?)*, *Time Management is Self Management*, *Image, the Silent Persuader*, *Three Essentials for a Happy Family*, *The Power of Listening*, and *Breaking the Golden Rule*. $61 for six cassettes (about five hours of listening time). [Source: Cathcart, Alessandra & Associates, Inc.]

101 Ways To Save Time—Like the title says, Time expert Harold Taylor gives over 100 time-saving tips under such categories as paperwork and correspondence, telephone, interruptions, visitors, meetings, travel, and delegation. Related is *Managing Yourself with Respect to Time*, on which Mr. Taylor gives a step-by-step explanation of how to get organized, clear away the backlog, and maintain control of your time and your life. $10 for either hour-long cassette. [Source: Time Institute]

Personal Time Management—A course on how to make more productive use of time by identifying and removing the major time wasters in both personal and professional life. $99.95 for four cassettes and instructional materials. [Source: Lansford Publishing Company]

I Would If I Only Had The Time—Three salesmen offer tips for making organization a habit, watching out for time stealers, and taking time to assemble the facts. $20 for three one-hour cassettes. [Source: Realtors National Marketing Institute]

Time Management for Today—If you can't manage your time, you can't manage your job. In this program, Dr. Merrill Douglas shows how to be on top of the job, rather than letting the job be on top of you. In six programs he shows how to find time to manage, how to organize desk and paperwork, how to eliminate timewasters, how to conquer procrastination, techniques of relaxation, and creative use of time. $65 for six cassettes in album. [Source: Time Management Center]

5 Steps to Success—Leo Hauser III has been there: at 28 he was national product manager for General Mills, at 33 he purchased a NYSE seat, he has been president of ASTD and the only American to head the Geneva-based international federation of training organizations. On this cassette he tells the steps that have led to his success in sales, marketing, finance, and human relations. $7.95. [Source: Hauser Productions, Inc.]

New Dimensions for Today—Christopher J. Hegarty offers pointers on how to increase self-direction, improve leadership qualities, train and develop others, and in general increase productivity, on four cassettes in album for $55. Related single cassette topics ($10 each) cover successful stress strategies, avoiding crises in communications, and managing the challenge of change. In *Timepower²* a four-cassette album, Christopher J. Hegarty shows how to manage your boss, enjoy being disliked, deal with workaholism, and generally how to use what you already know. $55. A related single cassette title is *Workaholism: The Cause, the Cure*, for $10. [Source: Christopher J. Hegarty]

Outstanding Contributors Series—Steve Becker conducts in-depth interviews with three men who have dominated and changed the training profession. Robert Mager has given form and substance to instructional technology, and in these interviews he shares his simple, intelligible systems and procedures to analyze performance, construct learning objectives, create instruction, and measure its effectiveness. Malcolm Knowles has done more than anyone to further the cause of self-directed learning and his name is virtually synonymous with adult education. Leonard Nadler is closely associated with the field of human resource development (a phrase he coined) and no one knows better how it can contribute to organizational goals. Each of these three interviews is on six cassettes and comes with a listening and reference guide in album, for $180. [Source: Learncom, Inc.]

How To Get the Breaks in Life—Some people seem to get 'all the breaks'. Lewis Timberlake shows what these 'breaks' really are, offers some methods to help people accomplish their own 'breaks,' and emphasizes the needs for successful communication skills to achieve success. $19.95 for a two-cassette album. To get those breaks you can take *All The Time You Need*: time management is the theme of this two-cassette album by Lewis Timberlake. On the first cassette he discusses different types of time and how to discover and manage those things that take up our time. On the second cassette, he tells the 11 major ways we lose time and money and outlines more than 60 ways to overcome time wasters. $19.95. [Source: Timberlake and Associates]

Career Management Cassette Series—Audio-cassette/workbook modules by distinguished authorities in career development that provide insights for increased self-awareness, guidance for greater on-the-job effectiveness, and individualized systematic help at critical career stages. Program titles are: *Finding and Getting the Right Job*, on the process of matching vocational preferences and abilities to specific jobs; *Managing Your Career*, giving the essential guideposts; *Life Planning*, looking at one's total life role; *Making the Most of Your Time on the Job*, on enhancing personal effectiveness through better allocation of time; *Dealing with Job-related Stress*, by a noted occupational psychiatrist; *Pre-retirement Planning*, on how to reduce the trauma; *Performance Appraisal*, making the interview benefit both management and the individual; *Management Assessment Centers*, and how they operate in the selection of managers; *Job Design*, to change boring jobs into productive ones; *Supervisory Training Through Behavior Modeling*; *Employee Privacy*, principles and procedures; *Goal Setting*, and how to apply it at the industrial level; *Morale Management*, on surveying and enhancing employee morale; and *Effective Leadership for Productivity*. $35 for each module of two cassettes and workbook in album. [Source: Management Decision Systems, Inc.]

Managing Time—Dr. Alec Mackenzie shows how to control the executive's greatest asset, his time, by identifying major time wasters and presenting ways to correct them. $395 for nine cassettes and workbook in album. [Source: AMR/Advanced Management Reports, Inc.]

ASTD Conference Cassettes—The best sessions from recent national and international conferences of the American Society for Training and Development. Some recent titles from 1982 conferences: *Training the Economically Disadvantaged, Quality*

Circles: A Unique Training Approach, Training for Increased Employee Involvement, Planning a Program for Increased Productivity, The Management Team of the Future, Strategic Planning Demystified, and *Measuring Results of Training*. $11.50 per cassette (less for members). [Source: ASTD Order Department]

Creative Problem Solving—Six cassettes and a workbook of activities and exercises deliberately planned to jar one's creative mechanisms and to start the flow of innovative ideas toward resolving problems. $145 for six cassettes and workbook, and quizzes that can be returned for scoring and evaluation. [Source: American Management Associations]

Cassettes for Success—Tailor-made for managers on the go, these programs are skillfully produced by the AMACOM Division of the American Management Associations, all packaged in albums with manual or workbook. Some of the titles: *Speech Power*, 12 cassettes, $99.95; *Writing Sense*, five cassettes, $95; *Reading/Plus*, six cassettes, $115; *The Comprehensive Exercise Guide*, three cassettes, $35; *Coping with Stress*, $74.95; *How To Improve Your Management Style* (using the Blake-Mouton Managerial Grid), three cassettes, $89.95; *Measuring Managers*, three cassettes, $79.95; *Career Success*, three cassettes, $39.95. [Source: American Management Associations]

Techniques

Audio-Forum—Single-cassette discussions about diverse facets of business and industry, such as *Decision Theory* by Colin C. Blaydon, *Understanding the Grapevine and Controlling Rumor* by Keith Davis, *The Role of Research in Industry* by Crawford H. Greenewalt, and many more. There are also two eight-cassette (12 hour) series (*Alphabet Soup: The Regulatory Agencies* and *The Future of American Labor Unions*) presented by the Center for Constructive Alternatives (Hillsdale College), for $70 each. And there are many more; write for the free catalog. [Source: Jeffrey Norton Publishers, Inc.]

Safety Tape Album Pack—Selling employees on the importance of safety is a never-ending job, requiring constant motivation for them (and for their supervisors). In this entertaining four-cassette program, Art Fettig covers motivation, communications, practical techniques, and interpersonal relationships—all intended to increase safety consciousness and save lives. $49.50. [Source: Art Fettig]

Somers H. White—A potpourri of interesting programs for the supervisor, manager, or executive. In *How To Borrow Twice the Money with Half the Work*, Mr. White tells how to prepare a commercial loan presentation, while the *Personalized Direct Mail Program*, especially aimed for those in real estate or insurance, shows how to produce significant increases in business at a very low cost. These are both four cassettes with workbook in album for $60. *How To Dress for Power, Success & Money* gives straight information for all men and women who are serious about making a success in business, on six hour-long cassettes for $80. Finally, John Moore joins Mr. White in telling *How Not To Be Ripped Off by Your Lawyer*, $70 for four hour-long cassettes in album. [Source: Somers H. White Co.]

Desk Top Seminars—*Handling "Problem Employees"* covers one of a manager's most dreaded obligations—correcting a subordinate whose off-the-job problems are interfering with on-the-job productivity. Two programs with legal overtones are *Conducting Lawful Interviews: Guidelines for Non-Discriminatory Hiring Practices* and *Motivating Employees: Understanding Legal Requirements*. Finally, *Telephone Dynamics* is a comprehensive program intended to increase productivity and profitability by making the most out of every phone contact. All four of these programs consist of two cassettes with manuals and/or leader's guide in album. All cost $125. [Source: Singer Management Institute]

Safety and the Supervisor—A self-instruction learning course that provides manufacturing supervisors with skills in dealing with the two factors—unsafe conditions and unsafe acts—that are involved in every accident. Essential in any industrial setting, there is considerable emphasis on the supervisor's responsibility under the Federal Occupational Safety and Health Act (OSHA). Because of the impact of OSHA standards, this course is suitable for both experienced and new supervisors and for trainees. $75 for five audio-cassettes and administrator's guide in album, $37 for the two workbooks, 146- and 166-pages. [Source: General Motors]

Seminar for Supervisors—Studio recorded highlights of a proved seminar, stressing motivation, getting your ideas across, and solving employee problems. $69 for six 40-minute cassettes in album. *Advanced Seminar for Supervisors* covers productivity, performance management, and employee improvement, in the same format, for the same price. [Source: Professional Training Associates, Inc.]

Professional Management Programs—Management development and improvement seminars and union-management relations programs conducted by Dr. John R. Van de Water, all aimed at helping to increase productivity, to more effectively utilize time, and actualize management potential. He offers nine 60-90 minute cassette seminars, covering the art and science of management, human values, communications, motivational factors, effective use of time, rational problem-solving and decision-making, creativity, goal development, managing by goals and results, and strategy in response to union organizing campaigns. A workbook included with each cassette facilitates study and preparation for individual and group improvement applications. $28 for each cassette, workbook, and transcript in album or all nine titles for $202.50. [Source: Learning Institute]

Management by Objectives—In these three 40-minute audio-cassettes, Peter F. Drucker and John Humble exchange ideas on: evaluating management potential and accomplishment; myths and realities of participative management/making teamwork effective; and management by objectives/management of the non-profit organization. $12 for each cassette. [Source: BNA Communications Inc.]

Effective Interviewing—Four programs are available, covering performance appraisal, career counseling, the selection interview, and the exit interview, each with two cassettes and extensive printed materials for $35. Each program provides a complete self-study skill-building course for managers or supervisors. [Source: Management Decision Systems, Inc.]

Fundamentals of Supervision—Three modular cassette-with-workbook courses in a self-paced format to provide maximum flexibility for individualized group training. *Supervisory Skills* and *Face-To-Face Human Relations & Communication* each consist of ten 3-hour modules, $380 for 12 cassettes, 10 modular workbooks in album; *Organizational Role of Supervisors* has eight 2-3 hour modules, $304 for 10 cassettes and workbooks in album. [Source: Practical Management Associates, Inc.]

PMA Seminars—Live recordings of one-day seminars for supervisors and managers. *Motivation & Discipline* covers common misconceptions about motivation, the basis of and the obstacles to achievement motivation, dissatisfiers, definitions of a job well done, and limits of discipline. *Use of Objectives in Planning for Results* covers the limits of the usual performance appraisals, why objectives work, and why they don't, rules for clear objectives, and causes of non-improvement. $125 for each seminar, on six cassettes (about 4½ hours). Also available are a series of *Management Discussions*, single-cassette discussions of practical, non-theoretical views of many functions and problems that managers face every day, $18 each, all 13 tapes for $200. [Source: Practical Management Associates, Inc.]

Self-Study Audio Cassette Programs for Supervisors—Each program contains a set of audio-cassettes corresponding to chapters in an accompanying text. After reading a chapter from the book, supervisors listen to the cassette's presentation of real life situations, and then completes assignments in the learning guide. All programs developed by (and accompanying texts written by) noted supervisory trainer Martin Broadwell. *The New Supervisor* package (14 cassettes) costs $235, *The Practice of Supervising* and *The Supervisor and On-The-Job Training* packages (10 cassettes each) cost $210. [Source: Resources for Education and Management, Inc.]

Audio Cassette Training Packages—Industrial and management training programs presenting basic concepts and ideas in a straightforward, logical way.

Intended for training classes but adaptable for self-study. Each package includes a comprehensive leader's guide with key thoughts, tests, and a complete script. Titles available are: *Communicating Skills*; *Interpersonal Relations*; and *Interviewing Skills* (each with six cassettes for $75) and *Managerial Skills* (five cassettes for $65). [Source: Resources for Education and Management, Inc.]

People, Productivity, and Profits—A 45-minute presentation on the changes that will be taking place in the practice of management during the 1980s; it provides a tool for examining operating practices and preparing for increased success. $11.95. [Source: Achievement Institute]

Executive Seminars in Sound—In this newly revised second edition a variety of business problems are depicted in twelve 45-50 minute sessions, and then pointers are given on how to handle them. Cassette topics are: how to get your ideas across, make the most of your time, your role as a decision-maker, guide to better people management, mastering the art of delegating, organizing your plans, strategies of moving ahead, and how to live with your own success. The goal of the program is to make one's role in the business world more effective, more profitable, and more personally satisfying. $95 for six cassettes with study guide in album. [Source: Nation's Business]

Project Management—These live recordings from seminars by Sydney F. Love tell how to bring in a project on time, within budget, and with the right results. He gives proved pointers in forecasting key resources (manpower, equipment, supplies) that will be needed, developing and using appropriate planning and scheduling tools, detecting trouble spots in advance, and more—all while never forgetting human frailties and organizational sensitivities. $95 for six cassettes in album. [Source: Advanced Professional Development Institute]

Practical Psychology for Managing People—Dr. Mortimer R. Feinberg, a well-known management psychologist, discusses his proved effective managerial strategies to boost employee performance. On eight live recordings, Dr. Feinberg covers: how to master the art of managing people, and how to use power and authority; how to select capable people, and how to appraise performance to improve results; techniques of executive decision-making and of persuasive communications; psychology in training and development, and an approach to handling stress. Individual programs $12.95 each, all eight in album for $99.95. [Source: Prentice-Hall Distribution Center]

Compleat Manager—Allan C. Filley helps improve the managerial skills used to lead more effectively, to motivate others better, and to become a better decision-maker, problem-solver, and time-manager, on 11 cassettes in album for $150. [Source: Research Press]

Job Design—A leading organizational psychologist, Dr. J. Richard Hackman, shows which aspects of jobs cause some employees to be highly productive and others to be apathetic, and then leads the listener through a model of work design for use in evaluating job characteristics as well as planning and implementing changes. $35 for two cassettes, study guide, and job diagnostic survey in album. [Source: Research Press]

Resources in Sound—Highlights from a decade of meetings and educational seminars of the American Society of Association Executives, with most cassette presentations aimed at improving the function of associations of all types and at upgrading the quality of their leaders. Topics include: improving effectiveness with chapters and affiliates, executive competency, role of an association's chief elected officer, how to sell a dues increase and build membership, building membership income, obtaining grants, going international, and having your members mind their own business. These range from $9 each from the 1981 annual meeting down to $5.95 for the few 1971 tapes available. The ASAE 1980 National Leadership Conference album contains six cassettes for $74, three 'pure gold' albums (highlights of past meetings) including Jim Low discussing associations, a management package, and a self-development package, for $40 each. Another special offering are two cassettes of Dr. Arthur B. Laffer talking about supply side economics, for $35. [Source: American Society of Association Executives]

Managing Fast Growth—CEOs from some fast growth companies (Federal Express, MCI, Pepperidge Farms) tell how they did it, the principles they used, and the pitfalls they avoided, on 16 cassettes in album and thick program guide for $495. Related advice is found in *Attacking the Competition*, on 12 cassettes in an album, in which a 'strike force' of experts tell how to identify which competitor to attack first, how to penetrate their key markets, how to get them off balance, anticipate their reactions, and much more. $495 including 'war manual', a copy of Clausewitz's book *On War*, and a poster of his maxims on guerrilla warfare. [Source: AMR/Advanced Management Reports, Inc.]

Management by Objectives—Seven complete courses for management training and self-development, conducted by George Odiorne, Dean of the School of Business Administration at the University of Massachusetts and "father of MBO." *Executive Skills*, aimed at top and middle management, and *Supervisory Skills*, designed for first-level and middle managers of people and situations, are each $196 for 12 C-30 cassettes and manual in album. *Training by Objectives*, covers a variety of basic training approaches, including the systems approach, and *Personnel Administration by Objectives* shows how to manage a personnel department effectively by using MBO techniques; these are both $98 for six C-30 cassettes and manual in album. *Managing the Non-profit Organization* teaches a two-stage MBO system of management by anticipation and by commitment, $98 for six C-30 cassettes and manual in album. *Successful Personal Selling Through MBO* shows how sales people can set objectives to become more self-managing and thereby more successful in selling, four C-30 cassettes in album for $68. Finally, *The Behavioral Sciences* gives managers at all levels the background for sharpening their interpersonal skills, $184 for 12 C-30 cassettes and study guide in album. [Source: MBO, Inc.]

Corporate Planning—19 top executives and educators present practical approaches to better business planning and more effective use of corporate resources. $385 for 16 cassettes in album. *Corporate Planning II* is presented in conjunction with the Planning Executives Institute to prepare management to cope with the complex markets and economics of the 1980s. $350 for 10 cassettes and workbook in album. [Source: AMR/Advanced Management Reports, Inc.]

Robert Townsend Speaks Out: How To Stop the Corporation from Stifling People and Strangling Profits—The author of *Up the Organization* is candid, caustic, and tells it like it is, from mistresses to mistakes, from nepotism to no-no's. $495 for 12 cassettes in album. [Source: AMR/Advanced Management Reports, Inc.]

Acquiring, Merging, and Selling Companies—A complete exploration of all practical and technical aspects from the viewpoints of experienced buyers and sellers. $350 for 12 cassettes and workbook in album. *International Mergers and Acquisitions*, recorded in London, in which a panel of U.S. and continental experts provide current strategies and techniques for the delicate steps involved. $195 for 6 cassettes and manual in album. [Source: AMR/Advanced Management Reports, Inc.]

Interviewing Skills and Techniques for Management—Experts use discussion and dramatized interview situations to demonstrate what not to do, what to do, and how to conduct productive interviews with subordinates, customers, and colleagues. $350 for six cassettes and 100-page workbook. Help with the hiring interview is included in *Hiring High Performers*, a program for managers who require outstanding performers—where to find them, the role of personal chemistry, how to interview them, checking references, making an offer. $295 for eight cassettes and comprehensive manual. [Source: AMR/Advanced Management Reports, Inc.]

Fundamentals of Finance—A course planned for those executives who are stymied by balance sheets, confused in budget meetings, shaky about financial analyses—to help them increase their effectiveness as managers and to develop professionally. $395 for ten

cassettes and workbook/test in album. Related financial management information is to be found in *Zero Base Budgeting*, which more and more companies are turning to as a tool to provide a systematic evaluation of all operations and programs, is here explained by Peter A. Pyhrr, "the first name in ZBB." $350 for ten cassettes and notebook in album. Also, there is *Capital Investment Analysis Techniques* with Raymond I. Reul offering a step-by-step method covering initial appraisal, rate of return, tax implications, and risk analysis. $350 for 12 cassettes and text. [Source: AMR/Advanced Management Reports, Inc.]

Managing by Objectives—Donn Coffee presents his unique system to improve both organizational effectiveness and individual performance. $350 for eight cassettes and workbook in album. [Source: AMR/Advanced Management Reports, Inc.]

Project Management—A detailed explanation of the critical points, the key concepts, and control techniques that are crucial to any manager or executive assigned a specific project. $395 for six cassettes and book in album. [Source: AMR/Advanced Management Reports, Inc.]

Audio Cassette Learning Programs—A host of top-quality, fairly priced seminars, based on the one-day management programs presented nationwide by Applied Management Institute. Each program consists of six hour-long cassettes with seminar notes in album, for $75. The titles (and speakers): *Assertiveness Training for Managers* (Sam R. Lloyd); *Communication Skills for Managers* (Hugh C. Rennie); *Customer Relations* (Carol Sapin Gold); *Effective Time Management* (Peter A. Turla); *Fundamentals of Accounting* (and also, *of Finance*) *for the Non-Financial Manager* (both by Dr. Robert P. Hungate); *Fundamentals of Data Processing for the Non-Data Processing Manager* (Dr. Bruce D. Sanders); *Fundamentals of Management and Supervision* (John R. Van de Water J.D.); *Fundamentals of Professional Selling* (Donald M. Dible); *Hiring, Evaluating and Firing* (Jill E. Shulman); *Increasing Productivity through Management by Objectives* (Dr. Joseph P. Yaney); *Management of Managers* (George L. Morrisey); *Managing People* (Dr. David L. Ward); *Practical Negotiating Skills* (Robert J. Laser); *Profit & Growth Strategies for the Closely-Held Company* (Donald M. Dible); *Profitable Telephone Marketing* (David Yoho); *Project Planning and Management* (Dr. Barry Z. Posner); *Psychology of Closing Sales* (Dr. Aaron Hemsley); *Quality Circles and Japanese-Style Management* (Larry L. Nelson); *Speed Reading Skills to Save Time and Improve Comprehension* (Kathleen L. Hawkins); *Stress Management* (Dr. Herbert S. Kindler); *Time and Territory Management for Sales Professionals* (Gladys Nicastro); and *Women in the Work Force: a Manager's Role* (Nicole Schapiro). [Source: Associated Management Institute, Inc.]

IBC Effective Management Program—Developed by John Sawatsky of International Behavioural Consultants, this 40-cassette program translates behavioral science concepts into practical, usable management methods. The program is composed of four integrated series, each in turn consisting of ten 12-minute cassettes. Titles of the four series are: *Managing Individuals Effectively* (increasing the effectiveness of managers), *Achieving Group Effectiveness* (learning how to develop and manage a team), *Developing Personal Effectiveness* (to be used by individuals for personal growth), and *The Leadership Guide* (guides for developing and training others). $100 for each series, or $12 per cassette. A related program, also applying behavioral science to management practice is *Effective Organization* in which management consultant Saul W. Gellerman describes how to use behavioral science findings to provide practical solutions to many of the issues involved in putting together an efficient organization, on six 30-minute cassettes, $12 each. [Source: BNA Communications Inc.]

Management Practice—John Humble joins with other management experts for thorough discussions that provide insights into the problems of company information systems and computers, creative marketing, and innovative long-range planning, on three hour-long cassettes, $12 each. [Source: BNA Communications Inc.]

Motivation and Productivity—Saul Gellerman and Emanuel Kay explain in down-to-earth language the fundamentals of employee motivation and how to use basic human understanding to boost employee output, on six hour-long cassettes, $12 each. [Source: BNA Communications Inc.]

Negotiating Leverage—A course to provide executives with practical strategies and skills for negotiations, by identifying the power and psychologic sources of leverage. 20 experts contribute, under the direction of Dr. Edward C. Caprielian. $395 for 16 cassettes and program guide in album. [Source: AMR/Advanced Management Reports, Inc.]

Executive Compensation—A program not only for executives receiving a compensation package but also for the specialist who must design the "right" individual pay package to hire, motivate, and retain essential management talent. $350 for 12 cassettes and manual in album. [Source: AMR/Advanced Management Reports, Inc.]

How Successful Managers Manage—This course shows trainees how to function in the management arena as it really is, not as it appears in textbook theory, by focusing on 'people and behavior' skills. Topics covered include learning objectives, managerial relationships, negotiations, realities of decision-making, solving problems through change, and working with the boss. The purchaser also chooses a seventh cassette covering management problems in:

banking, manufacturing, insurance, health care, government, or service. $275 for seven cassettes, 11 participant's workbooks and application manuals, 11 tests (the source scores and provides feedback), and leader's guide. Also they have *Four Essential Managerial Skills*, the ones involved in resolving these questions: what should we do? is it worth doing? how should we do it? how well are we doing? The components of this course are the same as for the previous one (including the seventh cassette of case studies in the area of the listener's interest), and the price is also $275. [Source: Management Resources.]

The Art of Negotiating Audio Program—Gerard I. Nierenberg, one of the country's foremost negotiators, has transferred his two-day seminar on negotiating onto 12 audio-cassettes, plus an easy-to-read, plain language manual. Together, they reveal the secrets, the strategies and counter-strategies, and associated techniques for becoming a winning negotiator. You can learn to estimate when your offer will be accepted, and when it will be refused—and the scope covers everything from million-dollar real estate deals to the best table in a crowded restaurant. $295 for 12 audio-cassettes, manual, plus three books by Mr. Nierenberg. [Source: Negotiation Institute, Inc.]

Management Classics—Two hours of listening to the original words of business pioneers—Adam Smith on specialization, Henry L. Gantt on morale, Frank G. Gilbreth on time management, Elton Mayo on human relations, and four others—to enhance understanding of the application of basic management to today's real business world, $15 each, $98 for eight cassettes in album. Related is Dr. Richard R. Gallagher's *Great Men in Management* (brief biographies of 12 innovators in management) and *The Art & Science of Shoveling* (Frederick Windslow Taylor's classic testimony before the U.S. House of Representatives in 1912), $15 each. [Source: Tutor/Tape]

Selection Interviewing Program—This step-by-step training course by Dr. John D. Drake can help the listener develop an effective systematic format for every kind of interview of every kind of applicant. The seven lessons cover practicing interviews, conducting the interview, how to get the applicant to open up, interpreting what you hear, the hiring decision, and avoiding discrimination. $295 for four self-study cassettes and two trainer's cassettes, trainer's guide, exercise workbooks, certificates, and text in slipcase. [Source: Drake Beam Morin, Inc.; also Management Resources]

Effective Negotiating—Dr. Chester L. Karrass is an expert on the strategies and tactics necessary to help people reach their objectives in business and personal transactions. On these 11 one-hour cassettes he gives a practical guide to negotiating techniques, countermeasures, and psychological insights into the negotiating process, for $310 including album, workbook, and two texts. *Winning in Negotiations* offers a condensed version of his principles on four cassettes with workbook in album, plus the same two texts, for $99. [Source: Negotiating Books]

Penton/IPC Management Courses—Programmed learning courses, each on three one-hour cassettes with workbook in album for $60. *Management by Objectives* emphasizes *what* must be done, rather than *how* it is to be done. *Management by Exception* shows managers how to confront, analyze, and resolve problems before they disrupt performance. *Fundamentals of Planning* provides detailed explanations of each step in long- and short-range planning. These three albums can be purchased together as the *Management Science Series* for $165. *Fundamentals of Cost Control* tells what it is, how to use it, and how to make the best decision based on the facts it gives you. *Fundamentals of Marketing* is simply "putting the right product in the right place at the right time at the right price supported by the right promotion." Finally, *Fundamentals of Sales Management* teaches the basics of how to get others to sell. [Source: Penton/IPC Education Division]

Tapes by Lawrence L. Steinmetz, Ph.D.—In *Fine Art of Delegation*, Dr. Steinmetz addresses the problems that managers and executives have in trying to be effective delegators, on six cassettes in album for $65. He tackles the problem related to *Managing the Unsatisfactory Performer*, also on six cassettes in album for $65. *First Line Management* was designed specifically for first level management people, and particularly newly appointed supervisory people, eight cassettes in album for $82.50. Finally, two live recordings by Dr. Steinmetz (four cassettes in album, $59 each) on *Managing a Fast Growing Retail Firm* and *Managing a Fast Growing Manufacturing Firm*. [Source: Horizon Publications, Inc.]

How To Interpret Financial Statements—Listen as experts talk you through balance sheets, income statements, statements of retained earnings, and statements of changes in financial position. Then, using analysis tools in the workbook, the listener applies the skills learned to an actual case history. $145 for six cassettes and workbook in album. Pre- and post-tests can be returned for scoring and evaluation. [Source: American Management Associations]

General Management Training—Basic courses intended for the new manager—*Concepts of Management, Motivation for Managers, Tools and Skills of Management, Communications in Management,* and *Getting Change Through Communication*—all $27.50 for each four-cassette course. *Selection of Men* gives a complete course in the fundamentals of personnel management, on 24 cassettes for $160. Specifically aimed at the retail manager are *Stop the Short Change Artist* (two cassettes, $12.95), *Stop the Shoplifter* (four cassettes, $27.50), *Dry Cleaning Sales and Service* (five cassettes, $37.50), *Service Station Job Introduction and Salesmanship* 12 cassettes, $60; and *The Secrets of Curly McAdams* (management of service stations, 10 cassettes, $55). [Source: Associated Educational Materials]

Audio-Cassette Library on Organization Development—The two latest additions to this large collection of presentations on organization development (OD) are *Concepts and Theories of OD* (on four cassettes for $63) and *The Practice of OD: What Do You Do When You Do OD?* (six cassettes for $106.50). Both these programs feature Dr. W. Warner Burke and Dr. James R. Marshall (Editor of *Development Digest*), and both are in the 'Programmed Divided-Attention Learning' format, with on-tape questions and exercises relating to the topics covered. Many other OD programs are available, covering overviews and critiques of OD, diagnosis, OD interventions, OD in non-profit organizations, and special OD applications in management. Individual tapes are $13.75. [Source: Development Digest]

Supervisory Success—How to make the changeover from worker to supervisor, how to work with the boss and with former 'buddies,' and how to share the problems of the boss, the workers, and the company—are all topics addressed on this course for new supervisors, pre-supervisors, and problem supervisors. $150 for six cassettes, seven trainee workbooks, and leader's guide. [Source: Management Resources]

Leadership and Motivation: The Influence Process—This program developed by Training by Design, Inc. teaches these how-to-do-it skills: developing personal leadership power, applying leadership to work situations, creating positive motivational climate, communicating leadership, understanding motivators and dissatisfiers, counseling poor or marginal employees, understanding and managing change, and building individual motivational strategies. $150 for five cassettes (including a tape for trainers), seven trainee workbooks, and leader's guide. [Source: Management Resources]

Effective Team Building—Jim Cathcart, in a live seminar, explains the essentials of helping people grow into a team, and discusses the strategic planning process that he conducts with major corporations each year. $25 for two audio-cassettes with article on planning. [Source: Cathcart, Alessandra & Associates, Inc.]

Management Basics for Women—A good introduction for women entering the business world, presented by Dr. Marion Wood, author of *Women in Management*. In this eight-cassette course, she places emphasis on time management, goal setting, priority planning, and the development of interpersonal skills. $67.25, including album. [Source: UCLA Extension]

Managing Conflict Productively—Any group or society that experiences declining resources will also
experience more conflict, for—according to Fred E.
Jandt, former director of professional development
at SUNY—conflict intensifies as resources become
scarce. In this program, Dr. Jandt demonstrates the
skills and techniques necessary to control potentially
damaging conflict situations and to make necessary
conflicts productive for everyone. $64.99 for four 60-
minute cassettes and workbook in album, $5 for
additional workbooks. [Source: Human Productivity Institute, Inc.]

Meeting Management—A noted professional conference planner, James E. Jones, gives pointers on
running a conference: site selection techniques, hotel
negotiations, meeting content, post-meeting evaluation, and much more. $16.45 for two cassettes.
[Source: Bayard Publications]

Project Management—Six cassettes, a 90-page workbook, and a text all coordinated to show how to
bring a project in on time, within budget, and with
the right results. This involves indepth coverage of
planning and scheduling, time management, budgeting and cost controls, 'hurry-up' measures, and the
use of computers in project management. $225 for
the set. [Source: Professional Cassette Center]

**Management Guide to Successful Recruiting and
Interviewing**—How to analyze the job requirements,
attract good candidates, identify their strengths and
weaknesses during screening and interviewing, and
finally, how to match the right person with the right
job—on two cassettes, workbooks, and guidebooks
in album for $95. [Source: Science Research Asso-
ciates, Inc.]

Better Than Money—Three programs developed by
John Tschohl that involve the use of 'strokes' (also
known as 'warm fuzzies' and loosely translated as
compliments, in contrast to 'cold pricklies,' or criticism) as management tools for immediate application in any company or organization. *Better Than
Money* shows managers and supervisors how to use
this non-financial compensation to the immediate
benefit of employee happiness, morale, and alle-
giance—on two cassettes with manual and stroke
cards in album for $42. *How to Score Through
Stroking* show how to build sales by enhancing
personal relationships, not only with prospects and
customers, but also with every daily contact—on one
cassette with manual and stroke cards in album for
$25. *Feelings* is a training kit (three cassettes, leaders'
and participants' books, and other materials in album) intended to show employees how to make their
customers feel good about the buying experience,
$119. [Source: Better Than Money Corporation]

Howard Shenson Consultant's Cassettes—Mr. Shenson is probably the nation's leading authority on
starting, building, and maintaining a professional

consulting practice. Here he offers several multi-
cassette albums, often recorded live during his seminars, with the essence of his experience and knowledge. He begins with a seminar on how to build and
maintain your own part-time or full-time *Consulting
Practice*, three cassettes, $69. The *Practice Building
Seminars* cover, on six cassettes, getting clients to
seek you out, the first client meeting, avoiding giving
away services, advertising, getting referrals and recommendations, and promotional brochures, $79.
You can learn *How Consultants Can Build a Lucra-
tive Paid Speaking Business* (with Dotty Walters) on
three cassettes for $59. *Selling Consulting Services* is
on eight cassettes, $89. *Grantsmanship Consulting* (by
Dr. Harry Murphy) is all about how to get government and foundation grants for yourself and your
clients, on eight cassettes for $89. Finally, there is a
seminar on *How To Start and Promote Your Own
Newsletter* for profit and/or personal image building,
three cassettes, $59. All seminars include album,
most include a manual or other printed materials.
[Source: Howard L. Shenson, Inc.]

Finance and Accounting—An overview for non-financial managers, specifically designed to teach the
principles, practices, and vocabulary of business
finance. Topics covered in the 12 units of study (one
on each side of each cassette) include influencing
operating profit, overhead, making current and fixed
assets work, improving return, and the investment
decision. $295 for six cassettes and comprehensive
workbook in binder. [Source: Forum/Schrello]

Management By Objectives . . . And Results—George
L. Morrisey gives a specially prepared distillate of
his authoritative seminar, describing how to establish
realistic management objectives, and then how to set
priorities so as to spend time, talent, and money only
on the 'critical few' actions that get the results
sought. $295 for six cassettes and coordinated work-
book in binder. [Source: Forum/Schrello]

Lansford Cassettes—An impressive collection of audio-cassette talks and topics with each cassette generally 40-60 minutes long and usually accompanied
by lecture notes or outline. Among the titles: *Management by Objectives*, three cassettes, $89.95; *Behav-
ioral Approach to Management*, four cassettes, $99.95;
Building Basic Management Skills, four cassettes and
resource package, $119.95; *Coping Effectively with
Difficult People* (with Robert M. Bramson Ph.D.), six
cassettes and workbook, $149.95; *The Supervisor and
The Supervisory Function*, four cassettes, $99.95;
Group Leadership, four cassettes, $109.95; *Reloca-
tion: A Corporate Decision* and *Where Do You Draw
the Line?*, both games with one cassette and instructions, $59.95 each; *The Art of Interviewing*, four
cassettes, $119.95; *Statistics for the Non-Statistician*,
two cassettes, $49.95; *Making Management Less
Complex and More Fun—With Better Results*, four

cassettes and workbook, $109.95; *Employee Motivation and Organizational Behavior*, five cassettes, $129.95; and *Management Techniques for Women*, six cassettes and workbook, $245.95. [Source: Lansford Publishing Company]

Frontiers of Professional Management—Eight leading experts—William Amberg, Joe Batten, Peter Drucker, Frank Goble, Harold McAlindon, George Miller, Tom Paterson, and Reed Powell—summarize their ideas about management, on eight cassettes in album for $89.50. [Source: Thomas Jefferson Research Center]

Productivity: Getting Employees To Care—In this four-hour album, some of America's leading executives and management consultants describe their experiences and successes in increasing productivity. The emphasis is on the workplace application of motivational research to increase productivity in private and public, profit and nonprofit organizations and at all levels of supervision. $99.95 for four cassettes and summary book in album. [Source: Thomas Jefferson Research Center]

How Successful Managers Manage—Real 'people and behavior' skills (not untested theories) in a cassette/workbook training program that teaches good management by practicing it, by using behaviors and responses called for in given situations. $125 for seven cassettes, workbook, and applications manual. [Source: Jeffrey Norton Publishers, Inc.]

Becoming a Successful Businesswoman—Business is a game, says Ms. Betty L. Harragan, and she gives concrete pointers on how to approach the challenge of job hunting, promotions and raises, and success in moving up the corporate ladder, all on a single cassette for $10.95. Other management topics from this source include *Building a Management Philosophy* by Harold F. Puff, *Leadership in Union-Management Relations* by Ross Stagner, *Executive Selection* by Robert N. McMurry, and more, all $10.95 per title. [Source: Jeffrey Norton Publishers, Inc.]

Audio-Cassette/Workbook Programs—Practical interactive programs designed to give one the tools and techniques needed to increase on-the-job effectiveness. All programs include six one-hour cassettes, a comprehensive workbook, pre- and post-tests to be returned for grading and evaluation, and an album, for $145. Completion of each course is awarded with one Continuing Education Unit (CEU). Some of the titles available: *Finance and Accounting for Nonfinancial Managers, How to Improve Your Memory, How to Interview Effectively, How to Be a Successful Public Speaker, Total Time Management, Computer Fundamentals for the Manager, How to Be an Effective Supervisor, Effective Team Building, Successful Delegation, Managing Conflict, Constructive Discipline for Supervisors, How to Improve Customer Service, Guide for Executive Secretaries and Administrative Assist-*

ants, Communication Skills for Secretaries, Personal Selling Skills, How to Market by Telephone, Understanding and Managing Stress, Management by Objectives, Using Managerial Authority, Fundamentals of Budgeting, Managing Cash Flow, Achieving Computer Security, Basic Business Psychology, and *Practical TA for Managers.* [Source: American Management Associations]

Managing the Unsatisfactory Performer—Larry Steinmetz takes a down-to-earth approach to translate broad management concepts into straightforward advice one can put to use immediately in dealing with the 'problem employee'—now or in the future. $65 for six cassettes in album. [Source: General Cassette Corporation]

Face to Face Management and Motivation for the 80's—Joe Batten, renowned author of *Tough Minded Management*, provides an up-to-date look at all of the most effective interpersonal management skills and methods, and introduces new pathways to productivity more complete and practical than the 'quality circles' now in vogue. $89 for eight cassettes in album. [Source: General Cassette Corporation]

Ojai Leadership Laboratories—Men and women from the upper echelons of corporate, governmental, military, and educational organizations meet every other year to examine the dynamics of group life and administrative human relations skills. Keynote lectures by Richard Farson, John C. Glidewell, William Crockett, Martin Nalder, Abraham Kaplan, and Sherman Kingsbury have each been captured on cassettes, $15 each, or all ten cassettes in album for $130. [Source: University of California]

Personnel Management—One of the manager's most sensitive and important jobs comes under the detailed scrutiny of an expert in four related programs: *Selecting Employees*—factual nuts-and-bolts information useful for anyone involved in searching for, interviewing, and hiring new employees. $80 for eight cassettes in album; *Hiring & Firing*—mistakes in employment and termination waste time, create undue stress, and cost money. This album of eight cassettes explains how best to find, screen, interview, and hire new employees, how to resolve performance problems and other conflicts, and how to terminate an unsuitable employee, $80; *Managing People*—to aid the manager to obtain results through the efforts of others, this program covers the reinforcement of positive management techniques and introduces new techniques to help defuse potentially explosive situations, to motivate problem employees, and to build assertive skills. $80 for eight cassettes in album, $20 for a one-hour cassette of highlights; and *Performance Appraisal*—designed to help get maximum productivity from employees, these eight cassettes in album offers problem-solving guidelines for collecting employee performance data, conducting annual performance interviews, and relating performance to pay. $80. [Source: Fred Pryor Resource Corporation]

Basic Supervision—An hour of pointers on how to make the transition from worker to supervisor, from getting the job done to getting others to get their jobs done, $20; and a related program, helpful in meeting and solving problems in supervision, *Creative Assertiveness for Managers* which tells how to handle such perplexing problems as the high performer who is always late, the untruthful subordinate, the employee who overreacts to criticism. $20 for one cassette. [Source: Fred Pryor Resource Corporation]

Leadership Skills—Discussions on improving productivity and labor relations, increasing morale and commitment, expectations vs. motivation, correcting and coaching, effectively communicating the management position. $80 for eight cassettes and study guide in album. [Source: Fred Pryor Resource Corporation]

Customer Relations—Pointers for anyone representing their company to the outside world: public contact skills, establishing rapport and trust, handling complaints, telephone techniques. $20 for a one-hour cassette. [Source: Fred Pryor Resources Corporation]

Productive Interviewing—Five 45-60 minute programs—*The Selection Interview, Appraisal and Career Counseling Interviews, The Problem-Employee Interview, The Exit Interview, The Information Interview*—combining actual interviews with perceptive comments. $34.95 each. Of related interest is *Handling Employee Questions About Pay*, a 60-minute cassette and manual for $34.95. [Source: American Management Associations]

Agryris on Organization—Any organization is fundamentally people, and that is what Chris Agryris discusses: the problems of human behavior in a company organization. $114.95 for four 60-minute cassettes and booklet in album. How to handle some of the problems created by that human behavior is dealt with in *The Likerts on Managing Conflict* which gives case histories presented by Rensis and Jane Gibson Likert that demonstrate how to resolve conflict within an organization for better performance, morale, and profits. $139.95 for five 45- to 60-minute cassettes with manual and album. [Source: American Management Associations]

Drucker on Management—Peter Drucker's books are milestones in management thinking, and here he engages in unrehearsed give-and-take with eight executives. $225 for eight cassettes (six hours) and brochure in album. Also available: *The "How To" Drucker*, how to put new life, new opportunities, and new triumphs into your job. $139.95 for four 60-minute cassettes and manual in album. They also have *Bennis on Leaders* featuring the president of the University of Cincinnati, Warren Bennis, discussing leaders as an endangered species, leader's overload, leadership requirements, and the personal side of leadership. $125 for five C-45 cassettes and two booklets in album. [Source: American Management Associations]

Condensed Audio Books—The bestsellers on management, all condensed onto one-hour cassettes, for $15.95 each. Some of the titles and authors: *No-Nonsense Delegation*, by Dale D. McConkey; *Power in Management*, by John P. Kotter; *Goal Setting*, by Charles L. Hughes; *Advertising Pure and Simple*, by Hank Seiden; *The Art of Decision-Making*, by John D. Arnold; *The Self-Reliant Manager*, by John Cowan, *Muddling Through*, by Robert A. Golde; *Shirt-Sleeves Management*, by James F. Evered; and *Mackenzie on Time*, by Alex Mackenzie. [Source: American Management Associations]

The "How" of Strategic Planning—Dr. George A. Steiner provides conceptual models for large, medium, and small companies to demonstrate flexible, adaptive planning in times of rapid economic, regulatory, and technologic change. $129 for four 60-minute cassettes and manual in album. [Source: American Management Associations]

New Supervisor Audio Cassette Program—A complete learning system for the newly-promoted supervisor. He reads a chapter in the book *The New Supervisor* (included) covering one aspect of his new job, listens to the corresponding cassette, then completes an assignment in the learning guide. Topics include the new attitude toward the job, his subordinates, and the boss, relations with coordinates, communications, setting up the work and getting it done, motivation, interviewing, training, running meetings, problem-solving, presentations, and self-development and self-evaluation. $225 for 14 cassettes, book, and learning guide. For the more experienced there is *Practice of Supervising Audio Cassette Program*. By means of correlated cassettes, text, and learning guide, Martin M. Broadwell provides ten instructive training sessions covering motivation, discipline, team building, role of the supervisor, getting along with management, and performance appraisal. The goal of the course is to make experienced supervisors more effective on the job, both by bringing them up-to-date on current techniques and by providing basic supervisory training that was never previously received. $200 for 10 cassettes, text, learning guide, pretest and posttest, and instructor's guide, in storage box. [Source: Addison-Wesley Publishing Company]

Performance Appraisal Instruction Kit—All a trainer needs to assist a group of trainees practice the developmental activities from George Morrisey's book titled *Appraisal and Development Through Objectives and Results*. $80 for 40-minute cassette, leader's guide, appraisal forms, and binder. Related are two overview cassettes—George L. Morrisey on

Management and Results Overview and Jack Fordyce on *Organizational Development Overview*—$17.95 for each 45-55 minute cassette. [Source: Addison-Wesley Publishing Company]

Cassettes for Success—Skillfully produced by the AMACOM Division of the AMA, all these programs are packaged in albums with manual: *Computers & Communications: Their Management and Integration*, three cassettes, $85; *Basics of Management* and *Basics of Marketing Management*, each three cassettes, each $69.95; *Basics of Finance and Accounting* and *Basics of Personnel Management*, each four cassettes, each $79.95; *Self-Discovery for the Manager*, three cassettes, $59.95; *Clues to Executive Time Control*, four cassettes, $114.95; *Tough-Minded Team Building* (with Joe and Hal Batten), three cassettes, $89.95; *Putting the Motivation Back into Work*, three cassettes, $80; and *Productivity: Getting Employees to Care*, four cassettes, $99.95. [Source: American Management Associations]

XIII.
Occupations and Employment

Communication Skills for Succeeding in the World of Work—Five self-contained instructional packages, each consisting of four cassettes, 30 activity booklets, and leader's guide. These programs are prepared for youths and young minority adults unprepared for job-seeking. Package titles include: *Listening on the Job* (learning to listen, getting the message, keeping an open mind, improving listening habits) *Speaking on the Job* (using standard English, speaking clearly, using the telephone, correct pronunciation); *Getting a Job* (finding and applying, making a good impression, handling the interview); *Getting Along with People* (remembering names, reading between the lines, small talk, being friendly); and *Advancing on the Job* (getting a promotion, giving directions, managing other people, defining success). $60 per package. [Source: McKnight Publishing Company]

Careers/Health Services—Each tape presents the nature of the work in a specific occupation, probable earnings, educational requirements, and future prospects. Programs are available for physicians, dentists, dental hygienists and assistants, RN, LPN, various medical technicians, optometrists, pharmacists, podiatrists, chiropractors, various health therapists, dietitians and other hospital staff. $105 for 24 cassettes. Career Aids has "career" packages similar to the above covering careers in transportation and communication services, sales and service occupations, sciences, business occupations, various other trade occupations, professional careers, machinist and mechanic occupations, and manufacturing and agriculture, all for $105 each. Other programs hone in on specific occupations—paramedic, broadcast technician, computer programmer, beautician, dental hygienist, automotive mechanic, and paraprofessional teacher—on two cassettes for $24 each. Still other programs are aimed at young people who are not familiar with the processes of locating and applying for jobs, and give practical pointers on how to get a job and then, how to keep a job. [Source: Career Aids]

Creative Learning Center—This excellent collection of titles falls into three categories. First are some programs to help one get a job, covering the changing job market, the employment application, the job interview, upgrading a career, dropping out, what to do if fired. Related to this are three structured cassettes to build vocabulary. All these are $9 each. Then there are over 100 cassettes explaining the nature of certain jobs, their places of employment, education and/or training, and working conditions. These are $8 each. There are 25 cassettes that give occupational outlooks by industry, $8 each. Finally, there are programs aimed for employed persons and their managers, covering such topics as dealing with the public (six cassettes, $54), understanding consumer credit (three cassettes, $9 each), better business by telephone (six cassettes and guides, $54), starting and managing your own business (seven cassettes with support materials, $60), and (for the truly successful) a five-cassette series on the New York Stock Exchange ($45) and a cassette telling the story of municipal bonds, for $8. [Source: Creative Learning Center]

American Occupations—198 careers analyzed on 99 cassettes, each carefully prepared and researched to give guidance to the quest for a career that will satisfy aspirations, expectations, and abilities. $6 for each 30-minute cassette, all 99 for $580. [Source: ESP, Inc.]

Job Hunting Cassettes—Cassettes for the job hunter, with each devoted to a particular aspect of the job campaign, and each with a correlated booklet. *How To Write Successful Job Resumes* provides a step-by-step guide to putting a resume together so that it will open the door to the interview. *How To Write Better Application Letters* tells what to say, and what not to say, to get good results. *How To Make Job Interviews Bring Job Offers* demonstrates kinds of questions that will be asked of beginners and executives, and describes the best kind of answers. *How To Carry Out Job Campaigns* outlines the three stages: learn about yourself, find and study prospective employers; and approach employers. *Women: Careers and Risks* is for women, at any stage of their lives, who would like to pursue a career or who are thinking about it. $13 each, 3 for $36, 5 for $55. [Source: Council for Career Planning, Inc.]

XIV.
Personal Development

Metaphysical Growth/Consciousness

Manly P. Hall Cassettes—Six titles from the contemporary philosopher and student of comparative religions: *Why I Believe in Rebirth*; *My Philosophy of Life*; *The Face of Christ*; *Personal Security in a Troubled World*; *The Spirt of Zen*; and *The Guardian of the Light*. $5 each, all six in album for $25. [Source: Philosophical Research Society, Inc.]

Teachings of the Ascended Masters—The words of Archangel Michael, Jesus, Ra Mu, Micah, Zarathustra, Pallas Athena, Gautama Buddha, El Morya, Saint Germain, Archangel Uriel, and other "great souls of all ages who have transcended the schoolrooms of earth to unite with the Presence of God and serve hunanity from accelerated planes of consciousness"—by means of dictation to their earthly representatives, Mark L. Prophet (now the Ascended Master Lanello) and Elizabeth Clare Prophet. She also lectures on subjects as ethereal as soul-testing and heightened consciousness, as earthly as the hazards of Salt II and the sins of marijuana, and as paradoxical as the religious philosophy of Karl Marx and the economic philosophy of Jesus Christ. Most discourses include an album, generally cost $5 to $6 per cassette. [Source: Summit Lighthouse]

A.R.E. Cassettes—The Association of Research and Enlightenment is an organization devoted generally to parapsychology and its spiritual dimensions, and specifically, to making practical use of the readings of Edgar Cayce. Categories of individual lecture tapes ($5.98 each) are: business, dreams, healing and health, life and death, love, meditation and prayer, prophecy and pre-history, psychology and self-help, reincarnation and karma, and religion. Home-study courses, all based on the Edgar Cayce works, include: *Universal Laws*, four cassettes (5 hours of lecture), $24.95; *Meditation Course*, six cassettes (10 hours of instruction), $39.95; *Awakening the Dreamer: Dream Interpretation*, six cassettes (9 hours of lectures), $49.95; *Dimensions of Love: Practical Steps in Loving*, six cassettes, $49.95; *Vibrations*, six cassettes (9 hours of instruction), $29.95; and *Beyond Sugar and Spice: How Women Grow, Learn, and Thrive*, six cassettes, $49.95. All A.R.E. home-study courses include albums, supplemental printed materials, and usually texts. [Source: A.R.E.]

Naropa Institute Recordings—Lectures and discussions by Gregory Bateson, Joan and Stanislav Grof, John Maraldo, and Chogyam Trungpa Rinpoche, and others. Also under this banner are poetry readings by members of the Jack Kerouac School of Disembodied Poetics of Naropa Institute: Anne Waldman, Allen Ginsburg, Ted Berrigan, William Burroughs, Philip Whalen, and Chogyam Trungpa Rinpoche. $10 per cassette. [Source: Vajradhatu and Naropa Recordings]

Seventh Sense Mind-to-Mind Healing Course—In this 10-cassette course, Ben Bibb shows how anyone can heal a diseased person by reaching the patient's inner mind, informing it of the danger to the body, and demonstrating a method that will lead to cure. In addition to this basic 'mind-to-mind' healing, Mr. Bibb also covers the uses of the aura to cleanse the body of impure cells and promote healing, and especially emphasizes correcting hormonal imbalances and rejecting cancer cells with psychic exercises. This one might be construed as a tiny bit unusual, but there are those who swear by it. $60 for 10 cassettes and reading materials in an album. [Source: Seventh Sense Institute]

Automated Learning—Gives you a variety of titles: *How to Develop Your Creative Mind Powers*, *How to Get Command Persuasion*, *The Universal Mind*, *Psychic Healing*, *Pyramid Energistics*, *ESP for Power-Making Decisions*, *Psi Talents*, *Psychic Energies Against Pain*, *Space-Age ESP*, *Alter Your Consciousness Without Drugs*, *The Amazing Fascitarr*, *Metaphysical Commands*, *The Secret of Perfect Living*, and *How to Rule Your Own Life*. [Source: Automated Learning, Inc.]

Learning Curve—One-hour mini-course consisting of a C-60 cassette, programmed exercise and test on *Facts of Astrology*. $9.98. [Source: Metacom, Inc.]

Rosicrucian Tape Recordings—Thought-provoking discourses that expound the Rosicrucian Order's metaphysical and physical philosophy and describe the significance and application of the cosmic and natural laws that surround us. Two lectures on each cassette, with total times ranging from 25 to 60 minutes. Some Spanish-language programs also available. $6.50 each. [Source: Rosicrucian Supply Bureau]

The Well of Wisdom—Anthony J. 'Tony' Fisichella (the 'Guru of Hicksville') leads the listener through an understanding of the world of esoteric thought and parapsychological principles, such as karma, reincarnation, the cosmic constitution of man, psychic healing, acupuncture, kirlian photography, altered states of consciousness available through various forms of meditation, and various mind-expansion techniques. $12.95 for each cassette, all ten in album for $129.50. [Source: ARC Systems]

Pathways to Mastership—A two-volume course developed by Jonathan Parker, a leading metaphysical counselor and teacher, intended to help the listener open new levels of awareness, consciousness, and personal growth. More than two dozen guided meditations to aid in releasing inner energies and creative powers, achieving freedom from guilt, fear, and worry, and gaining greater spiritual realization. $62.95 for each album of six cassettes, both albums for $101.95. [Source: Institute of Human Development]

Piercing Illusions—10 intensive one-hour presentations by Jonathan Parker, enhanced with meditations, giving indepth discussions on the nature of reality and illusion—an advanced metaphysical teaching program intended for those who have completed *Pathways to Mastership*. $83.45 with album. Designed to follow the *Piercing Illusions* course is *Epilogue*, a three-cassette course with album for $31.45. Less advanced metaphysical teaching is included in these three-cassette albums: *Recreate Your Future* (with guided visualizations and meditations); *Especially for Children* (six cassettes, $52.70); *Especially for Teens*; *Coping with Emotions*; *Love Series*; *Pathways to Power*; *New Age Hypnosis*; and *Land of Magic* (ancient Egyptian secrets). Individual tapes ($10.95 each) cover past and parallel lives, banishing evil, talking with animals, psychic powers, trance channeling, and more. [Source: Institute of Human Development]

Inner Circle Teachers of Light—Recordings of the voices of 16 beings from the past, speaking through a medium, Mark Probert, to give their interpretations of occult philosophy. The chief entity is Yada Di Shi'ite, who lived 500,000 years ago in the Himalayan civilization of Yuga; another is Alfred Luntz (1812-1893), an Episcopal clergyman in England. Each cassette covers one seance, runs from 30 to 150 minutes, costs from $11 to $20. Interesting catalog for $2. [Source: Universal Life Church, Inc.]

Lectures by Dr. Stephan Hoeller—Modern Jungian psychological views of modern and ancient religion, modern and ancient mystical traditions (including the Kabbala and astrology), and divination (including tarot and I Ching). Dr. Hoeller also discusses the Gnostic Gospels, Gnostic psychology, and Jungian parapsychology. $6 per cassette. [Source: Gnostic Society]

Encountering the Shining Stranger—A seminar by Winifred Babcock on Preston Harold and his unorthodox interpretation of Jesus and His mission, and from it, a new approach to the art of healing, the use of psychic power, and enlarged consciousness of self and the human potential. $42 for six cassettes, plus (if desired) $12 for transcript. [Source: Harold Institute]

Seminars with Seth—Seth is an entity who has lived all of his physical lives and now exists as an energy essence, speaking through medium Thomas Massari to help us realize our abilities and create our realities. Topics of the seminars include the death experience, healing (two parts), dreams (two parts), supplying the self with abundance, and spirituality and Jesus. These are $10 each. He also has four cassettes ($40) called *The Planets*, with a basic meditation on side 1, and on side 2 a trip to a different planet (conscious awareness, peace, subconscious understanding, and super-conscious love), which are all aspects of our being. [Source: Seminars with Seth]

New Age Light—Dr. Eileen Morgan offers tapes "to take you to Alpha and impress your subconscious mind with your desire". *Prosperity* attunes your mind to receiving money, *Perfect Mate* assures your inner conscious there is the right person for you in your life, and *Cosmic Light Attunement* is a meditation exercise to open the chakras. $10 each. [Source: New Age Light]

Living Library—Cassette messages by Dr. William Hornaday, leader of Science of Mind, the largest metaphysical church in the world. These are $7.95 each. *Golden Classics* are ten talks taken from the network radio broadcasts of Ernest Holmes, the founder of Science of Mind, for $6.95 each. Finally, *Explorations in Healing* are a collection of cassette recordings by pioneer leaders sharing their ideas, feelings, and discoveries about how the power of mind can accomplish mental/spiritual/psychic healing, $6.95 each. [Source: Science of Mind Publications]

Kathryn Kuhlman Cassettes—A collection of radio broadcasts with the lyric voice of the late Miss Kuhlman. Each 30-minute cassette contains two of her inspirational talks, sometimes with testimonies and music, for $5 donation. Longer cassettes—*Baptism of the Holy Spirit* and *An Hour with Kathryn Kuhlman*—are $5.25 each. [Source: Kathryn Kuhlman Foundation]

Vernon Howard Life-Healing Tapes—Mr. Howard is noted for the simplicity and directness with which he presents the most profound principles of inner development. Here he offers 40 90-minute messages aimed at helping people end their physical and mental roaming and begin focusing on their true purpose in life. Some typical titles? *Your Richest Investment in Life, How To Be Safe from Human Sharks, Practical*

Exercises for Inner Harmony, How To Turn Off Sinister Voices, End Mental Blocks and Soar Freely, and *Live with Yourself in Comfort.* $7 each. [Source: New Life Foundation]

Cornucopia Training Tapes—A wide selection of lectures, questions, and answers on a variety of topics for increased awareness, led by Ken Keyes, Jr., author of *The Handbook to Higher Consciousness,* and Carole Thompson, director and co-founder of Cornucopia. The tapes describe the skills that can be acquired through training for creating more happiness and prosperity. They teach how to relate to children, parents, lovers, spouses, and co-workers, and how to deal with addictions and other blocks to human creativity and potential. $5 for each 40- to 90-minute cassette. [Source: Living Love Publications]

Alphanetics—A technique for reprogramming both the subconscious mind (to obliterate the negative self-images imprinted during the impressionable childhood years) and the conscious mind (to permit controlled access into the 'alpha state', associated with creative periods). A "tax-deductible contribution of $121 to this nonprofit educational organization" (their words, not ours!) brings you 10 training cassettes in an album plus research reports, focalizer, booklets, membership certificate, and subscription to the official journal. [Source: Life Dynamics Fellowship]

University of the Trees Cassettes—Dr. Christopher Hills—yogi, philosopher, and scientist—discusses the nature of consciousness and teaches how to reprogram your subconscious mind with new essence knowledge. In *Awakening the Kundalini Fire* he shows how to use guided meditation to transform ordinary consciousness into bliss. *Faith in Self* teaches how to turn every problem in life into a joyous solution. Follow the guided meditation on *Opening the Intuition* and "drink in the cosmic fluids ... to fuel your etheric body." And there's more, all $8 for a 60-minute talk. [Source: University of the Trees]

The Discovery Program—A series of training exercises on six stereo cassettes with detailed guidance manual to permit full exploration of human mind potential. This is achieved by use of patterns of sound waves applied binaurally (different and independent signals in each ear) to synchronize the hemispheric activity of the brain. $95 for the set, in album. Less involved are their single-cassette packages: *Concentration* (to focus complete attention on any activity) and *Retain, Recall, Release* (total memory control), $11.95 each, both for $22; *Cat Napper* (relax and recharge in 30 minutes of special sleep), *Sound Sleeper* (a non-drug answer to insomnia), and *Super Senses—Touch* (to increase or decrease your sense of touch), all $11.95 each; and finally, *Under-Par Golf* and *Love Tennis,* to lower and increase your scores, respectively, $15.95 each. [Source: Mentronics Systems Inc.]

New Dimensions Tapes—"Not lectures, but rare glimpses into the essence of human consciousness," with Patricia Sun and her *Visions of Light, Dream Dynamics* with Michael Daddio, *Revelations* with Barbara Marx Hubbard, Stephen Levine and *Awakening to Life,* Ram Dass and *Notes Along the Way,* Salvadore Roquet and *Hallucinogens in Therapy,* and many more. These are $7.50 per cassette hour, with most presentations ranging from 1 to 2 hours in length. [Source: New Dimensions Tapes]

Motivation for Success

Human Motivation Cassettes—Programs developed by a clinical psychologist to aid those interested in self-improvement, each based on the latest principles of human behavior. Some of the topics covered: college stress, marriage and sex, self-hypnosis, relaxation training, weight loss and smoking cessation, executive and childhood stress. $25.95 for each hour-long tape. Other titles from this source: *Death and Dying* (with Edwin S. Schneidman), two cassettes and reprints, $65.95; *Skinnerism* (the analysis of behavior, mostly with Skinner himself), ten cassettes, $139.95; and *Goldstein: The Nature of Anxiety,* $19.95 for one cassette. [Source: Lansford Publishing Company]

True Cassettes—In these 30- to 50-minute self-development programs, Dr. Herb True alternates humor and motivational reinforcement ideas to provide stimulation for salespeople, managers, and parents. Mostly recorded before live audiences, some of the titles are: *Motivation* (secrets of using mirth to motivate, inspire, elevate); *Selling* (focusing on the human side); *Love* (replacing the love of power with the power of love); and *Management* (why people do what they do.) A couple of thought-starter cassettes (*Greatness/Boldness* and *Enthusiasm/Funnybone*) provide short vignettes for personal listening or group discussion stimulation. All cassettes $10 each. [Source: American Humor Guild]

Excel—An audio-cassette training program designed to help listeners increase personal performance and achievement by showing them how to make more effective use of their existing potential. Not just another set of inspirational messages, but an explanation of how obstructions are built into the human system to block effective performance, and how to overcome these blocks to achieve higher levels of performance and personal satisfaction. The *Basic Concepts Program* consists of two 60-minute cassettes and a reference guide, for $19.95. Then, for $9.95 each, there are 24 *Individual Specific Personal Performance* tapes covering such topics as: more effective memory, decision-making, salesmanship, problem-solving, communications; improving self-confidence, scholastic achievement, and constructive thinking; weight loss and control; better golf, tennis, bowling; and parent and youth effectiveness training, among others. [Source: Harris Communications]

Bob Richards—The Olympic champion offers ten cassette titles: *Just a Little More—Positive*; *The Greatness in You*; *Atmosphere of Greatness*; *There's Genius in the Average Man!*; *Life's Higher Goals*; *Will of a Champion*; *Response to the Challenge*; *Motivation for Living*; *Pride of a Champion*; and *The Best Is Yet To Be*. $15 for each C-30 cassette. [Source: Bob Richards Attainment Institute]

Success with People—Six half-hour motivational talks by Cavett Robert, emphasizing his point that sales people should know their product . . . but think people. On *How To Get What Ya Want . . . with What Ya Got!* he is joined by Merlyn Cundiff (an authority on body language) in a program of self-motivation for success. Both albums are $50 for six half-hour talks. [Source: Planned Achievements]

Success Cassettes—Two-cassette motivational albums of talks that expound the 'positive mental attitude' of Success Unlimited (and of its founder, W. Clement Stone). Mr. Stone capsulizes his beliefs in *Success System. Zig at the Rally* features Zig Ziglar recorded live before an SU rally. *Schuller and Peale* is a talk apiece by Dr. Robert Schuller ('life is filled with exciting possibilities') and Dr. Norman Vincent Peale ('free yourself from fears and self doubt'). Dr. Peale also contributes three albums, *Listen to Life*, that deal with self-fulfillment. George Odiorne has two albums on *Management by Objectives*, and Cavett Robert has one on *Prospecting and Human Engineering*. All albums are $19.95 each. Other individual cassettes of famous, classic, and inspiring motivational talks are available for $8.95 each—and some of these are also included in other two-cassette albums. Examples include *Diamonds and Power* (*Acres of Diamonds*, by Dr. Russell H. Conwell, and *Your Greatest Power*) and *Destiny and Compensation* (*As a Man Thinketh* and Ralph Waldo Emerson's famous essay on *Compensation*). Among the other individual cassette titles are *The Other Wise Man*, by Henry Van Dyke, *The Greatest Salesman in the World*, by Og Mandino, and *Think and Grow Rich*, by Napoleon Hill. Finally, Dr. George Odiorne reveals *Six Great Secrets of Personal and Business Success* on six cassettes in album for $39.95. [Source: Success Unlimited]

Getting Things Done—A step-by-step review by Ed Bliss of the techniques of time control that can help one overcome such problems as procrastination, paperwork, delegation, self-discipline, interruptions, planning, and much more. This program is guaranteed: if you don't gain at least an additional hour of productive time each day after listening to each tape three times, you get your money back. $59.50 for six cassettes in album. [Source: Edwin C. Bliss & Associates]

Strategies for Daily Living—Cornell psychiatrist Ari Kiev offers a variety of messages designed both to inspire people to move forward toward their most prized goals and to provide guidelines for effective

actions to accomplish those goals. He has messages on modifying behavior, developing self-reliance, conserving resources, improving relationships, managing time, fear, and stress, and helps with the specific problems of alcoholism, drug abuse, faulty communication, suicide prevention, and crisis intervention. $13.50 each, or any five for $52.50. [Source: Psychodynamic Research Corporation]

Thought Dynamics—Why hope that you 'have a good day,' when, by changing attitudes and developing new skills, you can 'make it a good day,' says psychologist William C. Tanner, Jr. Ph.D. He tells how to accomplish this by the use of three psychological techniques: picturing (affirmation-visualization), creative-relaxation (self-hypnosis) and assumption-assertion. The first four cassettes in this course show how to change attitudes, and the last six demonstrate how to apply them in specific areas: weight loss, communication in marriage, remembering made easy, and persuading and selling others. $10 each, all ten cassettes in album for $75. [Source: Thought Dynamics]

The Second Greatest Story Ever Told—In this four-cassette album, Lewis Timberlake stresses goal-setting and improved self-image. He shows that transforming one's self-image requires primarily an understanding of the self-image of others, discusses the principles that lay behind personal failure, gives keys to raising personal motivation levels, and offers the steps to use of your personal power to persist and to surpass. $39.95. [Source: Timberlake and Associates]

Goal-Achievement System—Ron Willingham developed this specific guide to goal setting, which can be used individually, with families, or in business. The two cassettes give a step-by-step process for defining objectives, building belief, developing necessary strength, and evaluating progress toward the goals. $22 including album. [Source: Ron Willingham Courses, Inc.]

Winning Behavior—"If you are not achieving the success in life you want, it's because your goals lack clarity, definition and direction," according to Greg Esch—and here he provides guidelines to help focus goals toward success, on five cassettes and text for $295. From the same source is a related program on *Personal Development and Successful Marketing* in which Greg Esch offers specifics to help individuals become motivated on a daily basis and thereby create an environment around them that can lead to greater marketing success. $375 for six cassettes and text. [Source: Goals Unlimited]

Live Long and Prosper!—Jerry Gillies, author of *Moneylove* and *Psychological Immortality*, gives strategies on how to have more money, success, time, creativity, love, and life. His emphasis is on life as an art, not a competition, and urges listeners to overcome their 'fixed income mentalities' and their parent-induced depression fears. Above all, he stresses that people who have fun earning a living earn the most. CIS recommends this one, especially for those in the throes of 'burnout' or those facing retirement. $59.95 for six cassettes in album. [Source: Jerry Gillies]

Nightingale-Conant Listening Library—*Lead the Field* is Earl Nightingale's all-time best seller, covering six different aspects of successful living, improving attitudes, setting goals, and improving earnings. *Great Ideas* is Mr. Nightingale's offering of ideas to enhance the image you project and to effectively communicate and sell your ideas to others. What is the greatest goal that you could possibly imagine yourself achieving? Dr. Robert H. Schuller (creator of TV's 'Hour of Power') shows how to use *Possibility Thinking* to turn it into reality. In *The Psychology of Winning*, behavioral scientist Dr. Denis E. Waitley discusses the 10 qualities of a total winner, then shows how to match winning attitudes with winning behavior for greater success. Dr. Wayne Dyer (author of *Your Erroneous Zones*) shows how you can control almost everything in your life and thus *How To Be a No-Limit Person*. *Success Is a State of Mind*, says noted psychologist Dr. Joyce Brothers, as she tells how to get the most out of every aspect of your life. *Earl Nightingale: Success Series* contains six classic talks by the master motivator covering ideas for achieving greater wealth, happiness, and peace of mind. In *Creative Thinking*, creative counselor Mike Vance offers practical, time-tested creative principles and procedures to enhance problem-solving skills and creative abilities. Dr. Sidney Lecker gives nine principles that can be learned and developed into a wealth-making system that works for you, in *The Science of Getting Rich*. These are both six-cassette albums for $60. *Kop's Keys to Success and Happiness* contains M. R. Kopmeyer's 71 lessons and 250 success methods for getting whatever you want out of life, $80 for 12 cassettes and guide in album. Finally, *Direct Line* is a series of three six-cassette albums offering ideas for speeches, meetings, dialogues, sales and management bulletins, business and social conversations, covering imaginative leadership, personal growth, economics, and study and planning. $60 for all courses, each consisting of six cassettes and guides in album. [Source: Nightingale-Conant Corporation]

How To Stay Motivated—Zig Ziglar, the "Will Rogers of the South", tells it all on eight cassettes (12 hours of material) plus a book and goal planner for $89.95. *The Goals Program* contains three cassettes on the why's and how's of goal setting and reaching, for $39.95 plus book. *Daily Christian Motivation* has six tapes by Mr. Ziglar on motivation from a Christian viewpoint, in an album plus a book for $49.95. *Motivation for Educators & Students* has two tapes by Zig Ziglar and one by Mamie McCullough in an

album for $19.95. *America the Beautiful* is a 90-minute motivational sales talk on the present and future of our country, while *Biscuits, Fleas, and Pump Handles* is 78 minutes of down-home advice on health, wealth, and happiness, $9.95 each. [Source: Zig Ziglar Corporation]

Neuropsychology of Achievement—A program that goes beyond relaxation and guided imagery to show how to use the five senses and the nervous system to focus the electromagnetic energy of the brain. The program first concentrates on 21 dominant characteristics, thinking patterns, and habits common among high-achievers, and then teaches the listener a step-by-step discipline that allows the brain to acquire, and assimilate, those ideal skills and behaviors and then transform them into reality. $150 for six one-hour cassettes and study guide in album. [Source: Sybervision Systems, Inc.]

Productivity and Your Self Image—45 minutes of sales ideas nd motivation by Tim Connor, author of *The Soft Sell*, $10. Related is *How To Overcome the Fear of Failure and Rejection*, also by Tim Connor, offering practical tips on how to deal with these demotivators and how to overcome them for a more productive career and life, $12.95. In the same vein is Dr. Richard R. Gallagher's *Motivation and Productivity*, analyzing the classical and current theories of Maslow, Herzberg, McGregor, Taylor, Argyris, and White, $15 with study guide. [Source: Tutor/Tape]

Challenge to Succeed—Jim Rohn offers practical guidelines that virtually anyone can use for improving attitude, performance, and lifestyle, in a motivating blend of inspiration, ideas and humor. $69 for six cassettes in album. Then there's the *Leadership Seminar with E. James Rohn*, a live 12-hour seminar that covers communication skills, effective leadership, financial independence, goal setting, time management, and game planning. $95 for eight cassettes in album. [Source: Professional Cassette Center]

Mark Victor Hansen—The noted speaker and motivator offers 3 four-cassette albums for $50 each: *How to Achieve Total Prosperity* teaches one to develop 'money consciousness,' earn and spend money profitably, and then use the prosperity philosophy to get rich and stay rich. *How to Outperform Yourself Totally* emphasizes a positive self-image, the constructive and creative use of your mind, the importance of setting high goals, and the importance of verbalizing and visualizing every desire in order to realize it. *Love 2 U* simply shows how anyone can become a nicer person, in the eyes of others, and far more important, in his or her own eyes. [Source: Mark Victor Hansen]

Success Motivation Cassettes—More than 100 cassette tape condensations of best selling books about success and sales, management, personal development, family life, and physical fitness: *I'm Okay— You're Okay* by Thomas Harris, M.D.; *The Magic of*

Believing by Claude M. Bristol; *The Greatest Sales-man in the World* by Og Mandino; *Think and Grow Rich* by Napoleon Hill; *Getting Through to People* by Jesse S. Nirenberg; *Passages* by Gail Sheehy; *Power of Goal Setting* by Paul J. Meyer; *Psycho-Cybernetics* by Maxwell Maltz, M.D.; *You Can Beat The Odds on A Heart Attack* by Irwin M. Levitas, and more, with new titles added each quarter. $11.95 each. [Source: Success Motivation International, Inc.]

SMI—An outstanding collection of leadership and personal development motivation courses from one of the pioneers in the field. The Success Motivation Institute Division offers *Success Planner, Dynamics of Goal Setting, Dynamics of Creative Selling, Executive Motivation Program, Dynamics of Financial Freedom, Dynamics of Personal Time Control,* and *Sales Manager's Motivation Program.* The Leadership Management, Inc. Division offers *Dynamics of Personal Leadership, Dynamics of Motivational Management, Dynamics of Supervision, Executive Motivation Program, Executive Time Management,* and *Skills for Dealing with People.* Both divisions also offer *Creative Family Living, Life in the Teens,* and *Adventures in Growth.* Each multi-cassette course comes with extensive workbooks, manuals, and texts. Prices range from $150 to $750 per course. Selected courses are available in ten languages in addition to English. [Source: Success Motivation International, Inc.]

Mindswap—A 40 to 60-minute monthly magazine in sound, presenting a variety of personal development and better living ideas, interviews with leading motivators and authors, excerpts from live motivational and personal growth seminars and recorded courses, and articles on goal-setting, time management, tax savings, sales skills, creativity, communications, and success. $89 a year for ten issues. [Source: General Cassette Corporation]

High Performance Behavior—James W. Newman shows how to use the PACE system to release the full scope of an individual's potential, and thereby allow him or her to reach goals with greater ease and speed. The program specifically aims at teaching individuals to respond to problems and pressures positively, so that they "turn you on rather than tie you up." $60 for six cassettes in album. There's also *The Maximum Performer* in which Dave Grant, founder of the Growth Process Institute, presents a comprehensive, action-oriented program that provides many specific how-to techniques: how to eliminate fear, make enough money, build lasting relationships, be the person you want to be, identify and understand other people's needs, and make things happen (things you want to have happen). $115 for 12 cassettes in album. [Source: General Cassette Corporation]

The Official Guide To Success—Motivational and inspirational techniques, with master sales trainer Tom Hopkins showing how to take control with positive attitude skills, and how to: increase self-image, function creatively without need for approval, control negative thought patterns, change behavior patterns, make procrastination pay, set priorities and use self-discipline, overcome worry, and more. $75 for six cassettes in album. [Source: Tom Hopkins Champions Unlimited]

Motive-Action—In this easy to listen-to cassette, Arthur Bauer explains his philosophy of motivation: persuade someone to do what *you* want them to do because *they* want to do it. He discusses the two types of motivation, the four motivators, 10 ways to kill motivation, 20 motivational techniques, and more. In *The Magic in Selling*, Mr. Bauer applies his fundamentals of motivation specifically to selling. $14.95 for each 30-minute cassette. [Source: American Media Incorporated]

Dave Johnson Seminars—Four six-cassette albums by the master motivator and salesman: *Super Thrust Goal Setting* (there are no unrealistic goals, only improper time frames), *Million Dollar Effective Sales Procedures* (steps and points to build rapport, overcome objections, and increase sales), *How To Turn Disgustomers Into Immediate Sales* (effective sales/educational/psychological formulas), and *Dare To Be an Inner Winner* ('you can't sell yourself to others if you aren't sold on yourself'). $65 each, three for $140, all four for $175. [Source: David Johnson Seminars]

Doc Blakely—Humorous yet inspirational talks, recorded live: *To Soar with Eagles* blends laughter and the philosophy of success, while *Accent on Laughter* features stories told in a variety of national dialects, including Texan. $10 each. [Source: Doc Blakely]

Bill Gove on Cassette—Motivating talks by the former 3M sales development manager: *Billy Be Yourself* (classic advice to his son); *Time—Its New Dimensions* (how to add minutes and hours to each day); *People Love to Buy* (verbal reminders); and *Whatever Sets You Free* (go into every relationship as an equal). $7.95 for each 20-40 minute cassette. A special offering is *H.I.T.* (*Hang in Tough*), a two-cassette mix of meat and humor that shows how to increase assertiveness and feel comfortable while doing it, $14.50 with album. [Source: Bill Gove]

Realizing Potential

Personal Adjustment—Dr. Carl Rogers discusses the importance of being the person you are, and of accepting and understanding your role as well as that of others. $84.50 for ten C-30 cassettes in album. Other topics by Dr. Rogers: *How To Use Encounter Groups* in two 10-cassette albums for $78.95 and one six-cassette album for $47.95 (all of them for $189.95); *Carl Rogers—Some Basic Views,* a dialogue with Paul Tillich, $59.50 for five C-60 cassettes with transcripts; and *Carl Rogers in Retrospect,* recorded between 1960 and 1964, $64.95 for six C-60 cassettes in album. [Source: Instructional Dynamics, Inc.]

Encountertapes—The result of a six-year research project on the self-directed or leaderless small group setting, these programs provide suitable opportunities for a person to participate directly in experiences which can contribute to his or her individual growth. Most require several sessions (although can be done in "marathon" settings), and are planned for groups of 6 to 12 people. Encountertapes are available for the following subjects: personal growth, ten cassettes and manual in album, $69.95; employee and team development, ten cassettes, manual, and 36 participant notebooks, $139.60; vocational education, four cassettes, manual, and 36 participant booklets, $79.50; and single adult groups, six cassettes, manual and 'Encounterbats', $74.45. [Source: Instructional Dynamics, Inc.]

Assertive Training for Groups—Discussions by two clinical psychologists plus exercises designed to facilitate the learning of assertiveness—standing up for what you think are your rights $89.50 for six C-60 cassettes and leader's guide in album. [Source: Instructional Dynamics, Inc.]

Workshop Cassettes—Talks on the human potential movement, mostly recorded during Esalen long-term and special workshops, and covering the current work taking place at Esalen Institute. Some of the single tape titles and speakers: *LSD and the Nature of Reality*, Albert Hofmann; *Zen*, Reb Andersen; *On the Evolutionary Bio-Process*, Frank Barr; *On the Evolution of Human Culture*, William Irwin Thompson; *Good and Evil*, Rollo May and Daniel Ellsberg; *Vitamin C and Cancer*, Linus Pauling; *Hasidic and Sufi Teaching Stories*, James Fadiman; and more. These are $9 for each 60 to 90 minute cassette. There are two-tape titles for $16 each: *Fairy Stories for Men and Women*, by Robert Bly; *Energy Awareness and Transformation*, George Leonard; *A Psychic Training Program*, Ann and Jim Armstrong; *Interplay of Mind and Body Realities*, Andrew Weil; *The Possible Human*, Jean Houston, and more. [Source: Dolphin Tapes]

Dolphin Series—A distinguished collection of personal growth talks, designed to enhance human potential. Titles of some of the talks, the speakers, and the number of 60 to 90 minute cassettes involved: *Transformations of Myth Through Time*, Joseph Campbell, 4; *Nature, Mind and Consciousness*, Stanislav Grof, 4; *Awareness Through Movement: The Feldenkraid Method*, Ruthy Alon, 6; *Insight and Ecstasy*, Joseph Chilton Pearce, 8; *The Pajaro Dunes Tapes: A Weekend Seminar*, Buckminster Fuller, 8; and many more. Cost is $10 per cassette prepaid, including an album. *The Gregory Bateson Archive Tapes* contain his 'informal Esalen lectures' (1975-1980) on two albums of six cassettes each, $60 each or both for $98. Finally, the *John C. Lilly Tape Series* is a collection of individual cassettes with the

distinguished scientist and mystic describing his work in dolphin-human communications, sensory isolation, mid-brain relationships, and mind-body explorations into inner space, all of them $10 per hour. [Source: Dolphin Tapes]

Pace-Setter High Performance Program—All of us have a lot of potential that we aren't fully using. This program shows how to release that potential, allowing one's ability to flow freely, spontaneously, naturally and consistently. $240 for 13 cassettes, chartbook, planbooks, exercise packets and reminders, plus affirmation review service. The two *Key-Point Review Tapes* offer a fast-moving review of the entire PACE program (80 minutes) for $25. *Releasing Human Potential* is a seminar led by Jim Newman (founder of PACE) presenting his concepts to a live audience, on four hour-long cassettes in an album for $62.50. [Source: PACE Organization]

Laughing, Loving and Living Your Way to the Good Life—Ed Foreman and his "Successful Life Associates" offer this course, subtitled 'How to Have a Good Day Every Day'. Their philosophy is that you must know specifically and exactly what you really want from life; when you do, their course will show how, consciously and subconsciously, to develop a plan that will take you, one small step at a time, to these goals. $69.50 for eight cassettes in album. Also available is a four-cassette album, *Winning is a Developed Habit*, featuring Ed Foreman, Zig Ziglar and Cavett Robert, for $35. You can have both albums for $95, and a one-hour highlights cassette costs only $10. [Source: Executive Development Systems]

Rochelle Myers—Ms. Myers offers tapes to help promote exploration, clarification and resolution of complicated issues in our lives. Some of her titles: *Finding Creative New Solutions to Stale Old Problems*; *All About Rejection*; *On Judgment*; *Happily Married, Happily Single*; *Listening As An Instrument of Healing*; and *On Making Good Mistakes*. $10 each. [Source: Creative Resources]

Self-Directed Assertiveness Training—A program for therapists and counselors, to help clients become constructively assertive. Using real-life situations, the program shows how and when to say 'no', when assertion is an appropriate positive response, and when not to be assertive. $45 for four hour-long cassettes, client workbook, and therapist manual in album. [Source: BMA Cassettes]

New Dimensions for Personal Development—Six cassettes, four workbooks, and a text provide a complete self-improvement kit for any achiever, with emphasis on taking charge, getting what you want, and handling change. $195 including two album/binders. [Source: Professional Cassette Center]

Assertion Training—This two-cassette program begins by defining assertive, non-assertive, and aggressive behaviors, and then shows how to develop an assertive stance and how to apply assertion in various situations, $69.95. A related topic is *The Shy Child In Us All*, with shyness pioneer Philip Zimbardo and Shirley Radl presenting the causes of shyness and telling how to overcome it, on two cassettes for $49.95. [Source: Lansford Publishing Company]

Positive Self-Concept—The emphasis in this four-cassette program is on what you can do to help yourself and others maintain a positive self-concept, $99.95. A related title is *Self-Concept: Psycho-Cybernetics and Positive Development*, with advanced techniques for enhancing positive self-image in six cassettes for $149.95. [Source: Lansford Publishing Company]

Art of Positive Living—Barby Eide offers some different techniques for personal and professional development, to aid the listener in understanding mate, children, friends and co-workers, and above all him or her self. $65 for six cassettes in an album. Other offerings include single cassettes on *You Don't Have to Be in Who's Who To Know What's What*, *The Art of Positive Nonverbal Communication*, *The Art of Positive Time Management*, *How To Be A Super Secretary*, and *Understanding Your Dreams*, at $10 each. [Source: Barby Fairbanks Eide]

Women's Liberation and the New Myths of Motherhood—Lectures by Shirley Radl, author of *Mother's Day is Over* on the perils of moving too rapidly into 'liberated womanhood' until the attendant problems have been studied and resolved. It's on two cassettes with a book of $65.95. [Source: Lansford Publishing Company]

To Be a Woman—Straightforward, understanding insights into the physical, emotional, spiritual, and relational dimensions of womanhood, by Dr. James C. Dobson. His themes include childbirth, dealing with daughters, premenstrual tension, overweight, submission, tough love, adultery, husband's mid-life crisis, the single mother, mothers of teens, widowhood, and more. $89.95 for 12 cassettes, transcripts, and discusson guides in album. Related is *His Stubborn Love*, Joyce Landorf's Christian-based messages of hope, self-esteem, and encouragement for women (soundtrack of her film series), six cassettes and study guides in album for $34.95. [Source: Word, Inc.]

Your Child's Self-Esteem—How to help your child develop this most fundamental basis for successful living. Also, *First Time Out*, for teenagers living away from home. $10.95 each for these single cassette condensed books. [Source: Metacom, Inc.]

Guided Visualizations—Personal guides to help create images 'in the mind's eye' that will help "achieve your goals, develop your imagination, awaken your intuition, expand your mind—and have fun doing it." Titles of the cassettes are *Exercise Your Inner Eye*, *The Force (and How To Use It)*, *ESP and Visualization*, *Getting Well with Healing Imagery*, *Creative Dreaming*, *Self-Relaxation Course* and *Attracting Your Perfect Mate*. $9.98 each, any three for $25. [Source: Guided Visualizations]

Balanced Living—Bob and Zonnya Harrington offer alternative solutions to the out-of-balance conditions that all of us experience at times. They offer these albums to show how to put 'balance' into your physical, mental, spiritual, social, financial, and family lives: *You Can Make 'It' Happen*, three C-60 cassettes, $29.95; *Balanced Living Is Success*, six C-50 cassettes, $79.95; and *Super Star Selling*, six C-60 cassettes plus workbook. Several single cassette programs—on how to develop self-confidence, increase thoughts and actions, handle depression, control stress, and enjoy better family relationships—are available for $10 each. [Source: Balanced Living]

Self-Assertion: Second Time Around—A program for persons who have developed some self-assertiveness but find it has slipped a bit and feel the need to get in touch with their assertive selves once again. $9.50 for a single cassette. [Source: Mozelle Bigelow Kraus, Ed.D.]

Developing a Positive Self-Image—Counseling psychologist Roy Trueblood Ph.D. designed this 60-minute program to improve self-confidence by means of self-learning but structured exercises, including personal assessment, determining the ideal self, acknowledging strengths, accepting self, and developing potentials. $9.95 including printed guide. [Source: Development Consultants, Inc.]

Assertive Training Series—The basic concepts of assertive behavior for both professionals and clients, with three cassettes recorded during actual training sessions and a fourth cassette on the training process itself, for $43.95 with album. Also available is a 60-minute tape of deep muscle relaxation, instructions and guided fantasies to reduce anxiety, $10.95. [Source: Research Press]

Lull-A-Baby—To start infants off with a good self-image from birth, this cassette combines traditional lullabys with positive affirmations. This cassette combines basic, wholesome thoughts with a selection of soothing, relaxing, old lullabies. Although comprising only about 10 minutes of this hour-long cassette, the affirmations (given in correct English, not baby-talk) instill positive thinking in the very young (and in their parents). $10.70. [Source: Joan Kennedy]

The Positive Mind—In these 12 messages, Bob Conklin outlines in step-by-step fashion how to set aside the fears, worries, doubts, and negative thoughts that may doom one to become a 'self-made failure.' This frees the mind, he says, to accept ideas of thought and behavior that will guide one toward a life of growth, accomplishments, and satisfaction. $45 for six cassettes in album. [Source: Personal Dynamics Institute]

Simon Says—In eight 45-minute lessons, Arynne Simon shows how to be assertive, effective without anger or fear, and emotionally independent for life. $39.95 for four cassettes and workbook in album. Ms. Simon also has individual cassettes on specific problem areas and solutions—holidays without stress, growing up not old, making an assertive deal, practical problem solving, hanging on to your own identity, playing the game of teamsmanship, assertive skills in business, and more—for $11.45 each. [Source: Simon Says]

Learning Assertiveness through CHAANGE—A cassette that provides the basics in assertiveness skills in an easy-to-learn step-by-step manner, with many practical examples presented in dialogue form. $15.50. [Source: CHAANGE]

The Magic Power of Successful Living—Nido Qubein offers 12 presentations, each aimed at enhancing a facet of your personality (developing leadership potential and a good self image, setting productive goals and getting more done, communicating and listening effectively, and more). These principles, he says, should lead to successful living and success in business. $69.95 for six cassettes in album. [Source: Creative Services, Inc.]

Self Improvement Through Assertiveness Training—DeAnne Rosenberg shows how to feel more self-assured and more self-confident in business relationships, and less intimidated and more secure in the job, by means of this complete assertiveness training course on eight cassettes with workbook in album. $83.95. [Source: DeAnne Rosenberg, Inc.]

The Love Tapes—Based on current brain/mind research (especially the use of both brain hemispheres) and valid psychological principles, these tapes are designed to overcome negativity and build self-esteem—which includes loving yourself. They use a combination of goal-oriented relaxation, mental imagery, affirmations, positive emotions, proved mind development techniques, and the power of love. Topics of individual tapes range from weight and smoking control and developing self-confidence and creativity to attracting money and love, overcoming worry, and effective study and test-taking habits. $9.98 each (messages usually identical on both sides for ease of repeating). [Source: Effective Learning Systems Inc.]

Assertive Training for Groups—Counsel by Dr. Celia Halas and Dr. Roberta Matteson on how to be decisive when confronted with choices, control situations rather than being controlled, demonstrate authority at work, handle unreasonable demands by

others, act on your rights—while all the time feeling good about yourself. $89.50 for six hour-long cassettes and course guide (for six more hours of group exercises) in album. [Source: Instructional Dynamics, Inc.]

Experienced-Based Learning Cassettes—The first side of each of these cassettes contains an informative lecture about the topic; the second side presents a guided imagery exercise that helps give you skills in the topic. Topics include: developing poise and self-confidence in stressful situations; overcoming discouragement and depression; increasing personal power; developing self-motivation; and building ego strength and self-esteem. $9.95 each, three for $27. [Source: Explorations Institute]

Memory Made Easy—A field-tested program developed and presented by Dr. R. L. Montgomery that can train one to remember all important details about clients and friends, be free of reliance on notes, be able to think and act fast with all vital data recorded in your memory. Three hour-long cassettes and guide in album for $85. [Source: Robert L. Montgomery & Associates, Inc.]

Personal Performance Improvement System—Guidelines for creating a successful self-image, changing destructive emotions, developing strong relationships, understanding and influencing others, communicating effectively, developing a strong willpower, and more, all for $24.95 for one cassette, transcript, and workbook in album. [Source: Performance Group Incorporated]

The Richer Life Course—An individualized personal development course led by Zig Ziglar, with 12 cassettes on self-image, attitude, and more, a creative ideas manual, goal planner, and book, all in a tote bag for $169.95. [Source: Zig Ziglar Corporation]

Omega System—Based on the research of Dr. Georgi Lozanof of the Institute of Suggestology in Bulgaria, this system gives an entirely new perspective for overcoming limitations by awakening the mind's inherent potentials. The program first teaches how to identify actual problems without lengthy analysis, and then how to remove these difficulties through reprogramming the subconscious mind in small and progressive steps ('micro-shifting'). The course takes about nine weeks to complete, and requires self-discipline by the listener to follow the instructions to acquire the necessary skills in reprogramming. $145 for 12 cassettes in album, two endless-loop repeating cassettes, instruction book, and stereo 'eyephones' (earphones that block sight and extraneous sounds for sensory isolation). [Source: ULC, Inc.]

Big Sur Recordings—With recordings from Esalen Institute, the Association for Humanistic Psychology, the C.G. Jung Institute of San Francisco, and other similar groups, Big Sur distributes lectures, seminars, and workshops in areas of physical, emotional, and spiritual well-being and growth. They offer programs under these headings: athletics, body-mind function, communities, death and dying, education, encounter, environment, esoteric schools, gestalt therapy, groups, imprisonment, intimate lifestyles, literature, meditation, parapsychology, philosophy, power, psychology (behavioral, East-West, humanistic, Jungian, primal, Reichian, transactional, and transpersonal), psychosynthesis, religion (Buddhism, Christianity, East-West, Zen), sexual attitudes, social commentary, and yoga. $9 per cassette. The catalog of over 500 titles ($2) documents the growth of the human potential movement from its inception through 1976. [Source: Big Sur Recordings]

Women in Change—Carol A. Codori and Constance W. Elsberg explore important themes facing women as they adapt to new forces shaping their lives. They discuss: negotiating change, learning to grow, maintaining health, being alone, and changing relationships with children, spouse, and self. $59.50 for six cassettes and guide in album. Related is *Developing Adaptive Skills*, advice by Richard H. Starkey on developing the necessary skills to adapt to the current business climate—especially the woman who is re-entering the work force or the one seeking a job change. This one is $68.45 for six cassettes. [Source: Instructional Dynamics, Inc.]

Perspectives for Men—A. Victor Kirkman, Jr., Ed.D. discusses the changing role of the American male and describes the new options that are available to him as husband, father, sexual being, career person. Special emphasis is placed on mid-life crises, conflict management, and lifestyle planning with suggestions on making needed role transitions. $109.50 for 10 cassettes and guide in album. [Source: Instructional Dynamics, Inc.]

Discover Your Hidden Talents—Guidelines to improving self-image, how to develop enthusiasm, how to turn shortcomings into advantages, and how to develop a more positive attitude—to enable one to achieve personal happiness and business success. Four cassettes, $27.50. [Source: Associated Educational Materials]

Self Control and Direction

Quitting for Good—A complete home program intended to help break the smoking habit, developed by Dr. Robert P. Baker at the Ochsner Foundation in New Orleans. The approach employs specific instructional materials, relaxation/meditation exercises, and additional psychological aids. $23.95 for two cassettes and manual in album. [Source: Self Control Systems, Inc.]

Psychology Today Cassettes—Provocative interviews with foremost social scientists, offering insights into issues that concern us all in our daily lives. Among a few of the titles offered: *Assertive Training*, by Robert Alberti and Michael Emmons; *Constructive Anger*, by George Bach; *Learning to Control Pain*, by David Bressler; *21 Ways To Stop Worrying*, by Albert Ellis, *Understanding and Coping with Anxiety*, by Rollo May; *What Hypnosis Can Do for You*, by Wiliam S. Kroger; and *Curing Depression*, by Nathan S. Kline. $10.95 each, with a 15% discount for 4 or more. [Source: Psychology Today Cassettes]

Overcoming Irrational Fears—Two series by Dr. Maxie Maultsby, Jr., with each cassette addressing a particular set of irrational fears and developing effective countermeasures. $78.95 for each series of ten C-30 cassettes in album. [Source: Instructional Dynamics, Inc.]

Colaxsus—A series of single cassette self-improvement courses that use COncentration to bring about complete reLAXation, creating a high degree of SUSceptability to internal, external, or tape-recorded stimuli. Topics include: stopping smoking, losing weight, improving memory, removing tension, overcoming insomnia, removing impotence or frigidity, stopping stuttering, bedwetting, snoring and many other woes. There are also cassettes on improving golf, bowling or tennis. $9.98 each. [Source: Institute of Colaxsus]

LeGrand Day—In *Jungian Hypnoanalysis*, Mr. Day explains how he integrates hypnosis with dream interpretation, dream recall, imagery and lifestyle analysis. *Hypnomeditation* guides the listener into an altered state of consciousness aided by the use of a mantra. *Seven-minute Meditation* has been specially designed for short-term meditations by using auto-conditioning with seven musical tones. $10 each. [Source: Le Grand E. Day]

Hypnosis Motivation Cassettes—Based on his 25 years of experience with over 9,000 subjects, Gil Boyne has developed a technique of 'power programming' to facilitate self-hypnosis and augment posthypnotic suggestions. He incorporates the concepts into cassettes ($11 each) covering such topics as self-confidence, concentration and memory, restful slumber, communications and expression, creative acting, creative writing, winning tennis, stopping smoking, sexual enrichment for men and for women, and relaxation for respiratory patients, among many others. [Source: Gil Boyne]

Bi-Modal Learning Systems—Motivational hypnotist Joseph P. Reel involves the listener directly as a participant in educating both halves of the brain—the left hemisphere that specializes in rational-logical-verbal thinking, and also the right hemisphere and its capability for creativity and intuitive wisdom.

The general purpose title program for personal growth uses hypnosis, metaphoric learning, Ganzfeld effect, meditation, guided imagery, and bilateral input to bring about increased confidence, self-esteem, creativity and motivation. The *Self-Hypnosis and Meditation Course* teaches how a person can use mental programming through self-generated auto-suggestion and meditation to improve daily life. Each of the programs contains 12 sessions on six cassettes in an album for $69.95. Single cassettes, also including the bimodal approach to achieving goals and changing habits, cost $14.95 each and cover: stopping smoking, weight reduction, improved memory, concentration, study habits, sleep, relaxation, meditation, self-confidence, creativity, overcoming jealousy, enjoying flying, prosperity, enhanced sexual relationships, and living alone. [Source: Human Development Training Programs]

Stop Smoking Thru Subliminal Modification—After a brief explanation, this cassette contains an hour of relaxing ocean sounds ... but hidden within those soothing sounds are messages which have been carefully worded with psychologic 'power-phrases' to replace one's willpower and to implant themselves directly into the subconscious to modify smoking behavior with no conscious effort. *Lose Weight Thru Subliminal Modification* uses the same format, with the messages directed toward avoiding excessive food consumption. The theory is that "it may be impossible to resist instructions which are not consciously experienced." Each tape is $17, with instructions. [Source: American Research Team]

Learning Curve—One-hour mini-courses, each with a C-60 cassette of programmed exercises and tests: *Developing Your Memory, Stop Smoking Now* and *Weight Control.* Each $9.98, any two for $15.98 or three for $22.98. [Source: Metacom, Inc.]

SCWL Subliminal Techniques—These programs use barely audible positive thought patterns (subliminal perception) to help persons eliminate unwanted habits and achieve special goals. Unlike hypnosis tapes, they involve no hypnotic or relaxation state nor special concentration, only a quiet relaxed atmosphere. The theory is that subliminal technique permits these recorded positive thoughts to enter the subconscious mind without the conscious mind having a chance to screen and possibly reject the favorable thoughts. Some of the topics covered: weight loss, smoking, memory, seduction, depression, happiness, motivation, shyness, creativity, sexual satisfaction, impotence, breast enlargement, drinking, alcoholism, hair loss, agoraphobia, and claustrophobia. $19.95 per tape. [Source: Midwest Research]

Rational Behavior Training Center—Maxie C. Maultsby, Jr. M.D., professor of psychiatry at the University of Kentucky, pioneered the development of emotional self-help techniques to improve personal problem solving skills and to increase joy of living.

In these 13 live 28- to 45-minute programs, Dr. Maultsby works with emotionally upset people to show them how to overcome such problems as depression, faulty parenting, fear of failure, overeating, and marital problems. $10 each. Caution: these programs are actually the audio tracks of videotape programs. [Source: Rational Behavior Training Center]

Weight Control for Women—Janet Kloster helps the listener to understand the emotional and physiological factors behind obesity, to learn to overcome them, and to find the inner strength to stick to that all-important diet. She covers the solo vs. group plans, and her dietary recommendations are based on Weight Watchers. There's even a segment on how overweight affects sexuality. $49.50 for four cassettes and exercise manual in album. Also from the same source is the *Guide to the Working Man's Diet*, a complete course in weight reduction by means of the 700-calorie diet by Dr. Siegfried Heyden, its originator and leading proponent. $54.50 for six cassettes, diary sheets, and guide in album. [Source: Instructional Dynamics, Inc.]

Clinical Hypnosis: Brief Treatment with Restructuring and Self-Management—This course by Herbert Spiegel M.D. and David Spiegel M.D. has two hallmarks: first is the use of trance as a diagnostic tool and to set the stage for short-term treatment; second is the use of patient self-instruction on practicing basic therapeutic lessons in real life. The first three tapes cover the instruction to therapists, and the last three clinical demonstrations of the use of hypnosis in treating insomnia, smoking, obesity, pain, and conversion reactions. $70 for six cassettes and manual in album. Other related titles include *Introduction to Hypnotherapy* by William S. Kroger M.D., *Hypnotic Induction: Concepts and Procedures* by Milton V. Kline Ed.D., *Hypnotherapeutic Approaches to Chronic Pain Management* by Joseph Barber Ph.D., and *Hypnotherapy for Children* by Sol Gould Ph.D., all $10.50 for one cassette. [Source: BMA Audio Cassettes]

Innerquest: A Biofeedback Program—Dorrelle Heisel uses biofeedback techniques to introduce the listener to greater sensitivity and relaxation. $59.50 for six C-30 cassettes and finger thermometers in album. [Source: Instructional Dynamics, Inc.]

Total Mind Power—The first 30 minutes of these hour-long cassettes contain the thoughts and insights of Donald L. Wilson M.D. about the topic or problem being considered, while the second 30 minutes consist of focused awareness and directed change of that behavior. Topics available include: improved sleep and dreams, changing weight, increased memory, stopping smoking, controlling pain, improved sports performance, lowering high blood pressure, improving eyesight, controlling a tumor, decreasing heart problems, slowing down the aging process, stopping fears and phobias, overcoming alcohol and drugs, increasing sexual enjoyment, improving mental and emotional stability, increasing ESP, enhancing religious experiences, and achieving better success. There are 11 additional programs in the 'Total Beauty' series, and 11 more in the 'Total Tennis' series. $9.95 per cassette. [Source: Total Mind Power Institute]

Institute for Behavioral Awareness—Dr. Frances Stern uses the technique of guided imagery to help listeners cope with life's problems. In *Successful Coping ... The Power of Positive Daydreaming*, she gives simple down-to-earth exercises in using this mental exercise and then leads the listener through 10 guided daydreams that show how to help oneself with individual problems. In *Mind Tripping ... How to Use Your Head to Reduce Your Body*, she applies these techniques specifically to the problem of weight control. $8.95 each. [Source: Institute for Behavioral Awareness]

UCanDoIt Programs—Behavioral scientists created these programs, utilizing a meditative frame of mind to facilitate the listener's reception of new ideas and information, thereby encouraging the desired behavior modification. Programs feature Drs. Thomas and Louise Lang and Dr. George Madison, and are available in a wide array of topics: overcoming obesity, smoking, alcohol; controlling blood pressure, jealousy, insomnia; preparing for court, the IRS, or dentistry; coping with shyness, allergies, asthma, speech impediments, fears of flying or of heights. Other topics include achieving self-confidence, improving memory and public speaking, taking tests and job interviews. Sports improvement programs cover bowling, tennis, skiing, and golf. The general premise is that "you are responsible for you, and only you can change you." These programs are $9.95 each, with every fourth program ordered free. They also have a complete hypnosis course, on 10 cassettes, for $49.95. [Source: Pivot Press]

Biogenics Cassette Tapes—Short relaxation and meditation talks and exercises (same message on both sides of tape) by C. Norman Shealy M.D., Ph.D. of the Pain and Health Rehabilitation Center for chronic pain and stress problems, for $6.95 each. Longer tapes on relaxation/meditation, self-health, basic Schultz exercises, stress reduction, and pain management cost $9.95 each. Some tapes are aimed for use by physicians and other health professionals: use of biofeedback self-regulation, basic relaxation and autogenic training, nutrition made simple, alcohol self-regulation, good sleep habits. These are also $9.95 each, some come with an explanatory booklet. [Source: Self-Health Systems]

Wider Horizons Hypnotic Sleep Tapes—These programs work on the theory that "what the subconscious mind can conceive and believe, the conscious mind can achieve", and that the quickest approach to the subconscious is by means of self-hypnosis.

Some of the topics covered by these tapes: memory and recall, study habits, sales motivation, public speaking, self-confidence, migraine control, relieving guilt, worry and fear, overcoming fears of driving or heights, becoming a nonsmoker or nondrinker, and achieving weight loss. $10 each. [Source: Wider Horizons]

Audiotape Symposium on Hypnosis—Five authorities give professional pointers: Theodore X. Barber Ph.D., *Word by Word Hypnotic Procedures and Suggestions* (four cassettes in album, $46); John F. Chaves Ph.D. *Techniques and Strategies of Clinical Hypnosis* (six cassettes in album, $69); Norman W. Katz Ph.D., *Self Hypnosis Skills: Theory and Application* (six cassettes in album, $69); William S. Kroger M.D., *Techniques, Inductions, and Suggestions for Hypnosis* (four cassettes, $46); Emmett E. Miller M.D., *Hypnosis Collection* (four cassettes, $53.80), all 24 cassettes in five albums for $199. Other speakers and topics on hypnosis: Donald B. DeRozier Ph.D., *Hypnosis for Students*, three cassettes; Errol R. Korn M.D. and George J. Pratt Ph.D., *Optimal Health & Hyposis*, eight cassettes ($9.95 each); Harley Stock Ph.D., *Forensic Hypnosis*, one cassette. All individual cassettes $11.50 each except as indicated. [Source: Proseminar]

Communications Enterprises—Clinical psychologist Dr. Tom Yarnell leads single-cassette courses in *Self-Hypnosis*, *Lose Weight with Hypnosis*, *Stop Smoking with Hypnosis*, *End Your Fear of Speaking in Public*, and *Self-Motivation*, and leads a complete deep relaxation procedure for *Stress Management*. $12.95 per cassette. [Source: Communication Enterprises, Inc.]

Medfield Foundation—Cassette tapes by T. X. Barber, generally designed to be used by therapists to aid clients with problems amenable to hypnosis and post-hypnotic suggestions. Titles of the four programs available: *Positive Suggestions for Effective Living/Philosophical Hypnosis*; *Verbatim Hypnotic and Self-Hypnotic Suggestions for Study-Concentration, Relaxation, Pain Control, and Mystical Experience*; *Deep Relaxation, Superaware, and Traditional Hypnotic Inductions and Modern (Permissive) Suggestions for Anesthesia, Hallucinations, Age Regression, Time Distortion, Etc.*; and *Hypnotic Suggestions for Weight Control and Smoking Cessation*. $10 each. [Source: Medfield Foundation]

Hypnosonics—Hypno-technician Hyman A. Lewis offers 51 motivational programs on a broad spectrum of topics: study skills and habits, concentration, typing, spelling, fingernail biting, stuttering, insomnia, a variety of sales topics, creative topics (painting, music, poetry, acting), good grooming, developing ESP, and improved athletic skills (golf, tennis, bowling, basketball, track, shooting, skiing, skating) and many others. Each message is 15 minutes, repeated on the second side. $6.95 for each program (any three for $20). [Source: Hyman A. Lewis]

New Life Institute—Self-hypnosis programs, led by hypnotherapist David Lee, covering six general areas to help people gain what they want out of life. There are educational programs (memory, concentration, and such), physical health programs, (weight loss, stop smoking, weight gain, relaxation, temper control, and others), emotional health programs (worry, guilt, loneliness), love and sex programs (attracting love, sexuality, and such), success programs (self-confidence, popularity, willpower, public speaking, and many others), psychic and spiritual programs (releasing ESP, dream control, astral projection, psychic healing, among others), and sports programs (bowling, golf, and tennis). $10 each, every fourth program free. [Source: New Life Institute]

Helpnosis—Ethical self-hypnosis programs designed by John L. Peakes to help listeners help themselves overcome costly, unhealthy habits. The two programs on smoking control and weight control are $14 each; the three on insomnia control, bed wetting control, and tension & relaxation are $11 each. [Source: Helpnosis]

Inner Mind Concepts—Clinical hypnotist Pat Carroll offers subconscious conditioning tapes to help one "accept your own potential to be all that you are capable of being in all areas of your life." Topics include: be your own woman, women and job stress, several tapes on weight loss and relaxation, weight maintenance for new non-smokers, insomnia, guilt, and grief. More advanced programs cover higher consciousness, past life, meditation, dreams, and intuition. All programs $10. [Source: Inner Mind Concepts]

Self Psych—On these cassette programs, TV personality Jim Hoke shows the listener how to simultaneously condition both the conscious and subconscious minds to help overcome negative hang-ups: worrying, nail-biting, stress, study habits, smoking weight control, sports improvement, depression, insomnia, shyness, exercises. He also tackles the weight problem with separate tapes on eliminating junk food, learning to hate sugar, positive food addictions, eliminating nighttime snacking,, and others. Associate Lenore Bechtel gives instructions on instant yoga and fighting facial wrinkles, Sue Weingarden on childbirth without pain, memory improvement for children, and overcoming test anxiety. $9.99 each, every fourth tape free. [Source: Self Psych, Inc.]

Applied Subliminals—Self-hypnosis tapes on a variety of topics, all with an induction procedure immediately followed by brief, direct posthypnotic suggestions. In addition, all programs are also available in 'direct subliminal' programming, with no induction phase: the conscious mind hears only a relaxing background sound while the subconscious mind extracts the message recorded within. Topics for both types of programming cover the gamut of self-improvement topics, from self-confidence, smoking cessation, weight control, and leadership, through sexual happiness, natural sleep, overcoming fear of flying, driving, or dentists, and improved golf, tennis, and bowling. All cassettes $9.95 each plus $1.50 shipping per order. [Source: Applied Subliminals]

Creative Hypnosis—A large collection of hypnosis programs by master hypnotist John M. Hudson, devoted to overcoming problems or enhancing desirable traits. Single cassette topics cover several phases of relaxation, how to overcome laziness, smoking, stage fright, how to develop confidence, recharge energies, bring about self-discipline, and quite a few on aspects of sexuality. These range from $5.95 to $14.95 each. *The Business Executive's Anti-Pressure Program* covers all aspects of relaxation, confidence-building, and personal development and interactions, on 9 cassettes for $110. Some other multi-cassette special programs include two-cassette sessions on smoking cessation, insomnia, and weight loss, for $19.95: sexual development on three cassettes for $29.95; a complete self-hypnosis course on six cassettes for $85; and nine cassettes that help get one through college by abetting memory, learning concentration, motivation, study habits, fighting procrastination, and taking exams successfully, for $59. And there are a lot more. [Source: Creative Hypnosis National]

The Damon Way to Self-Improvement—Ten non-medical habit control sessions that, when properly used, can help to control unwanted or negative habits. Topics available include control of smoking, eating habits, study habits, fingernail biting, and drinking habits, as well as self-confidence, memory retention, sales motivation, decreasing stress, and heightening sexuality. $10 for each cassette (each about 23 minutes long). [Source: Damon and Grace]

Randolph Tapes—Betty Lee Randolph Ph.D. leads the listener into a relaxed state of focused attention and changed concentration, helping to reprogram the subconscious mind to make it act on suggestions given it. Topics of the programs: weight loss/control, smoking, stress, sleep, tension headaches, memory, healing, sexuality (male and female), goals, sales, enthusiasm, relationships, anxiety, concentration, winning self-image, alleviate pain, positive thinking, and more. Some tapes have Dr. Randolph's instructions on one side and subliminal affirmations (heard only by the subconscious) set amidst sounds of the ocean on the other side; programs in this mode are the ones on weight loss, smoking, stress, memory, confidence, sales, and winning self-image. All tapes $9.98, every fourth tape free. [Source: Randolph Tapes]

Home Self Hypnosis Tapes—Tapes by three clinical psychologists and physicians—Lee Pulos Ph.D., Marlene Hunter M.D., and Robert G. Wilkie M.D.—with extensive experience and responsibility in all aspects of hypnosis. Side one of the tapes offers direct induction that is typical of traditional hypnosis; side two presents an indirect naturalistic approach using two voices—thereby benefitting both those who respond to a direct style and those who respond better to a more permissive mode. Also, most tapes are also available with subliminal messages and affirmations to increase subconscious acceptance of the suggestions on that program. The topics vary from the usual ones in regard to weight control, smoking cessation, relaxation, asthma control, and childbirth to some unique ones on preparing for surgery, self-healing, recovery from heart attacks, and pain control. These are all $13.98 each, $14.98 with subliminal messages added. Also available are some tapes of relaxing music with subliminals added, for $11.98 each. [Source: Mountain Glade Media Ltd.]

SOURCE Cassettes—Programs planned and narrated by Emmett E. Miller M.D. that can help accomplish personal change by replacing ineffective patterns of thought and behavior with those that lead to success and fulfillment. His secret is to use deep relaxation and selective awareness to 'quiet the chatter' of the conscious mind so that the unconscious mind can 'hear' the messages. On each cassette, Dr. Miller guides the listener through actual experiences and offers simple step-by-step routines that can be practiced and learned. A few of the titles: *Running Free* (imagery for competitive and recreational athletes), two cassettes, $16.95; *The Ultimate Student* (accelerated learning and high-performance test-taking), two cassettes, $16.95; *Freeing Yourself from Fear*, three cassettes, $27.50; *Loss and Letting Go* (loss, separation, and death as positive challenges), one cassette, $10.95; *Easing Into Sleep*, one cassette, $10.95; and many more (you really should ask for the free catalog). *Self-Hypnosis and Personal Development* is a live seminar by Dr. Miller incorporating many of his instructions, on seven cassettes in album for $97. [Source: SOURCE Cassette Learning Systems]

Quiet Decisions Success Programming Tapes—On these tapes, Dick Summer's soothing voice saturates both the conscious and subconscious minds with improved behavior programming. The goal of the tapes is to help you make the 'quiet decision' to change a behavior—and then give guidance and direction to help accomplish the decision. Topics cover smoking, weight loss, phobias/fears, insomnia, stress control/relax, memory/concentration, self-confidence, E.S.P., self-hypnosis, pain/headache relief, acne/rashes, sales power, assertiveness, past life regression, improved sexuality, and vocal production. $9.95 each. [Source: Quiet Decisions]

Dick Sutphen Tapes—Programs by Dick and/or Trenna Sutphen that include self-improvement by means of self-hypnosis, but go on to include psychic and metaphysical experiences facilitated by the hypnotic state. Some individual tape titles ($12.50 each)

selected at random from the free catalog: *Painless Childbirth Hypnosis, Overcoming Addiction, Loneliness, Shyness, Backache, Lowering Your Blood Pressure, Vision Improvement, Eliminating Phobias, Stopping Smoking, Increasing Efficiency, Astral Projection Preparation, Psychic Healing, Remembering Dreams,* and *Spiritual Protection from Psychic Attack.* They also have many two-cassette-with-booklet albums ($29.95 each, except as noted): *Past Life Therapy, Exploration Beyond Past Lives* ($24.95); *Lifestyle: Thin, Goal Achievement* ($24.95); *Assertiveness Training; Runner's Hypnosis; Martial Arts Hypnosis;* and *Higher Self Explorations* ($24.95). Some albums are also available by Brad and Francie Steiger: *Starbirth Odyssey* and *UFO Hypnosis Explorations.* [Source: Valley of the Sun Publishing]

Potentials Unlimited Self-Hypnosis Tapes—Over 112 programs by master hypnotist Barrie Konicov, each containing 40 to 45 minutes of suggestions (same message on both sides of the tape) to be played both during the day (to saturate the conscious mind) and at bedtime (to instill the message into the subconscious mind). A few of the topics covered in the Education Series include creative writing, good study habits, and taking examinations. In the Fear Series are tapes on overcoming agoraphobia, death, driving, flying, heights, water, and more. The Success Series covers, among other topics, creative thinking, effective speaking, fear of success, goal setting, overcoming procrastination, and will power. The Sports Series includes tapes on improving baseball (catching, hitting, or pitching), bowling, table tennis, and running. The Health Series considers drinking, drugs, tics, acne, sexual guilt, hearing loss, healthy teeth, hyperactivity, improving vision, jealousy, menstrual problems, back pain, stomach problems, and many more. Finally, the Psychic Series goes into astral projection, birth control, past life regression, psychic healing, and others. These are all $9.98 each. Some popular titles are available in Spanish, French, and German versions, for $15 each. Another group of tapes use subliminal messages buried in sounds of the ocean on the second side; these are $11.98 per tape. And finally, a couple of nice touches: tapes on recapturing youthful vigor and relieving arthritis pain will be sent for only a $2 handling fee to those over age 65 living on fixed incomes; the tape titled *Vietnam Veteran Come Home* is available to Viet veterans for just the $2 shipping fee. [Source: Potentials Unlimited]

Relaxed Meditation Series—Rather than hypnosis, Paul W. Schuette uses 'relaxology' as a new and pleasant approach to personal growth and motivation through relaxed listening which permits filling the subconscious mind with thoughts directed toward a happier, more abundant life. Titles of some of the programs: *Happiness on Tape, I Am Successful, Exams Are Easy, I Want to Quit Smoking* (and its companion *I Have Quit Smoking*), *Thinking Myself*

Beautiful (or Thin), Self-Confidence, Successful Retirement, I Love to Fly, Overcoming Procrastination (Stage Fright, Loneliness), I Am a Great Golfer (Bowler, Tennis Player), I Am Rich, Healing Meditation, and more. $10 each. [Source: Success Dynamics, Inc.]

New Age Hypnosis—Metaphysicist Jonathan Parker covers not only the standard topics of relaxation/insomnia, memory improvement, pain reduction, stop smoking/alcohol, weight loss, creativity, conquering bedwetting, and such, but he also goes on to harmony in marriage, living with a negative person, success for children, assertiveness, building your self-image, body beautiful, freedom from worry, improved sports performance, and positive expectancy for realtors. All $10.95 each. [Source: Institute of Human Development]

Hypnosis Workshop—A professional course, encompassing all areas of hypnosis, yet written for the layperson to aid in teaching techniques of inducing hypnosis rapidly and easily in oneself and others. This course was prepared by Self-Development Research Foundation, Inc. under the direction of Arthur Sontag and includes six cassettes and printed materials in album for $59.95. Mr. Sontag also has a single-cassette program, Learn To Use Self-Hypnosis, for $14.95. [Source: Automated Learning, Inc.]

Weight Control Through Self-Hypnosis—Arnold J. Polansky provides a down-to-earth, non-mystical approach to self-hypnotic techniques. On the first side of the 52-minute cassette he describes the principles of hypnosis, and on the second side, he shows how self-hypnosis can be applied not only to weight control but also to smoking, insomnia, and other human plights. Stop Smoking Through Self-Hypnosis follows the same format, but concentrates on helping the listener break the smoking habit through relaxation and self-hypnosis. $6 for each hour-long cassette. [Source: Hawthorne Hypnosis Studio]

Transitions—Master hypnotist Catherine Wiands has created 23 cassette programs, each designed to effect a specific change in the listener's life or habits, using a combination of relaxation, visualization, and auto-suggestion to change negative or restrictive behavior patterns. Topics cover confidence building, weight loss, improved relationships, overcoming procrastination, stopping smoking, sounding like a winner, improving concentration and memory, increasing prosperity, and more. These are $9.95 each, two for $16.95, three for $22.95. A program introducing self-hypnosis and relaxation is just $5.50, a two-cassette program on the use of affirmations is $14.50. [Source: Motivation Associates]

Success Tapes—Through the use of hypnosis, meditation, and other self-improvement systems, Bill Camp shows how one can take control of one's mind to lead to greater health, happiness, and success.

Topics of his tapes cover relaxation, beginning and deep meditation, weight control, better sports, decision making, self-programming, and command confidence. More metaphysical topics cover higher states of consciousness, E.S.P. and psychic development, distant healing, yogic breathing, astral projection, and chakra stimulation. $9.95 per tape, any two for $18, any three for $24. [Source: Success Tapes]

Sexuality

Audio Aphrodisiacs—Dr. Deborah Bright's audio treatment to physically and mentally stimulate active sensual awareness, two cassettes in an album for $30; and also Dr. Bright's Creative Relaxation with six cassettes in album for $60. [Source: Sales Communique Corporation]

Guided Sexual Fantasies—Aalsa Lee, a practicing sex-surrogate, created and narrates these tapes, sharing her expertise and professional skills in the world of sexual fantasy, to enable the listener to expand his/her potential. Available in men's and women's versions, for $14.95 each. Other self-hypnosis tapes, produced by Barry Konicov, Gil Boyne and Dr. George Madison, are also available. [Source: Self-Discovery]

Intimacy: How to Communicate Your Feelings and Needs—In plain everyday language, Dr. Nolan Saltzman offers a fuller understanding of what really happens in love relations, gives case histories of people who learned to restore intimacy to their love lives by expressing their feelings honestly, and suggests ways to overcome behaviors that avoid intimacy. $9.95 for a single cassette. [Source: Nolan Saltzman, Ph.D.]

St. Anthony Messenger Cassettes—A good source of practical, responsible programming, primarily for Catholic audiences. Clayton C. Barbeau has three series: The Male Condition, on male sexuality in a Christian world at $37.70 for six hour-long cassettes in a box; The Art of Loving, its definitions, mysteries, risks and rewards, $27.80 for four 90 minute cassettes in a box; and Creative Marriage, $41.65 for seven talks for premarried or long married. Nicholas Lohkamp, O. F. M., discusses Human Sexuality: Moral Dimensions on four C-60 cassettes for $23.80 in a box. [Source: St. Anthony Messenger Press.]

Overcoming Sexual Inadequacy—Dr. Stephen Neiger provides a comprehensive program for the man, woman or couple with sexual difficulties. The program is also useful for marriage counselors, physicians, clergy. $89.50 for 12 cassettes, with album. [Source: Instructional Dynamics, Inc.]

Human Sexuality Series—Each of these tapes by Dr. Milton Diamond features his discussion of one aspect of sexuality for 30 minutes, and then questions and/or a panel discussion of that topic, generally aimed at the college level audience. There are 30 topics available: $285 for the complete set, or $11.95 each. [Source: Jeffrey Norton Publishers, Inc.]

Enhancing Male Sexuality, Enhancing Female Sexuality, Couple's Sexuality—The most modern information and techniques on sex and love, written and compiled by Ann Hooper and Philip Hodson, editors of Forum magazine. $9.95 each, all three tapes for $26.50. [Source: Multi Media Resource Center]

Behavioral Learning Systems for Sexual Therapy—Short talks (7-14 minutes per cassette) by physicians intended for patients on various aspects of human sexuality: *Sexual Satisfaction*, *Learning about Self-Stimulation*, and *Teaching Your Partner about You* (each of these titles available in male and female versions), $5.75 each. Tapes on sex and pregnancy and on the pelvic examination are $6.50 each. All of these tapes include a transcript. Finally, a tape on male sexuality (including impotence, premature ejaculation, and sensate focus) sells for $9.25. [Source: Enabling Systems, Inc.]

Sex: Should We Wait?—Students at the University of Cincinnati engage in an honest, open dialogue with Dr. and Mrs. J. C. Willke on the medical, social, and psychological reasons for and against sex before marriage. $14.95 for two cassettes and accompanying manual. [Source: Hayes Publishing Company]

Understanding Our Sexuality—Frank, sincere, and reassuring talks by Regina Quinlan that give children in grades six through nine a good start on the road to healthy and positive attitudes regarding their sexuality. The program consists of a separate introduction for parents and teachers and four Christian-oriented talks directed to the students. $21.75 for three cassettes. *Young Adult Enrichment Program* moves on to the sexual concerns of adolescents. Two introductory talks for supervising adults show how the Church can give help and support in improving communications and in building personal responsibility. Four student-oriented talks take up a friendly examination of sex and sexuality, while marriage and adult sexuality are topics of two talks aimed at high school seniors. $29 for four cassettes. [Source: Family Enrichment Bureau]

Erotic Cassettes—Tape-recordings of the voices and sounds of people having sexual relations. Some of the presentations are of conventional love-making (although indulging in what some would consider unconventional techniques!), while others depict sado-masochism, sexual domination, and 'water sports.' We'll leave the rest of the descriptions unwritten; the tapes leave little to the imagination. The audio quality is excellent, as though the microphone was suspended directly over the participants—which it was. $9.95 to $15 each. [Source: Fantasia]

Stress Management

Daily Living—Coping with Tensions and Anxieties—Dr. Arnold A. Lazarus explains, in easily understood terms, how to deal more effectively with daily frustrations. $84.50 for ten C-30 cassettes in album.

Relaxation Exercises are another offering by Dr. Lazarus, on three C-30 cassettes in album for $37.95 [Source: Instructional Dynamics, Inc.]

Principles and Practice of Progressive Relaxation—Edmund Jacobson M.D. (the father of progressive relaxation), and F. J. McGuigan Ph.D offer a teaching primer on the techniques, with two cassettes and manual for the therapist, and two cassettes and manual for the client, all in an album for $40. Other single cassettes on relaxation cover sensory awareness relaxation, composite relaxation, auto-induced procedures for relaxation, breathing and meditative techniques, and many more. Also available from the same source is a short-term program by Dr. Thomas H. Budzynski, suited for individuals who suffer from psychological or physical disorders with stress or anxiety components, three cassettes and a manual in album for $31.50. Available with either male (Dr. Budzynski) or female (Judith Proctor) narration, and entitled *Relaxation Training Program*. [Source: BMA Audio Cassettes]

Quieting Response Training—A comprehensive stress control program by Dr. Charles F. Stroebel, using an innovative amalgam of established relaxation techniques to produce a solid base for continued progress. He concentrates first on developing greater awareness and breathing adjustments, and then methods for muscular and autonomic control. $60 for eight tapes, therapist manual, and self-instruction manual in album. Related is *Quieting Reflex Training for Adults* by Dr. Stroebel (narrated by Judith Proctor), intended to help people achieve reliable, positive response to daily stress situations. $50 for four cassettes and manual in album. [Source: BMA Audio Cassettes]

Nuclear Jitters—The Three Mile Island incident has created an environment of chronic stress for anyone living near a nuclear reactor. This one-hour program tells how to cope with this particular type of stress before it leads to physical and behavioral harm. $7.95 [Source: Creative Media Group]

Stress Management Exercises—Two cassettes in the series: on the first, Barby Eide provides simple techniques that effortlessly put you into a state of relaxation; on the second, she shows you how to use this natural state of rest to take control of your life. A third cassette, *The Art of Positive Stress Management*, offers an insight into the pressures of daily life and ways to use stress advantageously. $10 each. [Source: Barby Fairbanks Eide]

Q. R. for Young People—The quieting reflex is a self-enhancing response that teachers, parents, and counselors can teach children to substitute for temper outbursts, violence, headaches and other distracting behaviors. The tapes are suited both for normal youngsters and for those with emotional, behavioral, and stress-related disorders. This particular program is aimed at children age 9 and up; *Kiddie Q. R.* is the same program adapted for children 4-8. Either is $49.50 for four cassettes and booklets or manual in album.   [Source: Biofeedback Center of Berkeley]

Stress Management Training Program—A complete program designed to facilitate comprehensive education and training in relaxation and stress management. After teaching exercises to control muscle tension and to induce relaxation, the tapes focus on reducing autonomic arousal and cognitive anxiety. Topics of the eight cassettes in this package include: introduction, progressive relaxation, deep muscle relaxation, autogenic training, visual imagery training, stress management by automated systematic desensitization, and two home relaxation practice tapes. Each tape is about 30 minutes long, with a male narrator on one side, and the material repeated by a female on the other. $119 for the set, including album and conceptual and procedural manual. The cassettes are $12.95 each. [Source: Biofeedback Center of Berkeley]

CHAANGE Agoraphobia Treatment Program—Literally, 'agoraphobia' is fear of open places, but to most agoraphobics, it is the fear of leaving home because they fear the onset of a panic attack when they are not in a familiar place to deal with it. This course from the Center for Help for Agoraphobia/Anxiety through New Growth Experiences (CHAANGE) consists of a cassette and homework assignments, plus pamphlets and books when appropriate, sent weekly for 15 weeks, with much back and forth communication between the patient and CHAANGE. The purpose is to help agoraphobics stop frightening themselves so that they can get on with the business of being in control of their own lives again. The cost for the complete course of treatment is $425.   [Source: CHAANGE]

CHAANGE for the Fearful Flyer—Fear of flying is a learned condition, and this program teaches how to 'unlearn' it to change anxious, fearful feelings into calm and confident ones. The cassettes present a therapeutic dialogue among three people who have overcome fears of flying and their therapist. The program is structured to help one understand the fear and the physiologic reactions, and then to counteract them. $122.50 for a relaxation tape, practice tape, instructional tapes, plus workbook and other materials in binder. Related is *Preparing for Your First Flight Through CHAANGE*, a 30-minute cassette of explanation, relaxation, and practice for anyone who is anticipating flying and wants to experience an anxiety-free first flight. $10.50. For those who are fearful just staying on the ground there is *Driving Without Anxiety Through CHAANGE* for those who experience anxiety while driving a car (or as adjunctive therapy for agoraphobics). This cassette provides an understanding of the problem, a dialogue relating to driving fears, a relaxation segment, and practice in desensitizing the listener to the feared situation. $15.50. [Source: CHAANGE]

Relaxation Through CHAANGE—Two approaches to learning important relaxation skills: the first side features progressive muscle relaxation, guided by Lou Owensby, MSW; the second side offers relaxation through imagery, led by C. N. Owensby, M.D. $10.50.   [Source: CHAANGE]

Family Relaxation and Self-Control Program—Designed for parents and children by Mimi Lupin, this program includes music, environmental sounds, and separate instructions on relaxation and guided imagery to benefit both weary parents and overactive or aggressive children. The program comes in two volumes, each consisting of three cassettes in album with a guide to family and child relaxation and self-control procedures, for $29.95 each.   [Source: Stress Management Research Associates]

Stress Management Programs—Developed and tested by clinical psychologists, these programs give a comprehensive and practical treatment approach to a variety of stress-related disorders. Two programs are available: first is a hospital and clinic edition, with eight 30-39 minute cassettes of instruction (choice of male or female voice) in an album, plus a therapist manual, for $119.25. The home edition incorporates the relaxation and visual imagery sessions on three cassettes with album and guidebook for $29.95.   [Source: Stress Management Research Associates]

Coping with Stress—In this two-cassette program, psychologist Richard P. Issel addresses the common sources of stress in contemporary lifestyles, and how one can deal with it in a mature and positive way. A related program is *Psychology of Despair*, a live recording of Dr. Issel's discussion of what is despair and apathy, what causes it, and what can be done to combat it. $29.95 for each album of two 50-minute cassettes and guide. [Source: Learning Consultants, Inc.]

Tapes for Today—Psychologist Mozelle Bigelow Kraus Ed.D. offers three tapes that can provide new attitudes and new behaviors in everyday life: *Refreshing Relaxation* (for those who want to relieve tension and insomnia and increase feelings of success); *Relax and Relive—The Best Years of Your Life* (recall pleasant reveries from the past to start a new theme in life); and *Calorie Counting Can Be Fun* (helping to understand one's eating habits in a true, non-stressful perspective). These are each $9.50 for a single cassette. [Source: Mozelle Bigelow Kraus Ed.D.]

The Relaxation System—A 20-minute tape with a few simple techniques that, according to developer Ron Willingham, provides as much quality relaxation every day as one used to get only on long lazy Saturday afternoons. $11. [Source: Ron Willingham Courses, Inc.]

Reduce Stress Now—Two programs developed and recorded by Dr. Terry Chitwood, a clinical psychologist, from his extensive work in relaxation, yoga, and meditation. The first side of *Relaxation* is a passive relaxation exercise, with the vocal rhythms of Dr. Chitwood leading the listener into progressively more relaxed states; the second side uses active tensing and relaxing of major muscle groups. *Creative Imagery* leads the listener through imagined scenes in which he/she talks with various aspects of the inner self to learn secrets of self-healing, joy, humor, courage, and well-being. $11.95 for each 40-minute cassette. [Source: Polestar Publications]

DIMI-TAPES—Professional psychotherapist Richard L. Lutz offers relaxation therapy as a method of dealing with a variety of personal difficulties: anxiety, tension, various bodily aches and ills; conquer your shyness, depression, fears, and insomnia; control your cancer; conquer common sex problems. $8.95 each, two for $15, three for $21. [Source: DIMI]

I Never Stayed in the Dark Long Enough—A cassette desensitization course for those with phobias—fear of flying, fear of heights, fear of open places, fear of strangers, or any other phobia. Dr. Manuel D. Zane first introduces people talking spontaneously about their experiences in phobic situations (so the listener will realize that others with severe phobias have overcome them). Then Dr. Zane outlines six points to help control fear levels (by allowing fearful thoughts to come in ways that can be handled). $10. [Source: Phobia Educational Materials, Inc.]

Relaxation Cassette Tapes—Five tapes on relaxation and stress reduction, written by Matthew McKay Ph.D. and Patrick Fanning, that provide effortless, eyes-closed practice in: progressive relaxation and breathing; body awareness and imagination; autogenics and meditation; self-hypnosis; and thought stopping. $9.95 each, all five for $39.95. [Source: New Harbinger Publications]

UNstress for Business and Life—Some medical authorities say that 70-80% of all illness is stress-induced. This program is designed to lead groups or individuals into and out of a deep state of relaxation, with simple instructions and soothing sounds that not only counteract negative or excess stress/tension but also enable one to manage stress and use it to advantage to be more productive. $40.50 for four cassettes and 96-page book. [Source: Learning Programs of America]

Recharge Yoga and Tension Fighters—Stretching and relaxation are part of any good stress management plan. On the first half of this tape, Mardi Erdman leads the listener through ten basic Hatha Yoga postures that relax, 'recharge', and align anyone. On the second side, she focuses more on 'sneak a stretch' exercises for use in fighting tension during the day's hectic activities. $8.50. [Source: Soundmark]

Deep Muscle Relaxation—The soothing voice of Dr. John Marquis provides course of instruction that enables the listener to relax completely and thereby to free the body of all tension. Side A covers relaxation of the body muscles, side B is devoted to relaxation of the visual and vocal muscles. $10 for an hour-long cassette and brochure. [Source: Self-Management Schools, Inc.]

Self Control Systems—In *Striking Out at Stress*, Dr. Harold H. LeCrone, Jr. outlines the most significant facts about stress and shows how to handle it creatively. In *Parting with Pain*, Dr. LeCrone shares his technique of coping with pain by self-control and relaxation. In *Families under Stress*, Dr. Louis McBurney discusses, then shows how to control, the various stresses that confront a family and its members. In *Depression: Positive Strategies for Change*, Dr. Allan G. Hedberg gives a basic understanding of the nature of depression and provides resources for those who want to treat and prevent it. All of these are $23.95 for two cassettes and manual in album. For $25.95, in the same format, is Dr. C. Eugene Walker's *Stress Management: Everything You Always Wanted to Know about Tension But Were Too Uptight To Ask*. [Source: Self Control Systems, Inc.]

Astral Sounds—An hour-long cassette of computer-generated electronically created tones, notes, and sounds arranged in a specific pattern to stimulate the brain's 'pleasure center' to produce feelings of peace, happiness, emotional stability, and relief from pain, discomfort, stress, and anxiety. $17, with instructions. [Source: American Research Team]

Autogenic Training Cassettes—Autogenic training involves many of the principles of biofeedback training to overcome stress and release tension, but without the need for instruments. Rather, the person's own perceptions and images are used to dissolve learning blocks, improve concentration, and enhance physical well-being. Vera Fryling offers an introductory program, two specialized programs, and two advanced programs. $11.95 each. [Source: Creative Resources]

Beginning Stress Management Series—A basic program on two cassettes that gives, in over an hour of instruction, an explanation of the dynamics of stress, a stress evaluation to determine the levels and areas of stress in the listener's life, and then two relaxation exercises. $19.95 plus handling. [Source: SRR/Center for Stress Reduction]

Tension Easers—Severe tension is not something that can be eliminated, but it can be managed—contend the two clinical psychologists who with this program provide a three-step system to 'tame tension': first by relaxation, they by understanding one's reaction to tension, and finally by matching tension-easing exercises to one's individual stress patterns. $82.95 for four cassettes, two books, tension logs, and relaxation charts in box. [Source: Leadership Catalysts, Inc.]

A Stress Clinic on Tape—Tips to enable one to handle any kind of pressure, by learning the danger signals of over-stress, how to handle stress-inducing experiences, how to stay calm and avoid irritation in stressful situations, how to use the latest techniques of deep relaxation, and avoid or reduce dependency on alcohol, sleeping pills, and tranquilizers. $21.15. [Source: Audio Health Services]

Living with Stress Successfully—Author of *The Art of Hanging Loose in an Uptight World*, Dr. Ken Olson approaches stress by changing its causes, rather than treating its effects. In his simple, human, and practical manner, he describes and illustrates the changes that can be made to "manage stress before it becomes distress." $59 for four cassettes in album. [Source: General Cassette Corporation]

XV.
Philosophy

Existential Psychology Series—Well-organized lectures that provide a comprehensive explanation of the existential ideas developed by: Kierkegaard, Bugental, Heidegger, Binswanger and Boss, Sartre, Buber, Liang, Jourard, Husserl, Merleau-Ponty, Perls, and Frankl. $25.95 each. [Source: Lansford Publishing Company]

The Principles of Philosophy—Included on these six cassettes are the definition of philosophy, theories of metaphysics, dualism, materialism, idealism, ethics, and theories of knowledge. $149.95 for the six cassettes and guide. Related is *Philosophies of the Renaissance*, $49.95 for two cassettes and guide, and *The Great Philosophers*, six 50-minute lectures on the philosophy of Plato, Aristotle, Descartes, Kant, Hume and St. Thomas, $159 for six cassettes and handbook. *Ethical Issues and Dilemmas* considers the problem of ethical norms and models, responsible action, death and abortion as ethical concerns, and the ethical aspects of a quest for a satisfying personal lifestyle, on six 50-minute cassettes for $149.95. [Source: Lansford Publishing Company]

Esthetics Series—Lectures emphasizing the major contributions to esthetic thought made by: Plato, Aristotle, Freud, Jung, Croce, Cary, Bergson, Lange, Santayana, Vernon, Bullough, and Nietzsche. $25.95 for each cassette. [Source: Lansford Publishing Company]

Existential Philosophy and Psychology—Eight cassettes ($25.95 each) that explain the nature of existentialism, its historical background and importance for understanding the modern age, and its application to the behavioral sciences. [Source: Lansford Publishing Company]

Introduction to Logic—A complete course, covering uses of language, traditional vs. modern logic, theory of propositions, immediate inference, the syllogism, truth functions, formal proof, and scientific method, on six cassettes for $149.95. A more advanced course, *Informal Logic and Inductive Reasoning*, takes up identifying the problem, abstraction, reasoning by analogy, inductive and deductive reasoning, general assumptions, and informal fallacies, on six cassettes for $149.95. [Source: Lansford Publishing Company]

Audio-Forum—Individual lectures (generally $10.95 each) giving a vast number of philosophical viewpoints: Carlos Casteneda on *Don Juan: The Sorcerer*, Jacob Bronowski on *The Ascent of Man*, Victor E. Frankl on *Logotherapy and Existentialism*, Karl Hess on *The Future of Civilization*, Joseph Wood Krutch asking *What Does 'Human Nature' Mean?*, Ashley Montagu responding with *The Nature of Human Nature*, Arnold J. Toynbee describing *The Ancient Mediterranean View of Man*, W. T. Stace on *The Foundations of Ethics*, and many more. [Source: Jeffrey Norton Publishers, Inc.]

Basic Principles of Objectivism—Nathaniel Branden gives a systematic exposition of the fundamentals of the philosophy of objectivism, as originally expounded by Ayn Rand in her book *Atlas Shrugged* and by the Biocentric Institute. The complete course is on 20 long cassettes (24 hours of material) in albums for $212. These and other lectures by Dr. Branden are also available individually for $11.95 each. [Source: Jeffrey Norton Publishers, Inc.]

Livelong Learning—Conferences at the University of California Berkeley, expertly captured on audiocassettes. These aren't for the average high-school dropout. Some titles: *Martin Buber and the Life of Dialogue*, eight hours by Katharine Whiteside, $75; *Human Nature: Zen, Yoga, and Sufism*, four hours with James Fadiman, $48; *The Quest for Meaning*, seven hours covering woman's and man's quest, the quest through healing, the child's quest through sandplay, and the quest through religion, $75 (individual cassettes $15); and *Potential for Holocaust*, $13 for 38 minutes. [Source: University of California]

Tapes in Human Ecology—Short essays on man's nature in relation to his environment, and on the problems man must solve if he is to remain on earth—all by S. P. R. Charter (editor and publisher of *Man· On· Earth*). Each C-30 cassette contains five five-minute essays prepared to stimulate thought and discussion of each topic. The 52 tapes available are categorized into these headings: ecology, biology, sociology, political science, engineering, architecture and design, geography, business and economics, law and government, philosophy, and natural philosophy. $9 each.   [Source: Applegate Books]

Alan Watts Audiotapes—Virtually all of the recorded lectures and seminars of the philosopher and communicator are collected here. The lectures cover three basic areas: human consciousness, comparative religion, and arts and humanities; the lengths range from 16 to 75 minutes, cost $11 each, any four for $35. The seminars on the subject of comparative religion and human consciousness offer a deeper examiniation of the topics and demonstrate the

process of Alan Watts communicating with 25-30 of his students; most seminars consist of four 45-minute talks, $40 for the set.   [Source: MEA]

Alan Watts—Shortly before his death, Alan Watts recorded the basic tenets of his philosophy. These eight *Essential Lectures of Alan Watts* are now available on audio-cassettes, for $30. Other Alan Watts offerings include his eight-lecture courses on *Essentials of Buddhism*, *Philosophy of Religion*, and *Eastern Philosophy and Psychology*. Each lecture in these courses averages about 45 minutes. The cost of each course is $50, including album.   [Source: Essential Recordings]

XVI.
Public Affairs

Black Studies

Creative Learning Center—Biographies of noted black leaders (Banneker, Washington, Marshall, Bunche, Garvey, and King), stories of John Brown, the Scottsboro Boys, the KKK, and essays on black sports, black attitudes in white America, the color of equality, black revolutionaries, and black adoption. $9 each. [Source: Creative Learning Center]

Sounds of Black Heritage—An introduction to the historical development of black life and history, on six 30-minute programs: *Beginnings*; *Slavery*; *Civil War*; *Early Contributions*; *Reconstruction and After*; *20th Century*. $7.50 each. [Source: Sylvestre C. Watkins Co.]

Current Events and Issues

Opposing Viewpoints Cassettes—Short—8 to 12 minutes—these are stimulating debates by qualified people on pertinent topics: the U. S. policy of detente, with Senator Barry Goldwater vs. Senator Edmund S. Muskie; national health insurance, with Senator Edward Kennedy vs. Representative Philip Crane; affirmative action quotas, with Daniel C. Maguire vs. Sidney Hook; corporal punishment in the schools, with the Boston Globe vs. the Daily Oklahoman; the value-added tax, with Representative Al Ullman vs. Representative Barney Conable; and 55 more of similar interest. $5.98 per cassette (one debate to a cassette), free album with an order of any 10 cassettes for $59.80. [Source: Greenhaven Press]

New Directions in Program Design and Evaluation—In 12 taped talks, William Meyers deals with some of the most critical problems confronting social program effectiveness, $15 each, all 12 cassettes (13 hours) in album with bibliography for $160. [Source: University of California]

Informal Education—In this talk directed to parents, Howard Bonnell discusses the importance of preschool education. $10.95 for a single cassette. [Source: Howard W. Bonnell]

Tapes for Readers—Over 1,000 interviews with notable people conducted by reporter Stephen Banker, to provide an oral history of our times. All programs are grouped into ten subject areas: The Arts (including interviews with the likes of John Updike, Kurt Vonnegut, Jr., Saul Bellow, and Woody Allen); Black Studies (Alex Haley, Adam Clayton Powell Jr., and others); Consumer Affairs (Ralph Nader, Craig Clairborne, and others); Entertainers (Marcel Marceau, Zubin Mehta, and others); Human Behavior (Margaret Mead, B. F. Skinner, and others), Literature (James A. Michener, John Cheever, Herman Wouk, E. L. Doctorow, and others); Living History (Hubert Humphrey, Dean Acheson, John Kenneth Galbraith, and others); Native American Studies (Ladonna Harris, Tomas Sanchez, and others); Sports (Arthur Ashe, Muhammad Ali, Satchel Paige, and others); and Women's Studies (Gloria Steinem, Phyllis Schafly, and others). Each 25-45 minute tape is $10.95; 50¢ brings a list of speakers in each subject area, or $3.50 for all ten lists plus index. [Source: Tapes for Readers]

Firing Line—William F. Buckley, recognized for his debating skills and his command of the English language, interviews national and international figures on a variety of topics—from Vladimir Bukovsky on human rights in the USSR and Ron Dellums on the Black caucus to James R. Hoffa on himself and Bishop Abel Muzorewa on the Rhodesian dilemma. These are the audio versions of the popular PBS programs, complete from their start in 1971 to the present. $10 for each program tape plus $2 for a transcript. [Source: Southern Educational Communications Association]

American Awareness Audio Library—Sixty to ninety minute pro-American talks by various authorities giving the conservative view on many topics in the area of money and inflation, law and order, big business, federal agencies and big government, communism, American foreign policy, the United Nations, energy and ecology, education, and more. This is also a source for recordings by Robert Welch, founder and president of the John Birch Society: two albums of *Insights of Mr. Robert Welch* ($35 for a six-cassette album, $30 for a five-cassette one) and *The Blue Book*, read in its entirety (five cassettes, $30). [Source: Gary Allen Communications]

World Future Society—A collection of recordings, each consisting of two half-hour interviews, on future-related topics: worries and issues of the future; careers and education in the future; concerns about future resources and economics; the American value systems of the future; how futurists predict the future; nutritional alternatives and food technologies; and home energy uses. Each $6. Shades of the future, they also offer some programs on compressed tape, with each featuring four 30-minute interviews on a 60-minute tape: energy options; electronic office and intermation skills; alternative energy sources (fuel cells and coal). These are $7 each. Finally, *Effective Management of Change* is three cassettes and instruction manual designed to help future-oriented administrators and leaders plan and control and change and thereby reduce organizational 'future shock.' $70. [Source: World Future Society]

Audio Cassettes from the Center—Over 500 programs providing the listener with informative discussions on government and politics, law and justice, international relations, education, sociology, psychology, communications, philosophy, religion, science, technology, ecology, and future planning. Renowned leaders and specialists join Center for the Study of Democratic Institutions staff and associates in an open exchange of ideas. Cassettes run from 25 to 70 minutes, cost $8.50 each with discounts on large orders. Participants include Mortimer Adler, B. F. Skinner, Paul Ehrlich, Abba Eban, Cesar Chavez, Herbert Marcuse, William O. Douglas, Elizabeth Hardwick, Jacob Bronowski, Jacques Barzun, John Kenneth Galbraith, and many others. In addition to single programs in the areas listed above, special cassette series are edited from Center conferences, each covering a different aspect of the conference subject. Some of the albums available: *Crime—And What Can Be Done About It* and *The Family in a Changing Society*, each $47.60 for seven cassettes; *Critical Issues in Alcoholism*, seven cassettes, $45.90; *The Transition of Youth to Constructive Adult Life: The Role of the Public School*, ten cassettes, $72.25; *The Jewish Tradition and Its Relevance to Contemporary Life*, seven cassettes, $76; *The Future of the Criminal Justice System*, eight cassettes, $59.40. Other larger series titles include *Constitutional Principles: Their Validity and Vitality Today* and *Illegal Immigration*. All of these cassettes are also available individually, for $8.50 each. [Source: Center for the Study of Democratic Institutions]

National Public Radio—Over 500 programs, most originally broadcast to general audiences, are listed in their thick catalog, and the titles cover the spectrum of contemporary public affairs. The headings (amd major subdivisions) in that catalog cover education (issues, special aspects, theory and practice), humanities (sound portraits of 20th Century humanists, fine arts, performing arts, language and literature, media), science (general, natural, health, and medicine), and the social sciences (business and economics, history, political science, psychology, sociology including cities, family, and gerontology, and special interest groups including ethnic groups,

handicapped, and women). Most tapes are either 59-minutes long ($9) or 29-minutes long ($8). There are also some audio-print modules with teaching guides: *The Last of Jonestown*, 3 hours, $23; *Poland: A Time of Turmoil*, 84 minutes, $14; and *Power in America*, 6+ hours, $55. [Source: National Public Radio]

Public Policy Forums—The challenging roundtables and debates sponsored by the American Enterprise Institute (a conservative think-tank), feature face-to-face confrontations of advocates of differing points of view on major public policy issues, such as health insurance, inflation, the cities, tax reform, oil, social security, regulatory agencies, affirmative action, energy, nuclear power, foreign trade, and much more. Price is $7.50 for each C-60 cassette program, or any 10 for $50. [Source: American Enterprise Institute]

China Talks—America's leading sinologist, Harvard Professor John King Fairbanks, offers six lectures on the origins of Chinese culture and their impact on developments today. Lecture topics are: the Confusian social order; China and the barbarians; traders, missionaries, and diplomats; the revolutionary process; the People's Republic; and China's revolution in the 1970s. $60 for six C-60 cassettes with study guide in album. [Source: Harvard University Press]

Great Atlantic Radio Conspiracy—Thirty-minute programs originally produced for listener-supported radio stations, on a variety of New Left topics, under broad categories of: politics, political protest, the rulers and the ruled, the control of the media, revolution and counter-revolution, justice, food, health, ecology, women and men, racism, agism, radical alternatives, and radical arts. They are $5 per program, or two for $9 (on a C-60 cassette) for individuals, and for institutions $8.50 for a single program, $16 for two. [Source: Great Atlantic Radio Conspiracy]

Dr. Beter Audio Letter—Dr. Peter Beter offers a monthly hour-long report on how and why our nation is falling apart: the gold has been stolen from Fort Knox and replaced with plutonium; the Rockefellers and the Soviets have allied for world domination; NASA arranged a cover-up of the Columbia disaster; and how the collapse of the U.S. banking system was deliberately planned. The views expressed are somewhat unorthodox and thoroughly Cassandra-like. $35 for a 6-month subscription in U.S. and Canada; $19.50 for 3 months; single issues $7.50. [Source: Dr. Beter Audio Letter]

Lava Mt—Current history tapes: Richard Nixon's Checkers and resignation speeches and Spiro Agnew's Attack on the Media speech, $7.75 for each C-60 cassette. Then there are a flock of cassettes related to the JFK assassination: Dallas police transmissions, 90 min. $9; an interview and a debate with Lee Oswald before the assassination, each $7; Marguerite Oswald reading Lee's letters from Russia, $7;

CBS/NBC broadcasts from 11/22/63, 2 hours, $12; the Harold Weisberg "whitewash lectures," 6 hours, $30; James H. Lesar on the legal barriers to an investigation, $7; interview with Murray Jackson, Dallas radio dispatcher, $7; and an interview with Jim Garrison, $6. All the major public policy speeches of FDR are available on six hour-long cassettes, including all the inaugurals and the Day of Infamy speeches, among others, for $35. And then there is a horrifying cassette of the final 43 minutes at Jonestown, with Rev. James Jones admonishing his flock to begin their mass suicide, $10 including transcript. [Source: Lava Mt]

Space Shuttle: Voyage Into the Future—One cassette with book on the United States space shuttle project, complete with music and sound effects. $5.95. [Source: Magnetix Corporation]

Kennedy Space Center—The history and future of the space program at Kennedy Space Center is covered in this cassette and accompanying book. $5.95. [Source: Magnetix Corporation]

The American Woman in Fact and Fiction—An audiotape series created by Virginia Maynard documenting and dramatizing the changing status of the American woman from colonial times to the present, first broadcast over radio in 1958. $115 for 13 cassettes in album, $10 for each 30-minute cassette. [Source: University of California]

China: A Contemporary Assessment—A series designed to give a valid background for the literary, historical, religious, political, social and cultural realities of China. Each cassette is an independent study, and taken together they furnish a wide spectrum of Chinese culture, history, philosophy, and contemporary life. $12 per cassette. [Source: Everett/Edwards, Inc.]

Simplified Texts—A wide-ranging library of titles, generally grouped into series. The *Urban Problems* series covers ward politics, sweat shops, public schools, conspicuous wealth, and poverty. The *Terrorism* series gives an understanding of why violence happens, by analyzing the Haymarket riot, the Molly Maguires, the KKK, lynch laws, all four presidential assassinations, civil war draft riots, and looks at terrorism in the 20th century and crime in America. The *Middle East* series has 18 cassettes that explore the conflicts that have scarred the area, from Masada and Herod, wars of independence, Zionism and Islam, to Nasser, Arab nationalism, and looks at the future. *What the Jews Believe* gives the Jewish views on God, man, holidays, Bar and Bat Mitzvah, charity, non-Jews, rabbis, and men and women. All cassettes $10 each. [Source: Simplified Texts]

UNESCO Radio Programmes—The brilliantly produced UNESCO radio programs are available from Sound Information, a new Australian distributor/producer of audiocassette programming. The UNESCO programs cover a spectrum of topics of current events and interest: hydrology, man and the desert, oceanography, volcanoes, drug abuse, Karl Marx, Comenius, Rousseau, women's rights, the Galapagos—to name just a few. These are generally A$9.80 each; transcripts are available for A$2. Sound Information also publishes a catalog (A$2.50) listing the other 1,000 audiocassette programs they distribute, including some that they produce. [Source: Sound Information Pty Ltd]

Christopher Conversations—Discussions about a variety of contemporary topics, by notables in the field. A few of the 19 titles: *Aging in America*, with Garson Kanin and Dr. Dorothy Finkelhor; *Alcoholism—A Family Affair*, with Dr. Patricia O'Gorman; *Children are People, Too*, with Joan Ganz Cooney and Shari Lewis with friends; *Living with Cancer*, with Myr Leet and Robert Fisher; *Politics and the Press*, with Bill Moyers and Tom Wicker; and *Your Mental Health*, with Dr. David Viscott and Ann Sullivan. $5 for each 56-minute tape. [Source: The Christophers]

Pacifica Tape Library—Cassettes containing actual broadcasts from the non-profit educational FM Pacifica radio stations, the Pacifica News Service, and Pacifica affiliates. Topics covered are anthropology, art, black history, education, environment, economics, government, history, labor, law, literature, media, medicine, native Americans, philosophy, music, politics, psychology, religion, sociology, civil liberties, science, women, and world peace. The slant is usually distinctly liberal. The programs are of variable length, from 30 to 100 minutes, and cost from $10 to $21. [Source: Pacifica Program Service]

Women's Studies

Women: Perspectives on a Movement—A general overview to women in a format that promotes better understanding of the interaction of men and women in today's society. Separate sessions on psychology, biology/sexuality, socialization/education, changing life styles, theology/church, and politics/economics. $19.95 for three cassettes plus background readings, consciousness-raising exercises, and leader's guide. [Source: Thesis]

The Feminist Movement—A lecture on two 20-30 minute cassettes that covers the development of the movement, changing male-female roles, trends in discrimination, and new directions for modern women, for $65.95. [Source: Lansford Publishing Company]

XVII.
Recreation

Cooking

Cook International Tonight—Seventy-five recipes on six cassettes, with each side giving a complete menu and details for preparing a meal from one international area, including Greece, Vienna, France, Shakespeare's England, Mexico, Italy, Polynesia, India, Mideast, Spain, China. Also, Vincent Price gives background, serving, preparation and wine tips. $29.95 for six cassettes, and shopping guides in an album. [Source: Professional Cassette Center]

Vincent Price's International Cooking Courses—Twelve cassettes, each giving a complete menu, recipes and details on preparing a meal from one international area: Greece, Vienna, France, Shakespeare's England, Mexico, Polynesia, Italy, India Mideast, Spain and China. These are more than just 'how to' instructions: Vincent Price gives background preparation tips, serving and wine suggestions, and options for individualizing recipes and menus. $4.98 per cassette, any three for $9.98, and all 12 for $29.95. [Source: Metacom, Inc.]

Dance

How To Dance—Betty White, professional dance instructor and author, gives simple instructions on the tape correlated with simple drawings and diagrams in the instruction manual. Also covered are pointers on how to lead, how to follow, types of rhythms and breaks. There are 12 courses available: fox trot, waltz, cha cha cha, rhumba, mambo, tango, charleston, polka, lindy, merengue and samba, square dance, and party dances (bunny hop, Virginia reel, conga, Mexican waltz, la raspa). $7.98 each. [Source: Conversa-phone Institute, Inc.]

Dancercise Cassette Courses—From choreographer Jon Devlin's Dancercise Club in New York, four courses of music, instruction, and explanations that combine modern dance, yoga, and calisthenics to lose weight and gain grace are available: *Total Exercise*, with emphasis on supertoning exercises for the stomach, buttocks, and thighs and jogging to music; *Stretch Out*, a total body workout on the floor for limbering and toning the muscles and building strength; *Jazzerobics*, a basic jazz dance class designed for beginner, combining modern jazz dance

technique with toning exercises and an emphasis on aerobic movement; and *Hustle*, a basic introduction to disco dance steps. $10.95 for each kit of one cassette and picture instruction booklet. [Source: Dancercise]

Aerobic Dancing—has Barbara Ann Auer's carefully designed exercise programs to improve the cardiovascular system. Two programs, each with illustrated booklet, $6.98 each. *Recharge Yoga* is planned for the over-40 age group and provides deep breathing, proper spinal alignment, and stretching exercises without stress or strain. $4.98 for cassette and illustrated guide. [Source: Metacom]

No Fear Disco—Here is a program for self-conscious persons who would like to get out on the dance floor, but are sure they will make perfect fools of themselves. The first cassette is motivational and covers the six positive qualities of a successful dancer, plus relaxation exercise. Cassette two is a one-hour disco lesson with a qualified instructor teaching the 'double hustle.' $19.95 for two cassettes and pictorial study guide. [Source: Creative Media Group]

Exercise

Aerobics: The Science of Preventive Medicine—In six hour-long lectures, Kenneth Cooper M.D., the developer of aerobics, discusses the boom in preventive medicine, preventive cardiology, exercise and its relation to coronary risk factors, levels of fitness and coronary heart disease, testing aerobic fitness, and developing a personal fitness program. $39.95 for six C-60 cassettes in album. [Source: Institute for Aerobics Research]

5BX Exercise Plan—Dr. William Orban's famed plan, originally designed for the Royal Canadian Air Force, consists of scientifically designed exercises, each progressively more difficult as the subject improves physically. Dr. Orban explains it on this 60 minute cassette for $11.95. [Source: Jeffrey Norton Publishers, Inc.]

Beginning Yoga—Indra Devi, one of America's foremost yoga teachers, explains basic asanas with breathing instructions and step-by-step directions for all basic exercises. *Sai Yoga* covers advanced asanas, based on the teachings of Sai Baba. $10.95 for either 50-minute cassette. [Source: Jeffrey Norton Publishers, Inc.]

Comprehensive Exercise Guide—Dr. Michael J. Maloney leads the listener through a carefully structured activity plan, individualized to suit personal preferences, needs, physical capacity, and lifestyle. He paces one through the warm-up, a fitness test, and exercises for conditioning lower and upper body areas. $35 for three cassettes and instructional/record-keeping manual in album. [Source: BMA Audio Cassettes]

Ripped Seminars—Two informal, unrehearsed question-and-answer sessions with Clarence Bass explaining his 'ripped' body building philosophy, including protein and sodium requirements, supplements, maintenance and peaking diets, training routines for off-season and while peaking, and more, for the body building and fitness enthusiast. $13.95 each. [Source: Clarence Bass's Ripped Enterprises]

Power Focus Series—Peter Siegel explains how to become a better body builder by using his techniques to increase power, intensity, health, motivation, and concentration. Six sets are available: motivation series (4 tapes, $40); health series (7 tapes, $70); intensity series (4 tapes, $40); contest preparation (6 tapes, $60); women's training (5 tapes, $50); and contest preparation/women (6 tapes, $60). Any five tapes of your choice are $50, or $11.95 each. An instruction booklet is included with each order. [Source: Fitness Research Institute]

The Diamond Method—Stretching, fitness, and weight reduction exercises, led by Karen Diamond to the rhythm of spritely background music. Two half-hour cassettes are available, $9.89 each. [Source: Karen Diamond School of Exercise]

Mike Mentzer—A champion bodybuilder offers his weight training system to develop fullest potential in the shortest possible time. The single cassette covers exploring bodybuilding potential, proper diet to gain muscle without fat, new heavy duty methods (rest/pause, infitonic, omnicontraction training), carbohydrates vs. steroids, and 'the perfect routine.' $20.95 with written instructions. [Source: Mike Mentzer]

Games

Gambling Cassettes—Maximillion and Victoria Cabot have been beating the casinos at their own games for over 10 years, and now they share some of the simple techniques they have mastered to win, regularly and legally, at the gambling tables. In *Casino Gaming Expose*, they show how to beat baccarat, craps, blackjack, keno, roulette, and slots. In *Basic Roulette*, they teach betting strategy and progressive placement of wagers. *How To Win at Casino Blackjack* covers both card-counting and no-count methods of beating the house. In *Power Poker*, Max Cabot and George Percy reveal 'golden rules' and inside playing strategy to make one a consistent winner. These are all $19.98 per course of one

cassette, reference books, and other printed materials. Also available is *Backgammon in One-Hour*, with Bill Fox making you a solid tournament-level player in just one hour, for $4.98 for a cassette and illustrated guide. [Source: Metacom, Inc.]

Len Miller Casino Gambling Courses—The co-founder and editor of *Gambling Times* gives the secrets of transforming all the house odds and edges to your favor. Three courses are available—*Winning Dice*, *Winning Blackjack*, and *Winning Roulette*—each consisting of a cassette of instruction, board layout, and 'carry-to-the-casino' guide for $24.95 each; order all three for $64.85 and receive additional pointers on winning at keno and slots. [Source: Automated Learning, Inc.]

How To Play Chess—Chess Master Walter Hall explains the names and movements of the pieces, castling, capturing, check and checkmate, draws and stalemates, and more. 85-minute cassette and booklet for $11.95. [Source: Jeffrey Norton Publishers, Inc.]

Barrie Bridge Tapes—The fundamentals of basic and intermediate bridge, presented by bridge champion Billy Gough. *Basic Rubber Bridge* is a good basic course on the philosophy, objectives, techniques and scoring for rubber bridge. $14.95 for two cassettes (over two hours' instruction) with programmed booklet. *Introduction to Duplicate Bridge* gives all the information necessary for the rubber bridge player who would like to go to the duplicate bridge club, $8.95 for a 46-minute cassette and booklet. All highly recommended. Also, in *Introduction to the Chess Board*, chess master Walter Hall has prepared a program of fundamentals aimed at the absolute beginner. The first side describes the game and its concept, and introduces the pieces and their moves. The second side presents opening moves, offense, defense, and actual games. The course is programmed to an illustrated booklet, and it will teach you to play and understand chess. $9.95 for C-90 cassette with booklet. [Source: Barrie Sound Studios]

Backgammon—Instructor Bill Fox gives a private lesson in the increasingly popular game. The instruction moves at a comfortable pace, with both rules and strategy carefully explained. Suitable for learning alone or with an opponent. $7.50. [Source: Soundmark]

Music Instruction

Keys to the Keys: Self-Taught Piano Method for Adults and Teenagers, Vol I—This program by Gale Pederson is a basic study course with chord instruction, an easy and enjoyable self-study way to learn to play the piano. This practical course overcomes the problems of adults who think they are too old to learn or embarrassed at the thought of going to a class, as well as teenagers, who have little time for going to piano lessions. Progress is easily measured by the learner. Fourteen lessons are given in one 40-minute audio cassette with a 20-page illustrated, easy-to-follow book.

Correct seating and hand position, finger numbers, names of the white keys, legato finger action, note values, measures and counting, tie, cross-hand playing, hold sign, quarter rest, broken chord: it's all here. Upon completion of this volume the learner is able to play the following melodies in the right hand in combination with left hand C, F, and G7 chords: "Merrily We Roll Along", "Drink To Me Only With Thine Eyes", "He's A Jolly Good Fellow", and "Skip To My Lou". The order number is S1550, the price, $14.95. Volumes II (Lessons 15-23), and Volume III (Lessons 24-38) are in preparation. [Source: Jeffrey Norton Publishers]

Homespun Tapes—There is no finer source of instruction in authentic folk instruments than that provided by Homespun Tapes. The instructors are top professional musicians with many performance and recording credits—and the instruction is in an informal, relaxed manner that conveys the feeling that the teacher is a friend in your home. Except as noted, all courses consist of six hour-long cassettes (each with tablature and lyrics) that sell for $60 for the set, or $12 per cassette. Titles and instructors: *Guitar for Beginners, Lead Guitar,* and *Hot Licks for Guitar,* by Artie Traum; *Country Guitar Styles,* by Merle Watson (three cassettes, $30); *Pattern Picking* (three cassettes, $30), *Country Blues Guitar, Fingerpicking Series 1 & 2,* and *Flatpick Country Guitar,* by Happy Traum; *Advanced Flatpick Guitar,* by Russ Barenberg; *Flatpicking Fiddle Tunes,* by Dan Crary; *Ragtime Guitar,* by John James; *Electric Guitar* and *Rock and Roll Rhythm Guitar,* both by Amos Garrett; *Bottleneck/Slide Guitar,* by Arlen Roth; and *Basic Jazz Guitar,* by Artie Traum (three cassettes, $30). If interested in banjo and fiddle: *5 String Banjo Series 1 & 2,* by Happy Traum; *Clawhammer Banjo,* by Ken Perlman; *Bluegrass Banjo,* by Bill Keith, and *Advanced Banjo Workshop,* by Bill Keith and Tony Trischka; *Bluegrass & Country Fiddle,* by Kenny Kosek; *Texas and Swing Fiddle Styles,* by Matt Glaser; and *Irish Fiddle,* by Keven Burke. Still not satisfied? Then try: *Bluegrass Dobro,* by Stacy Phillips; *Blues Harmonica,* with John Sebastian and Paul Butterfield; *Bluegrass Mandolin,* by Sam Bush; *Blues Rock Piano* and *Ragtime Piano,* both by David Cohen; and *Hammer Dulcimer,* by John McCutcheon. On single cassettes with folio are *Strictly Folk Guitar* and *Gospel Guitar* ($12.95 each) and *Autoharp and Jew's Harp* with Mike Seeger ($12). $2.50 will bring you a cassette demonstrating the Homespun style of teaching guitar or banjo, mandolin, fiddle, and piano. [Source: Homespun Tapes]

Johnny Kemm Home Study Organ Course—A series of lessons by one of America's most noted organists, each consisting of two C-60 cassettes (voice-compressed) plus lesson plans and music, leading to

competency in any style of organ playing, from liturgical to jazz. Each cassette contains not only Mr. Kemm's verbal instructions but also organ demonstrations of the techniques under discussion. Titles include *The Art of Flipping Switches* (organ registration) *From Ears to Fingers* (playing by ear), both $20.70 each, and *Harmonic Ear Training* (playing chords by ear, to match any melody in any key), $24.95. All except the first one are also suitable for piano instruction, and all come with reference guides. [Source: Elizabeth Kemm]

Piano University—Everything but everything that the beginner would want to know about playing the piano, from *How To Play Chord Piano in Ten Days* and *Left Hand Bass Styles for 'Pop' Piano* to *Boogie Patterns* and *Hearing Rhythms, Identifying Patterns.* Other cassette courses cover improvisation, how to play and arrange various gospel hymns, how to get special effects on the piano, how to play ballads, honky-tonk, ragtime, blues, how to play a number of well-known classical songs, and much more. These are all taught by Duane Shinn. He also has cassettes on singing, songwriting, playing the chord guitar, courses in harmony and music theory in general, and courses frankly on how to make money in music, by writing articles about it, selling music by mail, and teaching music, all $12.95 each. A special offering is his program on *How To Write & Publish Your Own Book, Song, Course, Slide Chart, or Other Printed Product, and Make It Go!,* $99.95 for four cassettes and abundant literature and samples in binder. [Source: Duane Shinn Publications]

How To Make It in Pop Music—This is the generic title for a series of recorded 90-minute workshop cassettes offered by Songwriters Resources and Services, on song evaluation, music theory, voice, and the music business. Each cassette features experts with outstanding records and credits. Titles include: *You Ought to Be in Pictures* (music composition for films), *How to Make and Sell Your Own Record, The Art of Promoting Yourself, L. A. Country, The Track of Your Careers* (questions asked record producers), *Taking Care of Business* (the business of songwriting), and *Everything You Wanted to Know About the Music Business.* $11.95 each. [Source: Jeffrey Norton Publishers, Inc.]

Old-Time Radio Programs

Old Time Radio Programs—A good collection of original broadcasts from the 1940s and 1950s, during radio's 'golden age.' They have shows with Jimmy Durante, Eddie Cantor, and all the other headliners, a large collection of Bob Hope shows, and many of the old country music, big band, and other music shows. $4 for two half-hour shows of your choice. [Source: Cassette Library Center]

Golden Age Radio—Thousands of old radio shows in all categories—from Lux Radio Theatre and Glenn Miller to This Is Your FBI and Sergeant Preston of the Yukon (remember that theme song?). Free catalog. $6 per pre-recorded C-60 cassette (generally two shows) or four for $18. [Source: Golden Age Radio]

Great Radio Shows—A huge collection of radio programs from the past, with emphasis on the classic radio programs, such as Jack Benny, Fred Allen, Suspense, Fibber McGee, One Man's Family, and the like. They have all 114 X Minus One shows, for the Arch Oboler buffs, for example. All cassettes are $6.50 per hour of your choice. For $2.95 ($1.50 deductible from first order) you can get their ream-thick catalog containing a brief, literate synopsis of the plot, stars, and other pertinent information on each show; it is easily the best catalog of this nature we have seen, and worth the price just for the memories alone. [Source: Great Radio Shows]

Radio Reruns—Some of the best old-time radio programs, complete with commercials, including Fibber McGee and Molly, Burns and Allen, Amos & Andy, Jack Benny, and some of the best from Dragnet, Escape, Inner Sanctum, Suspense, Sherlock Holmes, The Shadow, and others. $3.98 for each 30-minute cassette, with every sixth tape free. [Source: Metacom, Inc.]

Radio Vault—Their large catalog of shows from the 'golden age of radio'—Our Miss Brooks and Ellery Queen, National Barn Dance, Spotlight Revue—is available for $2. All the shows are recorded from original transcriptions, so fidelity is very good to excellent on all. $3 per hour with a minimum order of two hours; order ten hours and get a free hour. [Source: Radio Vault]

Memory Lane—Programs from the early years of radio, from Burns and Allen and Escape to Fibber McGee and Molly. $5.25 per pre-recorded C-60 cassette containing two 30-minute shows. [Source: Audio Accessories Co.]

Mar-Bren—Specializing in vintage radio programs, Mar-Bren offers over 11,000 old-time radio programs, comprehensively described in their master catalog and supplements. They have Gildersleeve and Gunsmoke, Lux Radio Theatre and Backstage Wife. An interesting new offering is almost a complete day (August 10, 1945) in WEAF in New York, starting with H. V. Kaltenborn and more news, then Mary Margaret McBride, and on to innumerable soap operas, the six o'clock news, then musicals and a quiz show in the evening. Cost is $9.50 per C-60 cassette, with your choice of contents. [Source: Mar-Bren Sound Ltd.]

Golden Radio Library—One-hour preselected programmings, containing some of the finest moments in radio history. There are not only Jack Benny, The Green Hornet, Amos & Andy, Suspense, Charlie McCarthy, and Spike Jones (to name just a few), but

documentaries on Remember Radio?, famous radio fluffs, an hour of memorable commercials (like 'Rinso White' with Beverly Sills), and other anthologies. $5.95 each. [Source: Golden Radio Library]

Nostalgia Sounds—Certainly the lowest cost for any old-time radio cassettes that we have seen: $1.98 per C-60 cassette with your choice of programs. They claim to be the world's largest dealer in old-time radio shows, with over 15,000 titles in stock. Their catalog is $5, applicable to the first order. They have all the standards, a large collection of hour-long Lux Radio Theatres, and even some 1932-1933 Linit Bath House programs with Fred Allen as the star. [Source: Nostalgia Sounds]

Radio Tapes—Over 50,000 old radio programs, including not only the standards (Adventures of Harry Lime, Escape, Cavalcade of America, and Romance), but also probably the largest collection available of the early radio musical programs. $8 per cassette hour of your choice. $6 for a 500+ page catalog, or $3 for the latest supplement. [Source: Redmond Nostalgia Company]

Huckleberry Designs—A small but outstanding collection of old-time radio programming. Some of the highlights: Day of the Triffids, four 60-minute cassettes, $18.95; Lux's African Queen with Bogart and Greer Garson, and My Man Godfrey with Powell and Lombard, $5.95 each; I Love a Mystery's The Thing That Cries in the Night, three hours for $14.95; WW II news broadcasts with Murrow, Kaltenborn, Daly, Sevareid, and Winchell, $5.95, and some of the best of Rudy Vallee, Joe Penner, Jack Benny, Fibber McGee, Dr. I.Q., and X-1. [Source: Lava Mt.]

AM Treasures—Over 15,000 hours of radio shows from the '40s and '50s—Dragnet and Lights Out, Charlie McCarthy and David Harding, Counterspy—available for just $2.50 per hour-long cassette, plus 50 cents per order for handling. Catalog $1.25 [Source: AM Treasures]

American Radio—Over 8,000 shows available, including at least one of almost every radio show produced in the '40s and '50s, from Henry Aldrich and Young Widder Brown to United We Stand and Bob and Ray. $5.95 per hour of pre-recorded sets and collections. Catalog for $3.95. [Source: American Radio]

Once Upon a Radio—The full range of old radio programs in all categories—Fred Allen, Our Miss Brooks, Escape, Gunsmoke, Suspense, Hallmark, Lux, Capt. Midnight, Dimension X—for $8.50 per hour of your choice, or six hours for $40. $2 for thick catalog of titles. [Source: Once Upon A Radio]

Nostalgia Cassettes—137 professionally packaged and referenced old-time radio programs, each containing two half-hour pre-selected shows—Johnny

Dollar and Molle Mystery Theatre, Sergeant Preston and Nick Carter, Red Skelton and Big Town, usually with original commercials. $6.95 each. Also available are several complete serial stories: Superman, One Man's Family ('Book 80, Chapters 1-18'), and two I Love a Mystery stories, each on three cassettes for $20.85; and The Cinnamon Bear (classic Christmas story), six cassettes, $41.70. [Source: National Recording Company]

Old-Time Radio Tapes—About 8,000 old radio programs, including such standards as The Cisco Kid and Suspense to such rare ones as The Adventures of Frank Race and Ethel and Albert. They seem especially strong on adventure/mystery titles. $6.50 per hour of your choice. [Source: BRC OTR Distributors]

Voice From The Past—This source concentrates on special or documentary radio programs from the past, such as *Winston Churchill's Address to Congress after Pearl Harbor, Hitler's Inferno* (a narrated sketch of the rise and fall of the Nazi leaders interspersed with the voices of other leaders of his time), *Jack Benny Looking Back*, William Joyce (Lord Haw Haw) broadcasting from Berlin to North America, *Anti-Communist Voices of Yesterday* (1951-1952), *Nixon-Kennedy Debate, Nixon's Watergate Denial and 1974 Resignation Speeches, Yesterday's Headlines—Today's History*, and many more. Prices are $10.95 to $12.50 per cassette. [Source: Jeffrey Norton Publishers, Inc.]

Yesterdays Radio on Tape—A good source of 'theatre of the mind' programs, with over 20,000 old-time radio programs with all the standards, such as tense drama like Dimension X, hilarious comedy like Dennis Day, frightening fancy like City of the Dead, and astounding fact like The Passing Parade. $5.99 per cassette-hour of your choice (minimum of two cassettes), five cassettes for $25.25. [Source: Aston's Adventures]

Vintage Radio Programs—They have all the old standards, plus the unusual like Screen Guild Theatre and Screen Director's Playhouse, Box 13 and Sky King, two half-hour programs for the bargain price of $3 each. [Source: MB/JB Enterprises]

Sports

Goose Talk and **Duck Talk**—The basics of goose and duck calling, plus tips on the most effective decoy layout and hunting methods. Each C-25 cassette comes with a book and costs $12.10. [Source: G & H Decoys]

Instant Replay—Great moments in sports, such as the Cowboys winning the Superbowl, the return of the Yankees, the Trailblazers, Broncos, Raiders, Patriots, Ohio State—and play-by-play action, highlights, and interviews with most other sports teams who have won or nearly won a championship in the last decade. They also produce a program of sports highlights for each year, and special albums such as baseball's first 100 years, NFL memories, 25 years of the NBA, 50 years of the NHL. $6.95 each. [Source: Fleetwood Communications Co.]

Athletic Achievement—How-I-do-it talks by leading athletes and coaches, with emphasis on the mental attitude: Walter Alston on baseball, Lou Brock or Maury Wills on base running and stealing, Rod Carew or Pete Rose on hitting, Carlton Fisk on catching, Don Sutton on pitching, Joe Morgan on offensive baseball, Brooks Robinson on infielding, Joe Rudi on outfielding, John Wooden, Billie Moore, or Calvin Murphy on Basketball, Roy Emerson on tennis, Kyle Rote Jr. on soccer, Al Scates or Kirk Kilgour on volleyball, and Verne Wolfe on track and field. Then, there's football, with separate programs by Drew Pearson on wide receiving, Pat Haden on quarterbacking, Walter Payton or Chuck Foreman on running backs, and Ray Guy on punting. These are all $11.95 each. *The Making of a Champion*, a six-tape motivational program for young athletes, is available for $150. [Source: Success Motivation International, Inc.]

Learn From the Best—An excellent collection of talks by successful coaches and professional athletes about the art and science of their craft. There are four cassette (two hour) albums by John Wooden on Basketball, Billie Moore on women's basketball, John Robinson on football, Al Scates on volleyball, Walter Alston on baseball, Vern Wolfe on track & field, and Dr. Robert Kerlan on the prevention and treatment of athletic injuries. These are all $39.95 each. Then, there is a large library of various athletes talking about individual skills ($19.95 for two-hour album, $14.95 for a one-hour album): Rod Carew on hitting, Don Sutton on pitching, Lou Brock on base stealing, Brooks Robinson on infielding, Drew Pearson as wide receiver, Ray Guy on punting, Kyle Rote, Jr., on soccer, Roy Emerson on tennis, to name just a few. Finally, there is another 35 one-hour cassettes without albums ($9.95 each), featuring another host of athletes, including Pete Rose on hitting, Maury Wills on base running, Walter Payton on running backs, Bill Sharman on basketball shooting, Gordon Banks on soccer goalies, Nancy Lopez on golf. [Source: Let's Talk Associates]

Great Moments in Cubs Baseball—40 years of the Cubbies, narrated by Jack Brickhouse and 12 others, covering Ernie Banks' 50th home run, no-hit games, and the Cubs in the World Series (it does go back quite a ways!). $6.25 for C-40 cassette. [Source: Audio Accessories Co.]

No-Limit Tennis—You can benefit from the instruction of an experienced tennis professional in your office, living room, or car, without ever putting on your tennis shoes. John de Zeeuw developed and narrates this six-tape training series—covering general practice pointers, most common errors, motivation, strokes, services, spins, poaching, percentage tennis, singles tactics and practice, doubles tactics and practice, match play, court manners, and much more—all intended to make you a better tennis player. $27.50. [Source: Audio Tennis]

Theatre Arts

Walter Kerr's Guide to the Theatre—A complete, up-to-date course on the theatre, revealed in depth by a well-known and respected drama critic, all on six hour-long cassettes. Contents: What Theatre Is; Why Have Theatre?; The People Who Make Theatre; Inside the Play; The Changing Theatre; How to Judge Theatre. $60 for six cassettes with bibliography and glossary, in album. [Source: Educational Enrichment Materials]

Lehman Engel Musical Workshop—You sit in as a student while the 'Dean of American Musical Theatre' leads a 30-hour workshop of discussion, assignments, presentations, and critiques. You'll get practice in plotting, book, scene-by-scene synopses, and librettos, and receive pointers on song placement and scoring, ballads, 'long joke' and 'short joke' songs, and incidental and background music. $370 for 24 cassettes in albums, plus two books. [Source: Jeffrey Norton Publishers, Inc.]

The Business of Motion Pictures—Speakers involved in movie production provide perceptive insights into the way the movie industry functions. Survival tips come from Elia Kazan, David Susskind, Chris Preuster, Marin H. Poll, Arthur Manson, Donald Rugoff, Harry Buxbaum, Frank Perry, and Barry Yellen. Eight cassettes and booklet in album for $89.50. [Source: Jeffrey Norton Publishers, Inc.]

Scene Behind the Screen—Ten top professionals in the TV industry provide an in-depth examination of the programming process for network series, specials, children's TV, news, and sports. $76 for the set of eight tapes (12 hours), and also available individually for $10.95. [Source: Jeffrey Norton Publishers, Inc.]

Seven Arts Cassette Library—Programs covering legal aspects of the entertainment industry, with Walter Hurst and others giving sound counsel about the various legal pitfalls to be avoided. Some of the titles: *Artist-Recording Company Contract and Relationship*, four cassettes, $40; *The Songwriter as a Businessman*, two cassettes, $20; *Recording Session Budget and Checklist*, four cassettes, $40; *Overview of Tax Shelters*, especially for show business high earners, one cassette, $10, *How To Protect your Song*, one cassette, $10; *Copyright and the Movie Business* and *Copyright and the Music Business*, each $200 for 20 cassettes. [Source: Seven Arts Press, Inc.]

Times Cassettes—Prepared by members of The Sunday Times, some music and literature topics: *Enjoying Bach, Harpsichord Music, Enjoying Chopin, Enjoying Elizabethan Music, Enjoying Pop Music, Heroes, Villains, and True Love Conquers All* (Victorian melodrama), *An Hour with Edgar Allan Poe, An Hour with Damon Runyon*, and *Improving your Driving*. About $6 each. [Source: Drake Educational Associates]

Contemporary Drama Service—Aids for teachers of theatre arts and dramatic writing; *Basic Concepts for Beginning Actors* and *Basic Concepts for Beginning Directors*, $7.50 each for cassette, outline, and script; *How to Write your Own Short Plays and Skits*, $6.95 for cassette and synopsis; *14 Ways to Use Drama as a Teaching Tool* and *Using Simulations*, each $5.95 for cassette and outline or simulation game; *Acting with an Accent* (standard British, Irish, Italian, French), $18 each for one cassette with booklet. *The Adolescent in Literature* and *The Many Faces of Terror* (each with five classic stories on three cassettes in album for $17.50) help to develop critical thinking skills by writing critical analyses. In *Open-End Short Stories* ($9.50 for one cassette) students are asked to write an ending and then hear the authors' versions; careful study of *Styles of Comedy Dialog* ($12.50 for one cassette with scripts) will give student writers the basics to get started. *Reader's Theatre: Its Methods and Techniques* offers a complete course in this theatre form, for $5.95 for a single cassette. [Source: Contemporary Drama Service]

Travel

Sights and Sounds of Washington, D.C.—A guided tour of the most popular tourist attractions of the nation's capital. The White House, Lincoln Memorial, Washington Monument, and others are covered on this cassette with accompanying book. $5.95. [Source: Magnetix Corporation]

Let's Have Fun in Japan!—Travel writer Louise Purwin Zobel shows travelers headed to Japan how to prepare properly, then fully enjoy every moment in the Land of the Rising Sun. $9.95 for a single cassette with printed summary. [Source: Write To Sell]

Travel America—A complete library of walking-and-driving cassette tours through all 50 states, plus Washington, D.C. Your guide on the tape directs you through the cities and the countryside of each state, relates local history, points out historical sites, and often tells you the best places to eat and what to do in the evenings. $10 for each state's C-60 cassette, or $350 for all 51 programs. [Source: Cassette House, Inc.]

Auto Tape Tours—Your own 'audio escort' provides directions and describes the scenery as you tour various vacation areas. The national park series, prepared in cooperation with the National Park Service, covers Banff and Jasper (in Canada), Glacier, Grand Teton, Yellowstone, Rocky Mount, Great Smokey, and Gettysburg national parks. Also available are tape tours for the Lancaster Penn Dutch Country, Newport RI, and the seafaring towns of Mystic, Groton, Stonington, and New London CT. The California Auto Tape Tours are on 14 cassettes covering 1400 miles of scenic routes in California and Nevada, with your own 'tour guide' adding to the enjoyment of your drive. The England, Wales, and Ireland series (six different cassettes) offer recorded narration of history, geography, local color and legends, plus music of the area between informational passages. $10.70 each. These tour tapes can also be rented at various local sites for somewhat less than the purchase price, and a player is provided for all rentals except California, England/Ireland, and Yellowstone sites. [Source: Comprehensive Communications, Inc.]

All Roads Lead to Rome—This four-cassette album by Michael King takes the armchair traveler to 16 places in Rome—some famous, others little-known—to share the appeal of the Eternal City with the non-traveler and to aid the experienced traveler in planning a trip to Rome. $22.95. [Source: Alba House Communications]

XVIII.
Religion

Bible Study

Understanding the Bible I & II—Questions of interpretation and doctrine often arise in ecumenical Bible studies, and these teachings by Fr. John Burke OP and Fr. Thomas Kalita explains what the Roman Catholic Church teaches in the light of Vatican II and Catholic tradition. The first volume covers Bible sharing, the Gospel form, and introduction to Luke and the Pauline letters; the second volume covers literary form, the development of dogma and moral teaching, the prophets, and the writings of John and Paul. $39.95 for each nine-cassette album. [Source: SCRC Tape Ministry]

Believer's Bible Course—Messages by Rev. Kenneth Copeland are intended to build 'the solid foundation of faith in your heart'. The 66 cassettes in the series are grouped into such categories as Faith, Realities of Redemption, Healing and Love, Prayer Power, Forces of the Recreated Human Spirit, and Laws of Prosperity. $4 per cassette, or all 66 for $235. In *Advanced Bible Studies*, in-depth studies are taught by the same evangelist, intended for mature Christians seeking a deeper spiritual understanding of God's Word. There are 4 to 12 cassette messages in each study, mostly based on single books or chapters from the Bible. $4 per cassette. [Source: Kenneth Copeland Ministries]

Bible and Science—Dr. John C. Whitcomb, Jr., Professor of Old Testament at Grace Theological Seminary, discusses the Creation and the Flood in the Book of Genesis in the light of new scientific knowledge. $4.50 for each of twelve 60-minute cassette lectures with detailed outlines, $55 for complete set in album. In *Dinosaurs and Men*, Dr. Whitcomb uses evidence from the Book of Job, the Book of Genesis and modern discoveries to show that man and dinosaurs lived together on the earth after the Creation. Three 60-minute cassettes and outline in album for $16, or $4.50 for each cassette. *Solomon to the Exile* is a popular study by Dr. Whitcomb of Kings and Chronicles from the time of Solomon to the beginnings of the Babylonian Captivity. $4.50 each with outline, or all twelve of the C-60 cassettes and textbook with album for $55. In *The Second Coming of Christ*, the promised return of Christ, the judgment seat, Daniel and the Antichrist, and the Millenial Kingdom of Christ are all discussed by Dr.

Whitcomb on five cassettes with outline in album for $25, or $4.50 each. Finally, in *The Five Worlds of Bible History, Science and Prophecy*, Dr. Whitcomb describes the world of Genesis 1 and 2, the world before the Flood, the heaven and earth of the present, Christ's Kingdom, and the heaven and earth of eternity, on six cassettes with outline in album, $29, or $4.50 each. [Source: Dr. John Whitcomb]

Bible—George W. Sarris narrates the King James Version of the *Old Testament* on 48 cassettes for $169.95, the *New Testament* on 12 cassettes for $44.95, and *Old Testament Poetry* (Psalms, Proverbs, Ecclesiastes, Job and The Song of Solomon) on eight cassettes for $29.95. The New American Standard Version of the *New Testament* is available on 15 cassettes for $59.95. A new authorized version of the *Living New Testament* is available on 16 cassettes for $49.95, the *Living Old Testament* on 48 cassettes for $179.95, and *Living Old Testament Poetry* on eight cassettes for $32.45. All of these are narrated by George W. Sarris, and all sets come in albums. [Source: Master Productions]

New Testament—In the Revised Standard Version, accepted as an authoritative translation by most experts from both Catholic and Protestant traditions. $44.95 for 16 cassettes in album. They also have the *New Testament* with background music accompanying narration of the New American Bible Version, on 16 cassettes in album for $44.95. In the same version are *Psalms* and *Proverbs* from the Old Testament, on six cassettes in album for $29.95. [Source: Servant Publications]

Complete Old Testament—The King James Version, on 48 cassettes and in three albums, is narrated by Alexander Scourby for $68.75. Also available are some Old Testament selections: *Genesis-Exodus*, or six cassettes, $15.50; *The Three Kings* (Saul, David, Solomon), three cassettes, $9.50; and *Job to Jonah*, 18 cassettes, $43.75—all King James Version, all narrated by Scourby. *Exodus* is available on four cassettes in the Today's English Version for $8.20, and *Proverbs and Ecclesiastes* on two cassettes for $4.25. *The Complete New Testament* is available either in the King James Version narrated by Alexander Scourby or the Today's English Version narrated by Bud Collyer, on 15 cassettes and in an album for $35.50. [Source: American Bible Society]

Bible—Dr. Paul Mims narrates several editions of the King James Version of the *Old Testament*, in a deluxe edition on 72 cassettes in six albums for $189.50, and a regular edition on 48 cassettes in three volumes for $159.95. He narrates the King James Version of the *New Testament* in three editions: deluxe, 24 cassettes in two albums for $69.50; regular, 16 cassettes in one album for $49.95; and economy, 12 cassettes in album for $39.95. These portions of the Bible are available individually, all in album: *Psalms & Proverbs*, six cassettes, $24.95; *Psalms* alone, four cassettes, $15.95; *Proverbs* alone, two cassettes, $9.95; *The Gospel of John*, two cassettes, $9.95; *Romans*, one cassette, $6.95. From the same source many foreign language editions of the Bible are available and include two in Spanish, both narrated by Samuel Montoya: in the 1602 Reina-Valera Version, the *Old Testament* is on 48 cassettes and three albums for $159.95, the *New Testament* on 16 cassettes in album for $49.95; in the 1960 Reina-Valera Revised Version, the *Old Testament* is $165.95 on 48 cassettes in three albums, the *New Testament* is $54.95 for 16 cassettes and one album. Editions of *Genesis, Psalms, Proverbs*, and *The Gospel of John* are also available in both versions. Then, the *New Testament* is available in these foreign languages: French (Segond Version), 16 cassettes in album, $49.95; German (Luther Edition), 24 cassettes, two albums, $69.50; Italian (Riveduta Version), 16 cassettes in album, $49.95; Portuguese (Almeida Versao Atualizada), 16 cassettes in album; Arabic, 20 cassettes in album, $59.95; Korean, 24 cassettes in album, $69.95. *The Gospel of John* and *Romans* are also available in Chinese. [Source: Christian Duplications International, Inc.]

Bible—The Inspired Version (from the Reorganized LDS Church) of the *New Testament*, 14 cassettes and album for $49, of the *Old Testament* on 42 cassettes with three albums for $147. The 1980 Edition of the *Book of Mormon* is available on 18 cassettes with album for $63, the 1970 edition of *Doctrine and Covenants* on ten cassettes with album for $35. All narration is by Harold Whitehead. [Source: Herald House]

Bible—An authorized edition of the Alexander Scourby-narrated *Old Testament* (King James Version) on 48 cassettes for $119, of his *New Testament* on 16 cassettes for $39.95, and *Psalms and Proverbs* on six cassettes for $16.95. Efram Zimbalist, Jr. narrates Schofield's King James Version of the *New Testament* on 16 cassettes for $29.95, and *Psalms and Proverbs* on six cassettes for $29.95. The *New Testament* in the New American Standard Version is read by Al Sanders on 16 cassettes for $59.95. Then, there is a Spanish language version of the King James Version of the *Old Testament* on 48 cassettes for $159.95, the *New Testament* on 16 cassettes for $59.95. The *Living New Testament* is available on 16 cassettes for $59.95, *Living Psalms and Proverbs* on six cassettes for $29.95. Finally, *Living Christ* is a

dramatization of the life of Christ, on five cassettes for $35. All sets come in albums. [Source: Trinity Tapes, Inc.]

Home Study Bible Courses—Some of the correspondence courses conducted by the Moody Bible Institute are accompanied by audio-cassette lectures as a supplement to the course textbook. There is a wealth of low-cost information here (two to three hours of lectures by distinguished authorities, $9 for the set), if the purchaser understands that the recordings are correlated to the text (generally $7.95 to $9.75 each), and not necessarily a complete exposition in themselves. Titles include: *Survey of the Scriptures I, II, III, Genesis, Exodus, Psalms, Daniel, John, Romans, Galatians*, and *Hebrews*. Some non-Bible study titles are: *The Good News, A Reasoning Faith, First Steps in the Christian Faith, God's Will for Your Life, Successful Soul-Winning, The Cults Exposed*, and *The Person and Work of The the Holy Spirit*. [Source: Moody Correspondence School]

Bible—The complete King James Version of the *New Testament* on 12 C-90 cassettes for $39.95, $45.95 with album. *The Good News of Jesus Christ* (the Four Gospels) on six C-90 cassettes for $19.95, $23.95 with album. Finally, the *Book of Psalms* on four cassettes for $16.95. All narration is by Marvin Miller. [Source: Audio Book Company]

Bible—Bethany Fellowship offers the Bible in several versions and editions. It comes complete in the King James Version on 64 cassettes and four albums for $139.95; the *New Testament* alone is $39.95 for 16 cassettes in an album, the *Old Testament* on three 16-cassette albums, $39.95 per album. They have the *New Testament* in either the Revised Standard Version or the New American Bible version, each on 16 cassettes in album for $39.95. The *Dramatized New Testament* is $69.95 and the *Dramatized Psalms and Proverbs* is $29.95 (both in the King James Version, with background music and sound effects). The Modern English Version of the *New Testament* is $59.95. Finally, there is a Spanish language version of the *New Testament* (*La Biblia Hablada, Los Evangelios* and *Las Epistolas*), using the Antigua Version de Casiodoro de Reina, Revision de 1960, in two albums for $29.95 each. [Source: Bethany Fellowship, Inc.]

Dimension Tapes—A good collection of sermons, Bible studies, and theology by Arthur Bloomfield, H. J. Brokke, Larry Christenson, Loren Cunningham, James Bjornstad, Joy Dawson, T. A. Hegre, Malcolm MacGregor, Ray Mossholder, Ernest O'Neill, George Otis, Clark Pinnock, Paris Reidhead, Herman Riffel, Basilea Schlink, Arthur Wallis, and David Wilkerson, each $4.95 per cassette. This source also includes teaching and inspirational albums, such as these six-cassette offerings for $24.95 each: *Study in Romans* by H. J. Brokke; *Study in Ephesians* by Larry Christenson; *Victorious Christian*

Living by T. A. Hegre; *Before the Last Battle* by Arthur Bloomfield; *Best of David Wilkerson*; *The Occult & Confronting the Cultist* by J. B. Bjornstad; *Step Up to Life* by Elmer Murdoch; *What Happens When We Pray & Lord Change Me* by Evelyn Christenson; *Knowing God* by Joy Dawson; and *Cost of Discipleship* by Paris Reidhead. *Esther: A Study in Intercessory Prayer* by Larry Christenson is a three cassette album for $12.95. *Study in Revelation* (Volume I and II) by H. J. Brokke and *Fullness of Life in the Holy Spirit* (Volumes I and II) by Larry Christenson are all five cassette albums for $19.95 each. *Christian Family* by Larry Christenson and *Study in Daniel* by H. J. Brokke are seven-cassette albums for $29.95. *Christian Maturity & The Spirit's Power* by Herman Riffel and *Your Money Matters* by Malcolm MacGregor are eight-cassette albums for $29.95. *Faith and Reason* by Clark Pinnock is a four-cassette album for $16.95. And there are many more; write for their free catalog. [Source: Bethany Fellowship, Inc.]

Bible Study Cassettes—Bible studies by Dr. Donald Grey Barnhouse, founder of radio's Bible Study Hour, and by Dr. James Montgomery Boice, the present voice of the Bible Study Hour. Dr. Boice presents many studies on Genesis, Exodus, Hosea, Joel, Amos, Jonah, John, and Phillippians, as well as on the Foundations of the Christian Faith and other topics. Dr. Barnhouse has numerous studies of Mark, Luke, Romans, and Revelations, and miscellaneous other books. Both offer studies and sermons on Christian growth, end times, and doctrine. Also available are the proceedings of recent Philadelphia Annual Conferences on Reformed Theology. All cassettes are $4 each (usually with two Bible studies), or three for $11. [Source: Bible Study Hour]

Bible—You can get either the King James or Revised Standard Version of the entire *New Testament* for just $22.50, *Old Testament* for $69.25, *Psalms and Proverbs* for $11.50, or the entire *Bible* for $87.25; all sets include albums. The *Living New Testament* is $45.95, the *Living Old Testament* $133.85 (both with music and sound effects). Either the New American Standard or the New International Version of the *New Testament* are $39.95; the New International Version of the *Old Testament* is $133.85. The King James *Dramatized New Testament* is $49.95, *Dramatized Psalms and Proverbs* $20.95. A Spanish language *New Testament* (Good News Version) is complete for $32.50. Finally, the dramatized *Life of Christ* in album is $16.50. [Source: Oasis Cassette Library]

Bible Voice—Narrated by Jack French, the King James Version of the *Old Testament* is on 45 cassettes for $179.95, the *New Testament* on 15 cassettes for $59.95, *Psalms and Proverbs* on six cassettes for $24.95, and the entire *Bible* on 60 cassettes for $239.95. The *Living New Testament*, narrated by Cliff

Barrows and Jack French, is on 15 cassettes for $69.95, the Revised Standard Version of the *New Testament* also on 15 cassettes for $59.95. [Source: Omega Publications]

Book of Mormon—Dramatized Mormon scriptures, on 16 cassettes for $124.95. Also available are dramatized stories from the L.D.S. church history (16 cassettes, $124.95), the dramatized *Articles of Faith* (three cassettes, $21.95) and dramatized Bible stories (10 cassettes, $79.95). All sets include album. [Source: Promised Land publications, Inc.]

New Testament Greek for Beginners—This is an audio version of the text by J. Gresham Machen, including the Greek vocabulary and the answers to the exercises, as narrated by Spiros Zodhaites. He uses modern Greek pronunciation, rather than the Erasmic pronunciation commonly taught in New Testament studies. $31.95 for nine cassettes and guide in album (but you really should have the printed text as well, $21.95). *Vocabulary of the Greek New Testament* includes both the Koine words and other commonly used terms, specifically planned to assist every *Bible* student in knowing the *New Testament* better; $39.95 for eight cassettes and glossary in album. [Source: AMG Publishers]

Greek New Testament—For the person seriously interested in perfecting knowledge of New Testament Greek. Two versions are available, both narrated by Spiros Zodhaites: the Koine version, using the Nestle text, and the Vamvas translation for those who prefer a modern version. The prices for either: $41.95 for volume I (The Gospels, 10 cassettes), $48.95 for volume II (Acts through Revelation, 12 cassettes), $79.95 for the entire Greek New Testament. [Source: AMG Publishers]

Bible—Steven B. Stevens narrates the *New Testament* in three editions: the King James version for $39.95, the New International Version for $59.95, and the NIV dramatized version for $69.95. Reina Valera also narrates a Spanish-language version, for $39.95. The *Living New Testament* is available for $64.95. As for the *Old Testament*, Mr. Stevens narrates the King James Version for $119.95, the New International Version for $179.95, and the dramatized NIV version for $199.95. The *Living Old Testament* is available for $179.95. *Psalms and Proverbs* come in the King James version for $18.95, the New International Version for $24.95 (both narrated by Mr. Stevens), and the *Living Bible* version for $21.95. [Source: Word, Inc.]

Mission Tapes—A large selection of Bible study cassettes, featuring such speakers as J. Vernon McGee, J. Dwight Pentecost, Dr. Dave Breeze, Dr. Joe Temple, and many others, covering studies on virtually every book of the Bible. $1.75 per tape (most containing two messages) after payment of a $10 annual membership fee. Some tapes are available in Spanish. [Source: Mission Service Ministries]

New Testament—The King James version, on 12 cassettes in album, for just $19, after an annual membership fee of $10. Also available are *Proverbs*, *Ecclesiastes*, and *Song of Solomon* (King James Version), on five cassettes for $12. [Source: Mission Service Ministries]

Thomas More Cassettes—Todd Brennan reads books from the New Testament with introductions by scripture scholar John L. McKenzie: *Matthew*, *Luke*, *John* (each three cassettes, $24.95), *Acts* (two cassettes, $24.95), *Mark* (two cassettes, $17.95), *Revelation* (two cassettes, $16.95), and the *Parables* (one cassette, $9.95). John McGiver reads the texts of, and Fr. McKenzie offers reflections on, selections from *Psalms* and *Isaiah* (two cassettes each, $14.95 each) and *Job* (three cassettes, $16.95). Fr. McKenzie has two other talks about the Bible: *War and Peace in the New Testament* (one cassette, $8.95) and *Myths in the Bible* (one cassette, $9.95). [Source: Thomas More Cassettes]

Home Bible Studies—Two five-cassette, five-hour, verse-by-verse commentaries by Dr. Ralph Earle, for use in family devotions or neighborhood studies: studies from I John, for outreach families, and studies from I Thessalonians, for new Christians. $19.95 for each album. [Source: Nazarene Publishing House]

New Testament—Unabridged Good News for Modern Man Today's English version, $69.95 for 20 one-hour cassettes with reference guide in cedar wood case. Other offerings in the same version include: *Psalms and Exodus*, each $16.95 for four C-60 cassettes in album; and *Justice Now* (Hosea, Amos, and Micah), *Tried and True* (Job), and *Wisdom for Modern Man* (Proverbs and Ecclesiastes), each $7.95 for two cassettes. $1.25 for audition cassette of excerpts. [Source: Magnetix Corporation]

Evangelical Christian Cassettes—Bible studies and news reports by Herbert Henry Ehrenstein, Bible teacher and radio speaker: *Life of Christ*, $35 per 10-cassette album (8 albums available); *The Church—As It Was, As It Is*, 13 cassettes, $40; *The Holy Spirit*, 12 cassettes, $35; *The Mind of God in Print*, 2 cassettes, $10; *The True Lord's Prayer*, 3 cassettes, $12; *Praying Intelligently*, 2 cassettes, $10; *Death and the After-Life*, 2 cassettes, $10; *Isaiah 53*, 2 cassettes, $10; *The Book of Judges*, 12 Cassettes, $40; *The Book of Revelation*, 32 Cassettes, $100; *Corinthians*, 22 cassettes, $50; *To Everyone Who Asks* (Bible-related questions and answers), 4 cassettes, $20; *The Disciples' Prayer*, 4 cassettes, $20. Single-cassette titles for $5 (except as noted) include: *The Case for Biblical Inerrancy*, *the Resurrection Body* ($4), *The Cult of the Returning Dead* ($3), *The Charismatic Movement*, *Tongues-Speaking*, *The 23rd Psalm*, and four different questions-and-answers cassettes. Religious news cassette programs also available. [Source: Herbert Henry Ehrenstein]

The Chronological Bible—A different approach to the scriptures, presenting them historically, in the order of occurrence. $29.95 for 16 cassettes in album. More conventional is *The New Testament*, in the King James Version, read by Carl Richardson, in the same format and for the same price. *Wisdom of the Ages* contains the Books of Psalms and Proverbs, interpretatively read by Mr. Richardson, on six cassettes in an album for $20. *The Words of Jesus* read by Greg Oliver, are available on three cassettes for $12.95. [Source: Forward in Faith]

Lutheran Tape Ministry—About 300 hours of verse-by-verse Bible study, basics of Christianity, Doctrine, and other topics, all available without cost—but they understandably do seek donations to facilitate production of additional programs. [Source: Lutheran Tape ministry]

The Bible—The King James Version, narrated by Alexander Scourby. The *Old Testament* is in two volumes on 48 cassettes, $99.95, the *New Testament* in one volume on 16 cassettes, $49.95, both for $149.95. [Source: Episcopal Radio-TV Foundation]

The Bible—This source offers several sets. First are the *Living Old Testament* (48 cassettes in albums, $119.85) and the *Living New Testament* (16 cassettes in album, $39.95), each complete with music, dramatization, and sound effects. A companion album is *Living Psalms & Proverbs*, on six cassettes, $21.95. Also available are the *New International Version of the Old Testament* ($129.95), the *New International Version of the New Testament* ($49.95), and *Psalms and Proverbs* ($24.95). The *Dramatized King James New Testament* is $49.95. Next, there is Sir Laurence Olivier reading selected passages from the *Old Testament*, accompanied by music from the Holy Land, on six C-90 cassettes in album for $29.95. Finally, there is *Jesus: A Biography*, the dramatized story from birth to ascension, on five cassettes in album for $25.95. [Source: Living Scriptures, Inc.]

The Dramatized Bible—71 of the best stories of the Old and New Testament, each stressing such character-building principles as faith, obedience, repentance, and honesty, on 36 cassettes in three albums. $6.25 each shipped monthly, or $225 for the complete set. [Source: Living Scriptures, Inc.]

Contemporary Drama Service—Dramatized interviews with Bible immortals: *Living Interviews with Paul* and *with Peter*, each on three cassettes with study guide in album for $17.50; *Living Interviews with John*, two cassettes with study guide in album for $12.50; *Old Testament Immortals*, (Ruth, Jezebel, Bathsheba, Abraham, Daniel, Moses) on three cassettes with study guide in album for $17.50; and *An Interview with Jonah*, one cassette, $5.95. *Contemporary BC* are three cassettes of Bible-based discussion-starters for youth rap sessions and retreats,

$6.95 each. Dr. Martin E. Marty also has two discussion starts for youth or adults, *Christianity— Why?* and *Prayer—Its Power and Purpose*, each three cassettes with leader guide in album for $17.50. Then, there are two cassette study programs for Holy Week: *Five Views of the Crucifixion* (three cassettes in album, $16.50) and *Judas and Barabbas* (one cassette with guide, $6.95). Finally, three single cassette programs: *Thirty Ways to Use Drama in the Church* and *Contemporary Church Drama—How to Produce and Direct It* (each $5.95) and *The Art of Preaching* ($6.95). [Source: Contemporary Drama Service]

Creation-Life Cassettes—Lectures advocating the biblical philosophy of the creation and exposing the fallacies of evolution. The speakers are Henry M. Morris Ph.D. with 11 talks on science and the creation, plus the *Genesis Record Series* and the *Psalms Series*; Duane T. Gish Ph.D. with six titles devoted mostly to current science; Clifford Wilson Ph.D. has four titles on *The Illegal Trial of Jesus Christ* and three on *Encounter with UFOs*; A. E. Wilder-Smith Ph.D. the spectrum from black holes to cloning; and John D. Morris Ph.D. talks on the Ark and on Ararat. All cassettes $4.95 each, any six in album for $28, any eight in album for $35. [Source: CLP Publishers]

Covenant Recordings—Recorded religious, educational, and entertainment works, mostly on 90-minute cassettes. They have hundreds of spiritual selections, including: *The Old Testament* (with a free *New Testament*), $149.95 for 72 cassettes; *The New Testament*, $49.95 for 14 cassettes; *The Book of Mormon*, $69.95 for 17 cassettes; *Doctrine and Covenants* (plus *The Pearl of Great Price*), $39.95 for ten cassettes; *Jesus the Christ*, $59.95 for 16 cassettes; *Miracle of Forgiveness*, $39.95 for nine cassettes; and *Journey to Bethany* (life of Christ dramatized with over 100 actors), $34.95 for six cassettes. Also available are a variety of talks by LDS leaders and noted educators, dramatized productions, on one to four cassettes for $6.98 to $12.98. [Source: Covenant Recordings, Inc.]

Voices from His Excellent Glory—Fundamentalist Bible camp and gospel recordings, featuring such speakers as Calvin Simmons, Ray Alsobrook, Ferris Miller, Win Worley, and Carroll McCarrol, all recorded at the Arkansas camp ground. Prices vary, but average $4.50 per cassette. [Source: Lake Hamilton Bible Camp]

Word of Grace—Sermons by Dr. John MacArthur Jr., with lengthy series on Habakkuk, Zachariah, Matthew, Acts, Romans, I Corinthians, Galatians, Colossians, Hebrews, I & II Peter, I, II, & III John, Jude, and Revelation, plus major series of Giving, Security, the Body of Christ, Prophecy, Reliability of the Bible, God and Satan, and the Charismatic Movement, among others. Sermons by other preachers are also available, and some of Dr. MacArthur's sermons have been translated into Spanish. The suggested donation is $1.25 each. There are also subscription plans (the Sunday morning or evening sermon, as preached each week at Grace Community Church, for $1.25 a week, or both for $2.50 a week) and a lending service (one tape at a time, for an annual fee of $5, three at a time for a fee of $9, and so on). Many of the Bible studies and the major series are available in albums—again, at a very modest cost. [Source: Word of Grace Communications]

Pastoral Studies

Thesis Theological Cassettes—A monthly series of C-60 cassette programs that bring the essence of major lectures, conferences, and symposia to the pastor and the church with live presentations by outstanding scholars. Each program comes with supplement and discussion guide. $72 a year (12 issues), $39 for six months, $6.98 monthly. [Source: Thesis]

Thesis Study Units—Each hour-long study cassette contains four to six sessions by an outstanding leader with a discussion guide. Titles: *The Healing Ministry* by Dr. Francis S. MacNutt; *Transactional Analysis* with Drs. John and Dama Wilms of Purdue; *An Hour with Malcolm Boyd* and *Meditations with Malcolm Boyd*; *At the Frontier* (contemporary ethical problems) with Dr. Joseph Fletcher; *Jesus and Judaism* with Dr. Amy Faust; *On Being Gay* (views of homosexuality from within and without), and *Exorcism: The Devil, Demons and Possession*. Also in this series are three Bible studies: *Great Chapters from the Gospels* with Dr. Addison Leitch; *New Perspectives on the Parables* (two cassettes) with Dr. Kenneth Bailey; and *Focus on Philippians*, with Dr. Gary Demarest. And a most unusual offering, *God, Man and Archie Bunker*, contains live segments from the TV show and Spencer Marsh (author of the book by the same title) setting the comments in theological perspective. $8.95. Finally, there is *Developing Ministries with Young Adults*, which provides resource papers, a booklet of profiles on what young people are thinking and doing, and three cassettes of comments on strategies for ministry, all $35 in album. [Source: Thesis]

Competent To Counsel—Training materials that enable Christian leaders to counsel from Scripture. The eight 90-minute instructional cassettes give case studies dealing with problems of fear, worry, disintegrating marriage, alcoholism, and other problems— with the opportunity to discuss the problems and then hear typical approaches that others take. The cassettes are supplemented by a study guide, a leader's guide, pre- and post-training tests, and other materials, all in an album for $34.95. From the same source a related program, *Christian Counseling Course* features Dr. John Broger stressing self-confrontation. Ten cassettes for $35, with a useful syllabus for study available for $2.50. [Source: National Association of Evangelicals]

Biblical Hebrew—An easy-to-use course for beginners that provides sufficient basic instruction and exercises in Hebrew grammar and construction to permit a working understanding of Old Testament Hebrew. $20.30 for four cassettes and text. [Source: Nazarene Publishing House]

Dynamic Leadership Series—For Sunday school superintendents, pastors, and directors of Christian education, a three-hour course with leaders in Sunday school work talking about their successful and current ideas. $29.95 for six cassettes and listening guides in album. [Source: Nazarene Publishing House]

MTC—Minister's Tape Club—A monthly continuing education cassette service for ministers. $39.95 a year for 12 cassettes. [Source: Nazarene Publishing House]

Teacher Cassettes—For Sunday School teachers, a cassette that provides practical tips for session preparation, ideas for more effective teaching and counseling, and suggestions for in-class features and activities. Separate cassettes available for junior, teen, high school, and adult Sunday School teachers, for $6.95 each. Of related usefulness is *Suede-Graph Cassettes*, each cassette including a bible story plus sound effects, songs, activity music, to be played while the teacher arranges suede-backed figures (available separately for $2.45) on a flannelboard to dramatize the story. Useful in Sunday School, Bible School, and day care centers. $4.95 for each C-30 cassette. Several other cassette programs for pre-primary children are also available. [Source: Scripture Press Publications, Inc.]

Foundations—A meditation subscription series that features foremost Catholic scholars and teachers talking in depth about the central experiences of their faith: Eugene LaVerdiere on presence, Dianne Bergant on suffering, Joseph Grassi on teaching, and others on journey, hope, poverty, bread, works, prayer, and faith. Suitable for liturgy and retreat workers, ministers, and individuals seeking personal growth. $59.95 for ten tapes, one mailed each month, plus storage album. [Source: NCR Resources]

Liberation Media—Three audio-cassettes that explore the media issues challenging the world. In *The Electronic Heart of the 80's: The Ministry of Communications in a World of Rich and Poor*, Rev. Miles O'Brien Riley suggests that the flickering images of today's media are only a shadow of the real world. In *If News is Silenced, So Are We: Understanding the New World Information Order*, Sr. Camille D'Arienzo points out that information is power, and those in the first world who have access to the media have a power over those in the third world who do not. In *Liberating the Media: To Open the Eyes of the Blind and Ears of the Deaf*, Ruth Fitzpatrick looks at the role of the media in the liberation of oppressed peoples, and our role in liberating the media from its biases. $6.50 for each 48-minute tape, all three for $16. And to get down to practicalities there is *Communications Techniques in the Vocations Office*. On this 60-minute cassette, two religious media professionals discuss how to produce a slide show, how to write an effective brochure, and how to create a media strategy appropriate for the vocations message. $7. [Source: Center for Communications Ministry]

Hebrew Prophets and Christian Preachers—With humor and irony, Dr. John Whitcomb offers a study of God-revealed and unchanging techniques of teaching and preaching the Bible today, in this set aimed for pastors. $4.50 for each C-60 cassette with outline, or $27 for all six cassettes and album. In *Contemporary Apologetics*, Dr. Whitcomb discusses God-revealed methods of making Christianity believable in a secular society. $4.50 for each 60 minute cassette, or all four cassettes with printed text in album for $18. [Source: Dr. John Whitcomb]

Seminary Extension Independent Study Institute—Basic and advanced curricula for pastors and lay preachers, prepared by the Southern Baptist Seminaries. The courses can be taken for individual refreshers, or for certificates and diplomas. The basic (pre-college) courses cover biblical studies, pastoral ministries, and Ecclesiology, cost $22.50 per each of the 13 courses offered. The advanced (college-level) courses delve into specifics of Bible study, with three Old Testament Surveys, three New Testament Surveys, many programs on various books of the Bible, biblical history, theology, and many practical courses on pastoral duties, evangelism, leadership, and education. The advanced courses are $21.50 each plus the cost of the text for each course. [Source: Seminary Extension]

The Family—A realistic, practical, self-administered marriage enrichment program for pastors, social workers, and just plain people. There are two introductory talks for group leaders, ministers, and counselors, and then 14 talks covering the 'real' aspects of married life: communication, honesty, adult maturity, sex and love, children, and sex education. A Spanish-language version is also available. Each is $58 for eight cassettes. *Building Happiness* is a program to aid the minister or counselor in initiating small-group discussions to promote personal growth and marriage enrichment, but without manipulation and intimidation. $27 for three cassettes, leader's manual, and six 32-page participant handbooks. [Source: Marriage Enrichment Bureau]

Principles of Catholic Moral Life—Presentations from a week-long symposium on this topic, with presentations by leading theologians and scholars involved in the study of questions regarding formation and conscience, useful for retreats, seminary study, homily instructions, and catechisms. 17 cassettes in two albums, $60. [Source: Ministr-O-Media, Inc.]

Argus Communications—Quality programs to aid priests, pastors, and religious educators. The parables of Jesus challenged listeners to re-examine basic attitudes and values, and *To the Crowds in Parables* offers a similar experience with modern and biblical parables, $24.95 for two cassettes, book, and group activity guides. *The Fully Alive Experience*, based on the teachings and values of Jesus, provides materials for 10 two-hour sessions, each including an input talk by John Powell SJ and personal exercises by Loretta Brady, all on 11 cassettes, personal notebook and guidebook in box for $75; additional notebooks $2.50 each. In *Teaching Youths To Pray*, Mark Link tells how to integrate a prayer program into a religious education curriculum by emphasizing that prayer is the essential and vitalizing link of Christian living, $10 for two 90-minute cassettes. Finally, in *My Vision and My Values*, John Powell SJ discusses the dynamics of faith and love as the focal point of any personal relationship with Jesus, $20 for four 90-minute cassettes. [Source: Argus Communications]

Audio Communications—A good source of low-cost, high-quality programming for Catholic priests, nuns, religious educators, and some for the laity. Programs for priests include: *The Priestly Heart*, with Bishop James Griffin sharing inspirational thoughts and prayers on priestly life and ministry, $20.95 for four tapes; *Humanae Vitae*, with Anthony Iezzi Ph.D. presenting a positive and comprehensive discussion of the total document, $25.95 for five cassettes in album; *The Catholic Priest in the Modern World*, by Fr. Paul Hill, $15.95 for three cassettes; and *The Priestly Carnival*, by Howard Gray SJ, five cassettes, $25.95. Many single-cassette talks are also available, for $4.25 each. *Reaching for Community* is an album of threee tapes, with each tape containing a presentation on one aspect of community life, followed by reactions of sisters living in community, $18.95. *Gift of Ministry* is a series for all sisters who want to strengthen and intensify the service they give to others, five cassettes, $16.75. *Religion and the Elementary School Child* is an eight-tape program designed to answer the questions most asked by religion teachers, $39.95. *Parenting for Peace and Justice* is a five-cassette course for the entire family, $25 with album. In *Doctor Iezzi Discussing Human Life*, he covers quality of life, sexuality, abortion, euthanasia, population, and genetic manipulation, $20 for four cassettes. There are many more; write for their free catalog. [Source: Audio Communications Center, Inc.]

ReSource—A subscription series prepared for pastors by the seminary faculties of the American Lutheran Church, providing a continuing education program that is both theologically enriching and pertinent to today's issues. $35 per year for 12 monthly one-hour programs, each with printed outline. [Source: Augsburg Publishing House]

PRTVC Audio Cassettes—Programs on various aspects of church leadership by some of the most authoritative sources in the business, including Carlyle Marney, Wayne Oates, Martin Marty, Seward Hiltner, Elton Trueblood, and Jurgen Moltman, to name just a few. The cost is generally $4 per hour-long cassette, or $15 or $16 for a four-cassette album. Some of the individual cassette titles: *Our Ministry to a Changing World*, Ralph E. Dodge; *Are Religion and Science Compatible?*, William G. Pollard; *How I Preach*, William Sloane Coffin, Jr.; *Some of the Problems of Freedom*, William F. Buckley, Jr.; *The Human Response to Change*, Norman Cousins; and *Whatever Happened to Marriage?*, Richard A. Bollinger. Some of the album titles: *Christianity Confronts the New Religions*, Anthony Campolo; *Personal Crises of the Pastor*, Wayne Oates; *Preaching to the Limits of Your Vision*, L.D. Johnson; *Studies in Ephesians*, Dale Moody; *God the Problem*, Gordon D. Kaufman; *Preaching as Story-Telling*, Fred B. Craddock; and many more. Also available are the proceedings from such ministerial conferences as Emory Ministers' Week, Columbia Theological Seminary Forum, and the Furman Pastors School. [Source: Protestant Radio and Television Center, Inc.]

Discipleship Resources—Preaching, teaching, and evangelical aids for United Methodist ministers and other church leaders. *Looking at Leadership Through the Eyes of Biblical Faith* is a program that enables a pastor to pinpoint his strengths and needs through study of six biblical images: king, priest, prophet, wiseman, disciple, and servant, four cassettes and guide in album, $25.50. *Ways Persons Become Christian* uses active learning exercises, post-class assignments, and intensive Bible study to involve students and arouse their sensitivities in this area of their total teaching philosophy, $29.95 for four cassettes and guide in album. *Communicating the Faith with Children* is a series of four cassettes that will help leaders, teachers, and workers with children improve their skills, with workbook in album for $24.95. *Ways the Bible Comes Alive in Communicating the Faith* shows how to use scripture as a teaching tool, on for cassettes with book and guide in album for $29.95. *Evangelism Cassette Mini-Course* contains talks by 12 of the most knowledgeable pastors and teachers in the field of church growth and evangelism, $39.95 for 12 cassettes, each with study guide, in album. The *National School of Evangelism Lectures* consist of 23 additional talks by other church leaders, providing information for personal study and church growth, $5.50 each, all 23 for $94.88. *Worship and Preaching Cassette* contains addresses by Melvin Talbert, Reuben Job, and Robert Escamilla, designed for local church pastors and designated lay leaders in worship, $4. [Source: United Methodist Center]

Addenda—A subscription program designed to keep priests and pastors current on the latest developments in theology, liturgy, and religious sociology. Each hour-long program features speakers like Bishop Albert Ottenweller discussing the parish of the future, Rev. John Shea telling about trends in contemporary theology, or Fr. John Heagle takes up priestly spirituality. $49.95 for seven monthly cassettes, sent October to May. [Source: Thomas More Association]

Broadman Cassette Tapes—A large selection of Baptist-oriented messages, sermons, and other resources for use by ministers, Sunday school leaders, deacons, and other church leaders, and for presentation to Sunday school classes. There are tapes on establishing vacation Bible schools, on witnessing and evangelization, on home and foreign missions, on preaching and on the pastor's life. And finally, there is much in the Bible study field, both sermons and background talks on various books of the Bible, and on biblical history and geography. There is much here, in essence, for anyone involved in a Protestant (not just Baptist) church, Sunday school, or mission. Most cassettes are 60 minutes long, most cost $6.95. [Source: Broadman Consumer Sales]

Kyrkans Kassette-Radio—"Church Cassette-Radio" is a monthly Swedish-language information service of the Church of Sweden, dealing with social concerns and church matters, with editorial input supplied by various divisions of the Church. Price is 500 SW Cr (about $120) for ten 90-minute cassettes a year. [Source: Logos (Sweden)]

Sanders Christian Foundation—They record and distribute lectures, sermons, and discussions from the Peniel Bible Conference, the Gordon-Conwell Theological Seminary, and various conferences held by the Evangelistic Association of New England and other area churches and ministries. Their catalog lists an impressive number of speakers and topics, and the price is roughly $3.50 to $4 for each 60- to 90-minute cassette, plus postage. The tapes will also be loaned for a modest fee. *Sanders Soundings* is a bimonthly 30-minute cassette news service, containing excerpts from various messages, tips on tape use, and other pertinent information, $5 for one year (6 issues). [Source: Sanders Christian Foundation]

Talks on Spirituality and Prayer—Fr. William Wilson talks on prayer and aspects of the interior life, the religious notions of death, law and the Gospel, the Christian spiritual doctrine of humility, Christian spirituality based on 'inner peace' (the tradition of hesychasm), the theme of Apatheia, and many other series and topics. $3 donation. [Source: New Melleray Abbey]

Care Cassettes—Aimed at hospital chaplains but useful for parish pastors, members of religious orders, and laity, each monthly hour-long cassette provides clinical and theological insights and information from some of the most provocative minds in the field of pastoral care. $60 per year, including album if prepaid; can also be billed quarterly. Back issues are available for $6.50 each, less to subscribers. [Source: College of Chaplains]

Institute of Theological Studies—Recorded lectures by outstanding evangelical leaders, designed for Christian laymen, professional Christian leaders, and theological students (the program is recognized by eight seminaries, and their deans make up a governing Deans' Council). There generally are two 28-30 minute lectures on each C-60 cassette. Available for $34.95 are 6-cassette courses on: *Epistle of James, The Prophecy of Habbakkuk, Christian Evidences*, and (for $44.95) *The Book of Daniel*. Available for $64.95 are 12-cassette series on: *Christology, Soteriology, Neo-Orthodoxy, The Book of the Acts, The Book of Job, The Epistle to the Hebrews, Conquest and Settlement, The United Monarchy (Kingdom), The Divided Monarchy, The Book of the Revelation, The Book of Psalms, The Pentateuch, Messianic Prophecy*, and (for $79.95) *Understanding the Old Testament (A Survey of the History of Salvation in the Old Testament)*. Also available for $54.95 is a 10-cassette series on *The Sermon on the Mount*, and for $109.95 a 20-cassette series on *The Pastoral Epistles*. All prices include album and syllabus. Postage/handling $1.50 per album in U.S. [Source: Outreach Inc.]

Cassette Campus—A wide-ranging series of Christian support messages. Pastoral Tapes series offers two hour-long messages by Dr. Warren Wiersbe (*Helps for New Christians*, and *Helps for New Church Members*), each $4.95 or both for $8.95. Dr. Wiersbe also discusses the *Biblical View of Satan—Enemy and Deceiver*, on five cassettes in album for $23.95. There are two sets by Dr. John C. Whitcomb, Jr.: *The Genesis Flood* (three 45-minute cassettes) and *The Creator and Creation* (three 40-minute cassettes), each $12.95 or both for $19.95. In *Youthbeat*, Mel Johnson provides an hour of pointers for youth leaders, $4.95. Most of these programs are expertly voice-compressed, to provide maximum material without noticeable speeding-up.

MLR Cassettes—Useful, down-to-earth solutions to problems encountered by every minister, for $7 per cassette. Topics include: how to minister to the dying and the bereaved; how to know who you are; how to refresh your preaching; how to make worship meaningful; how to make sense when you open your mouth; how to do creative marriage counseling; how to deal with suicide and alcoholism; and how to help people come alive. There is also a two-cassette series on causes and cures of conflicts in local congregations, for $11. Next, there are two cassettes for $7 each and aimed at both the minister and the church board, and dealing with the breadbasket issue of a minister's pay: *A Better Pay Plan for Pastors*, and *How Do You Pay Your Pastor?* Finally, two cassettes to help the minister cope with his income tax—*Clergy's Tax Preparation* ($7.50, revised yearly) and *Housing Allowance* ($7). [Source: Ministers Life Resources]

St. Joseph's Abbey Cassettes—A talk by Fr. Thomas Keating on contemplative prayer, with historical insights in the Christian tradition, $5; a three-cassette series by Fr. William Meninger on contemplative prayer, based on the method used in the book *The Cloud of Unknowing*, $15; and another by Fr. Meninger on a practical approach to reading and praying the scriptures, $5. [Source: St. Joseph's Abbey]

Global Ministries Cassettes—Discussion starter programs, designed to familiarize listeners with the problems of less affluent cultures. Titles available: *Latin America, The Native American, Third World Women*, and *Persons in Mission/Salvation Today*. Another offering—*The Christian and Interreligious Dialogue*—compares the features of the world's great non-Christian religions. All cassettes 34 to 40 minutes each, all cost $3.50 each. [Source: General Board of Global Ministries]

Franciscan Communications—*Harvest Blessings* is a series of cassettes created to aid those who minister to the elderly, the housebound, and the nursing home patient with spiritual sustenance, three volumes of four 3-hour programs, $27.50. The *L.O.V.E. Ministry* (Lay ministry Of Visitors to the Elderly in Institutions) is a 2½-hour training program to acquaint people with the workings of the institution, misconceptions about the aged, and practical techniques for ministering to the aged, $26.95 with guidebook. Also available are individual cassettes and series by Father Alan McCoy (*Faith for the 80's, Pastoral Renewal for Priests*), Emery Tang OFM (*Renewal in Love, All that Matters*), Miles O'Brien Riley, and Father Ed Eschweiler (*Letters to Nancy*), all about $6 to $8 each. [Source: TeleKETICS]

Falcon AVA—A division of England's Church Pastoral Aid Society, Falcon Audio-Visual Aids produces low-priced cassette programs for pastors and parishioners. *One To One* is a range of pastoral cassettes intended both to help those in need of help and to provide useful insights for pastors and counselors; topics cover agoraphobia, death of a partner, facing incurable illness, loneliness, and death of a child, about $4 each. Related are *The Topping Letters*, the first of which is a group discussion starter on bereavement, about $7. Falcon has two confirmation aids: *Going Firm*, a 10-week course for teenagers on one cassette with worksheets, about $8; and two cassettes by David Watson on *Christian Foundations* and two more on *Christian Living*, each about $5. Dr. Marion Ashton has several talks on *The Christian Life*, combining spiritual insight with a deep understanding of human nature, about $5 each. Finally, *Believing the Bible*, a cassette "particularly suitable for an articulate group of agnostics," about $5, and *Not Me Lord*, a four-week course in group leadership for the laity, two cassettes and printed materials for about $14. [Source: Falcon AVA]

Benson Cottage Ministry—Four innovative programs created by Dennis C. Benson to reach young people. The *Complete Floyd Shaffer Clown Ministry Workshop Kit* contains six cassettes on which the

renowned theological clown has produced his whole workshop, leading listeners through the actual exercises involved in this unique ministry, for $44. In the *Dan Kamin Mime Workshop Kit*, the noted mime leads people through a six-cassette training session to learn the art and skill of mime, for $46.50. *Teen Talk I* and *II* are each three-cassette albums that are especially useful in programs geared toward working with children and youth in the prevention of addictive diseases, $21 each. Finally, Dennis Benson offers three cassettes with study guides to help church leaders plan their own *Creative Ministry with Senior Highs, Creative Ministry with Junior Highs*, and *Creative Retreats*; $8.95 each, all three in album for $19.50. [Source: Recycle]

Crux Cassettes—Well-prepared programs for Catholic priests, sisters, and laity: *Priest: Man of Prayer*, with Fr. Bernard Haring exploring the priestly life; *The House of Prayer Movement*, with Fr. Haring giving an inside perspective on the growing number of Christians in full-time lives of prayer; *How To Form a Prayer Center in Your Parish*, a practical, down-to-earth guide; *Guided Prayer Using Process Meditation*, with Sr. Vilma Seelaus; *Living in God's Presence*, with Sr. Seelaus bringing listeners a deeper awareness of God and themselves; and *Centering Prayer*, with Fr. Michael J. van der Peet introducing an uncomplicated, comtemplative prayer form. $7.95 each. [Source: Crux]

Alba House Cassettes—An ecumenical outreach of the Society of St. Paul, Alba House produces quality audio-cassette programs for religious education and instruction. Most are of a Roman Catholic orientation: *The Spiritual Exercises of St. Ignatius Loyola*, by George Twigg-Porter SJ, two C-60 cassettes in album, $15.95; *Pope John and the Popes John Paul*, by Rev. Bernard R. Bonnot, four cassettes (about 50 minutes each) in album for $24.95; and *What Is Celibacy—and Why*, by Thomas Dubay SM, three cassettes (about 3 hours) in album for $24.95, to name just three. And Alba House also has programs of more general interest: *Marriage: A Call to Sanctity*, by Tom and Lyn Scheuring, four C-60 cassettes in album for $17.95; cassette commentaries (2 to 9 cassettes each) on the books of the New Testament; and *Supporting the Separated and Divorced Catholic as Ministry*, by Sr. Paula Ripple, three cassettes in album for $24.95. [Source: Alba House Communications]

Abingdon Audio-Graphics—A variety of well-known personalities discussing subjects important in today's world. There is *Barclay Introduces the Bible*, a down-to-earth yet comprehensive discussion by William Barclay, $9.95 for two C-45 cassettes with user's guide. *Ways the Bible Comes Alive in Communicating the Faith* provides a unique teaching tool for religious education, $29.95 for four C-60 cassettes, self-instruction guide and resource book in album. In *Growth Counseling*, Dr. Howard J. and Charlotte H. Clinebell offer new insights and methods in human counseling, in two series, each $32.50 for four cassettes and guides in album, or $7.95 each per cassette. *Informal Conversations With Seward Hiltner* covers the charismatic movement, women's lib, serial monogamy, and other pertinent topics, $12.95 for two C-60 cassettes. John Killinger tells *How to Enrich Your Preaching*, on four 60-minute cassettes and guide in album for $29.95. [Source: Abingdon Press]

Institute on Religious Life—Tape series devoted to finding solutions to the problems confronting religious communities in accordance with the authentic teaching of the Catholic Church and of Pope John Paul II and his predecessors, to promote religious life, and to encourage vocations to it. Some of the multi-cassette series are title: *Catholic Faith Today, Spiritual Life, History of Religious Life, Catholic Doctrine,* and a number of tapes from 1976 and 1978 national meetings. Also available are conferences and homilies from the 1978 and 1979 *Retreat for Laymen.* All cassettes are $4.95 each. [Source: Institute on Religious Life]

American Church Growth Study Series—In *The Principles of Church Growth*, Paul Benjamin gives four talks: The Unfulfilled Commission, Jesus Christ Brings Us Together, Five A Prioris in Church Growth, and Guidelines for Witnessing, $7.95 for two cassettes in album. [Source: World Wide Publications]

ASPIRE Tape of the Month—A monthly series of programs on evangelism, counseling, church affairs, preaching, and sermons, prepared for Seventh-day Adventist ministers and other church leaders. $52.95 a year for two 90-minute tapes a month. Also available (from Adventist Media Center, 1100 Rancho Conejo Blvd., Newbury Park, CA 91320) are individual selections from the ASPIRE programs for $3.50 each, plus some special series: *H. M. S. Richards Remembers,* $10 for four C-90 cassettes, the *1974 North American Bible Conference,* 19 C-90 cassettes for $47.50, and the *1980 Meetings for Ministers' Wives,* four C-90 cassettes, $10. Also there is *Ministry Tape of the Month,* a monthly C-90 service for all ministers, designed to aid in becoming a stronger preacher, teacher, and counselor, a more effective leader of worship, outreach, and stewardship, a better administrator, yet more informed on theological issues. $45 a year. [Source: Seventh-day Adventists]

Sermons and Testimonies

St. Anthony Messenger Cassettes—Fr. Richard Rohr has two offerings: *The Great Themes of Scripture* (an overview of both testaments), $65.40 for twelve 90-minute cassettes in a box; and *Days of Renewal* (combining music, prayer, liturgical drama and preaching), five cassettes with lyrics, boxed for $39.75. *What Is the Spiritual Life?* contains responses to the question by Fr. David Knights with ten 45-minute talks on five cassettes in a box for $34.75.

That You May Believe gives 22 half-hour lessons covering the main outlines of Catholic doctrine with eleven boxed cassettes and a study guide for $65.45. Thomas Richstatter, O.F.M. discusses *The Sacraments: The Church at Prayer,* on five hour-long cassettes in box for $29.75. Fr. Richstatter describes *Today's Liturgy: New Style, New Spirit* on five cassettes for $29.95 boxed. Finally, Rev. James Bacik describes *An American Spirituality for the 80s* on a boxed set of four cassettes for $23.80. [Source: St. Anthony's Messenger Press]

Voice of Confidence—100 messages of Dr. Norman Vincent Peale, recorded just as he gave them at Marble Collegiate Church and over the air. Each message combines faith-inspired counsel with spiritual inspiration to provide practical solutions to life's everyday problems. $9.45 for each cassette containing two messages, two cassettes for $18.90, three cassettes with free album for $26.45. You can also get *Norman Vincent Peale on Positive Thinking,* six messages on three cassettes offering faith, courage, inspiration, excitement, enthusiasm, joy, insight, and assurance that with God you can make life a positive experience. $26.45 with album. [Source: Foundation for Christian Living]

Servant Cassettes—Albums that provide instruction on leading the Christian life, with most of the topics oriented toward the charismatic renewal, particularly within the Roman Catholic Church. In the Foundatons of Christian Living series are: *Basic Christian Maturity,* four cassettes and guide in album, $24.95; *Christian Marriage and Family Life,* seven cassettes in album, $39.95; *Emotions in the Christian Life,* six cassettes in album, $32.95; and three-cassette albums on *Christian Sexuality for . . . Married Couples, Single Men,* and *Single Women,* $19.95 each. There are several albums for leaders of charismatic renewal groups: *Spiritual Leadership* and *Working Together as Leaders,* each $24.95 for four cassettes; *A Crisis of Truth: The Gospel and the Church,* five cassettes, $29.95; and two four-cassette albums by Fr. John Bertolucci, *Spreading the Good News* and *Preaching the Gospel,* $24.95 each. Other album titles: *The Healing Ministry,* five cassettes, $29.95; *Spiritual Power for Prayer Groups,* four cassettes, $24.95; *Men's and Women's Roles,* seven cassettes, $39.95; *Life of the Spirit Seminars,* for cassettes, $24.95; and *Christian Unity: What Will It Take?,* four cassettes, $24.95. [Source: Servant Publications]

Start the Day—A series of 12 cassettes (one for each month) to aid those Christians who begin their day with Bible reading, meditation, and prayer. Each cassette contains 28 three-minute programs with readings from a book of the Good New Bible, a question-and-answer about the text, a prayer, and a thought for the day, about $8 each. This major English religious publisher also has many 'discussion starter' cassettes (about $8 each), and some 'personal insights' and family guidance cassettes (about $6 each). [Source: Scripture Union]

Family Life Cassette of the Month Club—Cassette messages by recognized authorities on personal and family relationships offering practical ideas for building better relationships, understanding oneself and others, and bringing greater love and harmony into one's family. Speakers include Henry Brandt, Howard Hendricks, David Hocking, Tim and Beverly LaHaye, John MacArthur, Henry Morris, Charles Swindoll, Warren Wiersbe, Rich Yohn, many others. Membership costs $6, which includes a special cassette containing three family life messages and a storage album. Thereafter monthly cassettes are $5 each. [Source: Family Life Seminars]

Catacomb Cassettes—Cassettes and albums for personal, study group, and church use, on topics such as education, ministry, social issues, evangelism, to meet the needs of both Christian laity and leaders. The speakers come from many religious traditions— Episcopal, Anglican, other Protestant, Roman Catholic, and Eastern Orthodox. Single lectures are generally $7 each for a C-60 or C-90 cassette, less in sets. *Great Words of the Christian Faith* features Donald Coggan, Archbishop of Canterbury, $15 for four cassettes. The previous Archbishop, Michael Ramsey, talks about *The Holy Spirit and The Christian Life*, $29.95 for eight cassettes in album. Everett L. Fullam tells *How To Run a Christian Organization*, $18 for three cassettes, and Michael Marshall explains *How To Do Evangelism*, $10 for two cassettes. *The Ten Commandments* are the subject of addresses by Stuart Blanch, Archbishop of York, on three cassettes in album, $29.95. Then there are the programs with C. S. Lewis: *The Four Loves* (four cassettes, $29.95); *Comments and Critiques* (three cassettes, $6.95 each); and *Mere Christianity* (read by Michael York, ten cassettes, $56.95). There are lots more, including these single-cassette titles: *The Church and Theology* (with Hans Kung), *New Testament Commentary*, *Sex and Homosexuality*, *The Sacraments*, *Today's Priest: His Temptations and Challenges*, *Young Children and the Eucharist*, and more. [Source: Episcopal Radio-TV Foundation]

Encounter Ministries—Expository sermons by Dr. Stephen F. Olford, former minister of Calvary Baptist Church in New York City and widely regarded as one of the finest preachers of our time. The sermons are from his Encounter radio and TV programs, his former church, and various conferences, and most are keyed to a specific verse in the Bible. $3 per sermon. [Source: Encounter Ministries Inc.]

Merton Tapes—Talks by the late Thomas Merton, given informally at the Abbey of Gethsemane. Although addressed to his fellow monks in the context of a traditional Roman Catholic spirituality, Father Merton speaks to all of us on the truths that he knew to be the foundation of life. He combines profound spiritual wisdom with an exuberant sense of humor. In *Life and Prayer* (*Series I*), he talks about the

various aspects of the monastic calling, $8.95 per C-60 cassette, $96.66 for all 12 cassettes in the series. In *Life and Prayer* (*Series 2*), he considers consent to God, the ways of God, God as father, life and afterlife, and love and hope, $8.95 for each C-60 cassette, $96.66 for all 12 cassettes. In *The Monastic Life* he discusses Sufism (the spirituality of the Moslem mystics) as a basis for talking about Christian mysticism, $8.95 per C-60 cassettes, $88.60 for all 11 in this series. [Source: Electronic Paperbacks]

Lamb & Lion Ministries—Talks and sermons by Dr. David Reagan and others on Christian themes primarily related to prophecy and the Second Coming, for $3 each. Several albums are available for $10 each: *Signs of the Times* (pointing to this age as the season of the Lord's return), *The Power of Prayer*, *Visions of Jesus in the Book of Revelations*, *Marriage as God Intended It*, and *Science in the Bible*. [Source: Lamb & Lion Ministries]

Faith Enrichment Cassettes—Programs with a Catholic orientation, prepared for use in religious instruction, either privately or in group situations. All titles consist of two cassettes for $10 (unless otherwise indicated). Bernard Basset SJ offers four titles—*The Parables Today*, *How To Pray*, *One Step Enough for Me*, and *The Golden Years*. Robert J. Faricy SJ discusses *Teilhard de Chardin's Spirituality*, and *Teilhard de Chardin Revisited*. Anthony Padovano considers *Thomas Merton's Spirituality* and *The Nature of Religious Experience*. Frank Sheed gives insights into the Book of Genesis in *Adam and Eve and Us*, and with some college students he goes *In Search of Jesus* (both $15 for four cassettes with discussion guides). In *Liturgies for Children*, Christiane Brusselmans describes how to make them significant personal experiences. [Source: Arena Lettres]

Companion Cassettes—*The Greatest Thing in the World* is Henry Drummond's masterful discourse on the passages of I Corinthians; *As a Man Thinketh* is another classic that proclaims that 'you are what you are,' and *The Living Fountain* brings to life the Sermon on the Mount and selected Psalms and other verses—all narrated by John Zaremba. Quite modern is *Finance & Business, Understood Metaphysically*, describing the application of many biblical quotes to today's economy. All these are $8.98 each. Also available are the biblical lectures by Edith Armstrong Hoyt on: *The Book of Job*, *The Sermon on the Mount*, *The Four Horsemen of the Apocalypse*, *The Ten Commandments*, *The Letters of Paul*, and *The Bible*, for $8.98 each, all six for $40.63. [Source: World Harvest Records]

Terry Cole-Whittaker Ministries—'Reverend Terry' believes that, with her insights, "you can cause your life to happen your way." Each $9.75 cassette contains two talks from either her Sunday church service or her television program. You can also sign up to receive each Sunday church service talk for a considerable discount. [Source: Terry Cole-Whittaker Ministries]

Abbott Loop Christian Center—Highlights of courses taught at the Charismatic Bible College of Anchorage, plus teachings on the structure of the church, body ministry, and other topics from sermons at the College's weekly services. Speakers are Dick Benjamin, Dick Strutz, Jim Feeney, John Custer, Wayne Coggins, and others. They also offer a special selection of talks by women to women, amplifying biblical principles to make women aware of their God-given role in the family $4 each, tapes may be exchanged for $1 each, all plus postage. [Source: Mail Order Ministry]

Family Life Christian Fellowship—Sermons by Francis P. Martin, espousing his charismatic views of the powers of the tongue, divine health, faith, and family. A selection of Bible study courses are also available. The cassettes are $4 each. [Source: Family Life]

Voice of the Martyrs—Lectures and sermons on religious persecution in Communist countries, by Rev. Richard Wurmbrand, Rev. Michael Wurmbrand, John Noble, and others. $2.40 each. They also offer the Dr. Fred Schwartz lecture series on *What is Communism* for $9 (four cassettes) and the *New Testament* (King James Version) on cassettes for $35. [Source: Diane Publishing Company]

Cassette Teaching Tapes—Sermons and messages by Elbert Willis, grouped into series of from four to 20 cassettes. Some of the series titles: *Faith, Jesus Way of Living, Men of Faith, Women of Faith, Christian Hindrances, God's High Standards, Keys to Growth, Miracles, Conquest of the Mind, Promises, Prosperity Insight, Churches of Revelation, Leadership Characteristics, Crisis in Conquest, Divine Healing, Financial Prosperity,* and *Devil and Demons.* $2.90 per cassette. [Source: Lafayette Charismatic Teaching Center]

Christian Cassette Ministries—Sermons, talks, testimonies, and witnessing on a variety of topics, themes, and scriptures, by Lynn Anderson, Landon Saunders, Ronnie White, and Prentice Meador, Jr., among many others. $1.50 per cassette containing two messages. [Source: Christian Cassette Ministries]

Campus Crusade for Christ—A wide selection of lectures on evangelism and discipleship for all ages and people. The notable *Foundations for Family Living* series includes *Oneness: God's Design for Marriage,* $25.95 for four cassettes and study guide in album; *Communication and Sex in Marriage,* $17.95 for two cassettes and study guide in album; *Dad, the Family Shepherd,* $19.95 for three cassettes in album; and *Preparing for Oneness,* $21.95 for three

cassettes and study guide in album. *Evidence for Your Faith* is a practical approach to Christian apologetics, $37.95 for seven cassettes in album. Representative of their many Bible study programs is *The Epistle of Paul to the Romans,* by Josh McDowell, on eight cassettes in album for $41.95. In the *Christian Living* album, Dr. Bill Bright, founder and president of Campus Crusade, tells how to lead a better Christian life, on five cassettes for $28.95. Dr. Howard Hendricks presents methods for developing relationships in *Design for Discipleship,* four cassettes in album for $26.95. And there are many more. [Source: Campus Crusade for Christ International]

Abiding Word Tape Club—A collection of over 1500 different teaching tapes in 85 categories, expressing wide denominational and doctrinal views, with speakers like John Bertolucci, Judson Cornwall, Joy Dawson, Dave DuPlessis, Kenneth Hagin, Francis McNutt, Bob Mumford, Derek Prince, Oral Roberts, and many others. You enroll for $6 (pastors $4) and receive three tapes of your choice, which can then be exchanged as often as desired for any other tapes in the catalog. Any non-copyrighted tapes may be purchased for $1.25 each, plus 50¢ postage for any three tapes ordered. Obviously, this is a non-profit ministry. [Source: Abiding Word, Inc.]

Integrity Publications—A ministry committed to cultivating Christian maturity through cassette messages by Charles Simpson, Don Basham, Ern Baxter, and Bob Mumford. The topics fall into these categories: basic instruction; salvation and Christian foundations; Holy Spirit baptism; tongues; gifts of the Spirit; present issues; covenant community; relationship and discipleship; dealing with reality; the Christian family and marriage; the Kingdom of God; prayer and praise; faith and faithfulness, spiritual maturity and righteousness; evangelism and productivity; God's provision; spiritual warfare; and leaders' messages. The talks are $4.95 each, less when grouped together into series (as 3 tapes for $12.95, 4 for $16.95, 6 for $24.95). [Source: Integrity Publications]

Cassette Tapes by Stephen Hill—Sermons by Rev. Hill cover faith-building messages, divine healing, principles of the deeper life, restoration, praise and prayer, and numerous Bible studies (Daniel, Joshua, Revelation, Song of Solomon, and much more). $4 for each tape. [Source: Sound Teaching Ministries]

Truth Tape Library—A fine collection of sermons and Bible studies, mostly by Gene Breed of Grace Baptist Church, Fayetteville, GA, and the late Dr. Ferrell Griswold of Clairmont Reformed Baptist Church, Birmingham, AL. Other major speakers are Ron Rumburg, R. J. Rushdoony, Harry Graham, John Reisinger, and Jack Seaton. This is a rental service and there is no charge, but they would accept donations. [Source: Truth Tape Library]

Christian Cassette Library—A free rental service (but goodwill offerings are appreciated) for tapes from many producers (Bethany Fellowship, Charismatic Renewal, Spring of Living Waters, Thomas More, and many others). Their catalog lists tapes under these headings: testimonies, youth, healing, family, Bible, occult, cults, prophecies, teaching, and Spanish tapes . . . altogether, an outstanding collection of titles and speakers. They also produce some programs of their own, and these (only) are available, for a donation of $3 or more. [Source: Christian Cassette Library]

Audiomessages—Voices of outstanding evangelical Christian leaders—D. Stuart Briscoe, Larry Crabb, Jr., G. Allen Fleece, James M. Hatch, Vance Havner, Robertson McQuilkin, Stephen F. Olford, Alan Redpath, many more—with key messages from Ben Lippen conferences and from the chapel at Columbia Bible College. Most cassettes are about 50 minutes long, and all have been lightly edited to remove extraneous noises—a sign of quality. $4.18 per cassette, discounts with volume purchases. Cassettes may also be borrowed for four weeks without charge (send to attention of Audiomessage Library). [Source: Columbia Bible College]

Foundation Library—A huge collection of sermons, testimonies, and Bible study from many other sources, available on a loan basis (four titles for 30 days for $1 postage and handling). The list of speakers is impressive. $3 for a thorough catalog, indexed by speakers and subjects. [Source: Discipleship Tape Library]

Inspirational Tapes—A large collection of interdenominational testimonies, Bible studies, teachings, and sermons, available either by purchase or on loan. The tapes can be purchased through the *Inspirational Tape Club* by contributing $5 (or more) and receive the first month's tape free and then a tape of your choice each month thereafter for $5.45. Quantity prices as low as $3.50 each. Or, the tapes can be borrowed from the *Inspirational Tape Library*, one at a time for $5 a year (or two at a time for $10, three for $15, and so on) plus $1 for each cassette loaned, with the borrower keeping all cassettes in his/her possession at the end of the year's membership. A thick catalog costs $2. [Source: Inspirational Tapes]

Brigham Young University—A collection of talks given at BYU as devotionals, firesides, and forum addresses by various LDS Church authorities, members of the University community, and guest speakers. Most carry a Mormon message, but they are interspersed with non-religious talks: Bob Richards on motivation, Howard Ruff on the economy, and Maria von Trapp on Maria von Trapp. All talks $4.75 each. [Source: Brigham Young University]

Assumption Abbey Cassettes—Talks by monks of Assumption Abbey and others on the charismatic renewal, scripture, religious life, and monasticism. $4.50 each. Also available is a free lending library of over 5,000 *other* talks on the same subjects. Free catalogs available for both services. [Source: Assumption Abbey]

Changed Lives—Ben Haden, once an associate evangelist with Billy Graham, is the pastor of the First Presbyterian Church in Chattanooga. Messages from his weekly half-hour *Changed Lives* radio-TV program are available on cassette for $4 each, or any four plus album for $16. [Source: Changed Lives]

Personal Christianity—On his *Healing Instruction* cassette, Dr. C. S. Lovett offers 50 minutes of private instruction on how to heal disease and discomfort and to prevent further ailments through the power of relaxation and faith, $5.95. *Heaven on Earth* is a 25-minute talk by Dr. Lovett on the Christian approach to improving marriage, $4.95. [Source: Personal Christianity]

Witness Ministries Cassette Library—Sermons by Noel Brooks, Vinson Synan, H.L. Moore, Bishop J. Floyd Williams, John Parker, and a series of doctrinal studies on sanctification by Don Wilkes, all $3 per cassette. They also offer a series of radio tapes, consisting of two sermons on each tape, for just $1 per cassette. [Source: Witness Ministries]

Meditations by Archbishop Fulton J. Sheen—14 meditations on seven cassettes, given at St. John's Abbey in Collegeville, Minnesota by Archbishop Sheen in 1973. $35 for the set. [Source: Diocese of St. Cloud]

Voices in My Mind—Voice-impressionist Frank Topping presents Christian messages with humor, music, and meditation, on five cassettes of mini-dramas, featuring characters speaking with both American and British dialects, and presenting both Bible stories and present day tales of faith and life. Suitable for discussion starters, devotionals, or thought-provoking insights. $5.25 each. [Source: CTVC]

Cassettes from the Little Land of Canaan—Messages by M. Basilea Schlink, interspersed with her songs sung by the Sisterhood of Mary. Many are in part spoken by Mother Basilea Schlink; others are given by Sisters of Mary and Canaan Franciscan Brothers. General topics include Love for Jesus, My Prayer Life, Triumphant in Suffering, Victorious Living, Faith and Trust in God, Preparing for the Future, and For Special Seasons of the Year. All cassettes are 60-minutes long, but the messages on them vary from 5 to 30 minutes in length. They are especially prepared for Bible study groups, hospital and home visits, and evangelization. $3 each. [Source: Canaan in the Desert]

Archbishop Fulton J. Sheen on Cassette—21 talks available by the noted speaker, including *The Rosary*, *The Parables of the Lost*, *The Foundation of Sanctity*, *The Meaning of Suffering*, and *Three Kinds of Love*. $4.99 each, or all 21 cassettes for just $69.95. [Source: Ampico Sound]

Decision Tape Library—*Billy Graham Sermons*, *Volumes I* and *II*, $14.95 each for four C-30 cassettes in album, *Volume III*, $7.95 for two C-30 cassettes in album. In *Four-Fold Miracle of Israel*, Roy Gustafson asks "Does Biblical prophecy concern Israel?" and then shares his findings on two C-60 cassettes in album for $9.95. *The Christian Life and Witness Course* was recorded during actual training sessions for counselors at Billy Graham Crusades, $19.95 for four C-60 cassettes. [Source: World Wide Publications]

Cassette Study Program—Lessons by Rev. Charles Roth, one of the outstanding teachers in the Unity movement, on meditation, prosperity, healing, and practical truths, $3 for each cassette containing two lessons. Then there are Rev. Roth's special series, on: *The TAB Technique*, one cassette, $3; *How To Meditate* (basic meditation principles), three cassettes, $9; *Prosperity Is Your Birthright*, four cassettes, $12; *A New Way of Thinking*, six cassettes, $18; *Hidden Powers of the Mind*, four cassettes, $12; *Ten Commandment Series*, five cassettes, $15; and *12 Power Meditation Series*, six cassettes, $18. [Source: Unity of Indianapolis]

Sacred Heart Rectory—Six cassettes of 12 talks given by Archbishop Fulton J. Sheen in 1974 on the occasion of the centennial of the founding of the Sacred Heart Parish. One cassette is addressed to teenagers. $29.50 for the set, or $5 each. [Source: Sacred Heart Church]

Cornerstone Select Tapes—60- or 90-minute tapes from "an independent ministry dedicated to proclaiming Jesus Christ and to upholding the inerrancy of God's Word." All titles are available individually, for $4, but most are grouped together into sets: *Hudson Taylor's Spiritual Secret*, *The Problem of Time*, and *Outreach*, $5.50 for two cassettes; *Christian Classics*, *Pilgrim's Progress*, *The Christian Family*, *UFO's and Their Mission*, *Christian Missions*, and *Gods from Outer Space* (a debate between Clifford Wilson and Erich von Daniken), $8 for three cassettes; *The Passionate Christian Life*, *Humanism and Christian Education*, *The Trial of Jesus Christ* (analysis based on today's legal concepts), *The Best of Dr. Henry Morris*, *Creation Versus Evolution*, and *Biblical Answers to Scientific Problems*, each $10 for four cassettes; *Christian Psychology*, *Spiritual Life Set*, *Demonology*, and *Keswick Set*, $12.50 for five cassettes; *Christian Finances*; $15 for six cassettes; *Great Bible Truths*, $22.50 for nine cassettes; and *Our Lord's Teaching on Hell*, $25 for 10 cassettes. [Source: Cornerstone Ministry]

Mount Paran Tape Ministries—The extended messages of Jesus Christ, as presented by Dr. Paul L. Walker and staff ministers of Atlanta's Mount Paran Church of God. On their subscription plan, one receives tapes of Dr. Walker's Sunday morning or evening sermons for $3.50 each, or either full service for $4.75, billed monthly. Individual sermons on faith, inspiration, and encouragement are available for $3 each, full service tapes for $4 each. [Source: Mount Paran Tape Ministries]

Teaching Tapes—A three-hour worship service—complete with songs, testimonies, and a sermon by Lloyd L. Goodwin—on each two-cassette set. Over 750 complete services are available, with sermons covering the entire spectrum of scriptural study. $5.95 for each service (two C-90 cassettes). [Source: Gospel Assembly Church]

Winning Forever—Gospel messages and testimonies of hope by athletes, coaches, and counselors of the Michigan Fellowship of Christian Athletes, generally recorded live at FCA conferences. $25 for eight cassettes in album. [Source: Michigan Fellowship of Christian Athletes]

Winning Women—Short recorded talks by women on how to find spiritual fulfillment, how to be an adequate wife and mother, how to find peace in the midst of confusion, and how to develop other principles for everyday Christian living. $2 per tape. [Source: Winning Women]

Living Messages Recorded Library—Over 1,000 C-60 and C-90 cassettes, containing worship services, evangelistic messages, Bible conference series, Abundant Life conferences, Keswick messages, and Bible studies on individual books and themes of the Bible, all done by outstanding pastors and Bible conference speakers in America and Great Britain. Prices run between $3 and $4, depending upon length of the program. [Source: Outreach Inc.]

Dick Mills Ministries—Personal messages of encouragement and inspiration from evangelist Dick Mills, covering such topics as bringing healing help to others, how to forgive, the price of worship, getting a second chance, and spiritual self-defense. $4 each. [Source: Dick Mills Ministries]

Spoken Word—Sermons, lectures, and messages by leading pastors and theologians of the Seventh-day Adventist Church. More than 30 albums and many individual cassettes are available. In *The Shadows of His Sacrifice*, Leslie Hardinge Ph.D. gives an in-depth study of the sanctuary and its services, on 12 cassettes (15 hours) in album for $40.70. Morris L. Venden taks up *The Shaking of Adventism* and *The Parable of the Vineyard* on six cassettes in album for $18.95. Dr. H. M. S. Richards, radio pastor of the Voice of Prophecy, discusses two of the most prophecy-filled books of the Bible, *Daniel* and *Revelations*. Many other Bible studies are also available, at comparable prices. [Source: Spoken Word]

Autumn Thoughts—A series of three cassettes, produced in England, with the purpose of adding a spiritual dimension to the lives of isolated, lonely, and elderly people. In *Prayer*, speakers from various Christian denominations show that there is not just one way to pray, but that in different ways one reaches an understanding of God. In *Faith*, speakers relate moving, real-life stories of ordinary people, showing that faith is believing and trusting in God. In *Change*, the evolution of the Catholic mass, and some reactions to the modern format, are explored. About $8 for each cassette, about $20 for all three. [Source: Mayhew McCrimmon]

Omega Advertising—Sermons and messages presented at past conventions of the Full Gospel Business Men's Fellowship International, under the headings of Christian life, healing, Holy Spirit, the word of God, love and faith, marriage, family and interpersonal relationships, personal evangelism, prayer and praise, and prophecy. $4.50 each, discounts in larger volume, plus 10% postage and handling. [Source: Omega Advertising]

Victory Ministries—Sermons by Jeff Barnett grouped into series covering faith, healing, Holy Spirit, prayer, spiritual warfare, financial prosperity, the coming of the Lord, end-times restoration, the deeper life, and charismatic errors. $4 each. [Source: Victory Ministries]

Grady Nutt—The Southern Baptist layman and entertainer skillfully blends humor and a Christian message on his tapes: *The Gospel according to Pinocchio*, *The Flip Side of Grady Nutt, Humorist!* and *God's Will for Your Life*. $7.80 each. [Source: McKinney Associates, Inc.]

CFN Cassettes—Messages on the life of Christ, gifts of the spirit, prophecy, and revelation, mostly by Gordon Lindsay but also by many other charismatic evangelists. $4 each plus 50¢ postage for first tape. [Source: Christ for the Nations]

Forward in Faith—Sermons and lectures, mostly by radio's Carl Richardson. Some titles include: *Disciples Multiplied* (workable principles of church growth), five cassettes for $20; *Campmeeting Live* (three cassettes for $12.95); *Your Family: How To Win Them to Christ*, four cassettes for $12.95; and *The Beginning of the End*, four messages on two cassettes in binder for $10. [Source: Forward in Faith]

Provision Tapes—Sermons and Bible studies by Agape Force evangelists and revivalists: Leonard Ravenhill, A. W. Tozer, Winkie Pratney, Tony Salerno, Juan Carlos Ortiz, Chip Worthington, and George Verwer. $3.50 per cassette, two or more for $3 each. [Source: Provision Publishers]

Teaching and Preaching Ministry of Robert Gass—Host of the weekly television program Celebration and former pastor of one of the largest charismatic churches in New England, Rev. Gass offers over 150 inspirational sermons and teaching messages, all with pertinent (and sometimes humorous) relevance to daily Christian living. $4 each, any four for $15. [Source: Bob Gass Evangelistic Association, Inc.]

Springs of Living Water Tape Library—Over 2,000 different messages, sermons, testimonies, Bible studies, and Bible passages by leading charismatic teachers and evangelists, covering all denominations, all faiths. All tapes can be borrowed two at a time by mail without cost (although good will offerings are appreciated). Borrowed tapes may be copied for non-commercial use without charge, or can be purchased for $4 each. [Source: Spring of Living Water]

Our Sunday Visitor—Eight cassette conferences in an album, containing the proceedings of an open retreat (priests, sisters, and laity were invited) in Gary in 1973, conducted by Archbishop Fulton J. Sheen. $19.95. [Source: Gary Sunday Visitor]

Les Parrott Library of Audio Books—Guidelines and insights for everyday Christian living, by Dr. Leslie Parrott, President of Olivet Nazarene College, $3.50 each or all seven cassettes for $21. Related is *The Fulfilled Life by Leslie Parrott*, his study of the sanctified life, how it relates to family relationships, and stressing his belief in sanctification as a practical way of life, $3.50 each, all four cassettes for $12.50. [Source: Nazarene Publishing House]

NavPress Cassettes—Cassette teaching programs developed by The Navigators for use in disciplemaking ministries. *Interpersonal Relationships* is a Bible study/cassette seminar that teaches the Bible's instructions for all our relationships, on four 60-minute cassettes with leader's guide and workbook in album for $29.50 (additional workbooks $2.50 each). In the six-cassette *Biblical Leadership* album ($29.95), Dr. Howard Hendricks and Doug Sparks each present three messages to challenge listeners in their leadership responsibilities. The 'word hand' illustrates the Navigators' five methods of learning from the Bible (hearing, reading, studying, memorizing, and meditating); the *Word Hand* cassette album of six cassettes features motivational and instructional messages based on the illustration, $23.70. The *Wheel* cassette album presents six messages on the six fundamental principles of the Navigators' symbol for a dynamic, balanced Christian life, $23.70. Finally, the *Classics* album contains 12 cassettes full of messages by Navigator speakers that have stood the test of time, $47.40, or $3.95 per cassette. [Source: NavPress]

Tape Ministers—Recorded sermons by Dr. David A. Seamands, pastor-counselor from the First United Methodist Church of Wilmore, Kentucky, and by

Rev. Ruben Welch, chaplain of Point Loma College, San Diego. Dr. Seamands has over 170 cassettes available, many dealing with the subject of Biblical psychology, on which he is an authority. One tape from this series, *The Healing of Damaged Emotions*, is rapidly becoming a classic. A recent four-cassette program is *The Great Phrases of Jesus*, $15. Rev. Welch specializes in Bible study topics. Each cassette generally contains two sermons or talks, and costs roughly $4 to $6 per cassette, less when various complete sets are purchased.   [Source: Tape Ministers]

Thomas More Cassettes—Authoritative speakers on a variety of relevant and provocative subjects, primarily of Catholic concern but almost everyone will find at least one topic of special interest. Lengths vary from 36 to 71 minutes per cassette, costs from $6.95 to $10.95 per cassette. Some examples: *The Storyteller of God*, John Shea; *The Social Mission of the Church*, Charles Curran, *The Real Mary*, John L. McKenzie, and *Sex for the Single Catholic*, Andrew Greeley. There is a large collection of cassettes by Fr. Henri Nouwen—*The Lonely Search for God, Prayer and Thought, Care and the Elderly, Compassion*, and *Celibacy and the Holy*, among others—that are intended more for those in religious life. [Source: Thomas More Cassettes]

Unity Cassettes—Lectures and sermons by Unity ministers and other New Thought scholars. Here are just a few examples from the variety of speakers and topics available. Marcus Bach offers his observations on how the power of God works in people's lives, 10 cassettes, $4 each. In two albums Jack Boland discusses *Prosperity*, 12 cassettes for $48 and *Unity and Alcoholism*, three cassettes for $12. Eric Butterworth has two three-cassette albums for $12, *Eckhart, Emerson, Thoreau, and Unity* and *The Master Formula for Demonstration*. Frank and Martha Giudici, the ministers of the Unity Village Chapel, offer three albums: *Love Yourself to Wholeness*, $9, *The World of Meditation*, $12, and *Successful Living Through Self-Awareness*, $16. On a single $4 cassette, Elmer and Alyce Green of the Menninger Clinic are interviewed about the Fillmore teachings and biofeedback. Three other albums: *Dynamics of Healing and Healing for Others*, by Kay Arndt and George Miller, two cassettes, $9; *The Bible Comes Alive*, with J. Sig Paulson and Rocco Errico, three cassettes, $12; and *The Quimby Writings*, by Dr. Ervin Seale, four cassettes, $16.   [Source: Unity School of Christianity]

People with Vision—A fascinating collection of talks by men and women who share with the listener "the real excitement of living as God meant us to live." In *Street University*, Arthur Blessit offers a crash course in the who, when, and where of sharing Christ, on six tapes. Gary Collins covers *Mental Health and the Bible, You Can Profit from Stress*, (both four tapes) and *People Helping in a Group* (six tapes). Dr. James Dobson offers several six-tape counseling sets: *Discipline from Cradle to College, Kids Need Self-Esteem*

Too, Preparing for Adolescence, and *What Wives Wish Their Husbands Knew About Women*. Dr. Howard Hendricks has six-tape albums on *Christian Marriage, Communications*, and *Management*, and four-tape sets on *Rearing Children* and *Creative Parenthood*. Also in the counseling realm are Dr. Tim LaHaye's programs on *How to be Happy Though Married, Spirit-Controlled Temperament* (six tapes) and *How to Win Over Depression* and *Transformed Temperament* (four tapes). Hal Lindsey discusses *Holy Spirit in the Last Days, The Late Great Planet Earth, Satan Is Alive and Well on Planet Earth*, and three volumes of *There's a New World Coming*—all six-tape albums. Walter Martin focuses on cults in *How to Witness to J.W.'s, How to Witness to Mormons, Martin Speaks Out* (in two volumes, on UFOs, reincarnation, TM, abortion, euthanasia, women's rights, and homosexuality), *The New Cults* (all four-tape albums), *World of the Cults* (two volumes), and *World of the Occult* (two volumes)—all on six-tape albums. Tim Timmons gives Bible-related counseling in *Maximum Manhood, Biblical Lovemaking* (both four-tape albums), *Maximum Marriage, Maximum Parenthood, Single's Solution*, and *Ultimate Lifestyle* (six-tape albums). All four-tape albums are $24.98, and the six-tape albums are $34.98. Each of these speakers also has many individual cassettes in their topics for $5.98 each.   [Source: Vision House Publishers, Inc.]

The Upper Room Cassette Edition—The world's most widely read daily devotional guide is available on two cassettes per month, for $21 a year, $49 for three years. Each month's tapes contains a daily meditation, prayer, meaningful Bible verse, scripture passage, thought for the day, and subject of intercessory prayer. Of related interest are *Living Prayer Cassette Tapes*, hour-long tapes with speakers from The Upper Room Prayer Meetings: *Back to Basics in Prayer*, featuring 'Spotty' and Miriam Spottswood, *Power for Ministry/Prayer Power*,, with Robert Standhardt and Jo Kimmel, and *You Can Pray as You Ought*, with Arnold Prater. $5.95 each. [Source: Upper Room]

World Evangelism—Sermons and rallys by Rev. Morris Cerullo, who calls upon his rich heritage in Judaism to become a dynamic Christian evangelist. Some of his album titles: *The New Anointing*, how to obtain answers to prayers, $25 for five C-90 cassettes in album plus book; *The Miracle Rally*, recorded live to inspire faith to new heights, on six C-90 cassettes in album plus book; *Revelation Healing Power*, sharing endtime truths at a personal level, $35 for seven C-90 cassettes in album; and these single-cassettes in album plus book (all $7.95): *Making Possible Your Impossibilities; Breakthrough in Prophecy, Wind Over the 20th Century, God's Master Plan of the Ages*, and *7 Steps to Victory*. Many individual cassettes also available, for $4.95 each. [Source: World Evangelism]

Word—*Improving Your Serve* is not tennis, but Charles R. Swindoll's exploration of the means, costs, dangers, and rewards of genuine discipleship, $89.95 for 12 cassettes in album. *Ask Him Anything*, says Lloyd J. Ogilvie, for God is not afraid of tough thinking, $89.95 for 12 cassettes in album. *A Gardener Looks at the Fruits of the Spirit*, by W. Phillip Keller, shows what the fruits really mean on a day-to-day basis in the life of the believer, eight cassettes with scripts in album, $59.95. *The Helper* is Catherine Marshall's study course on the Holy Spirit, $39.95 for three cassettes and workbooks in album. Who else but Billy Graham could describe *How To Be Born Again*, $39.95 for three cassettes, guides, and album. *Drumbeat of Love* is Lloyd Ogilvie and Bruce Larson's 'relational' study of the Book of Acts, three cassettes and manuals in album, $39.95. *Life-Lifters* are single cassette highlights of various Word, Inc. programs and speakers, such as: *Improving Your Serve*, *Straight Talk To Men*, *How To Be Born Again*, *Born Again* by Charles Colson, *Inside I Trembled*, by Keith Miller, *Losers Can Be Winners, Too*, by Dr. Robert Schuller, *Maximum Living in a Pressure Cooker World*, by Tim Timmons, and many more. [Source: Word, Inc.]

Truth Tapes International—Sermons and messages by younger missionaries and evangelists, focusing specifically on the spiritual needs of young people. Among the speakers offering Christian insights are Loren Cunningham, Joy Dawson, Winkie Pratney, Brother Andrew, Floyd McClung, Don Stephens, Campbell McAlpine, Jean Darnell, and Tony Salerno. $4 for each message. Also available is Gordon Olson's analytical study into the nature of God, the nature of man, the nature and extent of sin, and the nature of the Christian life, $119 for 44 cassettes. [Source: Youth with a Mission]

NCC Cassettes—Well-produced recordings of both traditional messages and modern concerns. In the traditional category are the four-cassette albums each featuring eight sermons by Dr. David H. C. Read, Dr. Fred B. Craddock, Dr. William C. Howland, Dr. Ralph W. Sockman, and Dr. Joseph R. Jeter, for $24.50 each. Dr. Read also has *To the Romans—and To Us*, on two four-cassette volumes, $17.85 each, both together for $34, and also *Finding Christ in the Fourth Gospel*, five cassettes in album, $34. Single-cassette titles include: *Prayer for Beginners/Meditative Prayer* (7.95); *How to Stay Married/12 Rules for Marital Fighting* ($5.50); *For Those Who Mourn* ($6.95); *Aging* ($7.95); *What is Spiritual Healing/Depression* ($7.95), and *Overcoming Our Fears* ($7.95). Albums on more modern themes cover *Consultation on Electronic Church*, four cassettes, $24.50; *Impact of New Technologies on the Church*, six cassettes, $39.95; and *Faith, Science, and the Future*, two cassettes (no album), $15. Individual titles: *The Church and Cable TV* and *Ethics and Trends in International Broadcasting*, both $4; *Understanding

the Systems Age*, $7.95; *Relationship of Christianity and Democracy*, $5.95; and *Sexism and the Bible*, $3.50. [Source: National Council of the Churches of Christ]

World MAP Tapes—Messages recorded at camp meetings of the World Missionary Assistance Plan by fundamentalist ministers and Bible teachers, such as Brian Bailey, Karl Coke, Kevin Conner, Judson Cornwall, David DuPlessis, Dr. Robert Frost, Ernest Gentile, Jack Hayford, Ralph Mahoney, Hal Oxley, Les Pritchard, Gerald Rowlands, and others. $4.50 per message. [Source: World MAP Tape Outreach]

SoundWord Tape Ministry—Messages by Pastor Jack Hayford of the First Foursquare Church of Van Nuys, CA, on a variety of teaching topics: new believers, Old Testament studies (Genesis, Exodus, Ruth, Nehemiah), New Testament studies (John, Romans, Corinthians, Ephesians, Hebrews, Revelation), domestic relationships, talks with men and with women, various seasonal messages, and many other subjects. $3 per message. [Source: SoundWord Tape Ministry]

Oasis Cassette Library—You pay a one-time lifetime membership fee of $5, and then can borrow without charge from their library of over 3,000 tapes, featuring speakers such as Chuck Smith, Bob Mumford, Ralph Mahoney, Don Basham, Fred Price, Jack Hayford, Roger Houtsma, Stephen Hill, and others. Non-copyrighted tapes may be purchased for $1.50. [Source: Oasis Cassette Library]

King Tapes—Inspirational Christian messages from a variety of points of view and from over 350 different evangelical speakers—a representative selection of just about everyone who has ever had a sermon or testimony recorded! Cost is $4.95 per selection, or $3.95 each when four or more are ordered at the same time. [Source: King Tapes]

Weekly Message Cassettes—Messages on a variety of spiritual and inspirational topics and Bible studies, with each cassette ($2.50) containing a message for each week of the year. They also offer collected titles from Theodore H. Epp's *Back to the Bible* radio broadcasts: *The Deceitfulness of Wine and Strong Drink*, nine messages on two cassettes, $5; *Marriage, Divorce and Remarriage*, four cassettes for $12.50, $3.50 each; *Portraits of Christ in the Tabernacle*, 35 messages on six cassettes in album for $18, $3.50 each. Warren W. Wiersbe describes how *The "Fear Nots" of the Bible* affected Abraham, Daniel, Peter, and John, and how they should affect us today, $7.50 for three cassettes. [Source: Back to the Bible Broadcast]

Melodyland Tapes—Every sermon and personal story delivered at the Melodyland Christian Center is available on cassette, with messages from leading evangelists, missionary statesmen, and Bible teachers—such as David DuPlessis, Michael Esses, Robert Frost, Roy Howes, Dick Mills, Hal Lindsey, Ralph Wilkerson, and many many others. $3.50 per cassette. [Source: Melodyland Tape Store]

Holy Spirit Center Tapes—Charismatic messages and testimonies by David Barnard (founder and pastor of the Holy Spirit Center in San Francisco), Dr. Dean Berger (psychologist and Bible-based counselor), Ray Bloomfield and Des Short (both from New Zealand), Chico Holiday (night club entertainer now with a music ministry), Joe Donato (former Mafia member), Georgio Tozzi (Met singer), G. B. McDowell (a Pentecostal authority), and others. All cassettes are $3.50 each, discounts with multiple purchases. [Source: Holy Spirit Center Tape Ministry]

Hour of Power—The stirring messages of Dr. Robert Schuller, recorded live at the Garden Grove Community Church and seen on nationwide TV. Among the albums (Tape Book) titles are: *Peace Through Possibility Thinking*, 12 messages on six cassettes, $25.95; *Power To Make Your Dreams Come True*, 10 messages on five cassettes, $22.95; *Your Key to Lasting Happiness*, 8 messages on four cassettes, $18.95; *Positive Ideas for a Happy Family*, six messages on three cassettes, $14.95; and seven others, all with album. A host of individual messages and sermons by Dr. Schuller are available on individual cassettes, for $3.95 each, including all of Dr. Schuller's 'Hour of Power' TV messages. [Source: Hour of Power]

Ministr-O-Media—Quality programs for both Catholic laypersons and those in the religious life. The witty English priest, Bernard Basset SJ gives an historical perspective in *Beginnings of the Faith in the New World*, four cassettes in album, $24.95. Father Basset has two other presentations: *A Weekend with Cardinal Newman* (seven cassettes in album, $34.95) and *A Parliament of Saints* (four cassettes in album, $24.95). Then, Juvenal Lalor OFM shows new techniques for praising God in one's own special way on The *Essentials of the Spiritual Life*, six cassettes in album plus bonus book for $29.95. They also have two albums of talks made at Maryland Right to Life Conventions, *Nurturing Families: Keystone of Society* and *Pro-Life Family: Beacon of Hope*, each consisting of 14 cassettes in two albums, $59. [Source: Ministr-O-Media, Inc.]

SCAN Cassettes—SCAN is a nationally syndicated 30-minute youth and young adult–oriented public service radio program produced weekly by the American Lutheran Church. Each program blends in-depth interview and contemporary music to tell the story of an individual problem, with its attendant struggles and growth potential. Nearly 400 programs have been produced, including such topics as alcoholism, family violence, global justice issues, personal relationships, disabilities, and self-image. Each

program is available on cassette for $5, with transcript and resource newsletter included. For $85 all the new SCAN shows will be sent for a year. Program lists available on request. [Source: SCAN/ALC Media Services Center]

Christian Classics—In *Pilgrim's Progress* (Books I and II), C. William Shaffer narrates Pilgrim's inspiring journey to the Celestial City. *The Holy War*, another work by John Bunyan, is also narrated by Paster Shaffer, and describes the battle against the city of Mansoul. A more allegorical narrative, *Hind's Feet on High Places*, describes Much-Afraid's journey to the High Places. $12.45 for each three-cassette album. [Source: Master Productions]

Archbishop Fulton J. Sheen—Recordings of talks, sermons, and retreats by probably the finest ecclesiastical orator of our times. The *Life Is Worth Living* collection contains two of his early TV talks on each cassette, $6 each or eight cassettes in album for $48. *Cor Ad Cor Loquitor* (Heart Speaks to Heart) are retreat messages for priests and all of us, eight cassettes in album for $34.95. *Renewal and Reconciliation* holds Archbishop Sheen's views on major issues facing us today, nine cassettes in album for $34.95. Other titles available include *Christ: His Passion and Death* (four cassettes in album, $24.95), *Trust in God* and *Tribute to a Pope* (one cassette each, $5.50 each), and *The Answers to the Seven Burdens of Life* (four cassettes in album, $24.95). [Source: Ministr-O-Media, Inc.]

Hosanna Tapes—One of the largest collections of sermons and testimonies on cassette, featuring virtually all of the leading lights (and some lesser ones) in the evangelical and charismatic movement, including many available from other sources. After a lifetime membership fee of $5, three tapes may be borrowed at a time without charge; most tapes are also available for purchase at $1.75 each. They also have a few low-cost albums available: *Jesus, Come Heal Your Family*, 16 tapes from the 1980 Catholic Charismatic Conference featuring Bishop Joseph C. McKinney and Mother Angelica, $22.50 with album; *Balance*, a Christian approach to financial planning, $34.95 for six tapes and book in album; *Let Us Reason Together*, a summary of Christian teaching by Rupert H. Schroeder, based on Luther's 'Small Catechism,' $8.95 for four tapes in album; *The Weightier Matters of the Law*, lawyers, judges, and ministers addressing themselves to the topic of Christian reconciliation, 12 cassettes in album for $17.25; *For Pastors Only!*, Iverna Tompkins talking to pastors on the topic of divorcees in the church, one cassette, $1.75; and more. [Source: Hosanna]

Logos Tapes—A host of albums, each containing six cassettes of related sermons by Malcolm Smith, $20 each, $15 for each additional album with same order. Individual teaching cassettes by Rev. Smith are $4 each, any three for $10 including album. They also feature cassettes by such well-known speakers as Iverna Tompkins, Judson Cornwall, Bob Mumford, Fr. Bertolucci, Jamie Buckingham, Agnes Sanford, and others, any three in album for $10. [Source: Logos Tapes]

Evangelization and the Scriptures—Drawing on his years of experience, Fr. John Burke OP provides a scriptural-theological perspective for the Catholic Church's current emphasis on lay evangelization. $25 for four cassettes and book in album. [Source: SCRC Tape Ministry]

Leadership Effectiveness Series—Based on biblical principles, this course covers three critical areas of leadership effectiveness: your personal development and growth, your ability to work with and motivate people, and your clearly understood purpose in society. The course is led by Dr. Howard Hendricks, Chairman of Christian Education at Dallas Theological Seminary; the eight cassettes cover: Daniel as a Leader I and II; becoming a person of influence; communicating more effectively; living by faith; significant steps for spiritual growth; becoming salt and light; and staying salty. $42. [Source: Leadership Dynamics International]

Leadership Dynamics Tape Series—Dr. Howard Hendricks and Bruce E. Cook combine forces to bring to executives the biblical concepts of management. Topics of the eight talks in this package include: characteristics of a leader, the world's greatest leader, personal decision making, knowing God's will, secrets of success, motivation or movement, motivational leadership, and focus on the family. $52 for eight cassettes. [Source: Leadership Dynamics International]

Practice the Word Series—Collections of talks by Jim Durkin: *God's Purpose & Vision*, an understanding of God's plan for your life, $15.95 for four C-60 cassettes in album; *Training Your Soul*, offering guidance in gaining control over destructive emotions and bad habits, $9.50 for two cassettes and book; *Believe, Confess & Act*, how to fill your life with blessing, $13.75 for three cassettes and book; and *Marriage, Childraising, and Sex*, with Jim and wife Dacie, married 30 years, sharing rich insights and experience about the adventures of family life, $14.95 for three cassettes in an album. Also available is the *Radiance Tape Library*, a free rental library of the practical Bible teachings of Jim Durkin and the men associated with him in the ministry of Gospel Outreach, stressing the realistic application of the action principles of God's Word. Two tapes are loaned at a time without charge for three weeks; they are also for sale at $4 each. [Source: Radiance]

Speaking Books—Dr. Jack and Cornelia Addington narrate their most popular books, on six 60-minute cassettes: *The Perfect Power Within You*; *The Hidden Mystery of the Bible* (six 90-minute cassettes); *Your*

Needs Met; *All About Goals and How to Achieve Them* (narrated by Dr. Thomas Hopper); and *The Joy of Meditation*. $35 each with album. [Source: Abundant Living Foundation]

Meditation Cassettes—21 presentations by Dr. Jack and Cornelia Addington (of the Universal House of Prayer) that explain the art and technique of religious meditation. All these hour-long programs have pauses at intervals for personal meditation. The Addingtons also have a series of lectures on self-improvement by prayer and relaxation. $5.95 for each C-60 cassette. [Source: Abundant Living Foundation]

Teaching Tapes by Derek Prince—Hour-long messages by an international interpreter of the charismatic renewal, in seven broad series: Systemic Theology; Salvation and Healing; The Holy Spirit; The Christian Life; The Church; Exorcism and Deliverance; and Prophecy. $4.95 for each C-60 cassette, each with printed analysis and outline. There is also *Update*, and in this bimonthly cassette letter, evangelist Derek Prince shares insights gained from his personal ministry on the need for prayer to overcome the problems and issues confronting this country and others around the world. $1 for the first issue, then $3.50 thereafter billed bimonthly, or $20 a year. [Source: Derek Prince Publications]

NCR Cassettes—About 500 titles, both single cassettes and albums, bearing a Roman Catholic orientation and dealing with adult religious education, liturgy, pastoral and sacramental aids, and personal development. Other topics covered include conscience/morality, ecumenism, marriage, family prayer, spirituality, women, death, and many others. Cassette lengths range from 20 to 90 minutes, and prices range from $6.95 to $8.95 (most are $7.95). Representative album titles: *Help For Christian Parents* by Dr. Henry Fischer, a clinical psychologist, $29.95 for four C-65 cassettes and study guide in album; *The Rites of Anointing: Pastoral Care of the Sick*, by Fr. Charles W. Gusmer, $24.95 for three cassettes and guide in album; *A Time to Grieve*, by Fr. Kenneth Czillinger, eight cassettes and study guide in album, $59.95; and *A Theology of Lost Mittens: Children and Penance*, Fr. Regis Duffy, $34.95 for four C-60 cassettes and study guide in album. [Source: NCR Resources]

Acceptance—The best-selling book by Vincent P. Collins, with the theme of peace of mind through acceptance of God's will, has been condensed into a 60-minute cassette. $6.95. [Source: Abbey Press]

Marital and Family Spirituality—David M. Thomas delves into the religious experience of American Christian families, on four 40-minute cassettes in album with study guide for $29.95. On *Single Parents*, Robert DiGuilio provides eight 20-minute talks to help Christian parents who are going' it alone to balance the demands of parenting and those of continued personal growth. Like all Abbey volumes, these are useful as group discussion starters. $34.95 for four cassettes with study guide in album. [Source: Abbey Press]

Parenting and Emotional Development—Larry Losoncy offers guidelines to enable Christian parents to respond sensitively to the changing emotional needs of their children. $29.95 for four 40-minute cassettes with study guide in album. A related series is *Parenting and Moral Development*, in which Andrew Thompson gives practical suggestions, in eight 20-minute talks, on how everyday family activities can be used to guide children on the path to Christian moral maturity. This is $29.95 for four cassettes with study guide in album. And in *Families Doing Things Together*, marriage columnists James and Mary Kenny detail their conviction that doing things together is the key to family strength, enrichment and blessings, on four 40-minute cassettes in album with study guide for $34.95. [Source: Abbey Press]

Herald House—Programs from the Reorganized Church of Jesus Christ of Latter Day Saints: sermons by Arthur A. Oakman, Harry Black, Eugene Austin, Lee Abramson, F. Edward Butterworth and other miscellaneous sermons and testimonies; a six-cassette album on *Know Your Church and How It Functions*, $27; a seven cassette album on *Family Ministries for the 80s*, $38.50; and a series of tapes on church history, covering the Nauvoo, Kirtland, and Lamoni eras. All cassettes $7.99 each, less in albums or with club membership. [Source: Herald House]

Tapes for Greater Living—Expository messages by Herb Ezell of the Harbor Christian Center, grouped under headings such as angels and demons, believers' ministry, the Bible as the word of God, water baptism, Christian agapé, fellowship, Christian standards of conduct, Christian discipline and divine order, encouragement and uplift, faith principles, physical healing, salvation, the Second Coming, spiritual worship, and total commitment. $4 donation for each 30-45 minute tape, $2.50 each when four or more tapes are ordered. [Source: Tapes for Greater Living]

Dramatized L. D. S. Church History—72 faith-building stories, beginning with Joseph Smith and the first vision and portraying all major events up to the present day, on 36 cassettes in three albums, $6.25 each shipped monthly or $225 for the entire set. [Source: Living Scriptures Inc.]

Spiritual Growth

14 Steps to Perfect Joy—A comprehensive and practical home program in yoga, developed by Swami Kriyananda for helping individuals develop growth potential. The set includes a 306-page practice manual of the 14 steps, and 14 cassettes to enhance and reinforce the learning experience, all for $157. A useful adjunct is a three-cassette album, *Yoga Postures for Self-Awareness*, $19.95 when ordered with the above, otherwise $25. This source also has Yoga seminars with Swami Kriyananda, recorded during Spiritual Renewal Weeks at the Ananda retreat, Rajo Yoga instructions, Kriya Yoga preparation, poetic readings, Sunday services, public lectures and evening satsangs. These are generally $6 for each 60-90 minute recording. [Source: Ananda Publications]

My Neighbor, My Friend, and My God—Concentrates on our being able to find happiness in these troubled times by living the way Jesus taught us to live with one another. Price is $36.25 for five cassettes. [Source: Family Enrichment Bureau]

Hanuman Foundation Tape Library—A major source of recordings by Baba Ram Dass (formerly Harvard professor Richard Alpert, Ph.D.), describing Eastern philosophy in terms Westerners can grasp. These include various lectures by Ram Dass, complete recordings of a karma yoga retreat at Lama Foundation, and a 26-hour course on the *Yogas of the Bhagavad Gita*. Other offerings include the complete proceedings of the *Vipassana Meditation Retreat*, led by Joseph Goldstein and Jack Kornfield. Cassettes vary in length, but the cost is a remarkable $3 an hour. [Source: Hanuman Foundation Tape Library]

Ashram Records—Talks by Swami Sivananda Radha on many aspects of Kundalini Yoga, mantras, meditation, relaxation, symbology. The approach used emphasizes the integration of Eastern spiritual wisdom with contemporary Western life and values. $6.50 for each hour-long talk, $8.50 for a 90-minute talk on Yoga, love, sex, and marriage. [Source: Timeless Books]

Emissary Cassettes—Each tape contains two hour-long services (usually, morning and evening services of the same day) given by the late Bishop Lloyd Arthur Meeker (Uranda) or by Bishop Martin Cecil, both of the Emissaries of Divine Light. These are $12 each. A *Basic Tape Series* of 12 cassettes giving the fundamental concepts and truths of the Emissaries of Divine light is available for $120 including album. [Source: Sunrise Ranch]

Unarius Tapes—2,000 teaching tapes that provide an understanding of the evolutionary development of man, using the principles of 4th dimensional physics as the foundation for learning the techniques of past life therapy. The course of study "provides for a scientific basis of healing of the past negative life experiences of the individual, and at the same time raising the consciousness of the student by the advanced information received." $7.95 for each 90-minute cassette. [Source: Unarius Educational Foundation]

Krishnamurti Recordings—Talks, discussions, and questions and answers by Krishnamurti, recorded live at various sessions in the U.S., Europe, and India. $5 to $10 per cassette. [Source: Krishnamurti Foundation]

Integral Yoga—Sri Swami Satchidananda speaks on deep relaxation and Integral Yoga Hatha for beginners and comments on the Yoga Sutras of Patanjali and on the Living Gita. Costs are $5 to $7 per cassette. [Source: Integral Yoga Publications]

Sathya Sai Baba—Discourses and bhajans by Sathya Sai, the founder of the Spiritual Advancement of the Individual Foundation, recorded live in India and Hollywood. Costs are roughly $4 for a 60-minute tape, $6 for a 90-minute one. [Source: S.A.I. Foundation]

SFF Cassette Tapes—An eclectic collection of talks giving insights into a variety of theologies, philosophies, spiritual theories, metaphysical considerations, and mystical and psychic experiences, recorded at various SFF conferences and retreats. [Source: Spiritual Frontiers Fellowship]

Sanatana Dharma Recordings—Talks and instructions by Yogeshwar Muni (and some by his guru, Svami Kripalvananda), including sadhanas (critical guides along the spiritual path), enlightenment, satsangas (sharings of the Truth), past life experiences, and science and truth. About $7 per hour. [Source: Sanatana Dharma Foundation]

The Sound of ECK—ECKANAR is "the most ancient spiritual teaching known to man (and) offers the ability to experience God in this lifetime, directly and personally through Soul Travel under the guidance of the Living ECK Master." On these tapes, the two most recent Masters, Sri Paul Twitchell and Sri Darwin Gross, offer this guidance on 'the path of total awareness,' recorded at regional seminars, workshops, and private recordings. $6.50 for each tape, usually about 90 minutes long. [Source: ECKANKAR]

MSIA Tapes—Discourses by John-Roger, the Spiritual Director of the Movement of Spiritual Inner Awareness, all focusing on bringing people into an awareness of 'Soul' and 'Soul Transcendence', and of the Mystical Traveler Consciousness that exists simultaneously on all levels and responds to those asking for its assistance. Tapes are $7 each. [Source: MSIA]

Quest Cassettes—Hour-long presentations aimed at aiding and abetting one's personal search for personal truth. Many of the talks are by Geoffrey Hodson: life after death and the pathways to perfection; reincarnation; the human aura and the powers of the human mind; psychic forces affecting health, happiness, and spiritual healing; perfected men on earth

and their disciples; the controversial occult power called Kundalini; and cruelty as cause of war and disease. N. Sri Ram discusses the evolution of consciousness and the significance of each moment. Richard Brooks describes occult ecology. Clara Codd reflects on yoga, and with Mr. Hodson talks about the science and process of meditation. Boris de Zirkoff discusses H. P. Blavatsky and Radha discusses Yoga. Finally, Phoebe and Laurence Bendit debate medical diagnosis by clairvoyance. $3.95 each. [Source: Theosophical Publishing House]

SYDA Tapes—Talks by Swami Muktananda given at intensives, informal interviews, and evening lectures, all addressing the human dilemma and its solution. Some talks are available in Spanish. $5.95 each. [Source: SYDA Bookstore]

Discovering Spiritual Values in Community—A 10-session program for those seeking to grow in religious awareness by exploring the spiritual values present in human existence. Not an advanced experience in spiritual growth, this program works best with nine or ten people, and makes an ideal weekend retreat. [Source: Instructional Dynamics, Inc.]

Bhagwan Shree Rajneesh—Lectures and discourses by the controversial spiritual mystic, both hailed as a sage and dismissed as a charlatan. There are many, many selections to choose from—fortunately, since Bhagwan is now speaking only through silence. The cassettes are $8.50 each. [Source: Chidvilas Rajneesh Meditation Center]

Findhorn Tapes—An interesting series of lectures—mostly with David Spangler, some by founders Eileen and Peter Caddy and a "Conference Series" by well-known speakers—that offer practical advice on living a spiritual and God-centered life in cooperation with man and the kingdoms of nature. Recorded at Scotland's unique Findhorn Community, which is imbued with these concepts. Costs are about $6.75 each, plus postage. [Source: Findhorn Foundation]

Nilgiri Press—In *Meditation*, Eknath Easwaran offers two cassettes on the purpose and practice of meditation, and two more on the disciplines which apply the energy and insights of meditation to daily life, $20 for four cassettes in clothbound case. Other titles, all on single 41- to 59-minute cassettes for $5, are *The Tree of Life, The Mystery of Time, Love Is a Precious Skill, Finding Time To Love, Living in the Present, The Transformation of Anger, Right Understanding, The House of the Mind*, and *The Force of Goodness*. [Source: Nilgiri Press]

Satsangs of Swami Amar Jyoti—Spiritual discourses and straight-forward guidance on the topics of the art of living, devotion and surrender, guru-disciple relationship, Kharma Yoga, mantra, meditation, principles and virtues, relationships, spiritual practice, true religion, and Vedanta. $8.23 each. [Source: Truth Consciousness]

Ashram Tapes—Yogi Amrit Desai, noted authority on yoga, explains the path of Kripalu Yoga, a unique form of meditation in motion that combines gentle stretching movements of hatha yoga with rhythmic breathing to bring deep peace and calm to body, mind, and emotions. Topics of his talks include: Kripalu Yoga, transforming stress, relaxation as a way of life, how to love and understand others, how to handle negativity, healing from within, improving communication, self-acceptance, and many others. They also have special series of relaxation and meditation tapes and yoga practice tapes. $6.50 for each cassette, with discounts for purchases of seven or more.   [Source: Kripalu Krishna Kala]

Integral Yoga—Swami Jyotir Maya Nandi gives personal guidance and instruction on attaining Total Enlightenment, ranging from guidelines on how to remove mental depression and how to overcome craving to controlling your own destiny and insights into death, plus instructions in various branches of Yoga. Also available are lectures or series on all the important Yoga scriptures, including *Raja Yoga*, *Bhagavad Gita*, *Upanishads*, and *Mahabharata*. $10 for any hour-long cassette.   [Source: Yoga Research Foundation]

SRF Recordings—Prayers, poems, and chants by Paramahansa Yogananda, founder of Self-Realization Fellowship; talks on the importance of God-centered living by Sri Daya Mata, his spiritual successor and now President of the Fellowship; and talks on the true guru, Kriya Yoga, and spiritual marriage by Brother Anandamoy, SRF minister. $4.95, $5.25, or $8.25, depending on the length. [Source: Self-Realization Fellowship]

Vajradhatu Recordings—Recordings of talks, seminars, and courses by Chogyam Trungpa Rinpoche, Jamgon Kontrul Rinpoche, Osel Tendzin, and His Holiness the Dalai Lama, all trained in the philosophical and meditative traditions of Tibetan Buddhism. Intended for students of Buddhism and spiritual development in general. $9 for each cassette. [Source: Vajradhatu and Naropa Recordings]

XIX.
Sales

Insurance

Consultative Selling Skills—An advanced course to enable insurance sales people to develop, through application to typical sales situations, the skills needed for a better performance. The aim is to gain proficiency in prospecting, securing appointments, gathering information during interviews and dealing with customer resistance. $270 for five audio-cassettes and 17 workbooks. [Source: Systema Corporation]

Great Sales Ideas on Cassette—In *Ben Feldman at Work*, the "world's greatest life insurance salesman" reveals his sales techniques in simulated interviews, $20 for two cassettes and workbook in album. *The MAGIC Split-Dollar Plan* is thoroughly discussed by Emil Budnitz, Jr., $19.95 for two cassettes. *Frank Weisz Discusses SuperTrust*, telling how this estate planning tool can have tax savings and other benefits for clients, $19.95 for two cassettes and workbook. In *Selling Smarter in the '80s*, Stephan R. Leimberg and Morey S. Rosenbloom offer advanced underwriting techniques in such areas as charitable gifts, split dollar, private annuities, grandfather trusts, and more, on two cassettes and loose-leaf book for $24.95. Mr. Leimberg also has a couple of single-cassette titles: *$1,000 A Minute*, $15 with charts; and *Ask For What You Want*, $9.95 with workbook. *Your Personal Growth and Achievement Program* is an eight-cassette course with Art Mortell exploring the reasons why salesmen have difficulty prospecting and closing, and so level off below their potential, $85 with looseleaf workbook. [Source: Farnsworth Publishing Company, Inc.]

Enterprise Records—'How I did it' talks by insurance professionals who have done it: *How I Sold $40,000,000 of Life Insurance in Two Years* and *How To Earn $100,000 a Year as a Salesman*, by Joe Gandolfo, CLU; *How To Get Daytime Life Insurance by Telephone* and *How To Hire and Train a Telephone Solicitor to Make Daytime Life Insurance Appointments*, by Frank C. Pfister, CLU; *How To Use Direct Mail To Sell $1,500,000 of Life Insurance Every Year*, by Jack Hartman; *How I Sell $3,000,000 of Life Insurance to the Town and Country Market Every Year*, by James C. Bradford; and *How To Increase Your Income and Accomplishments ... By Mastering Time Control*, by Robert H. Smith. $11.95 for each 45-minute cassette. [Source: Enterprise Records]

Chris Murphy Presentation and Training Program—A kit that includes an actual presentation by super-salesman Chris Murphy to a prospect plus a workbook, so that you hear, step-by-step and page-by-page, how Mr. Murphy leads his prospect to an eventual sale with an effective closing technique. This kit is not sophisticated, but workable. It doesn't complicate but simplifies the benefits of life insurance. All for $29.95. [Source: Richmar Productions]

Ben Feldman's Creating the Sale—Mr. Feldman is acknowledged as one of the world's greatest life insurance salesmen, having sold as much as $100,000,000 in a single year. In 12 sessions he presents his complete common-sense success system, covering planning, preparation, prospecting, making calls, researching, the interview, and the presentation. $49.95 for six cassettes in album. [Source: Richmar Productions]

MDRT Audio-Cassettes—Outstanding lectures from past annual meetings of the Million Dollar Round Table offer insurance people original ideas to help them grow personally and professionally. Major topic headings in their catalog are: agent as businessman, business insurance, communication, employee benefits & executive compensation, estate planning, gifts, group insurance, interview techniques, life insurance, motivation, pensions, personal and office efficiency, prospecting, and retirement planning. $7 each, $5 to MDRT members. [Source: Million Dollar Round Table]

Agency Management on Tape—A series of 32 cassette seminars for insurance agents and principals on various aspects of insurance management, ranging from mergers and acquisitions and legal considerations to agency tax strategies and marketing. $18.50 each. [Source: Independent Insurance Agents of America, Inc.]

Sales Interview Skills Training Program—Designed with the sole objective of helping new and experienced agents develop and add to their sales interview skills. $109.50 for six cassettes, eight workbooks, trainer's guide, and album. Also in the skills training line there's *Prospecting Skills Training Program*, an explanation of the prospecting process, how it works, how many prospects are needed for success, and the important point of prospecting by market, all on three cassettes and three workbooks for $58.95; and *Organizational Skills Training Programs* which shows how to organize for field efficiency, how to correctly complete an application, and how to apply after-the-sale activity in the life insurance sales process. $58.95 for three cassettes and three workbooks in album. [Source: R&R Newkirk]

Estate Planning Skills Training Program—A course that shows how to find estate planning prospects, and then what specific steps to take, from the initial phone call to working with the prospect's attorney and other advisors in implementing the plan. $142.95 for eight cassettes, workbooks, and other materials in album. [Source: R&R Newkirk]

In Sound—A quarterly cassette subscription service providing advanced underwriting news and marketing ideas. Side 1 of each 60-minute cassette discusses recent developments and current news of legislative changes, court rulings, regulations, and tax developments. Side 2 zeros in on one timely market or sales technique. $72 a year, including album and listener's guide for each edition. [Source: R&R Newkirk]

Telephone Skills Training Program—Appointments are crucial in insurance sales, and this kit gives agents pointers in improving their skills in making telephone appointments. $18.95 for cassette, telephone cue card, and sales guide. [Source: R&R Newkirk]

Business Insurance Series on Tape—Cassette/workbook mini-courses on nine aspects of business insurance: sole proprietorships, partnerships, professional corporations, closed corporations, key executive insurance, split-dollar insurance, deferred compensation, financial statements, and Section 79 plans. $15.50 each. [Source: R&R Newkirk]

Young Adult Sales Presentation—How it is done and what to expect, on a single audio-cassette, for $5.95. Other single-topic cassettes, sometimes with workbook, cover the '81 Tax Act, 'home assurance' sales presentations, balanced security, total needs, retirement, and IRA sales. A final offering is *Reflection & Directions*, by Benjamin N. Woodson CLU, $27.75 for three cassettes in album. [Source: R&R Newkirk]

Audio-Manual Courses—These are two-cassette basic overview courses on *Introduction to Insurance*, *Introduction to Life Insurance*, and *Telephone Customer Relations* (one cassette). $44 for each package of cassettes and workbook in albums. [Source: Merritt Company]

Life Sales Cassettes—A host of cassette-plus-workbook programs for new and/or experienced life underwriters. Most of these are $13 each, but sometimes more (as indicated) when additional training aids are included. First there is *The 1981 Tax Act*

Guide ($15.50) and up-to-date courses on *Individual Retirement Accounts*, *Keogh Plans*, and *Section 79*. Under the prospecting category (generally to train new agents) are *Who For You* (developing an initial list), *The Approach* ($19.95), *Referred Leads* ($21.95), *Target Marketing*, and *Agent Telephone Techniques* ($19.95). Titles covering closing include *A Process, Not A Problem*, *Removing Objections* ($21.95), and *Steps to Persistency*. There are these single cassette-plus-workbooks (all $13 each): *Mortgage Insurance, Family Income, Retirement Insurance, Converting Term*, and *Last Expenses*. Then, there are self-study training courses on agency management, consisting of a number of cassette-plus-workbook modules: *Agent Hiring Including EEO*, five modules, $110; *Agent Training & Supervision*, nine modules, $155; and *Agency Administration*, six modules, $117.50. The modules are available separately, for $15 to $30 each. [Source: Pictorial Publishers]

NU Cassettes—Sales messages, recorded live, about an hour each, $7.75 each: *The Easy Sale*, with John Savage pinpointing prospects that are almost pre-sold; and *Let's Get in Shape to Serve*, with Charlie Flowers presenting his views on the how and why to serve your fellow man. [Source: National Underwriter Co.]

To Market/To Market—Training courses that cut through legalese, dry doctrine, and mysticism to provide practical, relevant, and easily understood methods for insurance agents to apply in approaching three advanced markets: *Estate Planning for Life Agents* (12 cassettes and 18 workbooks in two binders for $97.50); *Business Insurance Perspectives* (10 cassettes and 16 workbooks in two binders for $97.50); and *Selling Qualified Retirement Plans* (six cassettes and 12 workbooks in binder for $79.50). [Source: Pentera Group, Inc.]

Legacy of Learning—From the General Agents and Managers Conference comes a series of monthly recorded interviews with leading insurance agency authorities, with each program covering one key area of building career agencies. Past volumes (each 12 cassettes in album) are $185 each. Volume V (1981) covers finding and selecting agency candidates, helping them develop and placing them in profitable areas, and identifying and aiding management assistants, all on 12 cassettes plus two bonus cassettes for $205. [Source: Wilson Learning Corporation]

Economic Recovery Tax Act of 1981—Neil E. Harl interprets the major estate, gift, and income tax provisions of this far-reaching legislation, in a 94-minute discussion on a single cassette for $19.95. [Source: Life Insurance Selling]

Advanced Sales Concepts Tape Program—Don Mehlig CLU shares his experience and creative selling approach to profit from current trends. Subjects of his hour-long talks, available for $20 each (except as noted): Section 79 and retired lives reserve, insurance in pension plans, executive benefit plans, split-dollar innovations ($22.50), and voluntary employees' beneficiary associations (VEBA) ($22.50). [Source: Life Insurance Selling]

Mail Order

Melvin Powers Mail Order Seminar—Melvin Powers, author of *How To Make a Fortune in Mail Order*, gives the listener a step-by-step explanation of how to buy space for the right price, selecting the proper mailing lists, how to test your ad, and finding the right products to sell. $25 for four 90-minute cassettes (recorded live) in album. [Source: Wilshire Book Company]

Mail Order Workshop—Duane Shinn, who has done very well in the music mail order business, tells how he did it and how you can do it, on a number of single cassettes (except as indicated): *How I Earn Over $1000 per Week Recording Cassettes at Home* (four cassettes and printed materials, $39.95); *How To Sell Your Product to Catalog Houses by the Thousands*, $23.95 with book; *How To Make a Small Fortune from Classified Ads*, $17.95; *How To Get Free Write-ups in Magazines and Newspapers All Over the U.S.*, $17.95; *How To Start Your Own Mail Order Business*, $9.95; *30 Businesses You Can Operate Without Leaving Your Home*, $17.95 with booklet; *Drop Ship Your Way to a Mail Order Fortune*, $19.95, and specific mail order businesses for writers ($17.95), songwriters ($17.95), hobbyists ($12.95), musicians, $14.75. [Source: Duane Shinn Publications]

Successful Mail Order Techniques—The secret, says Nido Qubein, is to offer the right products to the right people in the right way. Mr. Qubein draws upon his broad experience to tell how to start and organize a mail order business, how to select merchandise to sell, where to find it, how to advertise it, and how to process orders. $6.95 for six cassettes in album. [Source: Creative Services, Inc.]

Management

Managing Your Sales Force—William Welp and Christopher Hegarty discuss all the critical skills needed by the truly effective sales manager to meet the challenges of today's market. $350 for 12 cassettes and reference notes in album. [Source: AMR/Advanced Management Reports, Inc.]

Salesmanagement—A two-cassette album for $30 featuring J. Douglas Edwards. [Source: Sales Communique Corporation]

Manager's Guide to Higher Productivity—This has eight cassettes with workbook, by Danny Cox, $85; also there is *Basic to Basics Sales Management* by Fred Herman, with eight cassettes for $75; and *Art of Sales Management*, eight cassettes, $65. All courses include albums. [Source: General Cassette Corporation]

How To Permanently Motivate Sales People—Howard W. Bonnell draws upon 42 years of experience as Director of Sales Management Development for the publishers of the World Book Encyclopedia to offer this two-cassette seminar for sales managers. $21.90. [Source: Howard W. Bonnell]

Hiring Sales People—Master sales trainer Dave Yoho has four cassettes and a manual on personnel selection and evaluation, adaptable compensation system, and more, for $119, including album. [Source: Dave Yoho Associates]

Sales Management Performance Improvement System—A results-oriented course for the sales manager that combines logic and motivation to help build a high performance sales team, with discussions of objectives, training needs, sales meetings, profit motivation, time management, and standards of performance. $24.95 for one cassette, transcript, and workbook in album. [Source: Performance Group Incorporated]

Field Sales Managers' Self-Study Program—Six critical skill-building modules—covering field coaching, recruitment and selection, planning and conducting sales meetings, appraisal and the appraisal interview, sales planning and time management, and motivation, supervision, and counseling—each consisting of two cassettes and spiral-bound workbook in album. The highly interactive format permits on-the-job training as the sales manager applies the key concepts to his own district, people, and problems. $75 for one module, $60 each for two to five, $50 each for six or more. [Source: Porter Henry Knowledge Resources, Inc.]

Creative Recruiters—Four 'live' seminars, led by Gerald D. Oliver Sr., that give complete, step-by-step plans to use in building a large and successful sales force, all for $69.95 each. The titles are: *How I Created a Fortune Recruiting Salesmen*; *How I Created a Fortune Managing Salesmen* (in two parts); and *How to Create a Fortune Sponsoring Distributors*. The last one consists of eight cassettes, the others six. Another offering is *Mass Recruiting—How to Crack a New Territory Wide Open*, with Charles D. 'Chic' Statler, Director of Marketing for Roosevelt National Life, in a freewheeling roundtable discussion with his top 12 salesmanagers that reveals the ideas of some of the best recruiters in the country, $34.95 for three cassettes. [Source: Creative Recruiters]

How To Get Super Results from Average Performers—Robert G. Nesbit shows sales executives how to set up fair and meaningful performance standards for their sales force, isolate possible problem areas, identify signs of problems as soon as they appear, spot the symptoms of under-achievement, determine the cause, and finally, to get everyone to sell to their full potential. $99.50 for three cassettes and workbooks in album. [Source: Sales & Marketing Management]

Marketing

Computer Marketing in the 80's—Profiles of winning market strategies by leading computer companies, how to do market research, ground rules for success in computer marketing, and more. A companion program, *Computer Marketing for Salespeople*, focuses on prospecting and sales techniques, getting to the right people, reference selling, and winning computer sales techniques. Each is $120 for six cassettes and workbook in album. [Source: Professional Cassette Center]

Trade Secrets of Advertising . . . of Public Relations —Two six-cassette albums featuring frank, informal discussions by Gary Beals, giving helpful specifics on effective advertising and public relations techniques. These are especially geared for people in small or newly established businesses or non-profit organizations—people with limited budgets who seek easy-to-use ideas and techniques to create innovative programs. On advertising, Mr. Beals emphasizes the need to find differences with the competition's product, understanding the market, the message, and the media, and other vital advertising rules. On PR, he points out ways to develop creative skills, and techniques for getting news releases published and interview program bookings, as well as other useful tips. $59 for each six-cassette album with brochure, both for $99. [Source: Gary Beals Advertising & Public Relations]

C.A.M. Communications—*Advertising & Marketing Communications* offers the basic concepts of advertising and marketing of packaged goods. *Direct Marketing/Mail Order* tells how to get started in the mail order business, with growth and management tips, explanation of various techniques, and examples of success. Each of these courses is on a 60-minute cassette with outline and questions for $14. *Small Business Planning Guide* tells how to start a business of one's own, with a resource book by William E. Miller, two cassettesful of tips from a lawyer, a banker, and an accountant, two workbooks in album for $24. [Source: C.A.M. Communications]

Ad-Tapes—A wide range of recorded talks, panels, seminars, and interviews that initially covered (when started in 1967) advertising and marketing, and that now have expanded to include such fields as creativity, career management, motivation, communications, public relations, consumerism and government. Speakers include Ron Macklin, Charles L. Lapp, Ph.D., Lester C. Worden, Paul Rand Dixon, and many others. The times of single presentations range from 15 minutes to 3 hours, and costs range from $6 to $30. A special offering is an instructional course of professional public relations, sponsored by the Los Angeles Chapter of the Public Relations Society of America, in cooperation with UCLA, $80 for 12 cassettes, $8 each. [Source: Ad-Tapes]

Radio Spots—The International Newspaper Promotion Association has produced five different cassettes containing radio commercials that promote a newspaper's news, features, public service events, contest, and circulation, recruit carriers, or sell classified ads. $10 each. [Source: INPA Radio]

Effective Marketing System—An eight cassette program by Richard R. Gallagher, D.B.A. that covers the essentials of marketing, with learning enhanced by an extensive note-taking outline. Topics covered include marketing management and research, the product, place, price, and promotion, and an interesting cassette of case studies in marketing (Apple, Kroy, Virginia Slims, and others). $98. Dr. Gallagher also summarizes the course on *Basic Marketing* in an 80-minute cassette with outline for $15, and provides a *Marketing Management Checklist* in a short cassette for $12. [Source: Tutor/Tape]

Do-It-Yourself Seminars—Cassette studies to aid in the never-ending pursuit of public relations professionals for knowledge to further their careers. Some representative titles: *Electronic Publicity* (reaching the public through radio and TV); *Video for the PR Professional* (use of video for internal communication); *Making PR Profitable* (pointers by an accountant); *Marketing Public Relations* (using public information to reinforce an ad program); *Getting New Clients* (where to look and how to get them); *Mail Order Marketing* (a discussion of the myth vs. bonanza); and *Advertising Small Business* (for the small businessman). There is also a five-cassette series on *Basic Public Relations*, covering the role of PR, public opinion and change, opinion research, planned public relations, and effective communication. All tapes $15 each, every fourth tape free. [Source: Worldwide Associates]

Advertising for More—Dave Yoho gives over eight hours of useful information on the uses of direct mail, the Yellow Pages, newspapers and magazines, telephone aids, radio and TV, with the single intent of getting high exposure, low-cost publicity for your product. Six cassettes in album for $99. [Source: David Yoho Associates]

How To Get Free Publicity and Promote Your Products and Services—That title about says it all, but the six cassettes (by Ron Tepper, one of the men responsible for promoting the Beatles in the U.S.) cover: news releases, how $50 can double your business, print/TV interviews, getting newspapers to come to you, getting free TV time, and winning promotion tips. $95 for six cassettes and workshop in album-binder. Two-cassette packages (tapes 1 & 2, 3 & 4, or 5 & 6) are available with outlines and references for $30 the set. [Source: Van Den Berg Publishing]

Ideas in Sound—Hoke publishes *Direct Marketing*, *The Friday Report* and *Fund Raising Management* magazines, and their cassette offerings include advice and expertise of leading executives in the areas of direct mail, fund raising, sales promotion, and advertising. Some of these talks and panel discussions (generally 45-60 minutes long) are especially recorded for cassette, but most are recorded live at various direct marketing (and other) conferences and conventions. The format is often a company executive describing his techniques and success with direct mail or fund raising. Costs are generally $10 per cassette hour. [Source: Hoke Communications, Inc.]

Marketing for Non-Profit Organizations—Three cassettes that explain why and how price, product, place, and promotion may be used by public sector organizations to make their activities more effective, $79.95. [Source: Lansford Publishing Company]

Real Estate

How To Sell New And Resale Homes—Sales consultant Richard F. Russell covers theory, presentations, objections, and closes, on eight C-60 cassettes in album for $84.50. In *How To Rent and Lease Apartments*, he describes how to get the listings, how to market them, and how to convince the prospective renter/leaser to move in, on six C-60 cassettes in album for $84.50. *Sales Management for Net Profit Maximization* is really intended for the construction industry, covering supply and demand trends, fixed and variable costs, break-even analysis, and troubleshooting, all on a single cassette for $10. [Source: Russell and Associates]

Real Estate Listing Methods—A program to improve listing skills, on three 60-minute cassettes and workbooks, for $65. For the other half of the real estate business process there is *Real Estate Selling Skills*, a comprehensive self-study program, covering converting features into benefits, clarifying buyer and seller needs, presentations and objections, on eight cassettes and workbook for $60. [Source: Realtors National Marketing Institute]

The Here and Now of Listing and Selling—Top real estate professionals—Tom Hopkins, Del Bain, Danielle Kennedy, Richard Farrer—share their successful approaches to prospecting, listing, qualifying the buyer, and closing on four cassettes, $30. Also in the same theme is *Success Patterns in Listing and Selling*, which uses a dialogue approach, with 24 successful salespersons sharing their expertise by providing a variety of solutions to 25 common real estate problems. $30 for six one-hour cassettes. [Source: Realtors National Marketing Institute]

Memory Recall Training—An introduction to making use of thought associations and 'memory hooks' to visualize and retain information. $6 for a single one-hour cassette. [Source: Realtors National Marketing Institute]

The New Real Estate Survival Kit—Cavett Robert applies his principles of 'human engineering' to the arts of securing salable listings, showing property, making the offer and counter-offer, and other tips for real estate salesperson. $50 for six half-hour messages in album. [Source: Planned Achievements]

C.A.R. Cassette Albums—Sales training aids for both those interested in developing or pursuing careers in real estate, and for experienced professionals who wish to sharpen their skills and keep abreast of new trends. Most programs are recorded live at California Association of Realtors' meetings, and (except as noted) cost $37 for four 60-minute cassettes in album. The titles? *Five Keys to the 1980's*; *38 Ways to Help Buyers and Sellers Finance Homes*; *Real Estate Production* ($28); *The Here and Now of Listing Real Estate*; *Creative Financing with a Financial Calculator—HP 38* ($49); *For Sale By Owner*; *In Search of Agreement* (three cassettes, $28); *You Gotta Work the Territory*; *How To Negotiate in Listing and Selling Homes*; *Closing the Sale*; *Selling Income Property Successfully* ($40); and *How To Manage Condominium Developments*. Old but a bargain is *Condominium Conference*, six cassettes for $17. Then, some eight-cassette albums for $60: *Apartment Houses ... How To Invest, How To Sell*; *How To Convert Apartments to Condominiums*; *How To List and Sell Condominium Homes*; and *How To Manage an Apartment House*. [Source: California Association of Realtors]

Institute of Real Estate Management—This division of the National Association of Realtors publishes three audio-cassette programs. *How To Be a Successful Apartment Rental Consultant* shows rental agents how to get better results when showing apartments, two cassettes (85 minutes), $25. *How To Lease Office Space Profitably* has Duane F. Roberts discussing analysis of prospects and their needs, importance of showing suites aimed at meeting those needs, and descriptions of the necessary lease documents, three cassettes (110 minutes) for $30. Finally, *The On-Site Residential Manager Self-Study Program* offers a quick way to train present and future resident managers in management, administration, marketing and renting, housekeeping, resident communications, legal aspects and security, maintenance, fiscal procedures, and insurance, on 15 cassettes with 13 workbooks in a case for $150. [Source: Institute of Real Estate Management]

How To Become a Successful Real Estate Auctioneer —Not just the secrets of how to cry the auctioneer's chant, but also how to acquire listings, how to charge for your service, how to promote the auction, and how to conduct the sale ... all authored by one of the country's foremost auctioneers, Melvin A. Giller. The course includes a section on auctioning personal property. $89.50 for four cassettes and 76-page instruction manual in binder. [Source: National Institute of Real Estate Auctioneers Inc.]

Breaking Out!...The Effective Path for Today's Woman!—Designed especially for the woman real estate professional, this program provides specific methods for increasing effectiveness in personal and professional situations. On four cassettes with program guide, Gladys Nicastro shows how to develop self-confidence, independence, and the ability to relate to others, how to handle criticism, rejection, and anger, and how to get what you want without violating the rights of others. $55. [Source: Training Innovations]

Science of Persuasion—The emphasis is on 'closing confidence' in this six-cassette program recorded live by Roy Ruppert. It provides new insights into the psychology of persuasion and presents new methods, techniques, and strategies for closing more listings and sales. $65. [Source: Training Innovations]

Champions Unlimited—Real estate sales and management training programs, with Tom Hopkins ('the highest paid sales trainer in the world today') expounding his no-nonsense, tell-it-like-it-is approach. *How To Master the Art of Listing Real Estate* and *How To Master the Art of Selling Real Estate* each have eight 60-minute cassettes plus transcripts and flashcards in album for $120. Going one step beyond, Mr. Hopkins talks about *How To Master the Art of Selling Anything* (actually, a video soundtrack) on 12 cassettes with workbook in album, plus a book, for $183. *Attitudes for Success in Real Estate* covers the inner salesman—self-confidence, self-image, characteristics of a winner, and such—on six cassettes in an album for $75. Finally, *An Imaginar with Danny Cox* teaches the facets of real estate office management, including recruiting, advertising, meetings, leadership, and more, for eight tapes and workbook in album for $75. [Source: Tom Hopkins Champions Unlimited]

No-Fail Financing—Keith DeGreen first offers answers to such client questions as "How much do I lose by not buying now?" and "How much does it really cost?" Then he goes on to cover conventional secondary financing, blend rate mortgages, carrybacks, wraps, government insured and guaranteed loans, exchanges, renegotiable and other variable-rate mortgages, shared appreciation, land contracts and other installment sales, and residential purchase lease-backs and leases with options. $75 for six cassettes and workbook in album. [Source: DeGreen Corporation]

Real Estate Series—Up-to-date information for anyone involved in making real estate transactions: contract for deed and exchanges; real estate and construction financing; real estate taxation; Minnesota contracts; and Wisconsin condominiums and real estate forms. $40-$50 for three cassettes plus manual for $20-$30. [Source: Professional Education Systems, Inc.]

Realty Bluebook Seminars—A concentrated discussion and workshop on creative financing techniques, alternative mortgage instruments, calculating mortgage yields, remaining balance and equity build-up, present value at various inflation rates, multiple uses of annual constant table, plus solutions to other timely problems—all on two cassettes with workbook, album, and a copy of the current realty bluebook. $45. [Source: Professional Publishing Corp.]

Successful Selling is Fun for Realtors—According to Greg Esch, "productivity is a result of attitude; and if a person is a negative thinker it affects his end results. We all act as we think." Mr. Esch shows how to adopt a positive approach to real estate selling, on four cassettes with text for $75. [Source: Goals Unlimited]

Listing and Selling Real Estate—Shows you how to prevent failure and be successful in both aspects of the real estate business on eight cassettes in album, $65. [Source: General Cassette Corporation]

The Professional Real Estater—This is a complete real estate training course, featuring some of the most distinguished names in real estate sales, six-cassette albums for $80. [Source: Sales Communique Corporation]

Telephone Marketing

Selling Appointments by Telephone—A learning program with the basic purpose of teaching the most effective and up-to-date skills involved in making specific appointments by telephone with new prospects, existing accounts, and former accounts. $49.50 for one cassette, programmed instruction manual, structured role-playing sequences, critique sheets and planning guides. [Source: Reuben H. Donnelley]

Selling By Telephone—A course specifically designed to meet the needs of companies to train personnel in telephone selling. It covers how to plan and set measurable objectives, get decision-makers on the line, capture their attention and interest, probe for needs, spot buying signals, anticipate and overcome objections, and close strategically. $99.50 for two cassettes, workbook, role-playing book, an administrator's guide in binder. [Source: Reuben H. Donnelley]

Telephone Marketing Management Guidelines—Pointers on how to staff, structure, and run a successful telephone selling operation: sales planning, preparing sales presentations, establishing controls, producing sales aids, recruiting and selecting personnel, developing a suitable working environment, and designing special systems. $9.95 for a single cassette, instructions, and worksheets. [Source: Reuben H. Donnelley]

Telephone Marketing, Prospecting, and Selling—
Thom Norman, an expert on the use of the telephone, gives a complete roadmap to prospecting, getting appointments, and/or selling by telepone, with pointers on creating scripts, handling objections, and closing sales. Included are some live-recorded examples of his techniques. The course is complete on six cassettes with workbook and script in album for $75. Related is Don Huston's *Telephone Selling for Realtors* on six cassettes in album for $65. [Source: General Cassette Corporation]

Pay Phone Pay—In this self-training program for salesmen, Gordon Bethards (a top-producing salesman and now a sales manager for DuPont) explains how a traveling salesman can save himself many wasted miles and minutes through the use of the telephone. Well-produced with effective dramatizations of sales situations to emphasize the points. $25 for two C-60 cassettes in album [Source: Tape Productions, Inc.]

The Telephone: Profit and Problem Solving—Tom Hopkins and Danny Cox cover all aspects of the telephone as a sales tool: answering complaints, taking messages, calling FSBOs, canvassing, contacting customers, writing strong telephone ad copy—all intended to make the telephone start working for you. $65 for four cassettes and booklet in album. [Source: Tom Hopkins Champions Unlimited]

Selling Successfully by Telephone—Developed by Harrold H. Hayden, general manager of Universal Training Systems, this course offers nitty-gritty answers to three major problems: how to plan a telephone sales campaign, how to plan the individual sales call and how to get the selling points across and close the sale. $99.50 for 4 cassettes and 2 workbooks in album. [Source: Sales & Marketing Management]

Training

Sales Communique Corporation—Sales training and learning programs, featuring some of the most distinguished names in sales. Titles and contents of the six-cassette albums for $80 include: *Excel in Selling*, with J. Douglas Edwards, Dick Gardner, Bob Montgomery, Deborah Bright, Joe Gandolfo and Bob Richards; *The Making of a Salesperson*, with six sales messages, by J. Douglas Edwards; *Masters of Motivation . . . Ignite Your Aspirations*, with Dr. Murray Banks, Alan Cimberg, Ira Hayes, Dr. Charles Jarvis, Art Linkletter, and Dr. Arthur Secord; *Concentrate on Success*, with Dr. Kenneth McFarland. Also: *Telephone Prospecting for Greater Success*, with Thom Norman; *Closing Power*, with Zig Ziglar; *Psychology and Selling*, with Larry Wilson, Bill Gove, Zig Ziglar and Dr. Murray Banks; *Time Management and Closing Sales*, with Dick Gardner; and *New Dimensions for Today*, a look at self-improvement and personal development—these last five in four-cassette albums for $60. [Source: Sales Communique Corporation]

Never a Bee Back—A live Workshop on the newest methods of selling cars and trucks on six cassettes in album for $100 by Jack Cooper. [Source: Sales Communique Corporation]

NOPA Professional Selling Skills Course—An advanced course for the office products dealer, wholesaler, manufacturer, and outside salespeople. On the tapes, two office product salesmen discuss planning, selling strategy, problem-solving selling, finding and qualifying prospects, approaching the prospect, making the presentation, overcoming resistance, closing the sale, and time and territory management. A workbook provides transcripts, other data, quick quizzes, and action-planning exercises. Four cassettes and three workbooks in album for $90. The related *Product Knowledge Courses* tell everything the inside and outside salespeople and warehouse employees need to know about these office products: carbon and ribbons, data processing supplies, filing equipment and supplies, looseleaf supplies, marking devices, office papers and tapes, staples and fasteners, stock forms, tags and labels, writing instruments, and word processing supplies. One cassette per topic, with workbook and leader's guide, for $14; the complete set of 13 courses with album for $130. [Source: National Office Products Association]

Consultative Selling Skills—An advanced course that should enable salespeople to acquire knowledge of how to do their job better as they develop, through application exercises, the skill proficiencies needed for better job performance. The ultimate aim is to develop skill proficiency in prospecting, securing appointments, gathering information during interviews, and dealing with customer resistance. $270 for five audio-cassettes and 17 workbooks. [Source: Systema Corporation]

Professional Prospecting and Closing—is for salesmen, and gives eight effective ways to obtain unlimited numbers of prospects immediately, offers other innovative prospecting ideas, and 21 ways to close the sale and quash the hesitations and objections. $50 for a four-cassette album. [Source: Mark Victor Hansen]

Learning Curve—One-hour mini-course consisting of C-60 cassette programmed exercise and test on The Successful Salesman. Price is $9.98. [Source: Metacom, Inc.]

Sales Performance Improvement System—A one-cassette results-oriented course that gives pointers on becoming a master salesman by getting qualified appointments, creating desire for your product, making effective presentations and closes, and satisfying client's emotional needs. $24.95 for one cassette, transcript, and workbook in album. [Source: Performance Group Incorporated]

The Professional Image—The successful salesperson has a successful self-image, gives customers confidence, stays calm under stress, speaks and listens equally well, and builds client loyalty. These are all covered on this cassette, with transcript and workbook in album, for $24.95. [Source: Performance Group Incorporated]

Programming for Sales Success—On this eight-cassette program, Lee Boyan combines the most successful, tried-and-true principles and techniques of selling into one quick, clear, concise, sales producing program. He covers not only his methods of goal-setting, handling objectives, and making closes but also defines the successful sales personality and sales confidence. $85. [Source: Lee Boyan & Associates]

Selling Secrets on Cassette—Six new hour-long cassettes ($10.95 each), designed to hone the skills of selling professionals: *Les Dane's Master Secrets for Closing Sales*; *Kinesics: The Power of Silent Command*, or how to read the prospect's body language, and to control your own; *Secrets of Presentations That Sell*, with N. C. Christensen; *Secrets of Psychological Leverage in Selling*, to get prospects into a buying mood; *How To Sell the Tough Account*, with Lloyd Purves describing his specialized tactics; and *Strike-It-Rich Sales Prospecting*, by use of telephone and mail techniques, and 'bird dogs.' [Source: Prentice-Hall Distribution Center]

Effective Sales Techniques for Today—A six-cassette album, lead by Nido R. Qubein, that gives all of the important steps in selling, from finding and interviewing potential customers, giving demonstrations, listening, speaking, closing, handling objections, telephoning—and how to develop a 'selling' personality. $69.95 for six cassettes in album. [Source: Creative Services, Inc.]

Nine Keys to More Effective Space Selling—A cassette program designed for experienced salesmen and executives of special interest magazines, though it can also be used for sales training and stimulation. The 2-½ hour program was produced by Dave Hagenbuch, a distinguished media salesman. $110 for six cassettes, course booklets, and album. [Source: Dave Hagenbuch and Associates, Inc.]

Sales Human Engineering Motivation Course—The renown course by Cavett Robert that applies his principles of human engineering and motivation to sales training to "open doors of opportunity you didn't know existed." $50 for six C-30 cassettes in album. [Source: Planned Achievements]

Non-Manipulative Selling—Seven hours of live seminar training with Dr. Tony Alessandra, showing how to recognize and respond to different customer personality types and how to use effective communication techniques to detect and satisfy customer needs. Eight cassettes and workbook in album, $80. [Source: Cathcart, Alessandra & Associates, Inc.]

Dave Yoho Associates—Noted sales trainer Dave Yoho offers two cassette albums on sales training. *Closing the Sale* has him talking about closing at

your price and handling objections, plus more, on six cassettes for $69.75. *Managing Yourself and Others* teaches how the average individual can use the self-management concept to fulfill their goals and dreams by means of self motivation, on six cassettes with interactive manual, $69.75. [Source: Dave Yoho Associates]

Sandler Selling System—The old basic sales rules are totally out of step with today's sales realities, says David Sandler; today's salesman doesn't necessarily ask for an order, and he or she doesn't always emphasize features and benefits. What today's sales champion does do is maintain total control of the sales interview—and that is what Mr. Sandler teaches in this course, complete on six cassettes (12 workshop sessions) plus interactive workbooks and progress sheets in two binders. The cost is $95. [Source: Sandler Selling System]

Nightingale-Conant Listening Library—In *New Concepts in Selling*, Harold Gash shows how to put the customer's needs first, eliminate objections, and close the sale. *Winning Strategies in Selling* has Jack and Garry Kinder with Roger Staubach giving ideas to help you focus on your energies, build on your strengths, and achieve higher sales goals. In *Selling Techniques that Really Work*, Earl Nightingale and master sales trainer Fred Herman present 12 live seminars covering every essential step in making any sale, using the K.I.S.S. techique—keep it simple, salesperson. $60 for each program, including six cassettes and guide in album. [Source: Nightingale-Conant Corporation]

Salesmanship—Four-cassette packages ($37.50 each) aimed at providing the new salesman with basic skills in his new career: *The Power of Proposal Selling*, *The Three Keys* to effective salesmanship, *What It Takes To Make'Em Buy*, *Prospect Analysis*, *Pre-Approach*, *Approach*, *Socratic Technique*, *Creative Salesmanship*, *Care and Feeding of Customers*, *Communications* in improving sales results, *Listening/ Prospecting*, *Objections*, and *Coast to a Close*. [Source: Associated Educational Materials]

Building your Sales Career—Zig Ziglar, the "superstar of salesmanship" offers a complete sales training course on eight cassettes and career development manual including transcripts, for $99.95. *Sales & Motivation* features Mr. Ziglar at his best on his two favorite subjects, $19.95 for the two-cassette album. [Source: Zig Ziglar Corporation]

Sales Power Skill Builder Series—Cassette-with-text programs covering the art and science of: using questions in selling, selling by telephone, selling face to face, speaking clearly (all $100 each), guiding and controlling discussion ($150), and mastering and controlling your language (two C-50 cassettes, $150). [Source: Mills-Roberts Associates, Inc.]

Sales-Training Tapes—Ten 30-minute cassettes of instructional pointers for new or veteran salespeople: cold-call selling, saturated territories, when to say no, troubleshooting, the art of shutting up, persist and persuade, when your price is wrong, flexible presentations, closing, speaking tips. $49 for 10 cassettes in album, or $9.95 each. [Source: Bureau of Business Practice]

Winning Sales Techniques—According to the basic concepts of 'communicating styles technology' (CST), we all use a blend of four communicating or behavioral styles in our approach to life or work: intuitor, thinker, feeler, and sensor. This unusual program shows how to use CST concepts to strengthen personal and professional relationships, by recognizing and identifying a customer's basic communicating styles and then by adapting to the styles for more effective selling. This self-contained program is primarily geared to experienced sales marketing personnel. $70.50 for four cassettes, CST surveys, interpretation manual, and instruction sheet. [Source: Training Associates Press, Inc.]

Dr. Kenneth McFarland—Ken McFarland, who has received the National Leadership Award and his been honored as the Outstanding Salesman of America, believes that advertising and salesmanship are the gas and oil that fuel the American free enterprise vehicle. His philosophy is captured on these albums: *McFarland for Salesman* (the development of a successful sales career) and *Classic McFarland Speeches* (each $59.50 for six cassettes in album), *McFarland on America*, *Best of McFarland*, and *McFarland on Speaking* (all four-cassette albums for $45). Some individual talks are available on single cassettes for $12.95 each. [Source: General Cassette Corporation]

Selling . . . New Style—A demonstration by Robert L. Montgomery on how to use the new selling style—participative selling—to sell to today's better educated, more demanding customers. $12.95 for a 60-minute cassette. A companion program is *How to Sell in the 1980's, The Quick and Easy Way*, four cassettes on participative selling, with emphasis on 'how to question' and 'how to listen,' plus a cassette of 30 motivating pep talks, one for each day of the month, and a final cassette on advice for developing a winning personal appeal, $60 for six cassettes in album. [Source: Robert L. Montgomery & Associates, Inc.]

Why People Fail—Using both live seminar segments and step-by-step instructions, Dan Kennedy shows how to identify and eliminate the common causes of failure from your personality, life, and business—in a course expressly produced for people in multi-level sales businesses. $65 for four cassettes and workbook in album. [Source: General Cassette Corporation]

In-Store Selling Skills Course—Training for retail office products sales personnel in six important basic selling skills: nature of the business, opening the sale, presenting the merchandise, overcoming resistance, closing the sale, and increasing the sale. Three cassettes and summary booklet in album for $45. [Source: National Office Products Association]

Principles of Persuasion—A sales development program planned for the experienced salesperson who knows how to sell, but who wants to sell more. It incorporates new ideas from the fields of psychology and behavioral science, providing the listener with the scientific basis of human persuasion—and the art of professional selling. $195 for 12 cassettes (24 programs) and workbook in album. [Source: Burt Munk Productions, Inc.]

The Total Salesperson—A ten-cassette course specifically planned for use during the initial 3-6 months while a new salesperson is picking up knowledge and expertise about the company—a time when the partially trained salesperson represents a danger both to his company and to himself. Each module (cassette and manual) in this course covers one aspect of selling: a positive approach; sales communication and listening; prospecting & qualifying; the presentation; objections and negotiations; sales psychology; time and territory management; the first meeting; closing the sale; and customer maintenance. Each module $22.50, all ten in binder for $225. [Source: I. I. Goldmacher Publishing Co.]

You Can Sell Yourself Rich . . . If You Hammer Home the Difference—G. Worthington Hipple sums up the secret of his sales success—sell the difference, not the price—on a 90-minute cassette for $15.75. [Source: G. Worthington Hipple]

Creative Selling Seminar—Howard Bonnell, recently retired as Director of Sales Management Development for the publishers of the World Book Encyclopedia, shares his techniques and insights into the selling process. $44 for this four-cassette, four-hour album, including his famous motivational talk, *You Can Be Better Than You Are* (available separately on one cassette for $10.95). [Source: Howard W. Bonnell]

John Wolfe's Workshop for Sales Professionals—The man who coined the phrase 'sell like an ace, live like a king' offers a strong foundation in sales techniques for a beginning salesperson and builds confidence through the understanding that selling situations are a combination of knowing what to say and common sense. $65 for six cassettes and study guide in album. [Source: John Wolfe Institute]

Total Sales Person Program—10 high-quality, self-paced audio/print modules designed for individual instruction, applicable for enhancing the skills of experienced salespersons and for introducing new lines. Topics of the modules: a positive approach to selling, sales psychology, sales communications and effective listening, time and territory management, prospecting and qualifying, the first meeting, the presentation, closing the sale, dealing with objections/handling negotiations, customer maintenance/account management. $36 for each module (30-minute cassette and 16-page 'print component'), the entire set in album for $280. [Source: Cal Industries Inc.]

PROMPT—PROfessional Meetings with Professional Trainers—12 complete sales training courses, with a leader's script, each 45-minute discussion segmented into logical units and sequenced for periodic pauses to permit reaction, response, and discussion. Developed for Printing Industries of America (PIA) by The Professional Training Institute, the speakers are from the graphic arts industry but the sales training applies to almost any industry. $395 ($365 for PIA members) for 12 cassettes and leader's guide. [Source: Printing Industries of America, Inc.]

Effective Sales—A results-oriented program that will benefit the sales manager, experienced salesperson, and promising sales trainee. The program is designed to increase skills in communicating with the customer, establishing and maintaining trust, overcoming objections, negotiating techniques, and coping with discouragement and depression. $80 for eight cassettes and study guide in album, $20 for a one-hour cassette of highlights. [Source: Fred Pryor Resources Corporation]

The Psychology of Selling System—Ron Willingham has designed a system of selling that can help one to be more powerful and convincing in sales persuasion, and (one hopes) reach higher sales volume. $42 for four cassettes in album. [Source: Ron Willingham Courses, Inc.]

Be a Pro—It Pays (Well!)—As a sales/management trainer, realtor, and TV/radio personality, LilyB Moskal is billed as "the gal with the million $ attitude." Here, she offers a three-hour live seminar on listing, selling, and prospecting your way to success, $40 for three cassettes in album. In *Ya Gotta Believe*! she describes her psychology of believing in yourself, your profession, and your ability to be successful, on one cassette in album for $19.95. [Source: LilyB Moskal]

Selling Power of a Woman—Dottie Walters gives a six-hour course on how to develop the great selling power that is inherent in all women, on six cassettes in album for $69. Also available is Dottie Walker's single cassette on *7 Secrets of Selling to Women*, for $9.95. [Source: Royal Publishing]

Principles of Persuasion—A 12-cassette course that applies recent developments in psychology and behavioral sciences to the practical art of selling ... in 24 sales training sessions that get salespeople to take

a hard look at how and why they sell. Among the topics: getting appointments, stimulating and reinforcing customer response, anticipating objections, using objections to close, recognizing closing behavior, and improving an already productive territory. $225 for 12 cassettes and leader's guide. [Source: Singer Management Institute]

Speaking of Selling—A self-study program to help develop sales and presentation skills. Topics discussed by Thomas E. Anastasi, Jr. include how to make presentations work, how to prepare them, how to deliver them, and how to explain your ideas, and persuade others to heed them. $39.95 for three cassettes plus 40-page workbook. [Source: CBI Publishing Company, Inc.]

Today's Saleswoman—Women have some exceptional advantages in selling, but how do women enter the sales field and how are they trained for such a career? In this edited version of a live seminar, Beverly Kievman gives a realistic, intensive examination of these questions, and provides women in sales, or considering the field, with the answers. After covering the basic ground rules, Ms. Kievman focuses on selling skills and techniques, appointments, the presentation, and the close. $41 for five hours' training on three cassettes. [Source: Marketing Innovations Corporation]

Home Study Tape Library—Planned for both new and experienced salespeople, these sales training cassettes consist of live classroom situations that deal with six actual problems encountered every day in business: establishing preliminary rapport, fear of speaking (laliaphobia), negotiations, overcoming objections, closing techniques, and handling customer complaints. $125 for six cassettes with a comprehensive workbook for each cassette. Quizzes in the workbooks can be returned for grading and evaluation. [Source: Persuasive Communications]

Guaranteed Sales Success—Built around the master checklist evolved by George B. Anderson that includes every rule, technique and insight that goes into the making of a perfect sales presentation, and then presented with reinforced learning techniques. $179 for seven cassettes, 13 booklets and reminder cards in album. [Source: Dartnell]

Charles "T" Jones—The man whose name is synonymous with 'tremendous' gives eight hour-plus talks: *Managing Your Life I* and *II, Professional Salesmanship, The Price of Leadership, Where Does Leadership Begin, The Leading Edge, Dear Dad*, and *Learning ... A Tremendous Experience.* $10 each. [Source: Life Management Services, Inc.]

Targeted Selling Skills Program—Three modules are available, each focusing on one critical selling skill: key account selling strategies, selling to decision-making groups, and effective sales call planning.

Each module consists of a cassette with interactive workbook in binder. Cost of a single module is $75, $70 each when all three are ordered. [Source: Porter Henry Knowledge Resources, Inc.]

Lee DuBois Course in Selling Techniques—One of the all-time great sales trainers gives a 10-hour course to help salespeople become more professional and to sell automatically, habitually, and 'naturally.' The appropriate cassette can be reviewed just before making important calls and as a check after the sale to analyze what could have been done better. $130 (plus postage) for 17 cassettes in album, plus $16.50 for student workbook and reference manual. [Source: Milton O. Berry]

Symbiotic Selling—A comprehensive sales skills development review, on four 45-minute cassettes, that covers communications skills, motivation, career development, productivity, and confidence. $34.45 with album.   [Source: Z Incorporated]

Professional Sales Technique—Dr. Jack Schiff has produced a series of 12 audio-cassettes, each dealing with a major topic in sales—buying decisions, call planning, approach, presentation, objectives, closing, holding customers, home office back-up, finding new customers, roles in marketing and promotion, and continued self-development—all interwoven with a

232-page programmed learning course which takes salespeople through each stage of a successful sales call. $120 for 12 cassettes in album plus workbook. [Source: BNA Communications Inc.]

Selling is Easy—A successful consultant, lecturer, and seminar leader, Jules A. Marine shares his professional techniques for influencing people to 'buy' your idea, or service, or product. Really more than 'sales training,' he covers the development of a success formula for achieving both professional and personal goals. $51.50 for four cassettes. [Source: GBD and Associates]

You Can . . .—Five four-tape albums with booklet created and led by master motivator and trainer Joel H. Weldon, for $59 each: *You Can Sell More Professionally, You Can Prospect More Creatively, You Can Manage and Motivate, You Can Conduct Better Meetings and Speak with Confidence,* and *You Can Build a Better You.* Along the same line from Mr. Weldon is *Sell It with the Million Dollar Attitude!* with a fresh and creative approach to sales and prospecting, on six cassettes in album for $50. Then, he has two single cassette programs for $15 each: *Elephants Don't Bite* (a live recording showing how to make a training session more fun and more effective) and *Jet Pilots Don't Use Rear View Mirrors* (the benefits of looking ahead, as heard in-flight on American Airlines).   [Source: Joel H. Weldon & Associates]

XX.
Science and Engineering

Cooling of Electronic Equipment—A practical course, presented in electronic engineering terminology that describes all important methods of cooling used in electronic equipment: how to cool, heat conduction, fins, fan, cabinet, sealed cabinets, liquid or evaporation cooling, thermal measurements. $112.50 for eight 60-minute cassettes and illustrated workbook in album. The first cassette in the course is available for preview at $5. [Source: Enrichment Cassettes]

Instrument Society of America—Professional education programs in major instrumentation and process control subject areas. Most are on a single cassette with corresponding illustrated text: *Theory of Automatic Control in Simple Language* ($21.60), *Control Valve Sizing* ($24), *Flow Control, Rangeability, Characteristics and Leakage* ($24), *Process Electrochemical Instrumentation* ($24), *Fundamentals of Fluidics* ($24), *Fundamentals of Flow Measurement* ($24), and several more. The *Control Valve Study Package* has 12 cassettes, each with a topic ranging from valve sizing and valve types to selection factors and valve accessories, with workbooks in album for $240. Less for ISA members. [Source: Instrument Society of America]

Understanding Microwave Equipment—A six-session course that covers principles of operation, performance limits, and typical products of all the newest and important microwave systems and devices, described in simple physical terms without detailed mathematics. $112.50 for six 90-minute cassettes and illustrated workbook in album. As a preview, the first cassette in the series is available for just $5. [Source: Enrichment Cassettes]

Lifelong Learning—*The Future of Science* is discussed on four cassettes in album ($50) by Francis Crick, Philip Handler, and Mario Bunge. On seven cassettes, Gunther Sten covers *The Coming of the Golden Age* in two parts: *The Rise and Fall of Molecular Genetics* (4½ hours, $40) and *The Rise and Fall of Faustian Man* (3 hours, $30). In *Lost Worlds and Golden Ages* scientists from eight disciplines respond to the challenge of von Daniken and Velikovsky, eight cassettes, $85, $10-$13 each. Other scientists and scholars discuss *The Flood Myth: An Inquiry into Causes and Circumstances*, on seven cassettes, $80. [Source: University of California]

ACS Audio Courses—Professional education courses for chemists and chemical engineers, recorded by leading authorities in their own words and intended to expand, revise, and update the listener's knowledge. Here are just a few of the 55 courses in thier current catalog: *Basic Gas Chromatography*, six cassettes (4 hours) plus 110-page manual, $225; *Carbon-13 NMR Spectroscopy*, six cassettes (6.3 hours) plus 240-page manual, $265; *Essentials of Organic Chemistry*, eight cassettes (8.1 hours) plus 315-page manual, $310; *Free Radical Chemistry*, eight cassettes (6.9 hours) plus 285-page manual, $340; *Molecular Characterization of Polymers*, six cassettes (6.5 hours) plus 216-page manual, $280; *Chemical Bases of Environmental Issues*, six cassettes (6.2 hours) plus 173-page manual, $260; *Activated Sludge*, five cassettes (6.2 hours) plus 127-page manual, $275; *Chemical Abstracts: An Introduction to Its Effective Use*, two cassettes (2.3 hours) plus 214 page manual, $180; *The Effective Manager*, three Cassettes (2.3 hours) plus 104-page manual, $170; *Chemistry for the Non-Chemist*, eight cassettes (8 hours) plus 170-page manual, $360; *New Product Development*, seven cassettes (7.1 hours) plus 182-page manual, $345; *Practical Technical Writing*, eight cassettes (5.3 hours) plus 172-page manual, $245. Additional manuals are available separately. [Source: American Chemical Society]

Professional Study Seminars—From the American Institute of Aeronautics and Astronautics, technical lectures in specialized subjects: aeroelasticity, applied computational aerodynamics, fluid physics of pollution, high speed boundary-layer stability and transition, orbital and altitude dynamics, structural synthesis, transonic aerodynamics, gas dynamic lasers, and applied optimal control. Each topic consists of 9-12 cassettes (8½-12 hours) plus books and notebooks for $170. Two special programs are devoted to aerodynamic noise and mathematical biofluid-dynamics (each 5-6 hours with notebook for $90). Suitable for review or an introduction to a subject are the one-hour lectures on decision theory, dynamic programming, precise altitude determination of satellites, guidance and control systems concepts, rocket propulsion, low speed wing theory, the boundary layer (each $15.50 with notebook). Finally, the two-hour review or introductory lectures, on vortex waves of large aircraft, fracture mechanics, digital flight control, manual control, nuclear propulsion, and stability theory (each $29.50 for two cassettes with notebook). All prices less for AIAA members. [Source: AIAA]

Producers/Distributors

AAP Tape Library
2400 86th Street, Suite 30
Des Moines, IA 50322
515/278-8741
p. 36

Abbey Press
St. Meinrad, IN 47577
812/357-8011
pp. 127, 128

Abiding Word, Inc.
140 Franklin Avenue
New Rochelle, NY 10805
p. 120

Abingdon Press
201 Eighth Avenue South
Nashville, TN 37202
615/749-6451
p. 117

Abundant Living Foundation
PO Box 100
San Diego, CA 92138
619/271-1230
p. 127

Achievement Institute
Huron Towers West, Suite 201
Ann Arbor, MI 48105
313/769-9081
p. 69

Ad-Tapes
PO Box 66
Palos Verdes Estates, CA 90274
213/378-5865
p. 134

Addison-Wesley Publishing
Company
Reading, MA 01867
617/944-3788
pp. 7, 75

Advanced Professional
Development Institute
5519 Carpenter Avenue
North Hollywood, CA 91607
213/506-7765
p. 69

Affective House
PO Box 35321
Tulsa, OK 74135
918/743-8264
p. 48

AIAA
1290 Avenue of the Americas
New York, NY 10104
212/581-4300
p. 142

AICPA
1211 Avenue of the Americas
New York, NY 10036
212/575-5524
pp. 1, 19

Alba House Communications
PO Box 595
Canfield, OH 44406-0595
216/533-5503
pp. 108, 117

Aletheia Psycho-Physical
Foundation
515 N.E. 8th
Grants Pass, OR 97526-2194
503/479-4855
p. 22

Allen Visual Systems, Inc.
PO Box 8129
Northfield, IL 60093
312/441-5220
p. 27

Gary Allen Communications
7680 Wayland Road
Loomis, CA 95650
916/652-0650
p. 99

Alpha Recorded Tapes, Inc.
2970 Scott Blvd.
Santa Clara, CA 95050
408/727-8750
p. 51

AM Treasures
PO Box 192
Babylon, NY 11702
p. 105

American Academy of
Dermatology
PO Box 552
Evanston, IL 60204
312/869-3954
p. 24

American Academy of Family
Physicians
1740 W. 92nd Street
Kansas City, MO 64114
800/821-2512
p. 27

American Audio Prose Library
915 East Broadway
Columbia, MO 65201
p. 62

American Bible Society
1865 Broadway
New York, NY 10023
212/581-7400
p. 109

American Cancer Society, Inc.
777 Third Avenue
New York, NY 10017
212/371-2900
p. 26

American Chemical Society
1155 16th St, NW, Room 809-C
Washington, DC 20036
202/872-4588
p. 142

American College of Cardiology
9111 Old Georgetown Road
Bethesda, MD 20814
301/897-5400
p. 26

American College of Chest
Physicians
PO Box 93884
Chicago, IL 60670
312/698-2200
p. 26

American College of Hospital
  Administrators
840 N. Lake Shore Drive
Chicago, IL 60611
312/943-0544
p. 23

American College of Osteopathic
  Internists
Audio Education Service
PO Box 1411
Evanston, IL 60204
312/679-6030
p. 27

American College of Physicians
Audio-Visual Department
4200 Pine Street
Philadelphia, PA 19104
215/243-1200
p. 26

American College of Surgeons
55 E. Erie Street
Chicago, IL 60611
312/478-8787
p. 24

American Dietetic Association
430 North Michigan Avenue
Chicago, IL 60611
312/280-5000
p. 20

American Enterprise Institute for
  Public Policy Research
1150 17th Street, NW
Washington, DC 20036
202/862-5800
p. 100

American Hospital Association
PO Box 96003
Chicago, IL 60693
312/280-6000
p. 24

American Humor Guild
1717 East Colfax
South Bend, IN 46617
219/234-2340
p. 80

American Institute of
  Photography, Inc.
PO Box 26001
Sacramento, CA 95826
800/648-5000, 800/323-1717 in
  NV
p. 43

American Law Institute/
  American Bar Association
  Committee on Continuing
  Professional Education
4025 Chestnut Street
Philadelphia, PA 19104
215/243-1600
p. 58

American Life Foundation
9 Mojave Court
Corte Madera, CA 94925
415/924-7331
p. 45

American Management
  Associations (AMACOM
  Division)
135 West 50th Street
New York, NY 10020
212/586-5100, ext. 560
pp. 7, 54, 65, 67, 72, 74, 75, 76

American Med. Tech.
Box 238
Green Mtn. Falls, CO 80819
303/647-2324
pp. 26, 38

American Media Incorporated
5911 Meredith Drive
Des Moines, IA 50324
515/278-1078
p. 83

American Medical Association
Order Department
PO Box 821
Monroe, WI 53566
p. 23

American Personnel & Guidance
  Association, Order Services
5203 Leesburg Pike, Suite 400
Falls Church, VA 22041
703/820-4700
pp. 45, 48

American Radio
PO Drawer Z
Scottsdale, AZ 85252
602/991-5345
p. 105

American Radio Relay League
225 Main Street
Newington, CT 06111
203/666-1541
p. 44

American Research Team
256 S. Robertson Blvd.
Beverly Hills, CA 90211
pp. 88, 95

American Society of Association
  Executives
1575 Eye Street, NW
Washington, DC 20005
202/626-2742
p. 69

American Society of Clinical
  Hypnosis
2250 E. Devon Ave., Suite 336
Des Plaines, IL 60018
312/297-3317
p. 34

American Society of CLU,
  Continuing Education Division
PO Box 59
Bryn Mawr, PA 19010
215/525-9500
p. 18

AMG Publishers
6815 Shallowford Road
Chattanooga, TN 37421
800/251-7206, 615/894-6060
p. 111

Paul S. Amidon & Associates
1966 Benson Avenue
St. Paul, MN 55116
612/690-2401
pp. 13, 14

Ampico Sound
PO Box 55
Barrington, NJ 08007
609/546-7492
p. 122

AMR/Advanced Management
  Reports, Inc.
60 East 56th Street, 2nd Floor
New York, NY 10022
800/223-6787, 212/974-0800
pp. 4, 67, 69, 70, 71, 133

Ananda Publications
14618 Tyler Foote Road
Nevada City, CA 95959
800/824-9553, 916/265-5877
p. 128

Helen Antoniak, Ph.D.
7124 Caminito Olmo
La Jolla, CA 92037
p. 48

Applegate Books
PO Box One
Olema, CA 94950
p. 97

Applied Management Institute,
Inc.
623 Great Jones Street
Fairfield, CA 94533
707/422-6822
p. 5

Applied Subliminals
PO Box 135
Cresskill, NJ 07626
p. 90

ARC Systems
239 Glen Cove Avenue
Sea Cliff, NY 11579
516/671-0867
p. 79

A.R.E.
PO Box 595
Virginia Beach, VA 23451
804/428-3588
p. 78

Arena Lettres
PO Box 219
Waldwick, NJ 07463
201/445-7154
p. 119

Argus Communications
PO Box 7000
Allen, TX 75002
800/527-4747, 800/442-4711 in
TX
p. 115

Assertive Training Center
5444 Beaumont Avenue
La Jolla, CA 92037
619/459-7180
p. 31

Associated Educational Materials
PO Box 28167
Raleigh, NC 27611
800/334-4373, 919-828-1250
pp. 7, 8, 72, 87, 138

Associated Management
Institute, Inc.
1160 Homestead Rd.
Santa Clara, CA 95050
p. 70

Association of Trial Lawyers of
America, Education Fund
PO Box 3717
Washington, DC 20007
202/965-3500
p. 57

Assumption Abbey
Christian Life Center Loaning
Library
Richardton, ND 58652
701/974-3315
p. 121

ASTD Order Department
600 Maryland Ave SW, Suite 305
Washington, DC 20024
202/484-2390
p. 67

Aston's Adventures
1301 North Park Avenue
Inglewood, CA 90302
213/673-4455
p. 106

ATS-CLE Audiocassettes
PO Box 7158
Madison, WI 53707
608/257-3838
p. 58

Audio Accessories Co.
38W515 Deerpath Road
Batavia, IL 60510
312/879-5998
pp. 105, 106

Audio Alert, Inc.
108 Galewood Road
Timonium, MD 21093
301/252-8520
p. 18

Audio Arts
6 Briarwood Road
London SW4 9PX, England
01-720 9129
p. 62

Audio Book Company
PO Box 9100
Van Nuys, CA 91409
213/799-4139
pp. 60, 110

Audio Communications Center,
Inc.
2600 Lander Road
Cleveland, OH 44124
p. 115

Audio Digest Foundation
1577C East Chevy Chase Drive
Glendale, CA 91206
800/423-2308, 800/232-2165 in
CA
pp. 23, 24, 28, 33, 35

Audio Forum/Jeffrey Norton
Publishers, Inc.
On The Green
Guilford, CT 06437
203/453-9794
p. 40

Audio Health Services
PO Box 416
Temple City, CA 91780
213/574-7461
pp. 38, 96

Audio Learning, Inc.
1308 DeKalb Street
Morristown, PA 19401
215/279-9066
pp. 20, 27, 38

Audio Players
18349 Neeley Road
Guerneville, CA 95446
707/869-3559
p. 60

Audio Tennis
366 Spanish Trace Drive
Altamonte Springs, FL 32701
305/788-1645
p. 106

Audio Veterinary Medicine
810 South Myrtle Avenue
Monrovia, CA 91016-5727
213/303-2531
p. 28

Audio Visual Medical Marketing,
Inc.
404 Park Avenue South
New York, NY 10016
800/221-3995, 212/532-9400 in
NYC
pp. 25, 35

Audio Visual Productions
Hocker Hill House
Chepstow, Gwent, NP6 5ER, UK
02912 5439
p. 60

Augsburg Publishing House
PO Box 1209
Minneapolis, MN 55440
612/330-3300
p. 115

Automated Learning, Inc.
1275 Bloomfield Avenue
Fairfield, NJ 07006
201/575-8394
pp. 12, 44, 78, 92, 103

Ave Maria Press
Notre Dame, IN 46556
219/287-2831
p. 49

Back to the Bible Broadcast
PO Box 82808
Lincoln, NE 68501
402/474-4567
p. 125

Balanced Living
PO Box 7690
Clearwater, FL 33518
813/531-7793
p. 85

Bank Marketing Association,
    Training and Professional
    Development Department
309 West Washington Street
Chicago, IL 60606
312/782-1442
p. 16

Barrie Sound Studios
337 West Montgomery Avenue
North Wales, PA 19454
215/699-3646
p. 103

Batten Institute
518 Grand Avenue
Des Moines, IA 50309
515/243-0951
pp. 4, 65

Bayard Publications, Book
    Division
1234 Summer Street
Stamford, CT 06905
207/327-0800
p. 73

Gary Beals Advertising & Public
    Relations
4141 Fairmount Avenue
San Diego, CA 92105
619/284-1145
p. 134

Bedell Speech Training
    International
15213 72nd Avenue NE
Bothell, WA 98011
206/488-3702
p. 9

Bergwall Productions
PO Box 238
Garden City, NY 11530
800/645-3565, 516/222-1111
p. 10

Berlitz Publications
866 Third Avenue
New York, NY 10022
212/935-2000
p. 51

Bethany Fellowship, Inc.
6820 Auto Club Road
Minneapolis, MN 55438
612/944-2121
p. 110

Better Than Money Corporation
1101 West 78-1/2 Street
Bloomington, MN 55420-1083
612/884-3311
p. 73

Bible Study Cassettes
1716 Spruce Street
Philadelphia, PA 19103
p. 111

Big Sur Recordings
PO Box 91
Big Sur, CA 93920
p. 86

Biofeedback Center of Berkeley
2236 Derby Street
Berkeley, CA 94705
415/841-4333
pp. 93, 94

Biofeedback Recordings, Inc.
PO Box 1501
Monterey, CA 93940
408/373-2486
p. 37

Doc Blakely
Route 3, Box 208
Wharton, TX 77488
713/532-4502
p. 83

BLAT Centre for Health and
    Medical Education
BMA House, Tavistock Square
London, WC1H 9JP, UK
01-388 7976
p. 25

Edwin C. Bliss & Associates
El Rancho Loma Serena
Mountain Ranch, CA 95246
209/754-3560
p. 81

BMA Audio Cassettes
200 Park Avenue South
New York, NY 10003
212/674-1900
pp. 20, 22, 27, 32, 33, 34, 35, 36,
    37, 49, 50, 88, 84, 93, 103

BNA Communications, Inc.
9417 Decoverly Hall Road
Rockville, MD 20850
301/948-0540
pp. 3, 68, 71, 141

Bobbs-Merrill Educational
    Publishing
PO Box 7080
Indianapolis, IN 46206
800/428-3750, 317/298-5745 in IN
pp. 3, 27

Howard W. Bonnell
PO Box 3855
Chicago, IL 60654
312/245-3412
pp. 99, 133, 139

Books on Tape
PO Box 7900
Newport Beach, CA 92660
800/854-6758, 800/432-7646 in
    CA
p. 62

Lee Boyan & Associates
11813 Crawford Road West
Minnetonka, MN 55343
612/938-5904
p. 138

Gil Boyne
312 Riverside Drive
Glendale, CA 91204
213/242-3497
pp. 33, 87

BRC OTR Distributors
17173 Westbrook
Livonia, MI 48152
313/591-1074
p. 106

Brigham Young University
Media Marketing, W-STAD
Provo, UT 84602
801/374-2111, ext. 4071
p. 121

Broadman Consumer Sales
127 Ninth Avenue North
Nashville, TN 37234
615/251-2544
p. 116

Bruccoli-Clark Publishers
1700 Lone Pine Road
Bloomfield Hills, MI 48013
313/642-8897
p. 62

Bureau of Business Practice
24 Rope Ferry Road
Waterford, CT 06385
203/442-4365
pp. 8, 139

C.A.M. Communications
37 Woodland Road
Short Hills, NJ 07078
201/379-1948
p. 134

C.D.S., Inc.
1216 Stemmons Tower South
Dallas, TX 75207
214/630-0661
p. 45

Caedmon
1995 Broadway
New York, NY 10023
800/223-0420, 212/580-3400
p. 61

Cal Industries, Inc.
770 Broadway, 3rd Fl.
New York, NY 10003
212/685-0892
p. 139

California Association of Realtors
525 South Virgil Avenue
Los Angeles, CA 90020
213/739-8227
p. 135

Campus Crusade for Christ
  International
Arrowhead Springs
San Bernardino, CA 92414
714/886-5224
p. 120

Canaan in the Desert
9849 North 40th Street
Phoenix, AZ 85028
602/996-4040
p. 121

Career Aids
8950 Lurline Avenue
Chatsworth, CA 91311
213/341-8200
pp. 27, 30, 32, 77

Cassette House, Inc.
530 W. Northwest Highway
Mount Prospect, IL 60056
312/398-3838
p. 107

Cassette Library Center
PO Box 5328
Baltimore, MD 21209
p. 104

Cassettes Unlimited
Roanoke, TX 76262
817/430-1084
p. 4

Cathcart, Alessandra &
  Associates, Inc.
PO Box 2767
La Jolla, CA 92038
619/459-1515
pp. 7, 49, 66, 72, 138

CBI Publishing Company, Inc.
51 Sleeper Street
Boston, MA 02210
617/426-2224
pp. 12, 140

Center for Communications
  Ministry
1962 S. Shenandoah
Los Angeles, CA 90034
213/559-2944
p. 114

Center for Entrepreneurial
  Management, Inc.
83 Spring Street
New York, NY 10012
212/925-7304
p. 3

Center for the Study of
  Democratic Institutions
PO Box 4068
Santa Barbara, CA 93103
805/969-3281
p. 100

CHAANGE
1339 South Wendover Road
Charlotte, NC 28211
704/364-5026
pp. 86, 94

Changed Lives
PO Box 100
Chattanooga, TN 37401
615/756-0757
p. 121

Charles Press Publishers
Bowie, MD 20715
301/262-6300
p. 47

Chest, Heart and Stroke
  Association
Tavistock House North
Tavistock Square
London, WC1H 9JE, UK
01 387 3012
p. 38

Chidvilas Rajneesh Meditation
  Center
PO Box 12A
Antelope, OR 97001
503/489-3301
p. 129

Chiron Associates, Inc.
PO Box 2498
New York, NY 10163
212/876-1875
p. 15

Christ for the Nations
PO Box 24901
Dallas, TX 75224
214/376-1711
p. 123

Christian Cassette Library
2031 Hemlock Road
Norristown, PA 19401
215/539-4277
p. 121

Christian Cassette Ministry
PO Box 828
Missouri City, TX 77459
p. 120

Christian Duplications
  International, Inc.
1710 Lee Road
Orlando, FL 32810
800/327-9332, 800/432-5309 in
  FL
p. 110

Christophers
12 East 48th Street
New York, NY 10017
212/759-4050
p. 101

Citibank
PO Box 1250
New York, NY 10043
p. 16

Clarence Bass Ripped Enterprises
400 Gold SW, Suite 305
Albuquerque, NM 87102-3286
505/843-7676
p. 103

Clarity Tapes
PO Box 596
Templeton, CA 93465
805/434-1352
p. 22

Clearing House for Speech
  Humor
PO Box 15259
Seattle, WA 98115
206/522-8600
p. 10

CLP Publishers
PO Box 15666
San Diego, CA 92115
619/449-9420
p. 113

CMS Records, Inc.
14 Warren Street
New York, NY 10007
212/964-3380
p. 61

Cognetics, Inc.
PO Box 592
Saratoga, CA 95070
408/744-0919
p. 21

Terry Cole-Whittaker Ministries
Attn: Tape Department
PO Box 82138
San Diego, CA 92138
800/228-1999, 800/542-6120 in
  CA
p. 119

College of Chaplains
1701 East Woodfield Road, Suite
  311
Schaumburg, IL 60195
312/843-2701
p. 116

Columbia Bible College
Attn: Campus Bookstore
PO Box 3122
Columbia, SC 29230
803/754-4100, ext. 313
p. 121

Commerce Clearing House, Inc.
4025 W. Peterson Avenue
Chicago, IL 60646
312/267-9010
p. 19

Communication Enterprises, Inc.
PO Box 69
Ocean Springs, MS 39564
601/875-1734
p. 89

Communications in Learning,
  Inc.
2280 Main Street
Buffalo, NY 14214
716/837-7555
pp. 31, 39

Comprehensive Communications,
  Inc.
PO Box 385
Scarsdale, NY 10583
914/472-5133
p. 108

Condyne/The Oceana Group
75 Main Street
Dobbs Ferry, NY 10522
914/693-5944
pp. 57, 59

Confide
PO Box 56
Tappan, NY 10983
914/359-8860
p. 47

Contemporary Drama Service
PO Box 457
1529 Brook Drive
Downers Grove, IL 60515
312/495-0300
pp. 63, 107, 112

Continuing Education of the
  Bar—University of California
  Extension
2300 Shattuck Avenue
Berkeley, CA 94704
415/642-3973
p. 56

Conversa-phone Institute, Inc.
One Comac Loop
Ronkonkoma, NY 11779
516/467-0600
pp. 5, 51, 52, 102

Kenneth Copeland Ministries
PO Box 8720
Fort Worth, TX 76112
817/535-1920
p. 109

Cornerstone Ministry
PO Box 43189
Birmingham, AL 35243
205/967-6076
p. 122

Cortina Institute of Languages
17 Riverside Avenue
Westport, CT 06880
203/227-8471
p. 52

Council for Career Planning, Inc.
310 Madison Avenue
New York, NY 10017
212/687-9490
p. 77

Counseling-Learning Institutes
PO Box 383
East Dubuque, IL 61025
815/747-3071
p. 47

Covenant Recordings, Inc.
1345 Major Street
PO Box 26817
Salt Lake City, UT 84126
801/487-1096
p. 113

Creative Communications
  Associates
16126 Lomacitas Lane
Whittier, CA 90603
213/947-3445
p. 9

Creative Hypnosis National
14345 Friar Street
Van Nuys, CA 91401
213/786-1136
p. 90

Creative Learning Center
PO Box 5331
Baltimore, MD 21209
301/825-8036
pp. 32, 47, 77, 99

Creative Media Group
123 Fourth Street NW
Charlottesville, VA 22901
804/296-6138
pp. 9, 31, 32, 93, 102

Creative Recruiters
PO Box 2447
Springfield, IL 62705
217/529-3387
p. 133

Creative Resources
PO Box 4384
San Francisco, CA 94101
415/552-5045
pp. 20, 84, 95

Creative Services, Inc.
PO Box 6008
PO Box 6008
High Point, NC 27262
919/889-3010
pp. 9, 86, 133, 138

Crown Publishers, Inc.
1 Park Avenue
New York, NY 10016
212/532-9200
p. 53

Crux
75 Champlain Street
Albany, NY 12204
518/465-4591
p. 117

CTVC
Hillside, Merry Hill Road
Bushey, Watford, WD2 1DR
    England, UK
01-950-4426
p. 121

Damon and Grace
PO Box 1767
East Lansing, MI 48823
800/248-1530, 517/337-7471 in
    MI
p. 90

Dancercise
1845 Broadway
New York, NY 10012
212/245-5200
p. 102

Dartnell
4660 Ravenswood Avenue
Chicago, IL 60640
312/561-4000
p. 140

DeGreen Corporation
13444 North 32nd Street, Suite 19
Phoenix, AZ 85032-6085
800/321-5378, 602/992-5372
pp. 49, 136

Development Consultants, Inc.
2028 Powers Ferry Rd, Suite 190
Atlanta, GA 30339
404/952-0898
p. 85

Development Digest
PO Box 49938
Los Angeles, CA 90049
212/696-1610
p. 72

Development Publications
6505 Lamar Road
Bethesda, MD 20816
301/320-4409
p. 66

Karen Diamond School of
    Exercise
1616 Wisconsin Avenue, NE
Washington, DC 20007
202/965-7272
p. 103

Diane Publishing Company
PO Box 2948
Torrance, CA 90509
213/320-2591
p. 120

Diastole-Hospital Hill
PO Box 19682
Kansas City, MO 64141
p. 25

Dictation Disc Company
240 Madison Avenue
New York, NY 10016
212/683-9028
p. 5

DIDI
PO Box 3363
Salem, OR 97302
503/364-7698
p. 95

Diocese of St. Cloud
Communications Office
PO Box 1068
St. Cloud, MN 56301
612/251-3022
p. 121

Discipleship Tape Library
435 West Boyd
Norman, OK 83069
405/321-2817
p. 121

Dolphin Tapes/Paul B. Herbert
Hot Springs Lodge
Big Sur, CA 93920
p. 84

Reuben H. Donnelley
825 Third Avenue
New York, NY 10022
212/972-8396
p. 136

Dr. Beter Audio Letter
PO Box 276
Savage, MD 20763
202/659-3999
p. 100

Drake Beam Morin, Inc.
277 Park Avenue
New York, NY 10172
212/888-2816
p. 71

Drake Educational Associates
212 Whichurch Road
Cardiff CF4 3NB, UK
29414/24502
p. 107

East West Academy of Healing
    Arts
PO Box 31211
San Francisco, CA 94131
415/285-9400
p. 22

ECKANKAR
PO Box 3100
Menlo Park, CA 94025
p. 129

Education Research
PO Box 4205
Warren, NJ 07060
201/561-9344
p. 9

Educational Enrichment
    Materials
The New York Times
357 Adams Street
Bedford Hills, NY 10507
914/241-1350
pp. 13, 107

Educational Record Sales
157 Chambers Street
New York, NY 10007
212/267-7437
pp. 41, 63

Educational Reviews, Inc.
6801 Cahaba Valley Road
Birmingham, AL 35243
205/967-4711
pp. 12, 26

Educational Services
1730 Eye Street NW
Washington, DC 20006
202/298-8424
p. 53

Educulture, Inc.
1 Dubuque Plaza, Suite 150
Dubuque, IA 52001
800/553-4858, 319/557-9610 in IA
pp. 13, 63

Effective Learning Systems, Inc.
6950 France Avenue South
Edina, MN 55435
612/927-4171
pp. 21, 86

Herbert Henry Ehrenstein
PO Box 17240
Philadelphia, PA 19105-7240
p. 112

Barby Fairbanks Eide
PO Box 8524
Spokane, WA 99203-0524
509/535-2299
pp. 85, 93

Electronic Paperbacks
PO Box 2
Chappaqua, NY 10514
914/238-8661
p. 119

Enabling Systems, Inc.
PO Box 2813
Honolulu, HI 96803
808/536-6528
p. 93

Encore Visual Education, Inc.
1235 South Victory Blvd.
Burbank, CA 91502
213/843-6515
pp. 52, 54

Encounter Ministries, Inc.
Wheaton, IL 60187
312/690-7676
p. 119

Encouragement Associates
221 South 7th Avenue
West Reading, PA 19611
215/373-6858
p. 49

Encyclopaedia Britannica
  Educational Corp.
425 North Michigan Avenue
Chicago, IL 60611
312/321-6800
p. 8

Enrichment Cassettes
PO Box 11534
Palo Alto, CA 94306
p. 142

Enterprise Records
PO Box 395
Glenview, IL 60025
312/729-3380
p. 131

Episcopal Radio-TV Foundation
3379 Peachtree Road, NE
Atlanta, GA 30326
404/233-5419
pp. 112, 119

Epsilon Records
PO Box 626
San Jacinto, CA 92383
p. 44

ESP, Inc.
PO Drawer 5037
Jonesboro, AR 72401
800/643-0280
pp. 4, 10, 32, 37, 41, 43, 44, 52, 77

Essential Recordings
PO Box 361
Mill Valley, CA 94941
p. 98

Everett/Edwards, Inc.
PO Box 1060
DeLand, FL 32720
904/743-7458
pp. 42, 63, 101

Executive Development Systems
2995 LBJ Freeway, Suite 115
Dallas, TX 75234
214/620-0172
p. 84

Explorations Institute
PO Box 1254
Berkeley, CA 94701
415/548-1004
p. 86

Faces West Productions
10601 S. de Anza Blvd, #212
Cupertino, CA 95014
408/257-2796
pp. 37, 45

Falcon AVA
Falcon Court
32 Fleet Street
London EC4Y 1DB, UK
01-353-0751
p. 117

Family Enrichment Bureau
1615 Ludington Street
Escanaba, MI 49829-2894
906/786-7002
pp. 46, 48, 93, 128

Family Life
PO Box 52444
Lafayette, LA 70505
318/988-0030
p. 120

Family Life Seminars
PO Box 1299
El Cajon, CA 92022
619/440-0227
p. 119

Fantasia
PO Box 965
Melville, NY 11747
516/673-0330
p. 93

Farnsworth Publishing Company,
  Inc.
PO Box 710
Rockville Centre, NY 11570
516/536-8400
p. 131

Art Fettig
31 East Avenue, South
Battle Creek, MI 49017
616/966-5329
pp. 9, 10, 67

Findhorn Foundation
Audio Department, The Park
Forres, Scotland 1V36 0TZ
p. 129

Fitness Research Institute
2210 Wilshire Blvd., Suite 753
Santa Monica, CA 90403
213/470-2132
p. 103

Fleetwood Communications
  Company
PO Box 500
Revere, MA 02151
617/289-6800
p. 106

Folkways Records
43 West 61st Street
New York, NY 10023
212/586-7260
pp. 8, 52, 54, 60

Forum/Schrello
555 East Ocean Blvd, 4th Floor
Long Beach, CA 90802
213/473-2234
p. 73

Forward in Faith
1441 Gutherie Drive
Cleveland, TN 37311
615/472-3361
pp. 112, 123

Foundation For Christian Living
PO Box FCL
Pawling, NY 12564
p. 118

Foundation of Praise
PO Box 2518
Escondido, CA 92025
619/741-2755
p. 47

French & Spanish Book
  Corporation
115 Fifth Avenue
New York, NY 10003
212/673-7400
p. 51

G & H Decoys
PO Box 937
Henryetta, OK 74437
918/652-3314
p. 106

Gary Sunday Visitor
PO Box M-356
Gary, IN 46401-0356
219/886-3141
p. 123

Bob Gass Evangelistic
  Association, Inc.
1491 Rhododendron Drive
Acworth, GA 30101
404/428-3931
p. 123

GBD and Associates
22632 Claude Circle
Lake Forest, CA 92630
714/581-1073
p. 141

General Board of Global
  Ministries
United Methodist Church
7820 Reading Road
Cincinnati, OH 45237
p. 117

General Cassette Corporation
2311 North 35th Avenue
Phoenix, AZ 85009
800/528-5341, 602/269-3111 in
  AZ
pp. 8, 74, 83, 96, 133, 136, 137, 139

General Motors
Management & Organization
  Development Division
1700 West Third Avenue
Flint, MI 48502
800/521-5850
p. 68

Jerry Gillies
22541A Pacific Coast Highway
Suite 16
Malibu, CA 90265
p. 81

Gnostic Society
PO Box 3993
Los Angeles, CA 90028
213/465-9282
p. 79

Goals Unlimited
PO Box 8091
Roseville, MN 55113
612/488-4262
pp. 81, 136

Golden Age Radio
PO Box 25215
Portland, OR 97225
p. 104

Golden Radio Library
PO Box 3955
Rochester, NY 14625
716/288-3122
p. 105

I. I. Goldmacher Publishing
  Company
PO Box 447
Fresh Meadows, NY 11365
212/454-0137
p. 139

Gospel Assembly Church
7135 Meredith Drive
Des Moines, IA 50324
515/276-1331
p. 122

Gousha/Chek-Chart
PO Box 39118
San Francisco, CA 94139
408/296-1060
p. 44

Bill Gove
1A Atrium Circle
Atlantis, FL 33462
p. 83

Graves Medical Audiovisual
  Library
Box 99
Chelmsford, Essex, CM2 9BJ
0245-83351
p. 27

Great Atlantic Radio Conspiracy
2743 Maryland Avenue
Baltimore, MD 21218
301/243-6987
p. 100

Great Radio Shows
PO Box 254-T
Woodinville, WA 98072
p. 105

Greatapes
Law Enforcement Resource
  Center
123 South 12th Street
Minneapolis, MN 55403
612/339-1651
pp. 55, 56

Bill Tycoon Greene
PO Box 850
Mill Valley, CA 94942
415/383-8264
p. 18

Greenhaven Press, Inc.
577 Shoreview Park Road
St. Paul, MN 55112
612/482-1582
pp. 45, 99

Grolier Educational Corporation
Sherman Turnpike
Danbury, CT 06816
203/797-3500
p. 41

Grove Enterprises, Inc.
140 Dog Branch Road
Brasstown, NC 28902
704/837-2216
p. 43

Grune & Stratton, Inc.
111 Fifth Avenue
New York, NY 10003
212/741-6800
p. 27

Grupo Editorial QBD, Ltda.
Rua Caravelas 326
(Caixa Postal 30329)
Sao Paulo, Brazil 04012
011-570-6486
p. 28

Guided Visualizations
PO Box 28504
San Jose, CA 95159
p. 85

Dave Hagenbuch & Associates,
  Inc.
799 Bloomfield Avenue
Verona, NJ 07044
201/857-0548
p. 138

Halvorson Associates
PO Box 9975
Chevy Chase, MD 20015
301/654-1698
p. 64

Mark Victor Hansen
PO Box 7665
Newport Beach, CA 92260
714/759-9304
pp. 82, 137

Hanuman Foundation Tape
Library
PO Box 61498
Santa Cruz, CA 95061
p. 128

Harold Institute
PO Box 11024
Winston-Salem, NC 27106
p. 79

Harper & Row Media
Order Fulfillment/Customer
Service
2350 Virginia Avenue
Hagerstown, MD 21740
301/733-2700
p. 34

Harris Communications
17915-B Sky Park Blvd.
Irvine, CA 92714
714/979-9263
p. 80

Harrison Tyner International,
Inc.
PO Box 25083
Nashville, TN 37202
615/833-6693
p. 40

Harvard University Press
79 Garden Street
Cambridge, MA 02138
617/495-2438
pp. 46, 60, 100

Roy Hatten Enterprises
PO Box 6633
Jackson, MS 39212
601/372-0949
p. 46

Hauser Productions, Inc.
475 N. Ferndale Road
Wayzata, MN 55391
612/473-1173
p. 66

Hawthorne Hypnosis Studio
16 Hawthorne Lane
Valley Stream, NY 11581
516/791-3166
p. 92

Hayes Publishing Company
6304 Hamilton Avenue
Cincinnati, OH 45224
513/681-7559
p. 93

Hazelden Educational Services
PO Box 176
Center City, MN 55012
800/328-9288, 612/257-4010
p. 37

Health World
PO Box 4646
Westlake Village, CA 91359
213/889-1231
p. 21

Hear-A-Book, Inc.
31200 La Baya Drive, #304
Westlake Village, CA 91362
213/706-2234
p. 61

Christopher J. Hegarty
PO Box 1152
Novato, CA 94947
415/892-2858
pp. 9, 66

Heinle & Heinle Publishers, Inc.
51 Sleeper Street
Boston, MA 02210
617/451-1940
p. 54

Helpnosis, Inc.
2621 Libbie Drive
Lansing, MI 48917
517/322-0033
p. 90

Herald House
PO Drawer HH
Independence, MO 64055
800/821-7550, 816/252-5010 in
MO
pp. 110, 128

G. Worthington Hipple
8617 Dixie Place
McLean, VA 22101
703/893-8838
p. 139

Hoke Communications, Inc.
224 Seventh Street
Garden City, NY 11530
516/746-6700
p. 134

Holistic Health Resources Center
PO Box 20037
Seattle, WA 98102-1037
800/426-5515, 206/325-9077
p. 22

Holy Spirit Center Tape Ministry
PO Box 1127
San Francisco CA 94101
415/681-7900
p. 126

Homespun Tapes
PO Box 694
Woodstock, NY 12498
914/679-7832
p. 104

Tom Hopkins Champions
Unlimited
PO Box 1969
Scottsdale, AZ 85252
800/528-0446, 602/941-2000
pp. 83, 136, 137

Horizon Publications, Inc.
3333 Iris
Boulder, CO 80301
303/442-8114
p. 72

Hosanna
146 Quincy NE
Albuquerque, NM 87108-1296
800/545-6552, 505/266-8741 in
NM
p. 126

Hospital Financial Management
Association
1900 Spring Road, Suite 500
Oak Brook, IL 60521
312/655-4600
p. 23

Hour of Power
PO Box 1776
Garden Grove, CA 92642
714/791-4111
p. 126

Human Development Training
Programs
10701 Lomas NE, Suite 201
Albuquerque, NM 87112
505/292-0370
pp. 34, 87

Human Productivity Institute,
Inc.
1674C Lombard Street
San Francisco, CA 94123
415/775-5903
pp. 7, 10, 73

Humetrics Corporation
353 North Oak Street
Inglewood, CA 90302
213/673-3002
p. 30

I P O Associates, Limited
PO Box 281
Rocky Hill, NJ 08553-0281
215/836-2383
pp. 22, 23, 30, 31

ICLE
Hutchins Hall
Ann Arbor, MI 48109
313/764-0533
p. 58

Independent Insurance Agents of
America, Inc.
100 Church Street
New York, NY 10007
800/221-7917
p. 131

Infonetics Corporation
2921 South Main Street
Santa Ana, CA 92707
714/556-6136
p. 57

Informed Homebirth
PO Box 788
Boulder, CO 80306
303/449-4181
p. 32

Inner Mind Concepts
6515 Highland Road
Pontiac, MI 48054
313/666-3307
p. 90

INPA Radio
PO Box 17422, Dulles Airport
Washington, DC 20041
703/620-9560
p. 134

Inspirational Tapes
PO Box 2220
Payson, AZ 85541
p. 121

Institute for Aerobics Research
12200 Preston Road
Dallas, TX 75230
214/239-7223
p. 102

Institute for Behavioral
Awareness
PO Box 532
Springfield, NJ 07081
201/376-8744
p. 89

Institute for Language Study
71 Plymouth Street
Montclair, NJ 07042
212/582-3845
p. 51

Institute of Colaxsus
PO Box 543
Cohoes, NY 12047
518/237-4647
p. 87

Institute of Human Development
PO Box 41165
Cincinnati, OH 45241
800/824-7888, Opr. 256,
  800/852-777? in CA,
  800/824-7979 in AK or HI
pp. 79, 92

Institute of Real Estate
Management
430 North Michigan Avenue
Chicago, IL 60611
312/661-1930
p. 135

Institute of Theological Studies
PO Box 1000
Grand Rapids, MI 49501
616/363-7817
p. 116

Institute on Religious Life
4200 North Austin Avenue
Chicago, IL 60634
312/545-1946
p. 118

Instructional Dynamics, Inc.
666 North Lake Shore Drive,
  Suite 1100
Chicago, IL 60611
312/943-1200
pp. 13, 14, 34, 35, 36, 37, 40, 45,
  46, 50, 83, 84, 86, 87, 88, 92, 93
  , 129

Instrument Society of America
PO Box 3561
Durham, NC 27702
919/549-8411
p. 142

Integral Yoga Publications
PO Box 108, Route 97
Pomfret Center, CT 06259
p. 129

Integrity Publications
PO Box Z
Mobile, AL 36616
205/476-0496
p. 120

Inter Amar Specialties
PO Box 1900
Winter Park, FL 32790
305/629-1213
p. 52

International Institute for
Reading
4251 SW 13th Street
Gainesville, FL 32602
800/874-7877
p. 8

Japan Air Lines
Literature Distribution Center
PO Box 10618
Long Island City, NY 11101
p. 53

Thomas Jefferson Research
Center
1143 North Lake Avenue
Pasadena, CA 91104
213/798-0791
p. 74

Johns Hopkins University
Office of Continuing Education
720 Rutland Avenue
Baltimore, MD 21205
p. 24

David Johnson Seminars
40647 Canyon Heights Drive
Fremont, CA 94539
415/561-5346
p. 83

Josephson Center for Creative
Educational Services
10101 West Jefferson Blvd.
Culver City, CA 90230
213/558-3100
p. 56

Kelly Productions, Inc.
8 Howard Street
Aberdeen, MD 21001-2494
301/272-1975
p. 38

Elizabeth Kemm
625 N. Byers
Joplin, MO 64801
p. 104

Joan Kennedy
PO Box 12525
St. Paul, MN 55112
612/784-6211
p. 85

King Tapes
156 West Main Street
Mesa, AZ 85201
602/969-2956
p. 125

Kirkhon Publications, Inc.
PO Box 38569
Germantown, TN 38138-0003
p. 10

Mozelle Bigelow Kraus, Ed.D.
The Seasons, Suite 614
4710 Bethesda Ave.
Bethesda, MD 20814
202/296-8929
pp. 11, 85, 94

Kripalu Krishna Kala
PO Box 120
Summit Station, PA 17979
717/754-3051
p. 130

Krishnamurti Foundation
PO Box 216
Ojai, CA 93023
805/646-2726
p. 129

Kathryn Kuhlman Foundation
PO Box 3
Pittsburgh, PA 15230
412/391-1373
p. 79

Lafayette Charismatic Teaching
  Center
PO Box 53817
Lafayette, LA 70505
318/984-3367
p. 120

Lake Hamilton Bible Camp
PO Box 516
Hot Springs, AR 71901
501/623-2244
p. 113

Lamb & Lion Ministries
PO Box 527
Plano, TX 75074
214/424-0910
p. 119

Lansford Publishing Company
PO Box 8711
San Jose, CA 95155
408/287-3105
pp. 2, 12, 14, 15, 27, 35, 37, 41,
   45, 47, 56, 66, 73, 80, 84, 85, 97
   101, 135

Lava Mt
235 West 76th Street
New York, NY 10023
212/874-3631
pp. 62, 63, 100, 105

Law Distributors
14415 South Main Street
Gardena, CA 90248
213/321-3275
p. 57

LeGrand E. Day
3607-M West Magnolia Blvd
Burbank, CA 91505
213/848-2408
pp. 33, 87

Leadership Catalysts, Inc.
903 Edgewood Lane
Cinnaminson, NJ 08077
609/786-0695
p. 95

Leadership Dynamics
  International
5780 Peachtree-Dunwoody Road,
  NE
Suite 210
Atlanta, GA 30342
404/256-5110
p. 127

Learn Incorporated
113 Gaither Drive
Mount Laurel, NJ 08054
609/234-6100
pp. 8, 11

Learncom, Inc.
113 Union Wharf East
Boston, MA 02109
617/523-4160
p. 66

Learning Arts
PO Box 179
Wichita, KS 67201
316/682-6594
p. 10

Learning Consultants, Inc.
6600 North Lincoln Avenue
Lincolnwood, IL 60645
312/677-7116
pp. 3, 7, 15, 65, 94

Learning Institute
221 Wildwood Avenue
St. Paul, MN 55110
612/221-0214
p. 68

Learning Programs of America
3216 Diamond 8 Terrace, #102
St. Anthony, MN 55421
612/938-3230
p. 95

Bernard Lee
Rutgers Medical School
New Brunswick, NJ 08903
201/542-0032
p. 9

Let's Talk Associates
521 15th Street
Manhattan Beach, CA 90266
213/545-5997
p. 106

Hyman A. Lewis
24271 Blackstone Street
Oak Park, MI 48237
313/546-0815
p. 89

Life Dynamics Fellowship
2704 South Grand
Santa Ana, CA 92705
714/754-1779
p. 80

Life Insurance Selling
408 Olive
St. Louis, MO 63102
314/421-5445
p. 132

Life Management Services, Inc.
PO Box 1044
Harrisburg, PA 17108
717/763-1950
p. 140

Listen for Pleasure
PO Box 322
Lewiston, NY 14092
716/754-8750
p. 63

Listening Library, Inc.
PO Box L
Old Greenwich, CT 06870
203/637-3616
p. 62

Living Love Publications
790 Commercial Street
Coos Bay, OR 97420
503/267-6412
p. 80

Living Scriptures Inc.
4357 South Airport Park
Ogden, UT 84403
801/627-2000
pp. 41, 128

Living Scriptures, Inc.
PO Box 90776
Houston, TX 77090
800/231-0442, 713/893-1050 in
 TX
p. 112

Logos
Drottninggaten 35, 411 14
Goteborg, Sweden
031-17 17 70
p. 116

Logos Tapes
3103 Highway 35
Hazlet, NJ 07730
201/264-2759
p. 126

Longman, Inc.
19 West 44th Street
New York, NY 10036
212/764-3950
p. 53

Lutheran Tape Ministry
124 South 24 Street, Suite 202
Omaha, NE 68102
402/346-3313
p. 112

Magnetix Corporation
770 West Bay Street
Winter Garden, FL 32787
305/656-4494
pp. 101, 107, 112

Mail Order Ministry
Abbott Loop Christian Center
2626 Abbott Road
Anchorage, AL 99507
907/344-4577
p. 120

Management Decision Systems,
 Inc.
108 Old King's Highway North
Darien, CT 06820
203/655-4414
pp. 67, 68

Management Resources
155 East 56th Street
New York, NY 10022
212/935-4800
pp. 5, 7, 71, 72

Mar-Bren Sound Ltd.
PO Box 4099
Rochester, NY 14610
716/288-3122
p. 105

Marketing Innovations
 Corporation
1953 Piedmont Circle NE
Atlanta, GA 30324
404/873-6777
p. 140

Marriage Enrichment Bureau
1615 Ludington Street
Escanaba, MI 49829-2894
p. 114

Master Productions
Route 1 Box 66
Cozad, NE 69130
308/784-4471
pp. 109, 126

Math House
PO Box 411
Glen Ellyn, IL 60137
312/790-1117
pp. 12, 15, 44

Mayhew McCrimmon
10-12 High Street
Great Wakering, Essex SS3 OEQ
England, UK
0702-218956
p. 123

MB/JB Enterprises
PO Box 724
Spencer, IA 51301
p. 106

MBO, Inc.
PO Box 10
Westfield, MA 01086
413/568-1369
p. 69

McGraw-Hill Continuing
 Education Center
3939 Wisconsin Avenue NW
Washington, DC 20016
800/323-1717, 800/942-8881 in IL
p. 2

McKinney Associates, Inc.
PO Box 5162
Louisville, KY 40205
502/583-8222
p. 123

McKnight Publishing Company
PO Box 2854
Bloomington, IL 61701
309/663-1341
p. 77

MCLE-NELI Publications
44 School Street
Boston, MA 02108
617/720-3606
p. 58

MEA
PO Box 303
Sausalito, CA 94965
p. 98

Medfield Foundation
PO Box 312
Medfield, MA 02052
617/769-5230
p. 89

Medical College of Georgia
Division of Continuing Education
Augusta, GA 30912
404/828-3967
p. 25

Medical Group Management
 Association
4101 East Louisiana Avenue
Denver, CO 80222
303/753-1111
p. 23

Medical Information Systems,
 Inc.
185 Great Neck Road
Great Neck, NY 11021
516/466-3711
pp. 20, 24, 29, 31

Medifacts Ltd.
471 Richmond Road
Ottawa, Ontario K2A 0G3,
 Canada
613/728-4655
pp. 20, 29, 32

Melodyland Tape Store
PO Box 6000
Anaheim, CA 92806
714/991-7160
p. 125

Barnet G. Meltzer, M.D.
1011 Camino del Mar, Suite 234
Del Mar, CA 92014
619/481-7102
p. 21

Mentronics Systems, Inc.
PO Box 130
Nellysford, VA 22958
804/361-1500
p. 80

Mike Mentzer
PO Box 67276
Los Angeles, CA 90067
p. 103

Merck Sharp & Dohme
Attn: Supervisor, Postgraduate
   Program
West Point, PA 19486
215/699-5311
p. 27

Merritt Company
1661 Ninth Street
Santa Monica, CA 90404
213/450-7234
p. 132

Metacom, Inc.
1401-B West River Road North
Minneapolis, MN 55411
800/328-4818, 612/588-2781
pp. 7, 43, 53, 63, 78, 85, 88, 102,
   103, 105, 137

Michigan Fellowship of Christian
   Athletes
1316 W. Maple Street
Kalamazoo, MI 49008
616/345-7891
p. 122

Midwest Research
6515 Highland Road, Suite 203
Pontiac, MI 48054
313/666-1224
p. 88

Million Dollar Round Table
2340 River Road
Des Plaines, IL 60018
312/298-1120
p. 131

Dick Mills Ministries
PO Box 758
Hemet, CA 92343
p. 122

Mills-Roberts Associates, Inc.
1265 Broadway
New York, NY 10001
212/889-3990
p. 138

Milton O. Berry
614 Pauley Place NE
Atlanta, GA 30328
404/252-2515
p. 141

MIND
50 Washington St., Suite 1201
Norwalk, CT 06854
203/846-3435
p. 4

Mind's Eye
PO Box 6727
San Francisco, CA 94101
800/227-2020, 415/883-2023 in
   CA
p. 64

Ministers Life Resources
3100 West Lake Street
Minneapolis, MN 55416
612/927-7131
p. 116

Ministr-O-Media, Inc.
St. Joseph's Church
PO Box 155
Pomfret, MD 20675
301/870-3990
pp. 114, 126

Mission Service Ministries
Route 4, Box 384
Fayetteville, AR 72701
501/521-1758
pp. 111, 112

Montaigne Ltd.
157 Alfred Street
Pembroke, Ontario K8A 2Z9,
   Canada
p. 43

Robert L. Montgomery &
   Associates, Inc.
12313 Michelle Circle
Burnsville, MN 55337
612/894-1348
pp. 7, 8, 86, 139

Moody Correspondence School
820 North LaSalle Drive
Chicago, IL 60610
312/274-2535
p. 110

MOR Associates
PO Box 5879
Buena Park, CA 90622
714/995-1244
p. 65

Thomas More Cassettes
225 West Huron Street
Chicago, IL 60610
312/951-2100
pp. 112, 115, 124

Robert Morris Associates
   Cassettes
PO Box 8500
Philadelphia, PA 19178
215/665-2850
p. 16

LilyB. Moskal
2344 Hunters Square Court
Reston, VA 22091
703/860-9313
p. 140

Motivation Associates
PO Box 29289
Richmond, VA 23229
804/740-4299
p. 92

Mount Paran Tape Ministries
2055 Mount Paran Road
Atlanta, GA 30327
404/461-1116
p. 122

Mountain Glade Media Ltd.
1260 Hornby Street, 2nd Floor
Vancouver, BC V6Z 1W2,
   Canada
604/688-1714
p. 90

MSIA
PO Box 3935
Los Angeles, CA 90051
213/737-4055
p. 129

Multi Media Resource Center
1525 Franklin Street
San Francisco, CA 94109
415/673-5100
p. 93

Burt Munk Productions, Inc.
666 Dundee Road
Northbrook, IL 60062
312/564-0855
p. 139

Nadller Concepts
150-10 79th Avenue
Flushing, NY 11367
212/591-4167
p. 21

Nation's Business
Executive Seminars in Sound
   Division
1615 H Street NW
Washington, DC 20063
202/659-6010
p. 69

National Association of
   Accountants
Technical Information Services
919 Third Avenue
New York, NY 10022
212/754-9766
p. 1

National Association of
   Evangelicals
PO Box 28
Wheaton, IL 60187
312/665-0500
pp. 116, 113

National AudioVisual Center
General Services Administration
Order Section/RV
Washington, DC 20409
301/763-1896
p. 52

National Book Company
333 SW Park Avenue
Portland, OR 97205
503/228-6345
pp. 1, 5, 13, 17, 21, 28, 59

National Center for Audio Tapes
348 Stadium Building
University of Colorado
Boulder, CO 80309
303/492-7341
p. 53

National Council of the
   Churches of Christ
Communications Commission,
   Room 860
475 Riverside Drive
New York, NY 10115-0050
212/870-2574
p. 125

National Institute for Trial
   Advocacy
40 North Milton Street, Suite 106
St. Paul, MN 55104
612/292-9333
p. 58

National Institute of Financial
   Planning, Inc.
1831 Fort Union Blvd.
Salt Lake City, UT 84121
801/943-1311
p. 17

National Institute of Real Estate
   Auctioneers, Inc.
3400 Irvine Ave., Suite 218
Newport Beach, CA 92660
714/957-0045
p. 135

National Office Products
   Association
301 N. Fairfax Street
Alexandria, VA 22314
703/549-9040
pp. 137, 139

National Practice Institute
510 First Avenue North, Suite 205
Minneapolis, MN 55403
800/328-4444
p. 58

National Public Radio
2025 M Street, NW
Washington, DC 20036
800/253-0808, 616/471-3402
p. 100

National Recording Company
PO Box 395
Glenview, IL 60025
312/827-1715
p. 105

National Underwriter Company
Life & Health Publications Dept.
420 East Fourth Street
Cincinnati, OH 45202
513/721-2140
p. 132

NavPress
PO Box 6000
Colorado Springs, CO 80934
800/525-7151, 303/598-1212 in
   CO
p. 123

Nazarene Publishing House
PO Box 527
Kansas City, MO 64141
816/931-1900
pp. 112, 114, 123

NCR Resources
PO Box 281
Kansas City, MO 64141
800/821-7926, 816/531-0538 in
   MO
pp. 114, 127

Negotiating Books
390 SE St. Lucie Blvd.
Stuart, FL 33494
p. 71

Negotiation Institute, Inc.
230 Park Avenue
New York, NY 10169
212/986-5555
p. 71

Neuro-ophthalmology Tapes
9820 SW 62 Court
Miami, FL 33156
305/665-6827
p. 26

New Age Light
PO Box 24384
San Jose, CA 95154
p. 79

New Dimensions Tapes
267 States Street
San Francisco, CA 94114
415/621-1126
pp. 21, 80

New Harbinger Publications
2200 Adeline, Suite 305
Oakland, CA 94607
415/465-1435
p. 95

New Life Foundation
700 Wyoming Street
Boulder City, NV 89005
702/293-4444
p. 79

New Life Institute
PO Box 2390
Santa Cruz, CA 95063
408/475-2010
p. 90

New Melleray Abbey
Dubuque, IA 52001
p. 116

R&R Newkirk
PO Box 1727
Indianapolis, IN 46206
800/428-3846
pp. 131, 132

Newstrack
PO Box 1178
Englewood, CO 80150
800/525-8389, 303/778-1692 in
   CO
p. 2

Nightingale-Conant Corporation
3730 West Devon Avenue
Chicago, IL 60659
800/323-5552, 312/677-3100 in IL
pp. 13, 17, 82, 138

Nilgiri Press
PO Box 477
Petaluma, CA 94952
707/878-2369
p. 129

Jeffrey Norton Publishers, Inc.
On The Green
Guilford, CT 06437
203/453-9794
pp. 3, 10, 13, 15, 16, 17, 21, 34,
   41, 49, 50, 52, 53, 54, 62, 67, 74
   , 92, 97, 102, 103, 104, 106, 107

Nostalgia Sounds
PO Box 64
Keeler, CA 93530
p. 105

Oasis Cassette Library
3445 North Mustang Street
Las Vegas, NV 89108
702/645-5281
pp. 111, 125

Omega Advertising
3150 Bear Street
Costa Mesa, CA 92626
619/754-6399
p. 123

Omega Publications
PO Box 4130
Medford, OR 97501
503/773-8575
p. 111

Once Upon A Radio
PO Box 25066
Portland, OR 97225
p. 105

Orthopaedic Audio-Synopsis
   Foundation
PO Box H
South Pasadena, CA 91030
213/682-1760
p. 25

Outreach Inc.
PO Box 1000
Grand Rapids, MI 49501
pp. 116, 122

Pace Organization
11169 Weddington Street
North Hollywood, CA 91601
213/769-5100
p. 84

Pacifica Program Service
5316 Venice Blvd.
Los Angeles, CA 90019
213/931-1625
p. 101

Paulist Communications
2257 Barry Avenue
Los Angeles, CA 90064
213/477-2559
p. 48

Pentera Group, Inc.
6068 North Keystone
Indianapolis, IN 46220
317/259-8177
p. 132

Penton/IPC Education Division
1111 Chester Avenue
Cleveland, OH 44114
216/696-7000
p. 72

Performance Group,
   Incorporated
4950 Keller Springs Road, #480
Dallas, TX 75248
214/960-1045
pp. 65, 86, 133, 137

Personal Christianity
PO Box 549
Baldwin Park, CA 91706
213/338-7333
p. 121

Personal Dynamics Institute
5186 West 76th Street
Minneapolis, MN 55435
612/835-1020
p. 85

Persuasive Communications
1418 West Touhy Avenue
Park Ridge, IL 60068
312/298-8510
p. 140

Pfarrago Information Systems
4760 22nd Avenue NE
Seattle, WA 98105
206/522-4149
p. 33

Ph.D. Publishing Company
10860 Arizona Avenue
Culver City, CA 90230
213/204-1604
p. 18

Philosophical Research Society,
   Inc.
3910 Los Feliz Blvd.
Los Angeles, CA 90027
213/663-2167
p. 78

Phobia Educational Materials,
   Inc.
PO Box 807
White Plains, NY 10602
p. 95

Piano Playhouse
PO Box 54157
Tulsa, OK 74155

Pictorial Publishers
PO Box 68520
Indianapolis, IN 46268
800/428-1324, 317/872-7220 in IN
p. 132

Pivot Press
PO Box 940
Lakewood, CA 90714
213/867-1124
p. 89

Planned Achievements
PO Box 2029
Scottsdale, AZ 85252
602/994-8692
pp. 81, 135, 138

PM Incorporated
PO Box 2160
Van Nuys, CA 91405
213/873-4399
p. 25

Poets' Audio Center
PO Box 50145
Washington, DC 20004
202/347-4823
p. 60

Polestar Publications
620 S. Minnesota Ave, Suite 5
Sioux Falls, SD 57104
605/338-2888
p. 95

Porter Henry Knowledge
   Resources, Inc.
370 Lexington Avenue
New York, NY 10017
212/679-8835
pp. 133, 140

Post-Graduate Institute for
   Medicine
PO Box 158
Parker, CO 80134
303/841-5102
pp. 24, 25

Potentials Unlimited
4808 Broadmoor SE
Grand Rapids, MI 49508
616/698-7830
p. 91

Practical Management
  Associates, Inc.
6910 Owensmouth
Canoga Park, CA 91303
213/348-9101
pp. 12, 68

Prentice-Hall Distribution Center
Route 59 at Brook Hill Drive
West Nyack, NY 10995
201/767-5068
pp. 69, 138

Prentice-Hall, Inc.
200 Old Tappan Road
Old Tappan, NJ 07675
201/767-5000
p. 19

Derek Prince Publications
PO Box 14306
Fort Lauderdale, FL 33302
305/763-5202
p. 127

Printing Industries of America,
  Inc.
Management Services
  Department
1730 North Lynn Street
Arlington, VA 22209
703/841-8139
p. 140

Professional Cassette Center
180 East California Blvd.
Pasadena, CA 91105
800/824-7888, 800/852-7777 in
  CA
pp. 3, 8, 14, 18, 43, 49, 73, 82, 84,
  102, 134

Professional Education Systems,
  Inc.
PO Box 1428
Eau Claire, WI 54702
715/836-0060
pp. 16, 57, 136

Professional Information Library
PO Box 795129
Dallas, TX 75379
214/238-1819
p. 28

Professional Publishing Corp.
122 Paul Drive
San Rafael, CA 94903
415/472-1964
p. 136

Professional Training Associates,
  Inc.
1985 Spruce Hills Drive
Bettendorf, IA 52722
319/359-7133
pp. 3, 68

Promised Land Publications, Inc.
PO Box 269
Provo, UT 84601
801/225-2293
p. 111

Proseminar
75 Vandewater Street
San Francisco, CA 94133
800/227-4200, 415/421-7211 in
  CA
pp. 22, 89

Protape, Inc.
1540 Broadway
New York, NY 10036
212/575-1505
pp. 1, 13, 18

Protestant Radio and Television
  Center, Inc.
1727 Clifton Road NE
Atlanta, GA 30329
404/634-3324
p. 115

Provision Publishers
PO Box 386
Lindale, TX 75771
214/882-5571
p. 123

Fred Pryor Resources
  Corporation
2000 Johnson Drive
Shawnee Mission, KS 66205
913/384-4477
pp. 4, 46, 66, 74, 75, 140

Psychodynamic Research
  Corporation
150 East 69th Street
New York, NY 10021
212/628-4800
p. 81

Psychofeedback Institute
150 S. Barrington Avenue
Los Angeles, CA 90049
213/472-7254
p. 37

Psychology Today Cassettes
PO Box 278, Pratt Station
Brooklyn, NY 11205
800/431-2731, 800/942-1940 in
  NY
pp. 36, 87

Quiet Decisions
349 East 49th Street
New York, NY 10017
212/838-6083
p. 91

r.n. tapes, inc.
1400 Coleman Avenue (G-14)
Santa Clara, CA 95050
408/988-5351
p. 30

Radiance
PO Box Z
Eureka, CA 95501
707/443-6315
p. 127

Radio Vault
PO Box 9032
Wyoming, MI 49509
p. 105

Randolph Tapes
2108 Garnet Avenue
San Diego, CA 92109
619/276-9800
p. 90

Rational Behavior Therapy
  Center
University of Kentucky College
  of Medicine
2108 Nicholasville Road
Lexington, KY 40503
606/233-6009
p. 88

Realtors National Marketing
  Institute
430 North Michigan Avenue
Chicago, IL 60611
800/621-7023, 800/572-9484 in IL
pp. 66, 135

Recorded Books
6306 Aaron Lane
Clinton, MD 20735
800/638-1304, 301/868-7856 in
  MD
p. 61

Recycle
PO Box 12811
Pittsburgh, PA 15241
p. 117

Redmond Nostalgia Company
PO Box 82
Redmond, WA 98052-0082
p. 105

Reinforcement Learning, Inc.
PO Box 563
Upper Saddle River, NJ 07458
201/835-2244
p. 5

Research Press
PO Box 317760
Champaign, IL 61820
217/352-3273
pp. 14, 48, 69, 85

Resources for Education and
   Management, Inc.
544 Medlock Road
Decatur, GA 30030
404/373-7743
p. 68

Bob Richards Attainment
   Institute
15839 Sunset Road
Minnetonka, MN 55343
612/339-8123
p. 81

Richmar Productions
108 West Grand Avenue
Chicago, IL 60601
800/621-5199, 800/972-5855 in IL
p. 131

Rigby Publishers
176 South Creek Road
Dee Why West, N.S.W. 2099
   Australia
02-982-2344
p. 40

DeAnne Rosenberg, Inc.
28 Fifer Lane
Lexington, MA 02173
617/862-6117
p. 86

Rosicrucian Supply Bureau
Rosicrucian Park
San Jose, CA 95191
408/287-9171
p. 78

Ross Medical Associates
918 Red Fox Lane
Oak Brook, IL 60521
312/655-4456
p. 46

Royal Publishing
600 West Foothill Blvd.
Glendora, CA 91740
800/438-1242, 213/335-1855
pp. 9, 140

Russell and Associates
888 Sandcastle Drive
Corona Del Mar, CA 92625
714/640-1142
p. 135

S.A.I. Foundation
7911 Willoughby Avenue
Los Angeles, CA 90046
213/656-9373
p. 129

Elizabeth Sabine
7432 Mammoth Avenue
Van Nuys, CA 91405
213/989-4667
p. 44

Sacred Heart Church
1010 East Landis Avenue
Vineland, NJ 08360
p. 122

Sales & Marketing Management
Sales Builders Division
633 Third Avenue
New York, NY 10017
800/526-5368, 212/986-4800
pp. 133, 137

Sales Communique Corporation
PO Box 44
Franklin, MI 48025
313/661-4411
pp. 5, 92, 133, 136, 137

Nolan Saltzman, Ph.D.
25 East 86 Street, 13F
New York, NY 10028
212/876-4703
pp. 35, 92

Sanatana Dharma Foundation
3100 White Sulpher Springs Road
St. Helena, CA 94574
707/963-9487
p. 129

Sanders Christian Foundation
PO Box 348
South Hamilton, MA 01982
617/468-7306
p. 116

Sandler Selling System
PO Box 483
Stevenson, MD 21153
800/638-5686
p. 138

W. B. Saunders Company
West Washington Square
Philadelphia, PA 19105
215/574-4700
pp. 20, 24, 26, 29, 38

SBI Publishers in Sound
Willow Street
South Lee, MA 01260
413/243-3235
p. 63

SCAN/ALC Media Services
   Center
PO Box 122
Minneapolis, MN 55440
p. 126

J. Schimmel Associates
10251 Granada Lane
Overland Park, KS 66207
913/649-5743
p. 25

Science of Mind Publications
PO Box 75127
Los Angeles, CA 90075
213/388-2181
p. 79

Science Research Associates, Inc.
155 North Wacker Drive
Chicago, IL 60606
800/621-0664, 213/984-7000
pp. 8, 53, 73

Science-Thru-Media, Inc.
303 Fifth Avenue, Suite 803
New York, NY 10016
212/684-5366
pp. 29, 30

SCRC Tape Ministry
PO Box 45594
Los Angeles, CA 90045-0594
pp. 109, 127

Scripture Press Publications, Inc.
1825 College Avenue
Wheaton, IL 60187
312/668-6000
p. 114

Scripture Union
PO Box 38
Bristol BS99 7NA, UK
0272-771131
p. 118

Self Control Systems, Inc.
PO Box 7854
Waco, TX 76710
817/776-8110
pp. 46, 48, 87, 95

Self Discovery
PO Box 9786
North Hollywood, CA 91609
p. 92

Self Health Systems
Brindabella Farms
Route 2
La Crosse, WI 54601
608/786-0611
p. 89

Self Management Schools, Inc.
745 Distel Drive
Los Altos, CA 94022
415/327-7588
p. 95

Self Psych, Inc.
26555 Evergreen, Suite 1107
Southfield, MI 48076
313/358-4760, 800/521-3998,
    800/482-2467 in MI
p. 90

Self Realization Fellowship
3880 San Rafael Avenue
Los Angeles, CA 90065
213/225-2471
p. 130

Semantodontics, Inc.
PO Box 15668
Phoenix, AZ 85060
800/528-1052, 602/955-5662
pp. 5, 20, 45, 46

Seminars with Seth
PO Box 8146
La Crescenta, CA 91214
213/249-2791
p. 79

Seminary Extension
Southern Baptist Convention
    Building
460 James Robertson Parkway
Nashville, TN 37219
615/242-2453
p. 114

Servant Publications
PO Box 8617
Ann Arbor, MI 48107
313/761-8505
pp. 109, 118

Seven Arts Press, Inc.
6605 Hollywood Blvd.
Hollywood, CA 90028
213/469-7200
p. 107

Seventh Sense Institute
311 Gaymont Circle
Statesville, NC 28677
p. 78

Seventh-day Adventists
6840 Eastern Avenue NW
Washington, DC 20012
202/723-0800
p. 118

Shanti Nilaya
PO Box 2396
Escondido, CA 92025
619/749-2008
p. 46

Howard L. Shenson, Inc.
20121 Ventura Blvd, Suite 245
Woodland Hills, CA 91364
213/703-1415
p. 73

Duane Shinn Publications
PO Box 192
Medford, OR 97501
503/664-6037
pp. 104, 133

Simon Says
PO Box 2048
Rancho Santa Fe, CA 92067
619/753-1948
p. 86

Simplified Texts
8517 Green Lane
Baltimore, MD 21207
301/922-4378
pp. 41, 63, 101

Singer Management Institute
1345 Diversey Parkway
Chicago, IL 60614
800/621-1900, 312/525-1500 in IL
pp. 68, 140

Natalie Slohm Associates, Inc.
PO Box 273
Cambridge, NY 12816
518/677-3040
p. 60

Bob Snyder Enterprises
PO Box 15
Safety Harbor, FL 33572
p. 16

Sound Information Pty Ltd
PO Box 8 Broadway
Sydney 2007, Australia
02-698-8243
p. 101

Sound Teaching Ministries
311 Kincaide Street
Warsaw, IN 46580
219/269-1136
p. 120

Soundmark
4950-C Nome Street
Denver, CO 80239
303/371-3076
pp. 95, 103

SoundWord Tape Ministry
14434 Sherman Way
Van Nuys, CA 91405
213/785-8613
p. 125

Soundwords, Inc.
56-11 217 Street
Bayside, NY 11364
212/224-5310
p. 32

SOURCE Cassette Learning
    Systems
PO Box W
Stanford, CA 94305
415/328-7171
p. 91

Southern Educational
    Communications Association
PO Box 5966
Columbia, SC 29250
803/799-5517
p. 99

Spears Communications
    International, Inc.
5025 S. Orange Avenue
Orlando, FL 32809
305/855-7113
pp. 40, 61

Special Learning Corporation
42 Boston Post Road
Guilford, CT 06437
203/453-6212
p. 14

Spenco Medical Corporation
PO Box 8113
Waco, TX 76714-8113
800/433-3334, 817/772-7000 in
    TX
p. 32

Spirit of Life
PO Box 4002
Vero Beach, FL 32960
305/231-0162
p. 21

Spiritual Frontiers Fellowship
10819 Winner Road
Independence, MO 64052
816/254-8585
p. 129

Spoken Arts
PO Box 289, Dept. C
New Rochelle, NY 10802
914/636-5482
p. 61

Spoken Language Services, Inc.
PO Box 783
Ithaca, NY 14850
607/257-0500
p. 54

Spoken Word
PO Box 7269
Oxnard, CA 93031
805/483-6707
p. 122

Spring of Living Water
Richardson Spring, CA 95973
916/345-3310
p. 123

SSR/Center for Stress Reduction
2444 Moorpark Avenue, Suite 106
San Jose, CA 95128
408/275-6903
p. 95

St. Anthony Messenger Press
1615 Republic Street
Cincinnati, OH 45210
513/241-5615
pp. 92, 118

St. Joseph's Abbey
Mail Order Dept.
Spencer, MA 01562
p. 116

Stratford Publishing Company
PO Box 7077
Burbank, CA 91510
p. 44

Stress Management Research
   Associates, Inc.
PO Box 2232
Houston, TX 77001
713/890-8576
p. 94

Success Dynamics, Inc.
2633 State Route 59, Suite E
Ravenna, OH 44266
216/673-4114
p. 91

Success Motivation International,
   Inc.
PO Box 9125
Waco, TX 76710
817/776-1230
pp. 82, 83, 106

Success Tapes
103 Ash Avenue, Suite 5
Virginia Beach, VA 23452
p. 92

Success Unlimited
401 North Wabash Avenue
Chicago, IL 60611
312/828-9500
p. 81

Summit Lighthouse
PO Box A
Malibu, CA 90265
213/991-4721
p. 78

Sunrise Ranch
Cassettes—Kathleen McEleney
5569 North County Road 29
Loveland, CO 80537
p. 128

Sybervision Systems, Inc.
2450 Washington Avenue, #270
San Leandro, CA 94577
800/227-0600, 415/352-3526 in
   CA
p. 82

Sybex, Inc.
2344 Sixth Street
Berkeley, CA 94710
800/227-2346, 415/848-8233 in
   CA
p. 2

SYDA Bookstore
PO Box 6000
South Fallsburg, NY 12779
914/343-2000
p. 129

Systema Corporation
150 North Wacker Drive
Chicago, IL 60606
312/984-5000
pp. 7, 131, 137

Tape Ministers
PO Box 3389
Pasadena, CA 91103
213/794-4059
p. 123

Tape Productions, Inc.
60 East 42nd Street
New York, NY 10017
212/867-6038
pp. 9, 137

Tapes for Greater Living
1551 Wilmington Blvd.
Wilmington, CA 90744
213/835-5661
p. 128

Tapes for Readers
5078 Fulton Street NW
Washington, DC 20016
202/362-4585
p. 99

Tax Perspectives
2960 Camino Diablo, Suite 200
Walnut Creek, CA 94596
415/930-0648
p. 18

Taxwise Giving
13 Arcadia Road
Old Greenwich, CT 06870
203/637-4555
p. 19

Teach'em, Inc.
160 East Illinois Street
Chicago, IL 60611
312/467-0424
pp. 23, 24, 28, 29, 30, 31, 33, 38, 62

TeleKETICS
1229 South Santee Street
Los Angeles, CA 90015
800/421-8510
p. 117

Telstar
366 N. Prior Avenue
St. Paul, MN 55104
612/644-4726
p. 47

Theosophical Publishing House
306 West Geneva Road
Wheaton, IL 60187
312/665-0123
p. 129

Thesis
PO Box 11724
Pittsburgh, PA 15228
412/344-9449
pp. 51, 101, 113

Thought Dynamics
1100 El Centro Street, #101
South Pasadena, CA 91030
213/682-3441
p. 81

Thought Technology Ltd.
2193 Clifton Avenue
Montreal, Quebec H4A 2N5,
   Canada
514/484-0305
p. 36

Timberlake and Associates
PO Box 1571
Austin, TX 78767
512/837-1951, 837-4772
pp. 67, 81

Time Institute
2175 Sheppard Avenue East,
Suite 110
Willowdale, Ontario M2J 1W8
416/491-0777
p. 66

Time Management Center
PO Box 5
Grandville, MI 49418
616/531-1870
p. 66

Timeless Books
PO Box 60
Porthill, ID 83853
604/227-9224
p. 128

Toastmasters International
PO Box 10400
Santa Ana, CA 92711
714/542-6793
p. 9

Total Mind Power Institute
PO Box 545
Larkspur, CA 94939
415/924-6795
p. 88

Totaltape, Inc.
PO Box 1469
Gainesville, Fl 32602
800/874-7599, 904/376-8261 in
FL
pp. 2, 19, 59

Trainex Corporation
PO Box 116
Garden Grove, CA 92642
800/854-2485, 800/472-2479 in
CA
p. 31

Training Associates Press, Inc.
14455 Webbs Chapel Road
Dallas, TX 75234
214/484-4450
p. 139

Training Innovations
564 Stevens Avenue
Solana Beach, CA 92075
714/481-6473
p. 136

Trinity Tapes, Inc.
16604 Arminta Street
Van Nuys, CA 91406
213/786-5535
p. 110

Truth Consciousness
Gold Hill, Salina Star Route
Boulder, CO 80302
303/447-1637
p. 129

Truth Tape Library
PO Box 599
Fayetteville, GA 30214
404/487-4910
p. 120

Turning Point Programs
PO Box 1500
Woodland Hills, CA 91364
213/884-4050
p. 65

Tutor Tape Company Ltd.
2 Replingham Road
London SW18 5LS, UK
01-8704128/9
p. 54

Tutor/Tape
107 France Street
Toms River, NJ 08753
201/270-4880
pp. 1, 2, 13, 17, 41, 71, 82, 134

200-Language Club
PO Box 1727
Beverly Hills, CA 90213
p. 54

UCLA Extension
PO Box 24901
Los Angeles, CA 90024
213/825-7916
pp. 36, 50, 65, 72

ULC, Inc.
1605 NE 7th Street
Gainesville, FL 32601
p. 86

Unarius Educational Foundation
145 South Magnolia Avenue
El Cajon, CA 92020
619/447-4170
p. 128

United Methodist Center
Discipleship Resources
PO Box 840
Nashville, TN 37202
615/327-2700
p. 115

Unity of Indianapolis
907 North Delaware Street
Indianapolis, IN 46202
pp. 122, 124

Unity School of Christianity
Unity Village, MO 64063
816/524-3550
p. 124

Universal Life Church, Inc.
PO Box 11672
Palo Alto, CA 94306
415/965-6767
p. 79

Universal Training Systems
Company
255 Revere Drive
Northbrook, IL 60062
p. 6

University Associates
PO Box 26240
San Diego, CA 92126
800/854-2143, 619/578-5900 in
CA
p. 49

University of Bridgeport Law
Center
303 University Avenue
Bridgeport, CT 06601
203/576-4641
p. 58

University of California
Extension Media Center
Berkeley, CA 94720
415/642-1080
pp. 12, 15, 22, 28, 31, 36, 60, 74,
97, 99, 101, 142

University of California
Extension
Attn: Tapes
Santa Cruz, CA 95064
p. 22

University of Michigan
Michigan Media
416 Fourth Street
Ann Arbor, MI 48109
313/764-5360
p. 43

University of Pittsburgh
Division of Continuing Education
1022 Scaife Hall
Pittsburgh, PA 15261
412/624-2653
p. 28

University of the Trees
PO Box 644
Boulder Creek, CA 95006
408/338-2161
p. 80

University of Wisconsin-
  Extension
Extension Services in Pharmacy
425 North Charter Street
Madison, WI 53706
608/262-3130
p. 33

Upper Room
PO Box 189
Nashville, TN 37202
615/327-2700
p. 124

Vajradhatu and Naropa
  Recordings
1345 Spruce Street
Boulder, CO 80302
303/444-0210
pp. 78, 130

Valley of the Sun Publishing
PO Box 38
Malibu, CA 90265
213/456-5635
p. 91

Van Den Berg Publishing
9003 Reseda Blvd., Suite 205B
Northridge, CA 91324
213/885-6000
pp. 1, 3, 17, 134

Victory Ministries
PO Box 959
Warsaw, IN 46580
p. 123

Vision House Publishers, Inc.
PO Box 15163
Santa Ana, CA 92705
714/558-0511
p. 124

Visual Education Association
PO Box 1206
Springfield, OH 45501
513/864-2891
p. 54

Visual Education Corporation
PO Box 2321
Princeton, NJ 08540
609/799-9200
p. 40

Vocab, Inc.
3071 S. Broad Street
Chicago, IL 60608
312/254-8047
p. 10

Washington Audio Journal
1615 H Street NW
Washington, DC 20062
202/463-5858
p. 2

Sylvestre C. Watkins Company
PO Box 2532
Reston, VA 22090
703/620-9293
p. 99

Joel H. Weldon & Associates, Inc.
7975 North Hayden Road, Suite
  D-147
Scottsdale, AZ 85258
602/948-5710
p. 141

Well-Being
PO Box 105
Middletown, WI 53562
p. 21

Westerly Institute
11646 Chenault Street
Los Angeles, CA 90049
213/472-3244
p. 38

Western Tape
2761 Marine Way
Mountain View, CA 94040
415/969-0371
p. 4

Whirlpool Corporation
Literature Department, Parts
  Distribution Center
1900 Whirlpool Drive
La Porte, IN 46350-0927
219/325-2000
p. 44

Dr. John Whitcomb
Grace Theological Seminary
Winona Lake, IN 46590
219/267-8191
pp. 109, 114

Somers H. White Co.
4736 N. 44th Street
Phoenix, AZ 85018
602/959-9562
p. 67

Mike Whorf, Inc.
PO Box 1091
Birmingham, MI 48011
313/644-3370
p. 41

Wider Horizons
PO Box 3003
West Palm Beach, FL 33402
305/844-8100
p. 89

Ron Willingham Courses, Inc.
PO Box 8190
Amarillo, TX 79109
806/372-5771
pp. 81, 94, 140

Wilshire Book Company
12015 Sherman Road
North Hollywood, CA 91605
213/875-1711
p. 133

Wilson Learning Corporation
6950 Washington Avenue South
Eden Prairie, MN 55344
612/944-2880
p. 132

Winning Women, Inc.
18770 Farmington Road
Livonia, MI 48152
313/474-7271
p. 122

Witness Ministries
PO Box 12471
Oklahoma City, OK 73157
405/787-7110
p. 121

John Wolfe Institute
3935 Westheimer, Suite 301
Houston, TX 77027
713/960-1970
p. 139

E. F. Wonderlic & Associates,
  Inc.
820 Frontage Road
Northfield, IL 60093
312/446-8900
p. 4

Word of Grace Communications
PO Box 4000
Panorama City, CA 91412
213/764-5904
p. 113

Word, Inc.
Church Services Department
Waco, TX 76795
800/433-3327, 800/792-3210 in
  TX
pp. 49, 85, 111, 125

World Evangelism
PO Box 700
San Diego, CA 92138
619/239-4300
p. 124

World Future Society
4916 St. Elmo Avenue
Washington, DC 20014
301/656-8274
p. 99

World Harvest Records
474 East 17th St., Suite 203-A
Costa Mesa, CA 92627
714/631-7232
p. 119

World MAP Tape Outreach
900 North Glenoaks
Burbank, CA 91502
213/843-7233
p. 125

World Wide Publications
1303 Hennepin Avenue
Minneapolis, MN 55403
612/336-0940
pp. 118, 122

Worldwide Associates
3 Sandia Court
Edison, NJ 08817
201/494-9500
p. 134

Gordon Wright
55 Marchmont Road
Edinburgh EH9 1HT, Scotland
p. 51

Write To Sell
PO Box 1001
Carpinteria, CA 93013
805/684-2469
pp. 10, 107

Year Book Medical Publishers
35 East Wacker Drive
Chicago, IL 60601
800/621-9262, 312/726-9746
p. 28

Yoga Research Foundation
6111 SW 74th Avenue
Miami, FL 33143
305/666-1718
p. 130

Dave Yoho Associates
3930 Walnut Street
Fairfax, VA 22030
703/591-2490
pp. 8, 133, 134, 138

Youth With A Mission
PO Box 4600
Tyler, TX 75712
214/597-1171
p. 125

Z Incorporated
PO Box 5375
Madison, WI 53705-0375
608/831-8600
pp. 8, 10, 141

Zig Ziglar Corporation
13642 Omega at Alpha
Dallas, TX 75234
800/527-0102, 214/233-9191 in
  TX
pp. 8, 31, 82, 86, 138

Subject Index

Send me a free subscription to your newsletter, because . . .

HERE IS AN AUDIO-CASSETTE PRODUCER THAT ISN'T LISTED !

The following producer of spoken-voice adult-level educational or motivational audio-cassette programs is not listed in this directory:

(Please give the name and address of the producer and a brief description of that company's audio-cassette program. Enclosing a brochure, advertisement, or announcement from the producer greatly facilitates confirmation.)

After confirming that this company has not been listed in any previous editions of the directory or in past issues of the CIS newsletter, please send me with your compliments a year's subscription to the *Audio-Cassette Newsletter*.

NAME _____

ADDRESS _____

CITY / STATE / ZIP _____

Mail to:
Cassette Information Services, Box 9559, Glendale, CA 91206

TO HELP YOU KEEP CURRENT . . .
THE AUDIO-CASSETTE NEWSLETTER !

To keep up-to-date on what is available on educational or motivational audio-cassette programming, subscribe to the *Audio-Cassette Newsletter.* Each quarterly issue contains descriptions of new producers and their programs, information about new releases of established spoken-voice audio-cassette producers, plus developments in cassette hardware and other inside industry and consumer news. The cost is nominal, and your personal and professional benefits are guaranteed !

☐ Enclosed is my check for: ☐ $12 for a one-year subscription, or
　　　　　　　　　　　　　　 ☐ $23 for a two-year subscription.

☐ Please invoice me for:　　☐ $15 for a one-year subscription, or
　　　　　　　　　　　　　　 ☐ $28 for a two-year subscription.

☐ Please add $2 per year for addresses outside the U.S., Canada and Mexico.

NAME _____

ADDRESS _____

CITY / STATE / ZIP _____

Your check, payable in U.S. funds, should be made out to Cassette Information Services and sent to C.I.S., Box 9559, Glendale, CA 91206.

If for any reason you are not satisfied with your subscription, just return the first issue or two and *all* of your money will be refunded.